POLITICAL
RESEARCH

POLITICAL RESEARCH

*Design, Measurement
and Analysis*

DAVID C. LEEGE

&

WAYNE L. FRANCIS

BASIC BOOKS, INC., PUBLISHERS

NEW YORK

© 1974 by Basic Books, Inc.
Library of Congress Catalog Card Number: 73–82232
SBN 465–05937–6
Manufactured in the United States of America
DESIGNED BY VINCENT TORRE
74 75 76 77 10 9 8 7 6 5 4 3 2 1

TO THE ICPR

PREFACE

Although the "behavioral revolution" did not permeate most areas of political science until the early 1960's, isolated pieces of sound scientific research on politics could be found as early as 1910. Much of the scientifically respectable work in the intervening half-century was conducted by scholars whose disciplinary home was outside political science, most commonly in the fields of social psychology, sociology, or economics. Even when professional political scientists were responsible for an important piece of empirical research, they usually had received their research methods training outside the discipline.

By the 1960's the situation had changed substantially, and now most political scientists are familiar with some designs, methods, techniques, and statistical procedures by the time they are awarded the doctorate. Few departments of political science these days send their students to sociology or psychology departments for most of their training in research methods. Many offer some instruction in philosophy of science. A good share of them teach statistics as a part of the departmental curriculum. The products of such training regimens still, unfortunately, reflect the growing pains of the discipline as a whole. For scientific research on politics is only rarely taught as an integrated package. Statistics is often divorced from considerations of research design and measurement theory. Certain methods and techniques —e.g., survey research—are universally applied to any research problem. Time is needlessly wasted on arguments over "which method is *best* suited for political inquiry," as though *all* intellectual problems were amenable to analysis by the same method.

This book is an attempt to integrate a philosophy of science—multiple operationalism—with designs, methods and techniques of measurement, and statistical evaluation procedures. It is intended as a comprehensive guide through many of the models, methods, and techniques available for political research. It is methodological in orientation; instead of presenting designs and methods in a discrete fashion, it offers criteria for selecting an appropriate design and method and evaluates strengths and weaknesses in whole families of designs, instruments, or statistical procedures. It is not to be used as a cookbook; rather, the various sections and chapters build on methodological arguments developed earlier. The principal argument is that different intellectual concerns require the application of different designs and techniques; but in order to isolate and control various kinds of error, a variety of operations must be applied to the same phenomenon. The plausibility of any finding or interpretation is enhanced by mustering evidence which discounts rival hypotheses stemming from either substantive theory or method effects.

The book is aimed at two audiences: the scholar who is actually doing research, and the student who is learning about research in the classroom. While we feel the book should first be read in its entirety by both audiences, the practicing researcher may find of greatest value the criteria and evaluation section for a specific family of designs, samples, methods and techniques, and statistical evaluation procedures. Once familiar with the book, he or she may easily refer to the comparison of various measures of association, for example, or scaling models, and receive guidance relevant to his own specific research problem.

The book is primarily designed for the classroom. While usage may differ from campus to campus, we anticipate that heaviest classroom use will be found in the early years of graduate work. Students should have some familiarity with research methods and statistics prior to reading the book—perhaps a sophomore-level introduction to political research and a one-semester undergraduate course in elementary statistics. On campuses where undergraduates have an excellent foundation in modern mathematics, the book could readily be employed at the advanced undergraduate level.

Instructors will vary in their handling of the text. For those who wish to emphasize a particular set of designs such as experimentation, or a measurement model such as Q-methodology, supplementary handbooks will be desirable. But it is the stated purpose of this book to avoid overemphasis on a single method. In the dozen or so North American classrooms where many of the chapter drafts were tested, faculty have generally supplemented the book with occasional "how to" readings.

Instructors may also vary in their ordering of chapters. For some, a knowledge of statistical concepts and measurement theory should precede considerations of design and method. They may prefer a chapter sequence as follows: 1, 2, 9, 10, 11, 5, 6, 12, 13, 14, 3, 4, 7, and 8. Or, some other variant may be followed. Obviously, we prefer the present arrangement. Students will probably already know something about statistics or finite mathematics when they read this book, and when a statistical concept comes into the discussion in the earlier chapters, reference is made to the later chapter where it is discussed fully. There is no way the interwoven fabric of research decisions can be cut that will satisfy every researcher. In our own division of labor, Leege was responsible for drafting most of the early chapters and Francis the later chapters, but each of us required a full understanding of what the other was doing to be able to develop our own arguments. Some instructors may also find it best to extend usage of the book over a two-quarter or two-semester sequence.

Finally, the book is addressed primarily to political scientists but, we feel, could be fruitfully employed in sociology, social psychology, quantitative history, and even some areas of economics. While we have sought to deal with design and measurement considerations current to the mainstream of social research, some readers will note sections of chapters which are on the cutting edge of methodological problems and represent contributions not found elsewhere in the literature. Thus, we expect portions of the book to be dated as new methodological analysis occurs, and we urge readers not to use the book as a substitute for current reading in the methodology sections of journals.

As our own experience dictates, the best instruction in research methods comes from doing research. We hope this book can serve as the kind of companion to doing political research which will alert the scholar to the available options and the varying consequences of each decision.

ACKNOWLEDGMENTS

A book of this type reflects many intellectual influences. While the book would not have been written were it not for our frustrations in teaching political scientists how to conduct research with existing texts, nevertheless there is no doubt that those texts have structured part of our thinking.

Chapter drafts from the book have been utilized in a dozen and a half North American classrooms; feedback from these experiences has been helpful in suggesting revisions to the original drafts. But a number of scholars deserve singling out for particularly useful suggestions. These include: C. Richard Hofstetter of the Ohio State University, who sharpened up the arguments at several points in the manuscript; George Balch and Lyman Kellstedt of the University of Illinois at Chicago Circle and Lester Milbrath of SUNY-Buffalo, who clarified several difficulties in Chapter 5; George Modelski and Allen Pelowski of the University of Washington, who offered valuable comments in some chapters dealing with statistical analysis; and J. Merrill Shanks of the University of California at Berkeley, who made helpful suggestions in response to a convention paper that has been integrated into the book. Jon Cristopherson, a graduate student at the University of Washington, completed numerous computer runs for the factor analysis chapter, and Richard Li, now at the University of Wisconsin-Madison, offered expert help with the time-series literature. Ms. Anita Worthington of the University of Illinois at Chicago Circle and her staff faithfully typed various drafts of the manuscript. Martin Kessler, vice-president of Basic Books, has provided friendly encouragement to us as we have sought to realize the original goals of the book, and Ms. Charlotte Rosenberg, director of editorial services, has provided expert assistance in turning a manuscript into a published book.

Finally, we thank our families for tolerating the barricades of authorship. As one of our children wistfully reflected at the completion of the manuscript: "Now maybe Daddy won't have to think so hard anymore."

The book quite naturally is dedicated to the Inter-University Consortium for Political Research which—through its summer training programs, archival resources, and good offices in the social science research community—has had a more pervasive effect than any other single institution in nurturing whatever scientific research potential was to be found in the discipline of political science.

CONTENTS

PART
I

*Problems in
Scientific Inquiry*

Chapter 1

THE FORMULATION OF
RESEARCH PROBLEMS

Seldom does a published piece of research devote much attention to the actual reasons why the scholar undertook the project. Nor does it present much of the flavor of the human problems involved in formulating a researchable problem and executing the project. Public avoidance of such matters may be based on our desire to conform to prevailing misconceptions of a deductive scientific paradigm, where all hypotheses are spun out before the data are collected and the data, in turn, fall neatly into preordained cells. But we may also avoid such questions because, to be perfectly honest, we ourselves are not quite sure why we undertook the project and how the inquiry took on the focus it did. As Matthews mused when asked to describe how he got interested in the study of legislative politics, a question posed in that manner would lead to the same unpromising results a scholar gets when he asks a politician how he got interested in politics. Both questions ". . . run the risk of equally windy, self-serving, and unrevealing replies." [1]

We do sense that the discovery of regularities in human behavior is challenging in and of itself. In fact, Eulau and March, the co-chairmen of a major disciplinary review panel in the late 1960's, suggested that ". . . the search for patterns is the central task of political science."[2] Apart from the challenge of such an enterprise, we typically take other motivations to the intellectual task called "research."

Perhaps the major reason we have difficulty detailing why we settle on certain research problems and formulate specific research questions is that the process of doing research is endemic to human beings. From infancy to old age we puzzle, we reflect, we probe, we inquire, we try and often err. We seek to know. But we seldom seek knowledge simply to experience and enjoy something. We seek it because Western cultural values tell us that knowledge leads to power. Until environmentalists reminded us of other values, we studied nature to control it. In the Creation narrative, God told man to exercise dominion over nature. And we did. The scientist and the engineer collaborated in the development of theories and technologies which would enhance the ability of man to harness the world around him.

For social scientists and especially political scientists, however, the pursuit of knowledge is often suspect. In a social order that claims to be democratic, the "knowledge-control" linkage suggests a disturbing specter. Those who can "know politics"—who can find the patterns in matters politic—will exercise dominion over the political order. Indeed, one can argue, that is what the skillful precinct committeeman or campaign media specialist is doing. But scholars find it distasteful to be compared with hacks and hucksters. And so, we argue that the pursuit of knowledge for its own sake is the sole reward we seek. Or we evaluate proposed policy solutions to ever-present social, economic, or political problems, all the time denying that we are projecting our private values onto the public agenda. After all, we say, politicians and businessmen are selfish, while scholars are disinterested.

Perhaps that is what Matthews means about the fruitlessness of asking a scholar to trace the genesis of his research project. In doing what comes naturally—trying to know, trying to tease out order from disorder—we usually offer rather pretentious justifications. Yet our attempts to discover or impose patterns on our observations have a purpose, however ill-defined. By examining various purposes for the conduct of political inquiry we can shed light on (1) the many ways in which political scientists may formulate questions amenable to systematic and controlled inquiry and (2) the nature of the resulting contribution to knowledge, both in terms of its generality and plausibility. We have little doubt that self-conscious attention to the reasons for doing research and the manner of formulating research problems —at the beginning of inquiry—will help the scholar and the scholarly world to evaluate the end product.

Strategies for the Selection of a Research Problem

1 / DEVELOPMENT OF A BODY OF SCIENTIFIC KNOWLEDGE

Political scientists undertake research projects for a variety of reasons, none of them mutually exclusive. The development of a body of scientific knowledge is undoubtedly the reason offered most frequently by the scholar. When the corpus of scientific knowledge is at issue, theory is the point of orientation and theory is the goal. By "theory," we mean a collection of interrelated, warranted assertions about something. In a theory, at least two (and usually more) fairly abstract concepts are related to each other through a series of lawlike statements. These statements are warranted because: (1) they are logically implied by other statements in the theory and (2) the relationships between the concepts embedded in the theory are repeatedly confirmed by empirical observation of specific events. The former is called the test of deducibility; the latter, the test of tenability. Thus, both logic and experience are employed to develop a body of scientific knowledge. Existing knowledge is the customary starting point. What the scholar does with and to existing knowledge differentiates his approach to the development of scientific knowledge.[3]

The scholar may seek to *verify* (i.e., make more plausible) *existing knowledge through replication.* Replication is most commonly done after a new discovery has been made. A generation of scholars may repeat the initial inquiry to test the limits of generality and plausibility of the initial finding. Replication is not limited to duplicating the original investigation. Rather, other scholars will measure the concepts through different indicators, select different samples of subjects in different settings, and utilize different research designs. For example, on the basis of research in a housing project, a scholar may discover that influence in a social system is a function of physical centrality to a communications network. Other scholars may replicate the study in a controlled experimental laboratory setting with airplane crews, in a field setting with boys at a summer camp, or in the natural setting of a state legislature. While some indicators of "influence" and "physical centrality" in later studies will be identical to the original study, other indicators may be devised. The method of measurement may change from an interview to a questionnaire, to informants, to trained observers, to videotape. Additional hypotheses—e.g., that influence is related to perceived expertise, regardless of physical centrality to the communications network—may be tested. If, however, repeated investigations under both similar and altered arrangements continue to confirm the initial discovery, we will attach great confidence to the theory. That is, we will say it "explains" an important phenomenon—namely, influence—and we will attempt to utilize the theory to explain more and more political events.

Replication is essential to move a finding of limited generality to a higher level of theoretical abstraction. Rosenberg illustrates this move from a descriptive generalization to a theoretical generalization through a recurring finding in the early voting studies.[4] Over and over again, Catholics were found more likely to vote Democratic, and Protestants to vote Republican. To the campaigner that may be an important fact. But to the scholar interested in building a body of scientific knowledge which explains important political events, that finding is of little theoretical moment. If, as Rosenberg suggests, however, "Catholicism" and "Protestantism" and "Democratic" and "Republican" can be used as indicators of more abstract concepts, the finding will take on theoretical significance. A useful level of abstraction is offered in Mannheim's "theory of ideology and utopia." Lower-status groups, who suffer at the hands of the political order, support parties of social change; upper-status groups, who benefit from the present order, are likely to support parties of the status quo. If social status and ideology are useful concepts, and if we can employ "Catholic" as an indicator of "lower status,"

"Protestant" as an indicator of "upper status," "Democratic" preference as an indicator of "ideology of change," and "Republican" preference as an indicator of "ideology of status quo," we have a test of a hypothesis with considerable generality. But few scholars would settle for a single test. Not only would the study be replicated through time, but it should be replicated with other indicators of status—e.g., occupation, self-classification—and ideology—e.g., liberalism-conservatism scale, nature of organizational memberships—and the study should be done within subcultures and in other countries besides the United States. Furthermore, additional hypotheses involving either status or ideology should be deduced, and the behavior of Catholics and Protestants, and Democrats and Republicans, should be examined on these hypotheses. For example, one might predict that lower-status people would be more likely to join liberal groups and upper-status people, conservative groups. If Catholics do the former and Protestants do the latter, plausibility is added to the emerging theoretical generalization.

Sometimes replication with (1) other indicators, (2) other settings, (3) other samples, or (4) other deducible assertions raises doubts about the plausibility and generality of a theory. In that case the scholar may seek to *modify existing knowledge* by any of three strategies: (1) he may analyze the nature of the relationships by elaborating an entire argument and thereby discover spurious relationships, intervening conditions, or conditions that maximize or minimize the relationship; (2) he may pose new theoretical problems made possible through new methods or techniques of measurement; or (3) he may clarify ill-articulated concepts by noting inconsistencies between predicted performance and actual performance on the selected indicators for the concepts.

The inquiring mind is never satisfied simply to note an observed relationship. What mechanisms produced the relationship? Is it really there or is it a coincidence? Because one variable occurs with such regularity when the other occurs, can we really say that the other has in some sense "caused" that occurrence? Does an apartment next to the stairway "cause" its occupants to become influential in a housing project? Does responsibility for internal and external communications make the secretary the most influential person in an organization? Does previous experience on the bench condition judges toward judicial restraint rather than judicial activism? Are these relationships simply artifacts of a single measurement situation or are they regularities that occur over and over? Is the apparent relationship deceptive in that it hides another variable that is really the causal agent?

These questions call for the elaboration of an entire argument or, if you will, a causal chain. They are at the very heart of scientific inquiry. But they are also common to everyday life. For example, the parents of a red-haired, third-grade boy may be called to a conference with the youngster's neophyte teacher. The teacher points out how unmanageable the child is in the classroom: "He's full of it!" She has tried many times to discipline the child, but he continues to disrupt the class. The concerned parents ask for evidence so that they may deal with the situation. The teacher describes several situations and occasionally has recourse to the explanatory comment: "He's just like they said redheaded boys would be at that age. I have to watch him every minute!" That comment helps untangle the causal chain for the parents. For, while the teacher has noted a relationship between redheadedness in a third-grade male and disruptive behavior, the parents suspect that relationship is spurious. The teacher notes the disruptive behavior because she watches that child all the time, expecting him to act up, while paying little attention to the misbehavior of other children. We are likely to call her finding a *method effect*. But if we wanted to untangle the causal chain even more, we might find that the redheaded youngster is misbehaving, not because of the genetic trait of redheadedness, but because he perceives the teacher to be disciplining him unfairly relative to the other children. Thus redheadedness was a condition contingent to the causal agent—perception of the teacher's unfairness—which "caused" the misbehavior.

Many modifications of existing knowledge in political science begin with apparently spurious relationships and lead to the untangling of an entire causal argument. For example, the authors of the 1940 voting study in Erie County, Ohio, constructed the "index of political predispositions." [5] The index score—based on social class, religion, and urban-rural residence—correlated highly with candidate preference and was offered as an explanation for voter choice. In later work, however, Miller and Janowitz examined the relationship and found that these social characteristics "explained" nowhere near the amount of variation in voter choice that was explained by party identification, an enduring psychological trait.[6] And while party identification correlated highly with these social characteristics in Erie County, it was not so highly related elsewhere in the country. Thus, depending on the locus for generalization, the social characteristics might be antecedent conditions for the intervening variable—party identification—or they might simply be spurious characteristics confounded with the actual causal agent—party identification. It might even be argued that other social characteristics, such as region or race, might maximize or minimize the relationship between the original three social characteristics and voter choice. In untangling this chain, the scholar will seek the assertion offering greatest plausibility and generality. This generalization then modifies the existing body of knowledge.

Knowledge may also be modified because new methods or techniques for measurement permit the scholar to ask new theoretical questions. Consider, first, methods of inquiry. A *method* is a general approach through which the scholar structures observations, e.g., the dialectic. A *technique,* on the other hand, is a specific instrument for the generation and analysis of data, e.g., the semantic differential, factor analysis. Certainly available methods have set boundaries on what humans could say about the world they observe, for the questions we ask of that world specify the range of possible answers. Historically the methods we have used for asserting the truth or falsity of our statements have included (1) appeal to authority, (2) faith,

(3) magic and mysticism, (4) rationalism, and (5) the canons of scientific method.

There are many authorities that both learned and unlearned men use: Marx, Aristotle, the Bible, my psychiatrist, 40 million Frenchmen, scientists, and so on. Authority is invoked as a means of stopping challenges to an assertion; appeals to authority halt inquiry. In a social system where the norms prescribe clearly who is to be regarded as an authority, the appeal to authority will be taken as sufficient evidence that the assertion is warranted. However, where men disagree on the "authority" there is little chance of resolving the disagreement. Within an appeal to authority there is little room for extending the corpus of knowledge to incorporate new observations. An "orthodoxy-revisionist heresy" controversy is likely to develop. Appeals to authority are not uncommon in the works of scholars who deal in the history of ideas or the history of political philosophy. Some might argue that such appeals would not be found in the work of empirically oriented scholars. However, social science disciplines have ways of becoming tightly knit social systems with rigidly invoked norms. A disinterested observer may properly raise the question whether the search-of-the-literature section which begins each journal article or book is primarily an effort to locate intellectual problems so that research findings will be cumulative, or if it is an invocation of the discipline's gods which serves to justify the importance of the research. If this query has any substance to it, we must recognize that a discipline's folkways, as invoked by funding review panels or journal referees, often prescribe the method which we have called appeal to authority. As such, they may inhibit inquiry in much the same manner as do tribal chieftains or the Roman Curia. Knowledge is unlikely to be modified until the appeal to authority gives way to another method.

The appeal to faith is another method employed by men to ascribe plausibility to assertions. Whether the faith involves a supernatural power or simply intuition, an assertion is true because in the final analysis, "in your heart you know it's right." The person who takes this position is arguing that knowledge is not limited to what our senses can offer us. Thus, the knowledge system is essentially open-ended and there are no systematic criteria available for adding to or subtracting from the body of knowledge. This method is so boundless that most people who rely on it actually invoke authority or a sacred ritual to validate assertions.

The appeal to magic and mysticism usually prescribes performance of a ritualistic behavior as its own criterion for validation; this regimen, if executed faithfully, will result in the desired effect. Thus, a sacred rite of passage transforms a boy into a man, a girl into a woman. A divinely sanctioned investiture turns a novitiate into a priest. A rite of spring brings fertility to the soil, or a rain dance unlooses the firmament to drop life-giving moisture. A perceptive scientist, of course, will note the parallel between what he does and what the village shaman does. For common to both is the faithful learning and unfailing performance of the ritual at the right time. If manhood and womanhood are defined as capacities to produce children, no rite of passage will occur prior to puberty. Likewise, if a chemistry experiment is to produce the predicted results, precise control must be exerted over all compounds at all times. In science as well as in religious rite, however, the ritual can well become formalistic and meaningless. Thus, the political scientist who performs a factor analysis on every data set, who religiously uses the .05 level of significance as the ultimate test of truth, who offers the reliability coefficient alone as the sanction for his measures, is little different from the overly formalized bureaucrat in a transitional country aping Western models or from the village witch doctor. Ritual has no magical or mystical value for the scientist. It is a tool used consciously and publicly, applied sparingly and selectively, to produce knowledge. Magic and mysticism, where embodied in ritual, may well have efficacy in a closed knowledge system, where external conditions seldom change. As a method for modifying knowledge it is limited because it seldom penetrates to the elaboration of the entire argument needed for theory construction. On the other hand, one can certainly argue that successful exorcists of nature were early scientists, and that modern scientists always run the risk of becoming high priests, with all the attendant problems.

Rationalism as a method stresses reliance on human reason in dealing with ideas. As such, it is also an important part of the scientific endeavor. It takes concepts or other mental abstractions and looks for logical and illogical transfers. Once a system of logic is developed by the mind and is shared by other minds, men have criteria for evaluating arguments. Simple syllogisms, symbolic logic, and mathematical models all become useful tools within the rationalist method. Political philosophy through the ages has relied on rationalism. Empirical theory finds rationalism essential; as argument becomes more formal, political scientists will require increasing training in logic and mathematics. The rationalist method provides the criterion lacking in either raw empiricism or faith; it takes disparate pieces of experience and permits their evaluation in light of a logically sound conceptual structure. Thus, entire fields—voting behavior,[7] coalition behavior,[8] defense policy[9] —show the increasing application of formal models.

Few political scientists, however, would be satisfied with the development of a formal knowledge structure. They would ask that formal systems in some way "be faithful" to observable behavior. There is a strong component of practicality to this argument. Formal criteria are important in modifying knowledge but they offer little more than general guidance to us as we observe the ever-changing political world. Thus, typically we wed rationalism to empiricism through the canons of scientific method. These canons argue that whatever we "know" must be, at least in principle, observable. More important, the mechanisms for making observations and the means for making inferences from observables to theories must be public and open to discreditation. Scientific method is a means of controlled observation and controlled interpretation. Indeed it involves reason, ritual, and senses, but it insists on intersubjective knowledge. That is, the knowledge system is always open to modification by those who also use reason, ritual, and sense in a public way and can build a stronger case for the plausibility of rival assertions.

One can readily see that the move from one method to another leads to different kinds of theoretical concerns. For example, if the learned man asks only questions that involve appeals to authority or belief, divine right might well be taken as sufficient evidence for the authority of the ruler. However, if one is accustomed to following the canons of scientific method, he will look for empirical evidence of divine right. He may study the investiture ritual in relationship to sacred books; but he may find that task fruitless and turn to examination of the legitimacy of the ruler. Why do the subjects accede to his rule? What is the basis of his authority in their minds? What are the limits of his authority? How will the people or important sectors of the populace react when he exceeds those limits? Such directions for theory development move well beyond the content of sacred books, signs, or rituals, to the actual beliefs and manifest behaviors of the participants in the situation. New methods allow new questions.

New techniques also permit new theoretical issues to be raised and thereby to modify existing knowledge. When geologists developed trustworthy techniques to measure soil types, weather conditions, and growth patterns of different plants, the performance of sacred rituals in spring became less important to soil fertility than did the observation and manipulation of favorable production conditions. The earlier question—learning and exorcising the will of the gods—became less relevant than measuring and manipulating the ways of nature. In like manner, the new instrument permits new theoretical concerns to surface in political science. For example, on the basis of its national election studies, scholars at the Survey Research Center concluded that while issues might be an important determinant of electoral choice for some voters, among most of them the relationship between voter choice and the public policy performance and promise of candidates was not well articulated.[10] The technique which generated data for such an interpretation was primarily a series of forced-choice issue items developed by the study directors. However, RePass examined later SRC data sets and, by using a different measurement device, concluded that issue bases for voting choices were far more important than had been previously suggested.[11] He compared voters' responses to open-ended questions about issue salience with their responses on questions about candidate preference. This procedure permitted the modification of knowledge about issue voting. But still other measurement models which share the assumptions of RePass's work may allow us to say even more about the effect of ideology on voter preference. For example, Brown, using Q-methodology, and Marcus, Tabb, and Sullivan, using paired comparisons along with the INDSCAL model for analysis, have shown that ideology formation is a common property of nearly all voters and that it too has substantially more effect on voter choice than had been thought by Converse.[12] These newer techniques focus on mental patterning within the idiosyncratic individual, whereas the older techniques used a group norm to classify individual levels of development. Thus, in the field of voting behavior, not only do the new techniques permit modification of existing findings, but they facilitate research on theoretical concerns which the discipline has been very hesitant to address.

Finally, the scholar may modify knowledge because his replication of other studies points to ill-articulated concepts and inconsistent performance on the indicators that were intended to exemplify those concepts. The resulting research seeks to clarify both the concept and the operations used to generate data about it. Recent work by Balch is of this type.[13] He examines the concept "political efficacy" both through a meaning analysis and through performance data. (For a discussion of these terms see Chapters 2 and 5.) Using a sample of students located at several universities, he finds that political efficacy, as represented by the standard four-item scale developed by the Survey Research Center, is not unidimensional but has at least two dimensions. Two of the items correlate highly with items in a theoretical network involving social trust, while the other two items correlate highly with a theoretical network involving expressive activity. Neither pair correlates highly with the other. Balch concludes that what political scientists, in study after study, have called "political efficacy" needs considerable conceptual clarification and operational modification. Interestingly enough, Converse suggests a similar conclusion based on the more recent national election studies.[14] Many concepts found in political science literature—influence, alienation, participation, equality, sovereignty—are undergoing similar conceptual and operational analysis with a view to modification of existing knowledge.

On rare occasions, when scholars are seeking to verify or modify some aspect of the existing body of knowledge, an unanticipated discovery occurs which is of such scientific import that it may signal the development of new theory. In short, *the fortuitous discovery based on recalcitrant data leads the scholar to develop knowledge of a substantially if not radically different kind.* Walpole coined the term "serendipity" to describe such accidental discoveries. We are all familiar with such breakthroughs in the natural sciences: the miraculous discovery of penicillin or the Curies' remarkable discovery of radium. Rosenberg contends that two theoretically pregnant concepts in current social science literature came to us as serendipitous discoveries: relative deprivation and cognitive dissonance.[15]

Relative deprivation emerged from one of the largest personnel administration studies ever undertaken—*The American Soldier* studies.[16] Stouffer and associates were baffled by a recurrent finding: Northern Negroes stationed at Southern training bases showed higher morale (i.e., personal adjustment to Army life) than did Northern Negroes at Northern bases. Given the levels of overt racial discrimination in the two regions at that time, they had expected resentment to be much higher in the Southern camps. Yet after

11

reviewing the study design and other potential sources of error, the findings remained. Finally, the scholars concluded that Northern Negro soldiers were comparing their lot in life to that of Negro civilians. In the South, Negro soldiers' conditions were substantially better than those of Negro civilians; in the North the advantages were not that apparent. Hence, relative deprivation rather than objective deprivation affected morale. This hypothesis was tested and confirmed with several other samples in other settings. As a result, a concept which has served as the basis for much theoretical development was "discovered." Currently its utility can be seen particularly in studies of political violence and legitimacy.[17]

The concept of cognitive dissonance emerged from the discussions Festinger and his associates had about reports of Indians' reactions to a devastating earthquake in 1934.[18] People, already shaken by the earthquake, spread rumors of even worse disasters soon to come. Festinger and associates interpreted these rumors as "anxiety-justifying." If conditions were already unbearable emotionally, they might be made bearable through the threat of even worse conditions. The rumor served to reduce dissonance that people felt about their current rattled state. Cognitive dissonance and reinforcement theory has been applied to a variety of settings, especially in studies dealing with attitude stability and change. It has proven useful in the analysis of communications effects in political campaigns.[19] It has also been applied to studies of governmental policy impact on opinion change in the area of cigarette smoking and the Surgeon General's report about lung cancer.[20]

There is an important lesson to be learned from the examination of serendipitous discoveries. The discovery is an *ex post facto* interpretation. It is not yet a verified hypothesis. It is not the end product of research. Rather it signals the beginning of new theoretical developments. From it, new theory must be constructed which will pass tests of deducibility and tenability. A spate of studies must be undertaken which replicate the initial discovery but formulate explicit hypotheses to be tested. Only in that manner does the discovery become confirmed theory and take its place as a key organ in the body of scientific knowledge.

2 / MAXIMIZATION OF A SOCIAL, ECONOMIC, OR POLITICAL VALUE

Not all research has as its explicit purpose the development of a body of scientific knowledge. The point of origin for much research in political science is a pressing economic, social, or political problem; the purpose of the study is to conduct a systematic means-end maximization analysis. Typically some end or goal is posited as desirable; then a variety of means which might achieve it are examined. The study should show which means are most likely to accomplish the goal, usually with the least undesirable side effects. Often we call studies of this kind public policy analysis.

Within the public policy field, distinctive styles of research have developed. In one of these—cost-benefit analysis—once the ends and means are established, the analysis focuses less on data and more on logically sound strategic predictions. Its roots are in the rationalist method; occasionally, however, it will seek empirical data to test portions of the theory. For example, a number of political scientists do work in strategic analysis of national defense policy.[21] The end most frequently posited is peace, but other ends are also important—protection of spheres of influence, maintenance of territorial integrity, facilitation of free intercourse, and so on. If peace and the stabilization of current power relationships are posited as the goal, then a variety of means needs to be examined. One school suggests that strategic weaponry can serve as the best deterrent to war. A large nuclear arsenal will protect a nation from attack by an aggressor, particularly if that nation has a second strike capability which can wipe out the aggressor's civilian or military centers within a couple of hours. The certain likelihood of retaliation would leave the aggressor with a Pyrrhic victory and should be sufficient to deter his initial attack. Another school says that the best means for deterring war is arms limitation, particularly limitations on the weapons most devastating to civilian populations. They generally accept the view that arms are deterrents, but they argue that the risks attached to high-kill weapons are too great. Human miscalculations may lead to mistaken use of the weapons; politicians may suffer undue pressures to reach "final" solutions to recurring international crises; or the military may seek to escalate limited incidents into total war, which provides the ultimate challenge to their professional talents. Hence, while strategic nuclear arms might maximize the deterrent effect, the risks of total destruction are higher with that than with lower-kill weapons. Another version of this argument places great emphasis on diplomatic means for settling any conflict; sometimes the loss of some national initiative to an international regulating and peace-keeping organization is advocated. Still others argue that the best deterrent is a free and interdependent international economy, but to achieve this end some nations may have to give up current trade or monetary advantages. As one can see, each means for achieving the end has a cost. The task of the strategic analyst is to maximize the likelihood of achieving the end while minimizing the costs. Similar cost-benefit analysis is done on domestic policies—for example, studies of welfare reform.[22]

Closely related to cost-benefit analysis is policy impact analysis. The purpose of such studies has usually been less grandiose. Policy impact analysis is not strategic in orientation but is done after the fact. The goal for which a specific governmental policy was intended must be clearly specified; then controlled inquiry is undertaken to see whether that goal has been achieved and, if so, whether it was the policy or a multitude of other factors that led to successful achievement. If the goal has not been achieved, analysis is directed to uncovering factors which led to the policy failure. Curiously enough, with a few exceptions such as Harold Gosnell's 1927 classic, *Getting Out the Vote,* political scientists have not undertaken controlled inquiry of policy impact to the extent that social psychologists, educational psychologists, or sociologists have. A wide variety of evaluation studies by psychol ogist Donald Campbell and associates—ranging from police reform to educational policy—are now finding their way into political science literature. Similarly, the Coleman Report and other significant national policy studies done by sociologists appear to be receiving attention. Perhaps the principal reason political scientists have been slow to undertake policy impact analysis is that few of them have been trained in either experimental design or multiple regression analysis. That is likely to change within the next decade; there are already substantial signs of the discipline's awakening to opportunities for controlled evaluation of policy impact. Several illustrations are offered in Chapter 3.

An area that has attracted political scientists heavily in the past focuses on the systematic analysis of policy outputs. The discipline has always had a large component whose research interests centered on such matters as the forms of municipal government, legislative reapportionment, legislative procedures, and the like. But in recent years many scholars have systematically examined the relationship of these formal governmental structures, as well as a variety of social and economic environmental factors, to public-policy outputs.[23] For them, policy outputs are the dependent variable, while political, social, and economic factors are the independent variables. They ask, for example: What are the consequences of legislative apportionment on public policy? Do urban interests fare worse in malapportioned legislatures than in those that comply with the "one-man, one-vote" norm? Do states with strong two-party competition spend more per capita for education, welfare, etc., or is such spending more likely to be the result of the level of urbanization and industrialization in the state? Thus far, the studies have debunked a number of pet maxims about governmental structure which political scientists adopted from Progressive-era literature; generally economic factors have accounted for most of the variance in level of policy output. The studies must also, of course, address themselves to this question: Given a certain level of economic development, does governmental structure make any difference on policy output? The systematic analysis of policy outputs, like policy impact analysis, is an *ex post facto* procedure for determining *empirically* whether a specified goal is likely to be achieved by any of various means. It requires a high degree of control over the explanatory variables as well as possible extraneous variables.

Studies aimed at the maximization of a social, economic, or political value have had a preferred place in the discipline for many decades. Political scientists have often been political activists and many students are attracted to political science courses because they perceive that the discipline has an applied orientation. Public policy analysis, however, cannot proceed apart from the same rules that govern the development of a body of scientific knowledge. It is the function of theory to guide the scholar to relevant variables and expected relationships; it is the function of methodology to provide a rationale for the use of certain methods and techniques in making inferences from empirical observations. Without existing theory and methodology, the public policy analyst would be unable to specify relevant variables or to develop designs suitable for inferences. The product of his research may well be fed into the policy-making process; that is its purpose. But as a piece of controlled inquiry it also contributes to the existing corpus of knowledge.

All research on political phenomena involves the scholar in political and ethical questions. But in public policy analysis the scholar is more immediately aware of the acute nature of these questions because he has chosen not to divorce himself from the policy-making arena. If he has utilized inappropriate theory or exercised insufficient control over extraneous sources of variance, he is likely to give the administrator or policy-maker bad advice. Insofar as the policy-maker listens to him, not only dollars but human lives are at stake. Practically speaking, he forfeits the freedom to make a mistake that is afforded within academic walls. The policy analyst—whether with the Rand Corporation or the Institute for Social Research—is dealing with decisions about war, human potential, human freedom, life, and death.

His task is not made any easier by the milieu within which he must operate. For, as Campbell suggests, he is quite likely to be dealing with a "trapped administrator." [24] This administrator may see the value of sound policy analysis and will seek to subsidize such efforts. But the political order seldom takes an experimental approach to social change. It seeks answers right away. Changes occur slowly. If the administrator has gone out on a limb for a certain policy, then performance—i.e., social change—is seldom likely to match promise in the three-, four-, or five-year time span within which the political order will demand an evaluation. Consequently, analysis of the policy's impact is likely to make the administrator look bad. And the scholar, who regards this administrator highly because of his "rational" approach to policy-making, has contributed to his demise. Given these pressures, many agencies are likely to collect data only on those indicators which make them look good. The nation's health is measured by growth in GNP, not lakes recovered from eutrophication.

Not only does the public policy analyst recognize that he may well be contributing to the downfall of his allies in governmental circles; he may also be held suspect in academic circles for accepting "tainted" money. In the late 1960's a major issue on college campuses was the pervasive (and presumably perverse) presence of Department of Defense money underwriting research; people who accepted DOD funds were charged with selling out to a dehumanizing military-industrial complex. Antagonism toward the draft, the Vietnam war, and lost domestic priorities fueled these arguments. But as one political scientist of German-Jewish origin pointed out, "The United States fought another war once." The policy analyst, no matter how much he tries to divorce himself from other identities, is a citizen of a certain country. He must decide whose political purposes will be served by the product of his research and who will suffer as the result of it. He may have to determine, as with Project Camelot, whether he can ethically justify the pursuit of knowledge as a trade-off for supplying his government with that knowledge.[25] Particularly with research external to his national boundaries, he must decide whether his project will jeopardize the opportunities of other non–policy-oriented scholars to conduct research in foreign countries.

Finally, the policy analyst will have to live with the disturbing realization that the unanticipated consequences of policy change have a way of returning to embarrass him. He may be extremely resourceful in bringing extraneous sources of variance under the control of his design; yet no scholar is omniscient and thus able to anticipate all secondary effects. For example, most scholars would have anticipated that the Volstead Act would not significantly control alcohol consumption in the United States. And they would have argued that if alcoholic beverages were not marketed by legal sources, people would seek illegal sources. As a result, they would have predicted the rise of disciplined outlaw organizations—the Mafia, or what have you—to control distribution. Most of us would agree that the rise of organized crime in the 1920's was not such an unanticipated consequence.

Yet another consequence that has received little attention has to do with the leadership of big-city party organizations. Prior to Prohibition, many ward organizations began as beer-hall gangs, and the saloon keeper played a key role in politics. The organizations consolidated control, but Prohibition put the saloon keeper out of business. When one examines the ward and precinct-level organizations in city politics today, one finds very few saloon keepers. Did saloon keepers move onto the governmental payroll as a result of Prohibition? Did this lead to the rapid growth of urban bureaucracies? Did saloon keepers use their influence to get real estate or insurance licenses? Did this lead to the "politics of land use" as the principal locus for questionable transactions in cities? Did the extended absence of the neighborhood leader from his usual place of contact—the saloon—lead to the demise of party machines because they lacked friendly neighborhood contact settings? Such questions all stem from an unanticipated consequence of the Volstead Act.

At times it seems that the body politic is almost organic—change in one area will lead to wholly unanticipated change in other areas. If this is so, public policy analysis becomes a challenging and sometimes humbling area for research—humbling especially, because the policy analyst (as scientist) has less confidence than the politician (as advocate) in his answers. He is never certain that his theory and design have anticipated all relevant factors or that they have generality beyond his research setting.

3 / REALIZATION OF PERSONAL VALUES

Still another reason for the selection of a research problem can be found in the realization of personal values—principally the values of prominence in a professional network and security in a job setting.

Ideally all scholars seek, through controlled inquiry, to contribute to the body of scientific knowledge or to the maximization of a societal value. Yet they all live within constraints imposed by a disciplinary infrastructure and a job setting. Both reward published research. It is only natural, under such a reward structure, for quantitative indicators of research output to come into play. University promotions committees, try as they might, find quality an elusive trait; in disciplinary infrastructures, a recognizable name facilitates a career. While optimists continue to argue that the best work will eventually float to the surface and the rest will sink to the bottom like sediment, we are familiar enough with the mechanisms of career-building in academic and governmental circles to question whether a long curriculum vitae will direct us uniformly to significant scholarly contributions. Yet the constraints remain.

Under these circumstances, some political scientists may select a research problem because it deals with topics currently being examined by prominent scholars. Such a mechanism—some might hold that it has operated in the fields of voting behavior, axiomatic theorizing, and strategic defense analysis—should lead to a desirable cumulative effect. Yet in the younger political scientist's desire to follow recognized scholars' pathways to prominence, he may let their definition of the field's parameters determine his work. Other political scientists may choose a research problem because it is easy to do; the data are available—in government reports or social science data archives—and computer time is cheap. In contrast to other research problems, the research report can be offered for publication swiftly. Still other political scientists may select a problem because it is in a new area, easily preempted. Often the advice to the young scholar is heard: "If you're smart, you'll go out and study something nobody else is studying, and within ten years you'll be the recognized scholar in that area."

When one reflects on these purposes for scholarly undertakings, he can detect a conservative bias which may well impede the progress of a science. For example, in the 1950's Rossi criticized the major voting studies for relying solely on multistage probability sampling designs; he acknowledged that the studies have permitted a high degree of generalizability to local or national voting universes but argued that they have failed to provide the degree of precision that a factorial or rectangular sample would offer.[26] The studies, however, have been so readily available through the Inter-University Consortium for Political Research, that they have dominated research designs in the field. Interestingly enough, the Survey Research Center's 1972 sample design finally met Rossi's critique while maintaining the earlier generalizability feature; besides offering national probability estimates, the design generated a panel component and permitted precise analysis of both black and young voters.

In another critique of the voting studies conducted by the Bureau of Applied Social Research and, to some extent, the Survey Research Center,

Berns charged that their fixed-alternative questions failed to consider each voter's unique capacity for forming an opinion; the process of opinion formation internal to his mind could not be tapped by individual-difference psychology models.[27] While the polemical Berns' critique failed to comprehend fully the significance of SRC's modified Rogerian-type question, nevertheless it was not until Stephenson's and Brown's works, based on Q-methodology, were published in the late 1960's that the issue was enjoined frontally.[28] Nevertheless, many young scholars proceed with the archived voting studies, oblivious to the works of Berns, Stephenson, or Brown. While pathfinding scholars rightly deserve reputations for excellence, following in their footsteps because "that is what they are doing," or because "the data are there" does not necessarily advance a science. Intellectual issues must be enjoined. Nevertheless, the replication demanded by a hypothesis-testing, building-block scientific paradigm will require reworking the same or similar data with similar models.

How to resolve the dilemma between advance on the one hand, and necessary backing and filling on the other, usually is a decision the established scholars in a field must make. For the same people who are called upon to referee prospective journal articles are asked to serve on the governmental and foundation reviewing panels. As established scholars, they have set the thought patterns for the field; the burden of proof is placed especially on the aspiring scholar who seeks to challenge those thought patterns or to go outside them.

At times, pressure builds up to fund and publish research outside these thought patterns or in a completely new field. Again the journals and foundations must seek reviewers in whom they have confidence. And so they look to the young scholar who took the advice "to study something nobody else is studying"; he has embarked on a course of scholarship which will permit him to preempt the field. A new gatekeeper—whose work has probably not been subjected to careful scientific scrutiny—becomes a dominant force in funding and publishing circles.

The internal politics of scientific disciplines, of universities, and of governmental agencies are forces in the scientist's daily environment. A science demands replication and cumulation; established scholars must serve as gatekeepers. At the same time, scientists, young and old, are humans; they have aspirations not only for the "truth" but also for recognition. Under these circumstances, we must hope that the socialization of the scientist so ingrains the values of cosmopolitanism, curiosity, and intellectual openness that the personal gratifications which come from a job well done outweigh the seductiveness of prominence. In short, while the maximization of personal values is unavoidable, hopefully these can be made to coincide with the scholar's obligations to the body of knowledge and to societal values. The Velikovsky Affair is too recent an event in the politics of science to leave this point ignored.[29]

4 / SHEER FASCINATION WITH AN INTELLECTUAL PROBLEM

Some scholars select a research problem because they can't do otherwise. In their idle moments the problem continues to haunt them. For them, the problem becomes a matter of intellectual play; they must get to the bottom of it.

Idle curiosity has always played a major role in the selection of a research problem because scientists have always been fascinated with the aesthetic features of their work. They play around with a problem until an insight comes; they "tickle the data"; they tease out order from apparent disorder. There is a grand sense of design to political phenomena which comes from such play.

Often the fascination with an intellectual problem wells up early in the scholar's life. For example, Lipset, the senior author of *Union Democracy*, had a lifelong interest in the International Typographical Union.[30] While he was a boy, his father took him to monthly meetings of the local and he was always struck by the great sense of "occupational community" held by the members. Later, as Lipset became interested in socialist politics and at the same time discovered the Michels thesis—the iron law of oligarchy—he puzzled over the high degree of organized competition for office within his father's union. It appeared to be the deviant case; oligarchy had not invariably emerged. Why? The answer, he felt, was found in the determinants and consequences of the union's occupational community. Later, as a professional political sociologist, he returned with a controlled design to study the problem that had always fascinated him.

The crucial point in such a situation is reached when idle curiosity is transformed into controlled inquiry. Often idle curiosity leads the scholar to immerse himself in the phenomenon, to seek to understand it, to get at its genius. He will do exploratory work on the topic. But unless he can formulate the problem so that it leads to controlled inquiry and public inference-producing devices, the genius of the problem will follow him to his grave. Fascination developed early in life becomes a driving force in scientific inquiry, but it must be harnessed to a project that is public and nullifiable, and therefore replicable by other scholars.

Formulation of a Problem Amenable to Research

Encouraging the scholar to make private if not public confession about his motivation in undertaking a research project has a purpose. It is not that we want to create a generation of honest men, cleansed from guilt. That is the task of churches, psychiatrists, husbands, wives, and good friends. Rather, by asking that a scholar "know" himself, we are alerting him to common pitfalls in scholarly undertakings. Being aware of his values, he can have a better estimate of the generality of his work and can anticipate the barriers to scholarly confidence in his findings and interpretations.

A similar argument applies to the manner in which a problem is posed for research purposes. Once we have settled on a topic and begun to understand why we want to examine that topic, we can formulate it as a question, aimed at (1) simple description of the phenomenon, (2) relational analysis of various aspects of the phenomenon, or (3) causal interpretation of the phenomenon, its antecedents and its consequents. In actual practice, these three types of questions have a cumulative effect; causal interpretation cannot proceed without sound description and the noting of relationships. But the effect is not reversible; the scholar cannot hope to make plausible causal interpretations when he has developed a research design and observational techniques suitable only for descriptive questions or correlational analysis. The purpose of this book is to develop criteria for judging the strengths and weaknesses of various designs, samples, measuring instruments, and statistical models. At this point, however, the differences in the formulation of research questions can be presented and considered.

1 / DESCRIPTION

The beginning point in all research is the observation that something actually did occur or exist. The scholar should seek to document as completely and convincingly as possible how the event occurred or how the phenomenon existed.

Political science literature is replete with descriptive studies. Many scholars have sought to describe institutions. For example, they may look at how the Constitution, statutes, and practices have defined the contours of the U.S. Congress. The research question is posed in such a way that the full richness of detail about the institution may be brought together from all relevant sources. Other scholars deal with processes. Some studies, for example, will outline the copious steps by which a bill becomes a law in the Congress, a legislature, or a city council. Often such studies will offer comparisons of the process within several institutions; once comparison becomes rigorous, however, relational analysis is being done. Process studies are not limited simply to procedures within the formal institution. More frequently, "informal" actors are brought into the full description of a process. For example, in studies of the legislative process, the activities of legislators, lobbyists, interested executive agencies, the press, consituencies, and private citizens are all described. Still other scholars seek to detail the historical chronology surrounding an event or process. When a war develops they note various acts of hostility, the manner in which nations mobilize, the specific incidents that trigger the war, and the turning points in the conduct of the war.

Finally, some studies offer isolated facts which may be of interest to us. Frequently newspapers or scholars will detail the findings from a public opinion poll. A single question is presented and the distribution of responses follows. The following format is very common.

"If the election for President of the United States were held today, which candidate would you prefer?"

Candidate A	34%
Candidate B	25
Candidate C	16
Candidate D	9
Candidate E	6
Candidate F	5
All others	5
	100%

The findings are presented as a univariate distribution; that is, the table offers the number or the percentage of people in each response category for the single question asked of them. There is no attempt in such a presentation to analyze relationships; from it we infer the popularity of a candidate at the time the question was asked. We can infer nothing about which kinds of people in which parties or regions or occupations prefer which candidates.

Sometimes, however, data presented as though they were isolated facts are actually parts of observed relationships. For example, during the winter of 1971–72, the Gallup Poll and the Harris Poll reports on Presidential preferences consistently contradicted each other: Gallup said that among Democrats, Kennedy was the first choice; Harris said that among Democrats, Muskie received the plurality of preferences. The Gallup interviewers asked the question of all people who said they were Democrats. The Harris interviewers did the same, but before the data were published, Harris filtered out those Democrats least likely to be part of the active electorate. Thus, what Harris presented in newspaper reports was one-half of a bivariate relationship—showing only the preference of "active" Democrats. Had a univariate distribution lumped all Democrats together, the Harris reports might well have matched the Gallup reports. The important lesson, of course, is that a table that appears to present a univariate distribution may already be the product of cross-tabulational procedures; the reader must examine full documentation to decide what may be inferred from the table.

Limiting a research problem to a descriptive question does not preclude hypothesis testing. Rather, evidence must be offered to support the hypothesis that the descriptive facts are accurate and that they are based on appropriate sampling of observations. Furthermore, the nature of any preliminary relational and interpretive analysis of the observations—as in the Gallup-Harris controversy—must be clarified for the reader. We never observe without interpreting the stimuli perceived by the senses. But such interpretations do not necessarily force us to make cause-effect assertions. Acknowledging how our senses operate in conjunction with experience, we nevertheless sometimes limit our stated assertions to simple description of institutions, processes, chronologies, or isolated facts.

2 / RELATIONAL ANALYSIS

In relational analysis, systematic comparative judgments are made. The research question is posed in such a way that the scholar can determine whether two or more objects or events occur together or fail to occur together with some regularity. Among phenomena that differ in kind or *quality,* relational analysis will seek to show that one qualitative feature is most regularly associated with another feature and rarely associated with an opposite feature. Among phenomena that differ in magnitude or *quantity,* relational analysis will seek to show a regular pattern of association between phenomena. The pattern might be direct (an increase in the magnitude of one is associated with an increase in the magnitude of the other), inverse (an increase in one is associated with a decrease in the other), or a combination of the two. The kinds of evidence one would seek for relational analysis are illustrated in Figure 1.1.

FIGURE 1.1

A. Qualitative Association

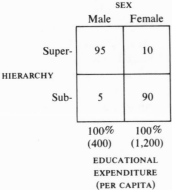

B. Quantitative Association

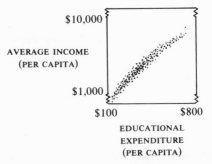

Status in Organizations by Sex, Governmental Agencies (hypothetical)

Educational Expenditures by Income American States (hypothetical)

Glock suggests that social scientists commonly undertake two kinds of relational analysis.[31] In one, the scholar examines covariation of *different* phenomena, e.g., sex of defendant and length of sentence. In the other, the scholar constructs a scale or index from *like* phenomena, e.g., "political participation" involving voting, working in campaigns, giving money, running for office, and so on. In neither case is relational analysis intended to suggest that one factor has "caused" another factor; other evidence is needed for that. Nevertheless, relational analysis provides crucial evidence for causal interpretations. It would be difficult to use cause-effect language when the patterns of conjoint association between two phenomena have not even been documented. Theory, regardless of whether it is a starting point in pure or applied inquiry, always casts a net. The net predicts conjoint association between certain dissimilar variables. But hardheaded measurement, as we shall see in later chapters, also insists that (1) more than one indicator be used to exemplify abstract concepts and that (2) each score somehow be a composite of performance across similar indicators. Both theory and measurement require that, for most research problems, both kinds of relational analysis be done.

Strictly speaking, relational analysis is as far as the political scientist can go in providing "hard" evidence for an assertion. In relational analysis we develop confidence in our finding by providing evidence (1) about the accuracy of each observation and (2) about the manner in which the magnitude of the observed relationship deviates from a "chance" expectation. That is, using certain statistical assumptions (see Chapter 11) we predict what kind of relational pattern might occur if, in fact, there were no relationship between the variables. Deviations from this norm are taken as evidence that the observed pattern is in fact worth studying. Causal interpretation, however, will seek to test out a large variety of factors which might account for the observed pattern. Perhaps the most common pitfall in social science is formulating a research problem amenable to a single relational analysis, but not amenable to systematic testing of a wide variety of possible explanatory factors—yet seeking to "explain" the event, i.e., asserting that one thing *caused* another.

3 / CAUSAL INTERPRETATIONS

The most difficult evidence to develop, of course, is at the level of a causal interpretation. Yet, that is the ultimate goal of political inquiry. Such evidence is difficult to come by because a multiplicity of factors may "cause" the same event, and each causal factor may, in turn, "cause" several other events. We have to be very clear just which factors and which events are the targets of our inquiry, and within that selected range of inquiry we must argue that the cause-effect relationships we have isolated are more plausible than other patterns which appear or might appear. Again, the machinery for such inferences constitutes the remainder of this book. However, we can point to ways in which a problem may be formulated *at its very inception* so that possible causes, effects, and complex processes may be anticipated. In the language of Blalock, this can be done by developing: (1) inventories of causes, (2) inventories of effects, and (3) models of complex processes, chains and loops.[32] From such inventories, hopefully, we can specify the conditions under which a variable is independent or dependent, antecedent or intervening (with maximizing or minimizing effects), or even extraneous.

When the scholar develops an *inventory of causes,* he searches existing literature, common knowledge, and hunch for all the possible factors which may lead to a specified outcome. Initially the possible factors may be labeled *independent* variables and the single outcome is called the *dependent* variable. At this point, two variants of the same strategy for formulating the research question may be used. In one, the independent variables are examined in relationship to each other to see whether any common factors among them have accounted for the relationship, whether some relationships are spurious, or whether one presumed independent variable has caused one of the other independent variables which, in turn, is the proximate cause of the event.

In the other variant an "accounting study" is done. All possible causes are enumerated and the amount of variation in the dependent variable attributable to each cause is partitioned off. If previous studies have already generated data for such purposes, statistical models such as the analysis of variance, partial correlation and regression (see especially Chapter 12 for a discussion of these models), and multiple regression analysis may be utilized to generate estimates of the relative impact of each independent variable. Schematically an accounting study might look like Figure 1.2. In this scheme,

FIGURE 1.2

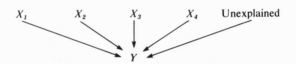

we have used shorthand to describe a very complex causal statement. It indicates that variation in each of the independent variables (X_1, X_2, etc.) has explained some of the variation in the dependent variable (Y). None of the independent variables alone has accounted for all the variation in Y. Nor have all the independent variables together explained all the variation in the dependent variable, because there is a residual term of unexplained variation. Finally, in this scheme the absence of any arrows connecting the independent variables to each other (e.g., $X_1 \to X_4$) indicates that none of the independent variables is related to any of the other independent variables.

Accounting studies help us to decide where there is a research payoff. Where we discover that most of the effect can be attributed to a single cause, we will probably examine that relationship more closely. Where we discover that the causal variables we have enumerated have accounted for little variance (a high unexplained residual), we would best start afresh with our attempts to explain the phenomenon. Accounting studies are most useful when a great deal of knowledge about a phenomenon already exists or large bodies of relevant data have been accumulated.

Accounting studies, however, rely on a sometimes deceptive assumption. They assume that all causes of an event are relevant and independent of each other. Seldom in social or political events is this the case. When the scholar

recognizes that his data might fail to meet this assumption, it is time to manipulate the inventoried causes to see how they relate to each other. It may be
found that the relationship between X_2 and Y is spurious, i.e., it is the result
of a factor hidden in X_2. It is entirely possible that the hidden factor is X_1 as
mediated by X_2, and if X_2 adds little to our understanding we may dismiss
it. Schematically the relationship would now approximate Figure 1.3. A

FIGURE 1.3

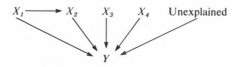

classic illustration of spuriousness would be the relationship between weight
and reading ability. Certainly an examination of patterns would show that
increased weights correlate with reading ability. But hidden in "weight" is
age and exposure to schooling. In fact, after a point there is no relationship
between weight and reading ability.

Another common result of such manipulations is to discover mechanisms
more general than those enumerated as causes which account for variation
in the dependent variable. The inventoried causes are mediated through them.
Blalock discusses Palmore and Hammond's formalization of important research on deviant behavior.[33] Initially, they suggest that background differences in sex, race, school success, family deviance, and neighborhood deviance account for the individual's deviant behavior. However, imposing on
the data two strands of theoretical development which seek to explain deviance by (1) blockage of legitimate opportunities and (2) access to illegiti-
mate opportunities, Palmore and Hammond suggest a model formalized by
Blalock as shown in Figure 1.4. Thus, an initial inventory of causes followed

FIGURE 1.4
Causal model of the Palmore-Hammond theory

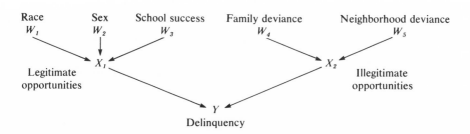

Reprinted from Hubert M. Blalock, Jr., *Theory Construction* (Englewood Cliffs,
N.J.: Prentice-Hall, Inc., 1969), p. 160, by permission of the publisher.

by a manipulation of variables to comply with theories at a more abstract level may lead to a more elegant causal interpretation.

Sometimes the scholar may seek to move back and forth between the earliest antecedent conditions to the more proximate causes for an event. In seeking to explain the relationship between economic conditions and the development of democracy, Lipset argues that economic conditions are well exemplified by the level of urbanization, education, and industrialization in a society.[34] But these conditions do not *cause* democracy; instead they lead to the development of certain values and behaviors which precipitate democracy. The latter include an open class system, equalitarian values, widespread sharing in economic wealth, literacy, high participation in voluntary organizations, and so on. Thus, the causes inventoried by Lipset involve a chain of both antecedent conditions and proximate causes leading to an effect. Each can be manipulated to measure its effect on the other factors as well as on the development of democracy.

An inventory of causes fairly begs the scholar to undertake an *inventory of effects*. Here the scholar identifies an independent variable and lists all of its possible consequents. The principal strategy for dealing with inventories of effects involves studying relationships between all possible values of an independent variable and a variety of dependent variables. One of the earliest works of this kind was Lenski's *The Religious Factor*. Kersten has capitalized on the Lenski model and more recent research in his *The Lutheran Ethic*.[35] As his independent variable, Kersten develops an index of religious beliefs. The index includes responses to items dealing with divine inspiration of the Bible, the historicity of the fall into sin, original sin, and the nature of salvation. The resulting scores are then characterized by the terms low, moderate, and high "theological conservatism." Kersten then relates an enormous variety of faith and life characteristics to these scores—e.g., membership in any of four Lutheran denominational bodies; attitudes on church practices, ecumenism, and morality; attitudes on political and social matters such as public welfare, foreign aid, civil rights, racial integration, and anti-Semitism; political ideology, party identification, candidate preferences, and others. In many instances the relationship between religious beliefs and these dependent variables is moderately strong and in the same direction. The more theologically conservative a Lutheran is (most Lutheran theologians would say these items characterize fundamentalism rather than orthodoxy), the more likely he is to be, for example, anti-Semitic or a Goldwater voter. On the other hand, the less theologically conservative he is, the more likely he is to favor, for example, ecumenical involvement and safeguards for civil liberties.

Designs such as Kersten's may be schematized as in Figure 1.5. The Kersten study relies on correlational models to document the association between values on the independent variable X and values for each one of the dependent variables Y_1, Y_2, Y_3, . . . Y_i. Such evidence alone is, of course, insufficient to permit causal interpretation. Rather, when inventories

FIGURE 1.5

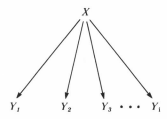

of presumed effects guide research, it is usually desirable to play with the effects in much the same manner we suggested for playing with causes. The scholar can see whether each effect is independent of other effects, whether some effects are in fact mediating others, or whether the effects are all resultant from common factors hidden in the presumed cause. For example, in the Kersten study one would like to see evidence that scores on the index of religious beliefs discriminate from scores on a test of closed-mindedness-openmindedness; if they fail to discriminate, the index has tapped a psychological trait rather than religious beliefs and has confounded the latter with the former as a causal agent.

Sometimes playing with the variables involved in an inventory of causes or effects will lead the analyst to examine conditions which seem to enhance or suppress, strengthen or weaken the relationship. The strategy here is to modify the independent variable in some way to see whether the relationship is strengthened or weakened. Examination of a scattergram will provide hints as to the desirability of such procedures; up to a point the relationship may follow a direct pattern, but beyond that point it may become inverse or weakened in strength. When this occurs, the scholar must examine the conditions that changed the relationship. Converse has provided an illustration of this strategy in his study of religion and politics in the 1960 election.[36] He notes initially that a sizable number of Protestant Democrats forsook their party identification to vote for Nixon, while some Republican Catholics also crossed over for Kennedy. The initial relationship between party identification and candidate preference is weakened by denominational affiliation. But Converse seeks to interpret more of the mechanisms which modified the initial relationship. He suspects that intensity of religious identification will enhance cross-over voting and uses both a behavioral measure—frequency of church attendance—and a psychological measure—communal involvement with the religious body—to study intensity. Indeed those with higher communal involvement—that is, closest friends from the same church—were more likely to forsake party identification in favor of consistency with religious identification. Several other variables including ethnic background, education, urban-rural location, and occupation are utilized; on some the importance of religious affiliation is increased, on others decreased. But by manipulating variables in this manner, Converse was not only able to isolate the conditions that would maximize and minimize cross-over voting rooted in religious identity, but he was able to suggest more useful measures of religious identity than simply "denominational affiliation." Inventorying both causes and effects is likely to alert the political scientist to more suitable indicators for key concepts and thereby increase the plausibility and generality of interpretations.

Once the scholar has begun to play with causes and effects, he or she is quite likely to *develop complex models* of causal relationships, some involving *chains* and *loops*. An exhaustive study of any phenomenon will involve the manipulation of variables in such a way that what was once taken to be an independent variable may now become an antecedent or intervening variable, or what was regarded as a dependent variable has feedback properties which give it almost independent variable status. In his model relating economic conditions to democracy, Lipset suggested that democracy in turn has a variety of consequences, some enhancing the continuation of democracy, others posing as threats to its continuation.[37] For example, an equalitarian value system operating through time in a democracy may become an egalitarian value system which threatens a capitalist economy. Widespread literacy, sharing in economic wealth, and high participation in voluntary organizations may eventually generate affluence and political apathy, or it may lead to a greater interest in governmental affairs. Thus, the same initial causes and effects in a complex model may generate positive and negative feedback. The task, of course, is to discover the conditions under which feedback is of one kind rather than another.

Complex causal models, drawn primarily from econometrics through the efforts of Simon and Blalock, have found their way into political science literature in recent years. Goldberg, for example, addresses familiar national voting study data with a variety of models aimed at discovering the most likely causal paths eventuating in voter choice.[38] The variables he selects —respondent's social characteristics, father's social characteristics, respondent's party identification, father's party identification, respondent's partisan attitudes, and candidate preference—reflect various strands of socialization theory and field theory. Goldberg tests six causal models, but one of them, presented in Figure 1.6, seems to have the best fit to the data. In complex multiple regression models such as this, the political scientist not only looks for the strongest path (i.e., highest path coefficient) between variables, but more importantly, he seeks evidence (i.e., low coefficients) that paths which his model has predicted will not be taken, are in fact not taken. If, for example, father's social characteristics are not predicted to have any effect on respondent's party identification, the coefficient between the two should approach zero. Furthermore, the multiple regression model used in these complex schemes allows us to note the cumulative effects of the variables.

In teasing out a causal interpretation, regardless of the model for dealing with causes and effects, the scholar can never in any final sense verify a theory. He seeks confirmation for a theoretical generalization by amassing

FIGURE 1.6

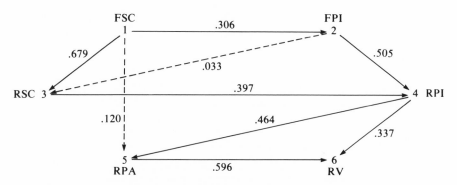

The beta weights of the implied linkages appear either immediately above or immediately to the right of their representational arrows. The beta weights of the linkages represented by solid arrows prove significant at the .001 level. Those represented by broken arrows prove significant at the .05 level but not at the .01 level. None of the possible linkages which have been omitted have beta weights which are significant even at the .05 level.

Key:　　　FSC = Father's Social Characteristics
　　　　　RSC = Respondent's Social Characteristics
　　　　　FPI = Father's Party Identification
　　　　　RPI = Respondent's Party Identification
　　　　　RPA = Respondent's Partisan Attitudes
　　　　　RV　= Respondent's Vote

Reprinted from Arthur S. Goldberg, "Discerning a Causal Pattern Among Data on Voting Behavior," *American Political Science Review,* 60 (December 1966), 913–22, by permission of the publisher.

many different kinds of evidence. Some of the evidence will show that the predicted relationships hold, apparently across several indicators and in several measurement situations. Other pieces of evidence will show that the relationships do not hold where they are not supposed to. Finally, still other evidence will show that other possible causal interpretations simply are not substantiated by the data. The causal interpretation offered by the scholar remains plausible. But the manner in which the question is formulated—the quality of the description, the strength and significance of the observed relationships, the handling of an entire network of presumed causes and effects —set the boundaries on the plausibility and generality of the research project.

NOTES

1. Donald R. Matthews, "From the Senate to Simulation," in Oliver Walter (ed.), *Political Scientists at Work* (Belmont, Calif.: Duxbury Press, 1971), pp. 9–10.
2. Heinz Eulau and James G. March, eds., *Political Science* (Englewood Cliffs, N.J.: Prentice-Hall, Inc., 1969), p. 11.
3. The following discussion is influenced heavily by Merton's classic suggestions

regarding the relationship between research and theory. Cf. Robert K. Merton, *Social Theory and Social Structure,* rev. ed. (Glencoe: The Free Press, 1957), pp. 85–117.

4. Morris Rosenberg, *The Logic of Survey Analysis* (New York: Basic Books, Inc., 1968), pp. 222ff.

5. P.F. Lazarsfeld, B.R. Berelson, and Hazel Gaudet, *The People's Choice,* 2nd ed. (New York: Columbia University Press, 1948).

6. Warren E. Miller and Morris Janowitz, "The Index of Political Predispositions in the 1948 Election," *Journal of Politics,* 14 (November 1952), 710–27.

7. See Anthony Downs, *An Economic Theory of Democracy* (New York: Harper & Row, 1957); Arthur S. Goldberg, "Discerning a Causal Pattern Among Data on Voting Behavior," *American Political Science Review,* 60 (March 1966), 913–22; see also several entries in C.F. Cnudde and D.A. Neubauer, eds., *Empirical Democratic Theory* (Chicago: Markham Publishing Company, 1969), and Hubert M. Blalock, Jr., ed., *Causal Models in the Social Sciences* (Chicago: Aldine-Atherton, Inc., 1971).

8. See Sven Groennings, E.W. Kelley, Michael Leiserson, eds., *The Study of Coalition Behavior* (New York: Holt, Rinehart and Winston, Inc., 1970).

9. See Herman Kahn, *On Thermonuclear War* (Princeton, N.J.: Princeton University Press, 1960); William W. Kaufmann, *The Requirements of Deterrence* (Princeton, N.J.: Center for International Affairs, 1954); Charles J. Hitch and Roland N. McKean, *The Economics of Defense in a Nuclear Age* (Cambridge, Mass.: Harvard University Press, 1960); Emile Benoit and Kenneth E. Boulding, *Disarmament and the Economy* (New York: Harper & Row, 1963); Amitai Etzioni, *Winning Without War* (Garden City, N.Y.: Doubleday & Company, Inc., 1964); David Mitrany, *A Working Peace System* (London: Royal Institute of International Affairs, 1946); Ernest Haas, *Beyond the Nation State* (Stanford, Calif.: Stanford University Press, 1964).

10. Angus Campbell et al., *The American Voter* (New York: John Wiley & Sons, Inc., 1960), especially Chapter 8.

11. David RePass, "Issue Salience and Voter Choice," *American Political Science Review,* 65 (June 1971), 389–400.

12. Steven R. Brown, "Consistency and Persistence of Ideology: Some Experimental Results," *Public Opinion Quarterly,* 34 (Spring 1970), 60–68; George E. Marcus, David H. Tabb, and John L. Sullivan, "The Structure and Content of Political Ideology: A Multidimensional Approach," mimeographed (Williamstown, Mass., 1971); Philip E. Converse, "The Nature of Belief Systems in Mass Publics," in David Apter (ed.), *Ideology and Discontent* (New York: The Free Press, 1964), pp. 206–61.

13. George I. Balch, "Multiple Indicators in Survey Research: The Concept 'Sense of Political Efficacy,'" (paper presented at American Political Science Association annual meeting, Chicago, 1971).

14. Philip E. Converse, "Change in the American Electorate," in Angus Campbell and Philip E. Converse, eds., *The Human Meaning of Social Change* (New York: Russell Sage Foundation, 1972), pp. 263–337.

15. Rosenberg, *Logic of Survey Analysis,* pp. 217–22.

16. See Samuel A. Stouffer et al., *The American Soldier,* 4 volumes (Princeton, N.J.: Princeton University Press, 1949); see especially Stouffer, "Some Afterthoughts of a Contributor to 'The American Soldier,'" in R.K. Merton and P.F. Lazarsfeld (eds.), *Continuities in Social Research* (Glencoe: The Free Press, 1950).

17. See Ted Robert Gurr, *Why Men Rebel* (Princeton, N.J.: Princeton University Press, 1970).

18. Leon Festinger, *A Theory of Cognitive Dissonance* (Evanston, Ill.: Row, Peterson, 1957).

19. Robert E. Lane and David O. Sears, *Public Opinion* (Englewood Cliffs, N.J.: Prentice-Hall, Inc., 1964), especially Chapter 5; Bernard C. Hennessy, *Public Opinion,* 2nd ed. (Belmont Calif.: Wadsworth Publishing Co., Inc. 1970), especially Chapter 20.

20. David C. Leege, "Missourians' Attitudes Toward Smoking, Lung Cancer and Governmental Regulation of the Tobacco Industry" (mimeographed report presented to the American Cancer Society, Columbia, Missouri, February 1966); Harold H. Kassarjian and Joel B. Cohen, "Cognitive Dissonance and Consumer Behavior," *California Management Review* (Fall 1965), pp. 55–64.

21. For illustrations, see footnote 9.

22. See Theodore R. Marmor, ed., *Poverty Policy* (Chicago: Aldine-Atherton, Inc., 1971); James L. Sundquist, ed., *On Fighting Poverty* (New York: Basic Books, Inc., 1969); Gilbert Y. Steiner, *Social Insecurity: The Politics of Welfare* (Chicago: Rand McNally & Company, 1966).

23. See Thomas R. Dye, *Politics, Economics, and the Public: Policy Outcomes in the American States* (Chicago: Rand McNally & Company, 1966); Ira Sharkansky, ed., *Policy Analysis in Political Science* (Chicago: Markham Publishing Company, 1970).

24. Donald T. Campbell, "Reforms as Experiments," *American Psychologist*, 24 (April 1969), 409–29.

25. Irving Louis Horowitz, *The Rise and Fall of Project Camelot* (Cambridge, Mass.: The M.I.T. Press, 1967).

26. Peter Rossi, "Four Landmarks in Voting Research," in Eugene Burdick and Arthur Brodbeck (eds.), *American Voting Behavior* (Glencoe: The Free Press, 1959), pp. 5–54.

27. Walter Berns, "Voting Studies," in Herbert Storing (ed.), *Essays on the Scientific Study of Politics* (New York: Holt, Rinehart and Winston, Inc., 1962), pp. 3–62.

28. William Stephenson, *The Play Theory of Mass Communication* (Chicago: University of Chicago Press, 1967); Brown, "Consistency and Persistence of Ideology," pp. 60–68.

29. See "The Politics of Science and Dr. Velikovsky," *The American Behavioral Scientist*, 7 (September 1963), entire volume.

30. Seymour M. Lipset et al., *Union Democracy* (Glencoe: The Free Press, 1956); Lipset, "The Biography of a Research Project: *Union Democracy*," and James S. Coleman, "Research Chronicle: *The Adolescent Society*," in Phillip E. Hammond (ed.), *Sociologists at Work* (New York: Basic Books, Inc., 1964), Chapters 4 and 8.

31. Charles Y. Glock, ed., *Survey Research in the Social Sciences* (New York: Russell Sage Foundation, 1967), pp. 8–12.

32. Hubert M. Blalock, Jr., *Theory Construction: From Verbal to Mathematical Formulation* (Englewood Cliffs, N.J.: Prentice-Hall, Inc., 1969), especially Chapter 3.

33. *Ibid.*, pp. 37, 159–62.

34. Seymour M. Lipset, *Political Man* (Garden City, N.Y.: Doubleday & Company, Inc., 1960), pp. 45–76.

35. Lawrence K. Kersten, *The Lutheran Ethic: The Impact of Religion on Laymen and Clergy* (Detroit: Wayne State University Press, 1970).

36. Philip E. Converse, "Religion and Politics: The 1960 Election," in Angus Campbell et al., *Elections and the Political Order* (New York: John Wiley & Sons, Inc., 1966), pp. 96–124.

37. Lipset, *loc. cit.*, especially pp. 74–75.

38. Goldberg, "Discerning a Causal Pattern," p. 919.

Chapter 2

THE INTEGRATION OF THEORETICAL LANGUAGE, EMPIRICAL OPERATIONS, AND STATISTICAL MODELS

In the conduct of inquiry, the political scientist is faced with a dilemma. He is seeking, in the first instance, to untangle fairly complex political events; so he develops abstract theories about these events. But theories are the products of the mind, and the political scientist wants to make certain that his or her theory can in some manner be substantiated by repeated observations of events. To do so, he can rely on some maxims commonly accepted within the scientific community. These maxims suggest the limits of confidence that may be ascribed to the integration of a theory with observation. The rationale for the selective application of these maxims to research problems is called *methodology*.

Unfortunately, methodological strictures are seldom met in fact. Most theories are likely to include terms without empirical referents or include other terms (concepts) that cannot be satisfied by observations on a single indicator or referent. Many theories, so-called, are not tight enough to be embraced by a logically coherent framework. Furthermore, most of the counting operations, summarizing devices, and quantitative comparison mechanisms used to analyze observations, while statistically sound, do not tell us very much about measurement error. Finally, there is the basic problem of translating verbal formulations of theory into mathematical and empirical operations, which may require a theory of correspondence.

Impaled on the horns of this dilemma, what is the political scientist to do? Should he or she become, as Dye fears, "methodologically constipated"? [1] Or should he unloose what he has to say about the political event all over the pages of a public journal? That is an agonizing decision, usually resolved by what a scholar's peers say about the proposed ideas and evidence.

It need not be so agonizing, however, if the scholar views the research process as a number of interrelated pathways, none of which very often leads to a dead end. Maxims generally accepted within the scientific community help the scholar to decide which way to go at each decisional juncture. While the maxims remain relatively constant, the range of possible pathways is ever shifting as we gain more knowledge about the strengths and weaknesses of each design, sampling plan, method and technique of observation, and statistical model. Furthermore, hybrids are frequently created and new instruments are constantly under development. Perhaps the most important decisional junctures can be located through Figure 2.1, which outlines the stages of the research process and some of the principal questions for which a methodological rationale must be offered. It is no coincidence that over half of the decisional space is devoted to precollection stages.

The most difficult task any scholar faces is that of not committing himself or herself too deeply to any pathway until the full terrain is explored. Collection, reduction, analysis, and reporting can proceed with alertness, confidence, and swiftness, once the analyst has thoroughly examined alternative theories relating to the problem at hand. For in them will come suggestions about appropriate designs, samples, measurement instruments, and formal analytical models.

One note of caution must be suggested in examining the steps outlined in Figure 2.1: Although we can reconstruct "stages" of the research process which usually precede or follow one another, in the course of any given research project, decisions seldom proceed this uniformly. Rather, a decision made in the design of the instrument or the analysis of the data will frequently cancel or modify a decision achieved earlier in the formulation of a research problem. It is the rare scholar who settles for answers only to the theoretical questions he initially posed.

This chapter introduces the reader to various stages of the research process but focuses primarily on general methodological questions surrounding the earlier stages of research. Later chapters will deal with specific methodological concerns at each subsequent stage of research.

The Nature of Theory

To summarize and elaborate on the discussion of theory in Chapter 1: By political theory, we mean a collection of interrelated lawlike statements or hypotheses which are intended to explain some political phenomenon or event. Each lawlike statement specifies relationships between or among fairly abstract concepts; usually the theory also specifies the *contingencies,* that is, the conditions under which these relationships are likely to hold. Thus, "given condi-

FIGURE 2.1

Stages of Research

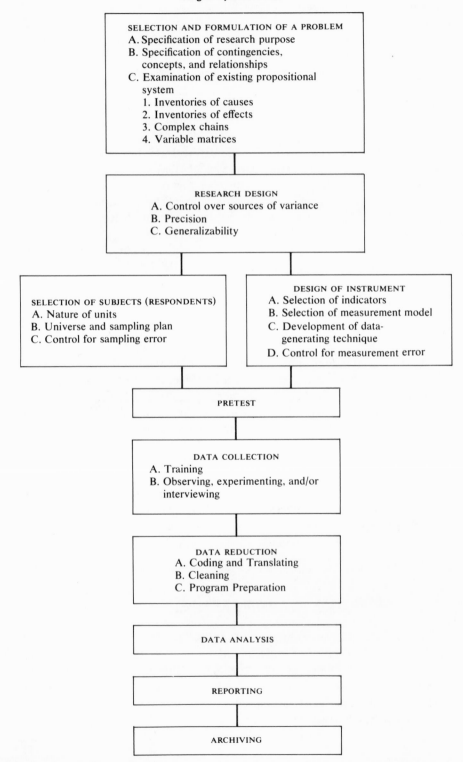

tions *a, b,* and *c, X → Y"* is a common form for a theoretical statement. Some statements in a theory will be *axiomatic,* that is, beyond logical derivation or empirical proof; all other statements are held together by a structure called deducibility. Generally, statements deduced from a theory must be confirmed or made tenable; *confirmation* occurs through empirical observation of the target phenomena. *Deducibility* occurs when, according to a prevailing system of logic, we can say that one statement implies another.

Scientific theories have both inductive and deductive components. The *inductive component* consists of a body of statements made tenable by empirical observation; that is, the events which were supposed to occur do occur and we have apparently uncovered a mechanism that leads to their occurrence. The *deductive component* consists of a body of statements which are deducible from other statements; they are valid. As Galtung notes: "An *inductive-deductive"* (hypothetico-deductive) system of scientific theory is a system where some valid hypotheses are tenable, and (almost) none are untenable." [2]

Both a *correspondence concept of truth* and a *consistency concept of truth* are involved in this approach to theory. But truth has no absolute character in either. A statement is "true" because (1) data conform to hypothesis and (2) a logical transfer has taken place. While on logical grounds we can certainly argue that a statement is falsified, we usually prefer to avoid a term like true in favor of terms like credibility or warranted assertions to describe the scientific theorizing process.

Whether a theory achieves widespread recognition usually depends on its *utility.* The utility of a theory may be determined by several criteria:

1. Is it *testable;* that is, is it possible to *verify* and *nullify* hypotheses stemming from the theory by examination of observables? Though the concepts embedded in the theory may be of sufficient generality to have theoretical import, can they point the scholar to specific empirical data suitable for test? Is it clear what is needed to prove or disprove the theory?
2. Is it *communicable;* that is, is it possible for other people in the scholarly community to understand the theory and the manner in which it was characterized by data and submitted to test? Is knowledge of the theory, design, measure, and finding transmissible or is it destined only to be understood by one man? Is it *intersubjective?*
3. Is it *fruitful;* that is, is it possible not only to reproduce the current hypotheses and tests but to *expand* the theory to embrace a larger number of phenomena in its explanatory network? In short, does the theory lead beyond repeated verification of current knowledge to new knowledge?
4. Is it *elegant;* that is, once the theory has proven its ability to expand knowledge, can it remain parsimonious and unified? Can it embrace a wide range of phenomena through a minimum of key concepts and relationships stated in formalized language? In short, is the theory, while general, still architecturally simple?

No theory is likely to pass all these tests, for any useful theory will be in a very fluid state of development. In fact, there are times when two theories —representing rival interpretations of the same phenomena—are allowed to exist side by side. For example, quantum theory and wave theory have both been found useful by physicists in describing the same phenomenon. Or in community power studies, elitists and pluralists are now emerging with highly similar findings, despite the fact that their interpretations of these findings are radically different. These interpretations or "proto-theories" may have become divergent because of the ideological controversies of our times, but the differences may also be traced to dissimilar research designs and data-collection operations. What is likely to occur when two theories continue to be applied to the same phenomenon is that either the limitations of one will become apparent so that it is seen as a special case of the other, or a more general theory embracing both will be formulated.

In political science literature at least four general patterns of theorizing may be found. Each has attractive and unattractive features. One general pattern involves *axiomatic* or *deductive* theorizing, in the strict sense. In this approach, an event is explained as a logical consequence of certain axioms and other lawlike statements. The tenability of the resulting theory is, for the time being, irrelevant. The scholar, acting as a logician, focuses only on the formal properties of his model. Downs' seminal work, *An Economic Theory of Democracy*, is of this type.[3] Downs begins with two elegant assumptions concerning rationality and uncertainty: Both individuals and political parties will act rationally—that is, engage in information-seeking about each other—in an effort to maximize utility income. However, both are faced with the condition of uncertainty; information comes only at a very high cost. The remainder of the theory involves the attempt to deduce propositions that help explain the behavior of individuals and parties in the electoral context. For example, given the high cost of information and the low return which comes from a single vote, it is not irrational for individuals to delegate to others (political parties, the press, etc.) candidate evaluation tasks; furthermore, the political party will attempt to maintain a more-or-less coherent ideology—that is, a general picture of the good society and how to achieve it—as a useful informational device for voters in the ongoing effort to corner their loyalty. Or, if the goal of the party is the maximization of an electoral majority so that it can exert control over the personnel and policies of government, and if information about each voter's preference comes at too high a cost, then it is rational for the party to try to occupy the issue space that the present successful party occupies; it would be rational to occupy a different issue space only if the party could show that a new majority, including substantially different voters, would be mobilized, or the current majority had partially shifted into a different issue space. In the decade and a half since Downs' theory appeared, political scientists have found in it a veritable gold mine of testable propositions.

Specialization of labor is not uncommon in any scientific enterprise.

Some scholars will limit their efforts to deductive theorizing; for them, the elegance of a tight theoretical network has its intrinsic rewards. But others will seek confirmatory evidence; they will submit many propositions in the network to empirical test. The important thing is that *both* must be done. Axiomatic theorizing or deductive theorizing is akin to a skeleton; it can indeed establish the form of a theory. But by itself it provides insufficient confidence about substance. Without empirical confirmation based on observation of political phenomena, deductive theorizing can hardly be labeled either scientific theory or political theory. But for the most part, this point attacks a straw man. Most current deductive theorizers serving the discipline have chosen to direct other scholars to data suitable for test, or they themselves, in other works, have conducted the test. At this point we do not fear that the interests of formalizers will lead to a divorce of formal theory from empirical research. Instead, we fear that too few empirical researchers understand either the fruitfulness of existing bodies of theory or the necessity of placing their findings within a logical structure. Perhaps deductive theorizing will remind the discipline of these components missing from so much current research. While the fruitfulness and elegance of deductive theorizing always commend it, nevertheless its testability and communicability must always be at issue. The formal theorizer must take seriously the obligation to point others to suitable data. More importantly, he must employ formal terms and tools of logic that communicate not only to other formalizers but also to those needed specialists who will submit theory to empirical test.

Probably the most common pattern of theorizing found in social science disciplines is *probabilistic*. Generally, this is the pattern we have in mind when we discuss the mixed inductive-deductive system of explanation. In it, propositions are either deduced from an existing body of theory or suggested by examination of data. Once formulated, however, the proposition is submitted to a number of tests, all of which are designed to make more plausible an interpretation of an observed relationship in the data. The tests usually predict what a "chance" association between two or more phenomena might be, and then the observed association is compared with it. The deviation of the observed relationship from the chance relationship is taken as evidence for the substantiation of the hypothesis. But careful scholars will not stop with a single such test. They will develop a more and more coherent body of predictions, involving many tests, so that the interpretation becomes increasingly plausible. The classic illustration of this pattern of analysis is Durkheim's *Le Suicide*.

Consider a contemporary political issue in the United States—population control. Let us suppose that in 1970 a demographer notes the following: The average white Protestant family has 2.5 children, the average white Catholic family has 3.0 children, and the average black family has 4.0 children. If we wish to interpret why this is so, we may develop a probabilistic explanation. One strand of theory may suggest fecundity. It is possible that the birthrate is higher in black families because a higher proportion of black females are in the customary childbearing ages of 15 to 45; to a lesser extent this might be so of white Catholic females. If these fecundity proportions did in fact occur as suggested, then we could not conclude that the birthrate differed by the race and/or religion of the family; instead we would argue that peculiarities in the age distribution of females in each class explained the differential birthrate. But our "probabilistic theory" would be based on the deviation from an expected "chance" norm and our observed relationships between religion/race, and age distribution.

In all likelihood, age distribution would not account for most of the differential birthrate. So, we turn to other strands of theory or hunch. Perhaps the differential birthrate is due to a physiological factor. Menstrual irregularity, hospitability of the uterus to a fertilized egg, conception-proneness related to customary position in intercourse, and so on—all might be associated with genetic or cultural traits of different races or religious bodies. Again, the evidence would be found in the configuration of numbers.

Most likely, we would seek an explanation for the differential birthrate in the modal attitudes and values of the three groups. One explanation might rely on differential usage of contraceptive devices. For socioeconomic reasons, blacks may be less likely to utilize the more effective procedures such as the pill, intrauterine devices, or voluntary sterilization. Catholic whites, on the other hand, may eschew such devices for religio-moral reasons. White Protestants, however, may view these procedures as morally desirable and may have educational and financial access to them. What would be needed to test this explanation would be both comparative statistical data on use of various kinds of contraceptive devices and attitudinal data toward their use.

Still another possible explanation for differential fertility may be found in courtship practices, particularly those relating to early cohabitation. Since other demographic data suggest that females who have children in their teens are more likely to have larger families, one might argue, it would be desirable to generate comparative statistical data by race/religion and courtship/cohabitation.

Others may argue that the birthrate differences can be explained by political factors. Both white Catholics and blacks are "threatened" minorities in this country, the latter more so. Therefore, as an instrument of political strategy, Catholic and black leaders will encourage large families and discourage family size limitations. Appropriate comparative statistical data for this test might include survey responses within each group as to whether their family size is in any way related to the need for more blacks or Catholics for political protection or influence.

Finally, other explanations might be found in the socioeconomic class itself or in migration patterns and settlement in urban or rural areas. Regardless of the explanation, the plausibility of the inference (and the confirmation of the theory) comes from the robustness of the deviation between observed and expected numbers of people, families, or whatever the sampling unit. And the more different kinds of statistical evidence the scholar can bring to bear on the problem, usually the greater becomes our confidence in the theory.

Probabilistic theories usually are attractive because of their testability, communicability, and fruitfulness. However, while it need not be so, in common research practice there is a tendency for probabilistic theorists to be less concerned about the logical structure of their theory and to let it inductively pick up excess baggage in the form of additional terms, conditions, and modifications. Thus, for the sake of the elegance and logical coherence of their theories, probabilistic theorists would do well to encourage formalizers to review their work from time to time. In general, however, this pattern of theorizing is the most common in social and political inquiry.

A third pattern of theorizing—*historical* or *genetic*—frequently appears in the literature. In this approach, an event is explained by examining its previous state: the conditions that regularly predict an event are best found in the temporal sequence antecedent to the event. Genetic theories have contributed such terms to political science as "incremental budgeting" and "sunk costs." [4] In the former, the best predictor of a legislative appropriation in a public policy area is the appropriation level in the preceding budgetary year. In the latter, the best predictor of resources available for economic development in a country this year is the level of resources available last year. Patterns in most human phenomena carry over from year to year with only minor changes.

A genetic theory might have been found useful in our previous illustration. Certainly one of the most reliable predictions of birthrate within a population class is the birthrate that class has typically had. Thus, black families are larger now because they have always been larger; white Protestant families are smaller now because they have always been smaller. But two questions immediately confront genetic or historical explanations: (1) so what? and (2) has it always been so? The machinery for handling such questions is found in Chapters 3 and 14, but here we can point in a general way to the strengths and weaknesses of this approach to theorizing.

We ask: So what? Who cares whether the birthrate or the appropriation or the level of resources is best explained by the level yesterday? There certainly is no question about the testability of such a theory, or its communicability, or its elegance. But is it really very fruitful? It points us only to the most obvious fact while typically overlooking the interesting nuances which explain the phenomenon. Unquestionably, appropriations for higher education this year are likely to be close to last year's level. But might the appropriation have been higher had the minority party been able to win control of the legislature? Might the overall level of increase through the years show a higher slope if the state had two competitive parties? What is the factor that maximizes or minimizes the overall relationship? The genetic theory is not likely to be fruitful on that score, and for that reason many scholars who rely on genetic theories will supplement them with probabilistic theories at key explanatory points.

One of those key points, of course, is addressed by the question: Has it always been so? To be sure, the rich get richer and the poor get poorer; but how did they get rich and poor to begin with? To be able to explain the crucial states of the organism—the take-off point where a potential begins to be realized—we must use something other than a genetic explanation. For example, it may be that the crucial factor in black family size is the role of the female in producing "property" centuries ago in the slave system. Because black women were obligated to have many children in slave days, blacks may have grown accustomed to having larger families, and thus, it seemed natural long after the Emancipation.

It is entirely conceivable that Protestant and Catholic family sizes were similar in Europe at one time. However, Protestants settled the United States earlier and gradually became a part of an industrialized, urbanized society; birthrates gradually decreased. Development may have proceeded more slowly in predominantly Catholic European countries, and when their emigrants arrived on these shores they were still accustomed to large families. Their families gradually decreased in size as well, but their take-off point was later than that for Protestant families. We have no idea whether such a theory would hold. It does, however, illustrate the crucial nature of explanatory factors at certain points in a time-series. Genetic theory is useful for many purposes, but its maximum utility comes when key stages of development are approached with supplementary probabilistic and deductive theories.

The final pattern of theorizing which appears frequently in social science literature is *functional* theory. An event is examined by locating it in a structured system; the consequences (function) of each component of the system (structure) are examined, usually by moving back from the function to the structure; finally, the balancing mechanisms by which the system returns to its approximate state under conditions of stress are explained. Often a functional theory will point out that several different structures can serve the same function (or have the same consequences); when one structure is removed from the system, another structure may take on its function. Thus, for example, in the healing system, medication may make a person well; however, a placebo might be used instead of the prescribed compound. The patient may get well simply because of the pill-taking ritual. In this illustration pill taking has a curative function regardless of whether an antibiotic with infection-fighting properties or a sugar pill is the structure utilized. Getting well is a psychological process which may or may not be related to induced physiological change.

Political phenomena lend themselves well to functional explanations. The multiplicity of causes for a political event and the frequent interchangeability of cause and effect render structural-functional models attractive. Functional theories are, of course, a more complex version of simple cause-effect models. In essence, a functional theory states that a function may be the result of several structures and that a function in turn has feedback effects on these structures. If one structure is destroyed (cause removed), another structure may take on more of that function (cause enhanced as the result of feedback within the system).

While political scientists are quite familiar with the general systems models of Easton, Levy, Parsons, or Loomis, many scholars in comparative politics and developmental administration have sought to formulate more manageable functional theories. Riggs, for example, notes how values that were served by prebendary and patrimonial bureaucratic structures in traditional societies are still served through rational-legal structures, as these societies adopt the symbols of modernity.[5] Ascriptive criteria may lead a civil service official to upgrade the test scores of people from his lineage. Or the ruler, while confiscating land and dividing it up among peasants, still consumes conspicuously in wives and wealth because such consumption was formerly a symbol of royalty. Easton points to Smith's study of lineage segmentation as the functional equivalent of pressure group formation.[6] And indeed, in many modern tribal-based polities, political interest groups—religious sects, labor unions, landholders' associations—are thinly veiled strongholds for an extended lineage. Splits within these groups and alliances among them may result from the political aspirations of half brothers or from strategic marriages.

In principle, functional theorizing should allow the scholar to meet all criteria for the utility of a theory. In practice, however, it has suffered from two weaknesses. First, many scholars have used functional analysis as little more than a shopping list. Any theory, of course, presents a conceptual map of the terrain, but a scientific theory moves on to empirical observation of that terrain and the testing of theory. Some functionalists, however, are so enamored of their models that they either forget to offer the scholar a host of testable propositions or fail to follow through with appropriate empirical research themselves. In short, not unlike some deductive theorists, some functional theorists fail to observe the criterion of testability.

Secondly, some functional theories are easily confused with normative injunctions. To state that a function is met by various structures is *not* to state that these structures are good and must persist through time. Voting might have permitted popular control over governmental policies at one time, but that does not mean that other structures could not perform the control function as well. Nor does it mean that if voters do not exert control over policy in the voting act, elections should be abolished; voting might serve other functions such as legitimizing a regime, developing allegiance to a political community, or providing catharsis for individuals who feel guilty about their negligible participation in policy-making. Functional theory is empirical theory; it partakes of the same descriptive, relational, and causal properties which characterize any scientific theory. Unfortunately, an assumption held by many functional theorists—namely, universal functionalism—contributes to the mistaken conclusion that "everything which *is* has a function; therefore, everything ought to be allowed to persist." To conclude thus not only would involve the scientist in premature theoretical closure but would lead him into advocacy of whatever exists. That in itself does not frighten us so long as the scientist does so openly. Unfortunately even when functional theorists have not had the intent of favoring existing structures, many of their readers have attributed it to their work. Thus, functional theory often suffers from problems of communicability.

The patterns of theorizing described above are not mutually exclusive. The same phenomenon can be approached through probabilistic theory at one time, functional theory at another. In fact a fruitful exercise in initially laying out a research problem is to develop theory about it through each of the four patterns. Each is quite likely to lead to different design, sampling, and measurement requirements and, as a result, more of the pathways through the terrain will be illuminated for the scholar.

The Test of a Theory

The dilemma posed at the beginning of this chapter is generic to social inquiry. We never actually *test* our substantive theory. Rather, through empirical operations we test a "test theory." [7] We test a posited relationship (or predictions) between sets of indicators which we feel exemplify each concept. Simply to note correlations between indicators would be inadequate for theoretical purposes. Instead we must include in our test theory a series of specifications which detail how we have moved from our general substantive theory down to the observables we claim to have measured, and vice versa.

The need for a test theory is based on three factors: (1) theoretically relevant concepts are usually more abstract than can be exemplified by a single measurable indicator; (2) some of the most theoretically relevant concepts—e.g., power, cause—are not directly observable; and (3) because of the first two conditions, an *a priori* unknown amount of measurement error is embedded in each empirical research effort. The test theory must first provide a rationale for the use of certain indicators for each concept; usually this is done through a *theory sketch,* or the construction of a *nomological network* of related predictions, and through careful explication of concepts; more is said about these tasks in the next two sections of this chapter and in Chapter 5. The test theory must secondly specify those concepts which are not directly observable and put them together in axioms; axioms will include all statements of cause and effect. Third, the test theory must specify what kinds of evidence might be taken as confirmation or disconfirmation of these axioms, *if* they were to be regarded as measurable. The kinds of evidence acceptable will have been suggested as covariation statements in the theory sketch or nomological network. But equally important to evidence about the predicted covariation between indicators is evidence about causal direction, about the effects of measurement itself, and about other possible causal factors of a substantive nature. Essentially, this third aspect of a test theory is a problem in research design—in the mechanisms by which we can make inferences from observations; some considerations about research design are introduced in this section and discussed in detail in Chapter 3. The first two aspects simply flow from the requirements that empirical research be theoretically rooted and that scientific knowledge be public in its development; these points are developed throughout the book.

Let us suppose that the set of predictions from our substantive theory has been upheld by the covariation pattern in our data. Typically we are likely to conclude that our theory has been confirmed, that it explains something. But such a conclusion would be erroneous without evidence that our entire measurement process has constituted a valid operationalization of the theory. When we get confirmation, we should do what we typically do when our predictions lack confirmation—namely, examine the integration of our theory and research to see whether: (1) the test theory, particularly with the indicators selected, did not really measure the substantive theory, or (2) the experimental or quasi-experimental design utilized for making inferences did not provide suitable controls over extraneous factors that got confounded with the test, or (3) the substantive theory was itself not credible. The first two challenges might be called "method effects"; the third might be considered a substantive challenge. The substantive challenge, of course, is the reason why we theorize and do research in the first place. We want to explain something. But our explanation may be an artifact of the way we have done our research. Thus, all three challenges must be dealt with.

There are many possible theories which could explain observed patterns of variation in data. If the observer cannot conjure up a variety of theories, it is doubtful whether he should be engaged in the scientific enterprise. Let us suppose we observe some events and label them C; we search around for possible explanations and decide that theory A offers a suitable explanation. This may be characterized: $A \leftrightarrow C$. Now, if we can find instances where theory A does not explain empirically observed events C, then we have induced evidence against the credibility of theory A. If we recurringly find instances where events C seem to be explained by theory A (at least in the way events C exemplify the concepts in theory A), we will regard theory A as credible. But *regardless of the outcome,* we want to know why theory A explains or fails to explain events C. Such curiosity will lead us into examination of (1) whether the entire set of predictions stemming logically from theory A applies to other events surrounding C and (2) whether the operations and indicators used in observation of C limit the applicability of theory A. The answers to these questions will determine the level of generality of the theory—both in terms of substance and method.

To deal with the questions of generality stemming from the integration of a theory with empirical observations, the scholar typically formulates specific testable hypotheses. The first hypothesis will seek to eliminate rival substantive theories. It will ask: Given events C, which theory, A or B, is a more plausible explanation? This may be characterized:

Although all rival theories should be tested as to their plausibility, generally the scholar should seek the most plausible rival theory for the "crucial experiment," as Stinchcombe and others have called it.[8] The task usually begins with the examination of the correlational patterns between *A* and *C* and *B* and *C*. Let us suppose we have called *C* the "process of modernization" and the events referred to are largely ones having to do with industrialization. Furthermore, let us suppose that theory *A* indicated, as Lerner has suggested, that modernization is the result of "empathy," the ability to imagine oneself in a setting changed not as the result of blind faith but because of conscious instrumental activity.[9] For the sake of further illustration, let us suppose that empathy must be a property of modal national character; that is, the largest sector of the populace must be empathic before a nation can modernize. Finally, let us suppose that we measured empathy through a battery of story completion tests on a survey addressed to several nationwide samples in modernized and traditional countries, and we found that there is indeed a pattern of covariation between empathy and industrialization; the correlation is high and positive.

Now the crucial test of the theory would occur when a strong rival theory was addressed to the same events *C*. Let us suppose that rival theory *B* stated that modernization results from the coercive actions of an industrializing oligarchy which decrees change and enforces it. And indeed on various indicators of coercive action by an industrializing oligarchy we find a high positive correlation with indicators of industrialization. Both theories seem to "explain" the same phenomenon. But which theory has more utility? We must now search around for other predictions which should stem from a theory about modernization. Modernization should also include changes other than industrialization; if modernization occurs, we might predict widespread literacy (as measured by the degree of mass sharing in a common national language or symbol system), urbanization (as measured by the proportion of the population living inside or within close proximity to metropolitan centers), functional specialization of governmental bodies, and so on. Now let us suppose we correlated indicators of empathy and indicators of coercive actions by an industrializing oligarchy with these other aspects of modernization. We might find that empathy as a modal national trait correlated highly with all other aspects of modernization, but coercive actions of an industrializing oligarchy did not. We would then conclude that empathy constituted a more useful theory of modernization.

The logic of the crucial experiment calls for both *convergent* and *discriminant* evidence. High correlations across all theoretical predictions provide convergent evidence which makes a theory more credible. Low correlations across some of the other predictions provide discriminant evidence that allows us to dismiss the rival theory. In this instance, modernization in all its aspects occurs only with empathy. The point about convergent and discriminant evidence from multiple indicators is vital to the understanding of social measurement and is developed more fully in Chapter 5.

It may commonly happen that existing theory is modified very substantially by a crucial experiment. For example, it is possible in our illustration that B causes C up to a certain point, and beyond that, part of C has a feedback effect that causes A and the rest of C. Coercive action by a few may bring about some industrialization, and further modernization may come about through changes in the social relations surrounding production and distribution; these changes in turn may lead to the development of an empathic modal national character, that is, a citizenry open to change. Or it may be that A (empathy) is necessary initially only in a small group (the industrializing oligarchy) and B (their coercive actions) causes modernization. One can readily see the utility of the problem-formulation procedures that in Chapter 1 we called "inventorying causes and effects." In the earliest research stages, rival theories may be suggested as well as a variety of indicators for each key concept. If existing theory is well developed, a nomological network relating many possible expectations about cause and effect may be fashioned. If it is less well developed, a more speculative theory sketch—a kind of proto-theory based on insight—can guide research. In either case, inventories of causes, effects, and feedback loops can guide the researcher to necessary empirical observations which will enhance the plausibility of his or her theory.

Illustrations of crucial experiments are difficult to find in political science literature of the past, but as the discipline makes conscious efforts to develop as a building-block science, they should be on the increase. An impressive recent effort of this kind is found in the research of Sullivan and Marcus.[10] The authors note that a great deal of scholarly attention has been addressed to the finding that most Americans cannot be characterized by "ideological thinking" or a "high level of conceptual organization" about politics. In one study they examined, Merelman had suggested a child-rearing or political socialization theory to account for this phenomenon. The theory involved a complex interaction of such factors as degree of parental warmth, method of child punishment, degree of identification with parents, degree of cognitive development, time of responsibility assumption, and degree of moral development—eventuating in level of ideology.[11] But Sullivan and Marcus return to the cognitive and developmental psychology literature where these concepts were first used, abstract from it a nomological network of interrelated propositions, submit them to empirical test, and find little confirmation in the data. In fact, the nomological network drawn from Merelman's model through the relevant theoretical sources itself led to inconsistent inferences.

Sullivan and Marcus then proceed through the test of several rival theories—social class, education, political activity, the functionality of ideology for information reduction, and level of political information. They find little support for complex models such as the socialization model or the functional model. Instead, they conclude that level of ideology is a simple function of level of information: the more a person learns about politics, the higher his level of conceptualization. The entire effort to weed out plausible rival hypotheses is based on the convergent and discriminant evidence approach we have urged above.

To this point we have suggested the formulation of specific testable hypotheses which are all substantive in character. Yet we have indicated that the generality which can be attributed to the integration of a theory with empirical observations is also a function of method effects. Thus, we must formulate hypotheses dealing with the measurement situation. We must be able to show that a theory explains the phenomenon across a reasonable number of different research designs, samples, methods and techniques for generating data, and statistical models for the analysis of data. Again, specific procedures for isolating and controlling method effects constitute the remaining chapters of the book; here we wish to introduce the general considerations.

Method effects result from our effort to link the imperfect measurement situation with our causal propositions or axioms. They occur when we seek evidence of *covariation, causal direction* of the relationship, and *nonspuriousness.*[12] To measure *covariation* we must, of course, assume that there is a range of possible values for each variable; we cannot work with a set of events for which there can be only one classification, a simple identity. Each variable will require a variety of values. Covariation will show the extent to which these values vary in predictable patterns. Covariation can be observed through two principal designs: (1) designs permitting *active control* and (2) designs permitting *passive control.*

In designs permitting *active control*—usually variants of the classic experiment—the researcher himself introduces the causal variable; this design permits him to manipulate the causal ("treatment") variable, so that for each value of it, he can measure the value of the dependent variable. Through randomized assignment to control and experimental groups, the design is intended to permit control over all contingency conditions, so that only the manipulated effects of the causal variable are observed in the values of the dependent variable. Specific experimental arrangements are evaluated in Chapter 3; various observational techniques suitable for active control are discussed in Chapter 7; and statistical models for dealing with covariational effects are described in later chapters, particularly those dealing with partial correlation and analysis of variance.

Designs permitting *passive control,* on the other hand, usually involve observation of natural change mechanisms or *ex post facto* attempts to reconstruct the change through either published records or self-reported data. Often, these designs do not allow the degree of precision and control found in the active control designs, but they do permit inferences to be drawn. Many quasi-experimental designs discussed in Chapter 3 are of this kind, especially those building on time-series data and correlational machinery. Multiple regression analysis, discussed in Chapter 12, is proving an increasingly powerful statistical model for exerting passive control over data. The whole range of observational devices running from participant observation to survey research to public documents may be used to generate data; each device, of course, has measurement errors to which it is particularly prone and these are discussed in Chapter 7.

The *causal direction* of a relationship may be uncovered through a variety of strategies, most of which have to do with *temporal sequence*. In the designs permitting active control, temporal sequence is manipulated by the researcher himself. The premeasure establishes the prevailing values of the dependent variable; then the experimenter introduces whatever value of the causal treatment he wishes, and the change in value on the dependent variable is recorded.

In designs permitting passive control, other strategies for handling temporal sequence must be devised. One strategy is to use ascriptive traits—characteristics inherited by the sampling units prior to any impact by a causal treatment—as theoretically relevant explanations of effects. Attitudes or political values might be treated as the result of race or sex or parental social class, all of which preceded them in time. Unfortunately, few of the theoretically relevant linkage mechanisms which relate ascriptive traits to attitudes or values are clarified by this procedure. In fact, overreliance on "demographic characteristics" as explanations may lead us to misunderstand the very phenomenon we are trying to explain. For example, some argue that educational achievement is largely the result of inherited native abilities which differ by race; it is far more likely, however, that educational achievement is the result of social values which limit the aspirations and access of certain racial minorities. It may even be the result of built-in racial biases in the criterion used to measure educational achievement. Thus, passive control over time sequence is not by itself sufficient evidence of causal direction.

Another strategy for dealing with directionality is to take full advantage of existing knowledge about theoretical linkages. For example, if one cannot control the causal variable but can manipulate a variable which is always associated predictably with it, he can manipulate the latter and measure changes in value on the dependent variable. As Stinchcombe suggests, we may not be able to control sunshine but through the use of a hothouse we can control temperature. Now if plants grow predictably by temperature regardless of the presence or absence of sunlight, we can certainly conclude something about causal direction—plants do not cause sunlight. Interestingly enough, we might conclude also that heat, not sunlight, is the causal agent, and thus modify our theory.

In a similar manner, if we cannot actively manipulate values on the causal treatment, we might be tempted to control values on the dependent variable and reconstruct the value of the independent variable. Then if covariation occurs, we might conclude that the latter is indeed the causal variable. But without additional knowledge about temporal sequence, we cannot do so. Our "dependent" variable may actually be the causal variable. Such additional knowledge may come from the entire theoretical network which surrounds a relationship. Let us suppose we know that candidate preference varies predictably with the strength and direction of party identification. It also varies with the salience of issues and the charismatic appeal of candidates in a given election. Furthermore, let us suppose we know that the latter two factors are weak in a given election. Finally, we know that party identification is developed long before the individual has knowledge of candidates or issues. Then, we can reasonably conclude that party identification typically "causes" candidate preference rather than the causal direction being reversed. Thus, even when passive control over one or both variables is the best the scholar can exert, sound theory can help the scholar assert the direction of causality with some confidence.

Finally, evidence of *nonspuriousness* can be developed in much the same manner as evidence for covariation and causal direction. Through active introduction and manipulation of suspected spurious variables the scholar may see where the stronger relationship exists—with the causal one or the spurious one. Through the randomized assignment of subjects to groups that receive the experimental treatment and those that don't, the scholar may assume he has allocated possible spurious factors equally. Randomization is most likely to control for spuriousness in those experimental designs (discussed in Chapter 3) which make special allowance for reactive measurement.

In passive control designs the machinery of elaboration, presented in Chapters 1 and 3, also permits control for spuriousness. In particular, standardization, partial correlation, multiple and partial regression, and the varieties of path analysis found in causal models provide appropriate statistical devices for control of spuriousness; all are discussed in later chapters. One major source of spuriousness is the set of indicators utilized by the scholar to exemplify each concept; convergent and discriminant evidence models for the control of measurement error are discussed in Chapter 5, and the manner by which variables for distinct concepts may suffer from the same confounding source of measurement error when generated by identical operations is discussed further in Chapter 7.

Throughout this book, we espouse the *multioperational* strategy—for design, sample, method and technique, and statistical model. This strategy is the one most likely to enhance the credibility of our integration of theory and research. A test theory that spells out as clearly as possible the implications of the theory and relevant rival theories, and that permits comparative assessment of possible measurement errors stemming from each design and measure, builds confidence in theoretical assertions. In fact, the more complete a test theory, the more it resembles all possible pathways to the solution of an intellectual problem.

The Flow from Concept to Variable

Concepts are the stuff of theory. No concept is "real" except in a semantic sense; a concept is a word or "term." But it is a special kind of term. A concept is an abstraction from observables that provides a theoretically useful symbol for the simple properties of empirical things. The definition of the concept points to whatever properties of objects the investigator wishes to examine. Some concepts are not very abstract and can be easily and directly observed. Others are more abstract and may require indirect observations and very complicated inferences about the presence or absence of the empirical properties. No useful concept exists apart from theory. Theory joins these specially defined synthetic words called concepts to other concepts through logical connectors.

It is important that concepts refer to phenomena which are, at least in principle, observable. We could and do employ unobservable concepts—e.g., causation, function—but we do not find it useful to employ them apart from observables. We might say that "a premier can change the course of history." This means that individual acts can cause collective change. But that is different from saying that "the Divine Will for the nation is carried out by guardian angels." While we have concepts of "Divine Will" and "angels," it is far more difficult for us to agree in our observations of them than in our observations of premiers' actions and collective human change. The latter lead us to the kind of indicators we are likely to call variables in our test theory. The flow from concept to variable has involved social scientists in some of the knottiest epistemological controversies known to philosophers. For that reason, we need to state the position implicit in this book, particularly as it undergirds Chapters 5, 6, and 7.

Controversy has not settled primarily on the general criteria for evaluating concepts; instead it surrounds the process of concept formation. Most scholars would probably agree with Dumont and Wilson that useful concepts must show *epistemic significance* and *constitutive significance*.[13] The epistemic significance of concepts is shown when ". . . the concepts are connected, either directly or indirectly, with observables by rules of correspondence that have been empirically justified. . . ." The constitutive significance of a concept is shown when it ". . . enters into a sufficient number of relations with other terms in the theoretical laws of the postulate network, and contributes to the explanation and prediction of observable events."

A concept with epistemic import will have explanatory power. The concept provides a useful tool for characterizing similar events. It not only helps the scholar to decide what to observe but it repeatedly permits him and other scholars to characterize these events in an interpretable manner. Observation of these specified properties will permit the test of hypothesized relationships between one concept and another. Through repeated observations of behavior the community of scholars can come to some collective judgment about the utility of observing the properties to which the concept corresponds.

But we ask not only that the correspondence between concept and behavior be empirically confirmed repeatedly; we also require that the concept not be isolated, that it be usefully embedded in a theoretical network of some generality. Any science is, after all, reductionistic and expansionistic at the same time: through a minimum of primary concepts and relationships, we seek to enclose a maximum of sensory experience. Consider a concept like "short-term effects" from the voting behavior literature. This concept can direct us to some observable voting phenomena; we can observe them and agree on what we have observed. But does the concept really play a key role in voting theory or in related psychological theories? Does it have the constitutive significance of concepts such as "dissonance" and "reinforcement" in studies of attitude stability and change? If not, would it not be better to take concepts which already have shown widespread utility in related bodies of theory, and apply them to voting phenomena? Often the use of concepts with limited constitutive significance forces the scholar to repeat definitions of what *he* means by the term. The efficiency and clarity of the knowledge-development enterprise is generally better served by the use of concepts which are commonly found in existing theoretical networks. This does not mean that a moratorium should be imposed on the creation of new concepts. Indeed new discoveries may require new concepts. Rather, it means that we should carefully explicate current and past meanings and observe the behaviors to which existing concepts refer before inventing new ones. There is a lesson for scientists in the ancient story of the Tower of Babel.

The real issue, as stated previously, is not what we seek in a useful concept, but how best to go about formulating it. In political science this controversy has been manifested in the conflict between some early behaviorists and some traditionalists. But as Kalleberg, in a particularly insightful article, pointed out, the opponents usually charged each other with either the most extreme version of Watsonian behaviorism or the most subjective of the *verstehen* positions.[14] In more recent practice, however, the schools have not been that far apart epistemologically.

The early behaviorists, such as Bentley, argued that all we could study was the overt behavior we could observe. Insofar as we were concerned with the intentions or social and psychological meanings actors impute to their behavior, we had to rely not on *their* intentions but on the objective meaning their behavior suggested to the observer. So that the observer would not be confounded by words which had a meaning in common parlance as well as a peculiar scientific meaning, it was thought desirable to create a new vocabulary of concepts, which would be removed as far as possible from common parlance. The resulting theories would be at a very high level of abstraction and objectivity.

Traditionalists, who rallied around Strauss, Voegelin, and others, argued that behaviorists could never penetrate to the real meaning of an event. Furthermore, by their emphasis on *objective* understanding, behaviorists were divorcing political science from the everyday political issues which required value commitments as well as intellectual discourse. According to this school, the only way to reach the essential meaning of a political event was to experience it; meaning came from active commitment, from immersion, not from cool withdrawal. "Sympathetic reconstruction" of an event came only from subjective experience, from knowing what it means *to me*. The meaning of the event to other actors was best grasped by *personal* immersion and introspection.

The position we espouse for the actual practice of research draws from both logical positivism and recent application of phenomenology.[15] We feel it is consistent with what both modern-day behavio*r*alists and traditionalists *do* instead of what earlier antagonists *said* they were doing. For us, concept formation is best done through:

1. Analysis of meaning at two levels:
   (a) Usage in theoretical literature
   (b) Usage in common parlance
2. Analysis of empirical performance data

In utilizing any concept, the scholar might first ask how other scholars have used it. This involves a survey of appropriate literature. Quite likely, subtle differences in usage will become apparent. For example, for some scholars "power" is a potentiality, for others an actuality. For some, the term social class involves occupancy of an objective position along a social ranking system, a hierarchy. For others, social class implies a ranking system but it also includes a subjective consciousness-of-kind shared by all people at the same rank. The differences in usage, of course, will suggest different predictions about observables. It is entirely possible that contradictory findings about the antecedents and consequences of social class would emerge depending on which meaning a scholar intended.

Indeed, analysis of usage in theoretical literature will have far-reaching impact on the research design and measurement model a scholar will develop. If social class refers to a ranking, then nominal level measurement would be inadequate; the measurement model must be ordinal, that is, it must permit distinctions of "more" or "less" rather than simply "has it–doesn't have it." If "consciousness-of-kind" is not required by the prevailing usage of "social class," objective indicators such as amount of income may be adequate; data collection could be limited to published census documents. However, if consciousness-of-kind is intended, then additional survey or observational data must be gathered so that the scholar can infer class consciousness. Or to use another example, if we were assessing national power, an additive model based on military hardware and preparedness, economic development and self-sufficiency, and popular support for governmental decisions would be inadequate. Syntactically, power suggests a relationship, not a summation. Thus our measurement model would have to include products, functions, weights, and so on. *In the syntax used to define a concept is found the most important suggestion for appropriate design, sample, measurement, and statistical model.*

The formation and explication of a concept, however, is not simply a bookish exercise. Meaning analysis—and here is the important contribution of the *verstehen* proponents—must also occur at the level of ordinary language and common usage. What Morgenthau or Kahn means by national power is important; what diplomats, military strategists, and heads of state mean by national power is even more important. For, in developing concepts with constitutive significance, we must never forget their epistemic significance. The concepts must correspond to behaviors, including mental and verbal behaviors; the intentions of the actors are usually instructive in this regard. For some purposes, of course, it may be desirable for us to overlook the intentions of the actors. If we want to study the consequences of racism, we probably will overlook whether or not the person intended his acts to be racist, in favor of observations of what he actually did. Even then, a concept like racism would probably be of limited utility unless the ordinary actors had some shared meaning for the term. But many other concepts important to political inquiry do require knowledge of intentions, not just observation of behavior. Most of the behavioral movement itself is addressed to psychological phenomena. Certainly such key concepts as power, control, justice, equality, legitimacy, group, decision, polity, and so on deal with meanings.

Meaning resides in both the actor and the observer. Depending on the concept, however, we are suggesting that the observer attempt to find and understand meanings commonly shared by the actors. For research on recent phenomena—that is, events occurring in the current historical epoch—that should not be an unreasonable demand. Scholars generally share enough of the prevailing cultural values that they can identify with their subjects. Their commonalities in socialization through parents, schools, and society outweigh their differences. They act in the same time and space, share the dominant mental paradigms. Thus, terms used in ordinary parlance which have some efficacy—that is, which suggest some expectations or predictions about behavior to the ordinary speaker and listener—are likely to be amenable to meaning analysis. "Conservative," "authoritarian," "activist," "influential," "heretical"—all are found in common parlance. The tools of ordinary language philosophy on the one hand, and survey research with partially structured questions on the other, can combine to help the scholar find out what people mean by discourse with these terms. Sometimes there are differences between the definition of a concept offered by scholars and the meaning attached to it in ordinary parlance. The resolution of such differences cannot be made according to *a priori* rules. Instead, the scholar must decide what the consequences for his rules of correspondence will be if he favors one meaning over another.

Social scientists should admit candidly that when they move beyond the direct observation of behavior—of physical acts and interactions—to intentions or social meanings, they are following different epistemological rules than are natural scientists. The natural scientist could not care less what the molecule (whatever that *is*) means by the term molecule, or what H_2O thinks about H_2O. But for many social scientific problems the extra stage involving the subject's meaning is crucial. This point will be especially pertinent in Chapter 7 where we discuss different modes of generating data. Perhaps the failure of some behavioralists to grasp this point has precipitated the almost polemical overreaction found in some current works on grounded theory and ethnomethodology.[16] To our thinking, most research questions posed by political scientists require meaning analysis both at the level of existing theory and at the level of common parlance.

The second principal stage of concept formation, the analysis of performance data, flows very readily from the need to examine common parlance. However, what we have in mind here involves a series of structured tasks with well-formulated procedures. Performance data are analyzed by: (1) selecting specific indicators for concepts, (2) making empirical observations on these indicators, and (3) combining the indicators into indices, scales, or types which can represent the meaning of the concept in a more-or-less homogeneous manner. If the concept is useful, it can point to a series of mental or physical behaviors which can meaningfully be combined into such indices, scales, or types. Sometimes the term "variable" is applied to the single indicator, but often it is used for the composite index or scale. Regardless of the usage, a *variable* refers to a set of empirically observable behaviors which vary, which have different values. Relationships among these variables are what the scholar in actuality tests with his statistical models. Operational definitions of concepts will often suggest that several indicators be combined; performance data are the empirical evidence of whether they can in fact be combined. These data provide the ultimate test of the epistemic significance of a concept. Extensive discussion and illustration of the analysis of performance data are reserved for Chapter 5; at this point only some general considerations are suggested.

Seldom is a single indicator considered adequate to exemplify a concept. Multiple indicators, then, usually compose the variables of social research. Multiple indicators are necessary for at least two reasons: (1) a concept is usually more abstract than can be embodied in a single fact or datum; and (2) our measures are unlikely to be free enough from either systematic or random error to permit reliance on single indicators. If only one indicator were used, we would have no way of estimating how much error is confounded with the performance score on that indicator; other indicators serve as criteria. And other indicators serve to represent other aspects of the abstract concept. Thus, multiple indicators permit the evaluation of *reliability* and *validity,* two important measurement maxims discussed in Chapter 5.

There are two common approaches to the combination of indicators into a composite score. In one we seek to put *homogeneous* indicators together into a single scale with several values. In the other, we seek to construct an index or typology from combinations of *unlike* indicators. When the former is done we look for a great degree of commonality in performance across all indicators. A variety of psychometric scaling models and homogeneity tests—including item analysis, Guttman scaling, factor analysis, latent structure analysis, multidimensional scaling, and others—are available for this purpose. (Some are discussed in later chapters.)

When unlike indicators are used to construct a typology, we are less concerned with homogeneity than we are with reducing data to a manageable set of types. So long as we can predict something about behavior from the types —that they refer to behaviors which, while unlike, do generally occur together—we are engaging in a useful enterprise. For example, Eulau and Eyestone sought to discover the antecedents of different stages of policy development in city councils. "Policy development" referred to "a set of policy outcomes which follow each other sequentially through time." [17] Using "planning expenditures" and "amenities expenditures" of a sample of city councils in the San Francisco Bay area, they tried to develop profiles; yet the two types of data would not permit homogeneous measurement. Instead, three homogeneous stages were identified—retarded, traditional, and advanced—but between the stages were some heterogeneous and relatively unstable behavioral phases labeled "emergent" and "maturing." Thus, for the remainder of their analysis, they utilized the five *types* rather than values on a single unidimensional scale.

Generally indices and typologies are useful in the early exploratory and mapping phases of an intellectual problem: not enough knowledge about the problem is accumulated to permit the use of homogeneous scales, yet some general patterns appear in the data, and the indices and typologies can predict well to these patterns. As more is learned, common properties are discovered, more general dimensions are developed, and measurement is refined, the inadequacies of constructed typologies become apparent. Thus, for example, Max Weber's rational-legal bureaucratic typology was used for several decades. However, research reported by Blau and Scott suggests that Weber's single type might better be subdivided into "professional" administrative organizations and "bureaucratic" administrative organizations, depending on the professional values of the staff and the freedom of action allowed within the hierarchy.[18] Several illustrations of the process of index and typology development are presented in Chapter 6.

Analysis of performance data is the necessary culmination of the process of concept formation. When the data are recalcitrant, the scholar questions the epistemic significance of his concept. When the data correspond to the strictures of the concept's defining phrases, the scholar is likely to accept that as evidence of epistemic significance and will seek ever wider constitutive significance for the concept. And as the concept, now empirically grounded, enters a wider number of relationships, the body of theory is developed and refined.

Variable Matrices, Syllogisms, and Diagrams

A procedure which combines many of the demands of a test theory with the desirable features of deductive theorizing can be found in the construction of a variable matrix. The variable matrix allows the scholar to formalize existing knowledge in a set of predictions, to note logical inconsistencies in predictions from different sets of empirical findings, to uncover gaps in the knowledge structure, and to scrutinize the variables which have been used in previous tests of theory.

A variable matrix is an organizing device used frequently in correlation analysis, but helpful in deductive theorizing as well. The reader may wish to turn to Tables 13.1 and 13.2 for examples of variable matrices containing statistical correlations; note that the correlations are expressed in positive and negative quantities, and that the values above the diagonal constitute a mirror image of the values below the diagonal. In constructing a theoretical system prior to an empirical investigation, the same organizing principal can be employed. However, it is obvious that precise correlations are not known; at most, the analyst is willing to assert only the direction of the relationship between two variables, positive or negative.

Suppose that a particular investigator identified ten variables and then proceeded to guess whether each pair of variables was directly or inversely related. He would have to make 45 guesses, or $(N^2 - N)/2$, to fill in each cell of the variable matrix with a + or – sign. The exercise might prove useful, but one might wonder about its purpose. Making 45 individual predictions, without any theoretical underpinning, seems a bit extravagant. But let us suppose that the problem did not develop in this manner. Instead, a number of postulates were created, from which the remaining relationships were deduced. The deductions follow from two types of syllogisms:

(1) *A* varies directly with *B*
     B varies inversely with *C*
     $\therefore$ *A* varies inversely with *C*

(2) An increase in *A* leads to an increase in *B*
     An increase in *B* leads to a decrease in *C*
     $\therefore$ An increase in *A* leads to a decrease in *C*

The first may be called a *covariance syllogism,* and the second, a *causal syllogism.* The logical rule is that the sign of the deduced relationship is the product of the signs of the postulated relationships. The three possibilities are: (1) $(+)(-) = (-)$ as above; (2) $(+)(+) = (+)$; and (3) $(-)(-) = (+)$.

Using this powerful logical rule greatly reduces the number of intuitively derived predictions. Letting N = the number of variables, only $N - 1$ postulates are necessary to fill in the signs of the remaining paired relationships, with the restriction that each variable must appear in at least one postulate. Thus for ten variables, only nine postulates are necessary to determine the signs of the remaining 36 relationships (45 − 9). Basically, the logical rule yields a propositional system with hierarchical efficiency, a characteristic of most advanced theoretical systems.

Propositional systems of the above type are becoming common to the theoretical literature in sociology; however, the formulators of these systems have been taken to task by statistically oriented sociologists who have been critical of some of the applications.[19] To summarize briefly, the critics have pointed out that the syllogisms make sense only if the theorist uses *causal* syllogisms, as in example (2) above. Only if the postulates express causal relationships can the deduced relationship *necessarily* follow. Unless the underlying correlations for the postulated relationships are very high, the sign of the deduced relationship will necessarily follow only *if* the postulated relationships are truly causal. Otherwise, one might find that the correlation between A and B is +.50, between B and C, +.50, and between A and C, −.20.

Of course, the critics are concerned more with formal statements of theory than with the heuristic value of organizing a problem through a set of syllogisms or a variable matrix. The analyst might begin with a set of propositions reflecting how pairs of variables covary and then later convert the statements to causal inferences. Or it may be that the purpose of the exercise is to determine whether certain important relationships have been ignored, or to determine whether "apparent logical inconsistencies" exist. In addition, frequently a variable matrix will be the quickest way to decipher a long list of propositions. To illustrate the heuristic value of a variable matrix, we can take an example from theory about legislative behavior, described in more detail in the original source.[20]

The problem focuses upon the analysis of coalition behavior in American state legislatures, and especially the attempts of party leaders and leaders of potential blocking coalitions to seek legislative rewards either through the winning of votes or concessions in the normal conduct of legislative business. We illustrate by simply stating the basic postulates or hypotheses, without detailing why they are selected:

1. The size of the legislative chamber will inversely affect the proportion of relevant information legislative participants think they possess. (−)
2. The degree to which legislators have had the opportunity to observe the behavior of other participants (legislative experience) will directly affect the proportion of relevant information they think they possess. (+)
3. The proportion of relevant information legislative party leaders think they possess will inversely affect the proportion of membership support they will seek. (−)
4. The proportion of relevant information legislators think they possess will inversely affect the number of supporters they perceive necessary to form an effective blocking coalition. (−)

5. The percent of seats in the majority party will directly affect the number of supporters legislators perceive necessary to form an effective blocking coalition. (+)

6. The percent of seats in the majority party will directly affect the degree to which majority party leaders withhold shares (utilities) from members of their party. (+)

7. The proportion of membership support sought by majority party leaders will inversely affect the degree to which they withhold shares from members of their party. (−)

8. The number of supporters legislators perceive necessary to form an effective blocking coalition will inversely affect their propensity to defect. (−)

9. The degree to which majority party leaders withhold shares from members of their party will directly affect the propensity to defect among their members. (+)

10. The number of supporters legislators perceive necessary to form an effective blocking coalition will directly affect the proportion of membership actually sought by coalition leaders. (+)

11. The degree to which legislators have had the opportunity to observe the behavior of other participants (legislative experience) will directly affect the degree to which they feel they possess power in their party. (+)

12. The degree to which legislators feel they possess power in their party will directly affect the degree to which they feel they are part of the party leadership. (+)

13. The degree to which legislators feel they are part of the party leadership will inversely affect their propensity to defect. (−)

It can be seen that the propositional inventory is getting out of hand, even when limited to propositions that cannot be derived from others in the set. To decipher the system, the variables embodied in the propositions can be listed:

1. Size of legislative chamber
2. Opportunity to observe
3. Self-perception of information level
4. Proportion of membership support sought by *party leaders*
5. Proportion of membership support sought by *coalition leaders*
6. Number of recruits perceived necessary to block
7. Percent of seats in majority party
8. Self-perception of power in party
9. Identification with party leadership
10. Propensity of *majority party leaders* to withhold shares
11. Propensity to defect

The variable listing reveals that the propositional system contains more than the minimum number $(N - 1)$ of propositions, and that three of the variables are particularistic in nature, as noted in italics above.

FIGURE 2.2
Variable Matrix Display of Postulated Relationships

	1	2	3	4	5	6	7	8	9	10	11
1. Size of chamber			−	⊕	⊕	⊕				⊖	
2. Opportunity to observe			+	⊖	⊖	⊖		+	⊕	⊕	
3. Self-perception of information level	−	+		−	⊖	−		⊕	⊕	⊕	⊕
4. % membership support sought by PL	⊕	⊖	−		⊕	⊕		⊖	⊖	−	⊖
5. % membership support sought by CL	⊕	⊖	⊖	⊕		+	⊕	⊖	⊖		⊖
6. # of recruits perceived necessary to block	⊕	⊖	−	⊕	+		+	⊖	⊖		+
7. % seats in majority party					⊕	+			+		
8. Self-perception of power in party		+	⊕	⊖	⊖	⊖			+	⊕	⊖
9. Identification with party leadership		⊕	⊕	⊖	⊖	⊖		+		⊕	−
10. Propensity of MPL to withhold shares	⊖	⊕	⊕	−			+	⊕	⊕		+
11. Propensity to defect			⊕	⊖	⊖	−			−	+	

In the variable matrix presented in Figure 2.2, the uncircled signs represent the postulated relationships. Now we may note that all of the propositions were stated in cause and effect form, such that one variable directly or inversely affected another. Suppose, however, that they were stated as simple covariance propositions, employing the terms "varies inversely with" or "varies directly with." Via the sign rule, the analyst might syllogistically fill in the remaining cells of the matrix. It would be his misfortune to find that there are contradictions in the system, a possibility whenever more than the minimal number $(N-1)$ of postulates are stated. For example, it is possible to deduce, through propositions 11, 12, and 13, that the opportunity to observe the behavior of other participants is *inversely* related to the propensity to defect. But through propositions 2, 3, 6, and 9, it is possible to deduce that the two variables are *directly* related. What is the response to this dilemma?

The alternatives are: (1) discard the problem; (2) discard the extra propositions; (3) discard the confounding variables and the corresponding propositions; (4) restate one or more of the propositions to yield the opposite sign; or (5) restate each proposition so that it gives a causal direction, as in the actual listing of propositions. Taking the last alternative, we can construct a representative diagram showing how the variables are sequenced in the propositions, as in Figure 2.3. The diagram indicates, for example, that the propensity to defect is affected by the opportunity to observe, through two parallel chains, explaining why the sign rule contradiction was encountered in the simple covariance framework. One chain has a negative impact and the other a positive impact upon the propensity to defect. Without actual data, the sign of the relationship between opportunity to observe and pro-

FIGURE 2.3

Unidirectional Description of Determinants of Coalition Change in the Legislature

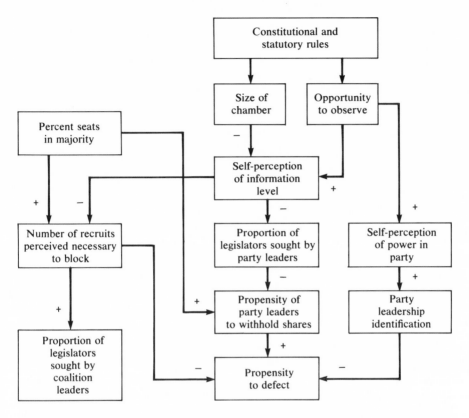

Reprinted from "Coalitions in American State Legislatures: A Propositional Analysis" by Wayne L. Francis in Sven Groennings, E. W. Kelley, and Michael Leiserson, *The Study of Coalition Behavior,* copyright © 1970 (New York: Holt, Rinehart and Winston, Inc., 1970), p. 423. Reprinted by permission of Holt, Rinehart, and Winston, Inc.

pensity to defect is indeterminate. In fact, the signs of several relationships are indeterminate. The signs that actually can be deduced are circled in the variable matrix, 28 in all above the diagonal. The signs for the blank cells are indeterminate.

Figure 2.3 contains three *exogenous* variables—that is, variables not affected by other variables in the system—percent of seats in majority, size of chamber, and opportunity to observe. There is no basis for concluding how they are related, unless, of course, a new variable is added. For example, constitutional and statutory rules generally provide longer terms for smaller state senates and shorter terms for the larger lower bodies; hence, one might wish to note that size of chamber and opportunity to observe are negatively related, but such a relationship cannot be deduced from the propositional system in a meaningful way.

The logic of causal inference is such that it is possible to deduce the sign of the relationship between two variables in two types of situations, in a sequence as follows,

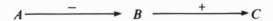

$$A \xrightarrow{\quad - \quad} B \xrightarrow{\quad + \quad} C$$

where the sign between A and C is the product of the two connecting signs, and in the following case,

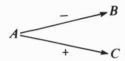

where the product of the two specified signs will give the sign between B and C. To be correct, a pre-empirical causal theory must be consistent with these sign rule applications.

The important notion to remember is that while theory construction prospers from conceptual clarity, the rules of logic adopted make a considerable difference at the prediction stage. At the present time, statistical theory is capable of testing causal constructs of the type illustrated here (see Chapter 12), but of course there is the important intermediate step of collecting information in a manner that will facilitate statistical evaluation. Carefully constructed *a priori* theory in any case can be very helpful. It is not restricted by the accessibility of information. This approach "forces" the researcher to consider what information would be necessary in the ideal research project, and perhaps provides clues as to why accessible indicators do not fall neatly into some defined statistical pattern. Many of the perceptual variables in Figure 2.3, for example, have not been measured; yet if the formulation is correct, one should not expect the immediately measurable variables to provide a very satisfying statistical confirmation of a theory that ignores the perceptual variables.

Nevertheless, it is still possible to determine whether the measured or indexed variables relate to each other in a way that appears to be consistent with the *a priori* construct. For example, the variable matrix in Figure 2.2 suggests that the signs of the relationships between percent of seats in the majority party and propensity to defect (cell 7, 11) and between opportunity to observe and propensity to defect (cell 2, 11) are indeterminate, at least from the logic of the system alone. From each prior variable, both positive and negative paths lead to the "propensity to defect," as illustrated in Figure 2.3. In a study of 50 states it was found that there was relatively high factionalism in *majority* parties containing less than 60% of the seats, perhaps indicating the willingness of rank-and-file legislators to defect when they do not need many recruits to be effective. Factionalism was least in majority parties containing between 60% and 70% of the seats, but in parties containing between 70% and 80% of the seats it was even higher than in the small majority parties; and it was highest of all in parties containing between 80% and 90% of the seats.[21] The increased factionalism in these larger parties may indicate the willingness of majority leaders to withhold shares (committee assignments, patronage, favors on bills, and the like).

Similarly, it was found in a study of 14 chambers of the Indiana state legislature that defection from party voting correlated highly with the percent of seats controlled by the majority party. In the same study it was found that legislative experience (a proxy for opportunity to observe) was curvilinearly related to defection from party voting. Freshman legislators tended to vote the party line, perhaps due to their low information level (self-perceived). Somewhat more experienced legislators tended to deviate more, whereas highly experienced legislators deviated less than those with middle-range experience, perhaps indicating their self-perceptions of power in their party and their identification with the leadership.[22] Thus while the evidence falls far short of a convincing confirmation of the *a priori* construct, the results are sufficiently consistent to warrant further investigation.

By regularly beginning a research project with an exercise such as the construction of a variable matrix, we feel that an investigator will be alerted to many methodological and substantive problems likely to occur in the project. It sensitizes him or her to the interrelated concerns of theory, logic, design, and measurement in the conduct of political inquiry.

NOTES

1. Thomas R. Dye, "Politics, Economics, and the Public: Looking Back," in Oliver Walter (ed.), *Political Scientists at Work* (Belmont, Calif.: Duxbury Press, 1971), pp. 140–41.

2. Johan Galtung, *Theory and Methods of Social Research* (New York: Columbia University Press, 1967), p. 453.

3. Anthony Downs, *An Economic Theory of Democracy* (New York: Harper & Row, 1957).

4. See Ira Sharkansky, *The Politics of Taxing and Spending* (Indianapolis: The Bobbs-Merrill Co., Inc., 1969); Arthur L. Stinchcombe, *Constructing Social Theories* (New York: Harcourt, Brace & World, Inc., 1968), especially pp. 120–29.

5. Fred W. Riggs, *Administration in Developing Countries: The Theory of Prismatic Society* (Boston: Houghton Mifflin Company, 1964).

6. David Easton, "Political Anthropology," in B. J. Siegel (ed.), *Biennial Review of Anthropology 1959* (Stanford, Calif.: Stanford University Press, 1959), pp. 210–62; M. G. Smith, "Segmentary Lineage Systems," *Journal of the Royal Anthropological Institute,* 86 (1956), 39–80.

7. The position taken in this book on the "operationalist" controversy is similar to that of Blalock and others, although they prefer different terms such as "auxiliary theory." See Hubert M. Blalock, Jr., "The Measurement Problem: A Gap Between the Language of Theory and Research," in Hubert and Ann Blalock (eds.), *Methodology in Social Research* (New York: McGraw-Hill Book Company, 1968), pp. 5–27; Hubert M. Blalock, Jr., *Theory Construction: From Verbal to Mathematical Formulation* (Englewood Cliffs, N.J.: Prentice-Hall, Inc., 1969), especially Chapters 1 and 2.

8. Stinchcombe, *Constructing Social Theories,* especially pp. 18–28.

9. Daniel Lerner, *The Passing of Traditional Society* (Glencoe: The Free Press, 1958).

10. John L. Sullivan and George E. Marcus, "The Development of Political Ideology: Some Empirical Findings," mimeographed (Williamstown, Mass. 1972).

11. Richard M. Merelman, "The Development of Political Ideology: A Framework for the Analysis of Political Socialization," *American Political Science Review,* 63 (September 1969), 750–67.

12. One of the most useful summaries of control over method effects is found in Stinchcombe, *Constructing Social Theories,* pp. 32–38. Our discussion, while expanding well beyond this summary, draws heavily from it.

13. Richard G. Dumont and William J. Wilson, "Aspects of Concept Formation, Explication, and Theory Construction in Sociology," *American Sociological Review,* 32 (December, 1967), 985–95. The definitions following in the text are drawn from p. 987.

14. Arthur L. Kalleberg, "Concept Formation in Normative and Empirical Studies: Toward Reconciliation in Political Theory," *American Political Science Review,* 63 (March 1969), 26–39. We draw heavily from Kalleberg's characterization of the conflict.

15. See Rudolph Carnap, "Methodological Character of Theoretical Concepts," in Herbert Feigl et al., (eds.), *Minnesota Studies in the Philosophy of Science,* Vol. 1 (Minneapolis: University of Minnesota Press, 1958); Carl G. Hempel, *Fundamentals of Concept Formation in Empirical Science* (Chicago: University of Chicago Press, 1952); Ronald D. Laing, *The Politics of Experience* (New York: Ballantine Books, Inc., 1967); Alfred Schutz, "Common Sense and Scientific Interpretations of Human Actions," *Philosophy and Phenomenological Research,* 14 (1953), 1–37.

16. See Anselm Strauss and Barney Glaser, *The Discovery of Grounded Theory* (Chicago: Aldine-Atherton, Inc., 1967); Harold Garfinkel, *Studies in Ethnomethodology* (Englewood Cliffs, N.J.: Prentice-Hall, Inc., 1967).

17. Heinz Eulau and Robert Eyestone, "Policy Maps of City Councils and Policy Outcomes," *American Political Science Review,* 63 (March, 1968), 124–43.

18. Peter Blau and Richard Scott, *Formal Organizations* (San Francisco: Chandler Publishing Company, 1962).

19. For example, see O.D. Duncan, "Axioms or Correlations?" *American Sociological Review,* 28 (June 1963), 452; Herbert L. Costner and Robert K. Leik, "Deductions from 'Axiomatic Theory,'" *American Sociological Review,* 29 (December 1964), 819–35.

20. Wayne L. Francis, "Coalitions in American State Legislatures: A Propositional Analysis," Chapter 21 in Sven Groennings, E.W. Kelley, and Michael Leiserson (eds.), *The Study of Coalition Behavior* (New York: Holt, Rinehart and Winston, Inc., 1970). The reader is also referred to the examples evaluated by Hubert M. Blalock, Jr., in *Theory Construction* (Englewood Cliffs, N.J.: Prentice-Hall, Inc., 1969).

21. Factionalism dropped in parties holding more than 90 percent of the seats. For possible explanations see Francis, "Coalitions in State Legislatures," pp. 417–18.

22. *Ibid.,* p. 415.

PART
II

---

*Acquisition
of Information*

Chapter 3

RESEARCH DESIGNS

Logicians sometimes tell the story of the problem drinker. A pathetic figure, he was in danger of losing his job, his marriage and family. His friends told him that he felt the way he did each day because of his heavy drinking on the previous night. But being of a scientific bent, he decided to measure just what was causing his woes. The first night he drank scotch and soda; the next morning he was unable to report to work and he abused his wife and children. The second night he drank bourbon and soda; the next morning he experienced the same unfortunate effect. And so it was each night—brandy and soda, rum and soda, etc.—always with the same aftereffects. At the end of the week he felt confident that he had the answer to his problem: cut out the soda!

Naíve, you say. Everyone knows that scotch, bourbon, rum, brandy, and others have a high alcohol content, and that it was his alcohol consumption that led to his drunkenness, meanness, lassitude, or whatever the state. We say his finding was *spurious* because it attributed the effect to the wrong cause. His research design called for very gross measures of one variable—soda—while they failed to penetrate precisely to the common factor—alcohol—hidden in all the other variables—scotch, bourbon, etc.—which he was treating as independent of each other. Thus, we decide that his research design and manner of measuring variables led him to the wrong conclusion. But was it?

Perhaps if he had consumed each kind of liquor straight or on the rocks, he might have found it unpalatable. Cutting out the soda might have led him to reduce or cut out completely his alcohol intake. A research design to measure this hypothesis would focus on the interactive effects of alcohol and soda and their joint contribution to the observed effect.

Or, perhaps we want to untangle the entire chain of factors that related his drinking to his unfortunate states. We may still note the apparent contribution of alcohol to his problems. But we now want to know why he ingested large quantities of alcohol. Did he dislike his job? Were his wife and children too demanding and inconsiderate? Was it something physiological? If any of these factors led him to drinking, would he have harbored the same feelings and acted the way he did toward job, wife, and family without the aftereffects of alcohol? Did the alcohol consumption actually alleviate instead of induce pathological social, psychological, and physiological states? To answer these questions we move well beyond a simple cause-effect research design to a very complex one.

In the first instance, the problem drinker attributed the effects to one of apparently several independent variables. Yet we argued that there were only two relevant independent variables present and that the other one had actually caused the results. In the second instance, however, we must develop a research design which not only calls for careful measurement of all variables but plays around with them—at one time making an independent variable dependent, at another time making it independent again; a variable may sometimes be treated as antecedent to the independent variable–dependent variable relationship, and at other times it may be intervening between the two. As a different level of explanation is sought, the variables change their location in the research design. Planning for the specification and manipulation of these variables constitutes the logic of a research design.

As a logic, each research design is like a blueprint that tells us how to reach plausible answers to research problems. There are three questions we may ask of the blueprint or research design: (1) Will the design provide plausible answers (a) at *the desired level of explanation* and (b) in a highly *sensitive* way? (2) Does the design permit control over extraneous sources of variance? Does it allow for the *test of plausible rival hypotheses* that (a) an observed finding is really the result of some substantive factor other than the one we have hypothesized (*extrinsic factor*) or (b) an observed finding is simply an artifact of the research design and measurement method we have used (*intrinsic factor*)? Psychologists sometimes call this "separating the main effects from the confounding variables." (3) Is the design *practical* and *ethical?* Does it lead us to the appropriate data in an efficient and morally acceptable manner?

The crucial point of any scientific endeavor remains the statement of the problem. The concepts and their relationship to each other must be spelled out clearly and unambiguously. One must know beforehand the function of each term in the statement, i.e., whether it is intended to be an independent variable, a dependent variable, an antecedent variable, an intervening variable, and must know the pathways to be followed among all the variables. When the logic of this aspect of the research design is outlined, the analyst can then make other research design judgments—about the sampling of objects and subjects needed, about methods and techniques for generating data, about the measurement model which will be used to analyze the data, and about the financial and moral cost of the entire enterprise. Each of these concerns will be discussed in later chapters. This chapter, however, seeks to reconstruct and evaluate a number of designs used or useful in political inquiry.

66

The Evaluation of Selected Research Designs

Any research design, whether based on methods of active control or methods of passive control, will have as its objective the objectives generally set for an experiment: ". . . variables are manipulated and their effects on other variables observed." [1] The manipulation must allow us to determine *how much* of the observed variance of the dependent variable can be attributed to the independent (experimental treatment) variable, and how much can be attributed to (1) other substantive variables (*extrinsic effects*) and (2) the research design itself (*intrinsic effects*). The first section below, based heavily on the work of Campbell and his associates, deals primarily with intrinsic effects. The language is that of experimental design but applies also to *ex post facto* experiments based on survey or aggregate data. The next section deals especially with extrinsic effects; it points out similarities between experimental designs and *ex post facto* designs when the scholar examines the effects of other substantive variables as well as method effects *after* the experiment is completed or the survey is done. A variety of other designs stemming from regression models are reserved for Chapters 12 and 14. This arrangement is not to suggest that regression-based designs are inferior to "true experiments." Quite the contrary—such models allow us indirectly to explain variance in the dependent variable with a high degree of precision. We have placed them in later chapters because of their statistical complexity.

INTRINSIC EFFECTS

In discussing factors intrinsic to the research design itself which confound the test of a hypothesis, Campbell distinguishes between internal validity and external validity. *Internal validity* is concerned with whether the experimental variable has led to a certain observed effect or whether, in fact, the effect was simply an artifact of the experimental design. *External validity* has to do with generalizability, ". . . the threats to valid generalization of the results to other settings, to other versions of the treatment, or to other measures of the effect." [2]

The following list * presents one of Campbell's inventories of threats to internal and external validity.

A / Factors Threatening Internal Validity

1. *History:* events, other than the experimental treatment, occurring between pretest and post-test and thus providing alternate explanations of effects.

2. *Maturation:* processes within the respondents or observed social units producing changes as a function of the passage of time per se, such as growth, fatigue, secular trends, etc.

* Reprinted from Donald T. Campbell, "Reforms as Experiments," *American Psychologist* 24 (April, 1969), 411–12. (Copyright © 1969 by the American Psychological Association. Reprinted by permission.)

3. *Instability:* unreliability of measures, fluctuations in sampling persons or components, autonomous instability of repeated or "equivalent" measures. (This is the only threat to which statistical tests of significance are relevant.)

4. *Testing:* the effect of taking a test upon the scores of a second testing. The effect of publication of a social indicator upon subsequent readings of that indicator.

5. *Instrumentation:* in which changes in the calibration of a measuring instrument or changes in the observers or scorers used may produce changes in the obtained measurements.

6. *Regression artifacts:* pseudo-shifts occurring when persons or treatment units have been selected upon the basis of their extreme scores.

7. *Selection:* biases resulting from differential recruitment for comparison groups, producing different mean levels on the measure of effects.

8. *Experimental mortality:* the differential loss of respondents from comparison groups.

9. *Selection-maturation interaction:* selection biases resulting in differential rates of "maturation" or autonomous change.

B / Factors Threatening External Validity

1. *Interaction effects of testing:* the effect of a pretest in increasing or decreasing the respondent's sensitivity or responsiveness to the experimental variable, thus making the results obtained for a pretested population unrepresentative of the effects of the experimental variable for the unpretested universe from which the experimental respondents were selected.

2. *Interaction of selection and experimental treatment:* unrepresentative responsiveness of the treated population.

3. *Reactive effects of experimental arrangements:* "artificiality"; conditions making the experimental setting atypical of conditions of regular application of the treatment; "Hawthorne effects."

4. *Multiple-treatment interference:* where multiple treatments are jointly applied, effects atypical of the separate application of the treatments.

5. *Irrelevant responsiveness of measures:* all measures are complex, and all include irrelevant components that may produce apparent effects.

6. *Irrelevant replicability of treatments:* treatments are complex, and replications of them may fail to include those components actually responsible for the effects.

As will be seen in our application of this inventory to specific designs, few designs control for all sources of design effects. Generally, the further we move from the "experimental group–control group, premeasure–postmeasure, randomized assignment model," the more difficult it is to control for design effects. And unfortunately, there is a tendency for internal validity and external validity to work at cross purposes: often, the greater our control over threats to internal validity, the less the generalizability of findings. In studies of human conflict, for example, the artificial laboratory setting may permit the greatest control over assignment to groups and precise introduction of the experimental treatment; yet it is very difficult and often invalid to generalize from these findings to situations of intergroup or internation conflict. On the other hand, observations of several actual school integration compliance situations may give us greater confidence in our generalizations, but they seldom allow us much control over the introduction and phasing of governmental actions, nor can we readily assign school districts in a random fashion to alternate kinds of governmental actions. As scholars, we typically have to settle for the "second best"; yet, we are obligated to explore the strengths and weaknesses of all designs and to alert the consumer of our findings to *plausible* sources of error. The fact that error occurs does not worry us. That is the very nature of scientific measurement situations. That some sources of error at times lead to more plausible explanations for our findings than we have hypothesized does worry us. The most serious threats will be examined with each design.

In the following discussion of research designs, the conventional notation system is used:

X refers to the experimental treatment (independent variable)

O refers to an observation on the dependent variable

$O_{1, 2}, \ldots$ refers to the time order of observations, the subscript indicating the order

R refers to assignment to groups by randomization

--- refers to nonrandom group assignment

1 / THE ONE-SHOT CASE STUDY

$$X \quad O$$

This design, perhaps the most common one appearing in political science literature of the past, involves the careful examination of only *one group,* event, or phenomenon *at a single point in time* after a presumed causal event has occurred. Any apparent change in behavior is attributed to the causal agent. We are familiar with "common sense" interpretations of current events: crime rates are soaring because young people aren't taught respect for authority anymore; black ghetto dwellers riot because the white establishment doesn't allow them self-determination; young liberal clergymen are engaging in social action programs because communists have infiltrated the seminary faculties; the divorce rate is phenomenal because of early sex education in the schools. In each instance, we observe an event and link it to a probable cause. We interview criminals and note that most of them have little respect for authority; yet crime rates may be soaring because of different methods of reporting crime, or perhaps noncriminals also have limited respect for authority. We examine the social and political life of black ghettoes and find them characterized by absentee landlordism, and blame rioting on that fact. Yet had we examined certain white ghettoes we might have found the same phenomenon—with no rioting. Or we find rioting has characterized only a portion of the black ghettoes. When we blame the clergy's social action programs on communist infiltration of seminaries, we forget that clergy engaged in social action long before Karl Marx was born, witness the *Acts of the*

Apostles. Sex education is occurring early in the schools; so is the new math, reading with the ITA system, and so on; why is early sex education to be singled out as the causal agent? Perhaps divorce rates are soaring because more divorced people (who are prone to further divorces) are remarrying again and again.

We may argue that the one-shot case study is reserved only for those who use "common sense." Yet we find it widely used in such diverse fields as public administration, policy process, public law, area studies, international relations, and political history. The Inter-University Case Program approach to teaching public administration has been frequently employed and has stimulated considerable research in the policy-making process; Moses on the Green and the King's River Project sensitized many political scientists and practitioners to such matters as the inseparability of formal administrative structures and informal political processes.[3] Yet no single case study could by itself constitute sufficient data for a test of any proposition derived from organization theory. Descriptions of the big steel confrontation in 1962 or the Berlin crisis in 1961 tell us something about the limits of a President's power but, singularly, each does not provide adequate evidence to develop and test theory about the behavior of chief executives. Area studies bring out every cultural nuance of a particular nation-state, yet immersion in no single national culture is adequate for explaining the process of political development. Political historians have offered keen insights through the biographies of great men; yet without collective biography we have little confidence in, for example, the relationship of the frontier to social mobility.

In fact, case studies are foreign to the very way we perceive events. We are always implicitly ordering events according to a standard: What was the state of the phenomenon prior to the causal event's occurrence? What is the current state of similar phenomena which have not been exposed to the causal agent? In short, we become accustomed to moving beyond simple or even exhaustive description to *comparison*.

The one-shot case study, no matter how laboriously and insightfully done, is likely to lead, as Campbell argues, to "misplaced precision." It provides for virtually no controls over plausible rival substantive hypotheses or method effects. From the standpoint of hypothesis testing, it is rendered useless. Even from the standpoint of discovery it is of limited utility because it provides no control within itself for the possible falsification of a finding. It would be more useful to spend intellectual and financial resources on a limited sampling of variables utilizing either a premeasure on the dependent variable, or a postmeasure on a control group (not exposed to X), or both.

2 / THE ONE-GROUP PRETEST–POST-TEST DESIGN

$$O_1 \ X \ O_2$$

In this design, a single group is compared with itself. A measurement is taken before a causal event occurs and then after the causal event occurs.

The difference in scores from t_1 to t_2 is attributed to the causal event. Note that no comparison is made with scores for a group that did not experience the causal event.

Despite some readily apparent weaknesses in this design, it also commonly appears in political science literature. In policy impact analysis, a time-series truncated around the policy is sometimes used. For example, in evaluating the Connecticut auto speeding crackdown, a public official might note that 324 traffic deaths occurred in 1955; the crackdown is introduced in 1956; 284 traffic deaths occur in 1956; the conclusion: the speeding crackdown has reduced traffic deaths. Or, one might note that in 1970 a Republican-controlled state legislature appropriated $6.2 million for a public welfare assistance program whereas in 1971 a newly elected Democratic legislature appropriated $6.9 million; conclusion: Democrats are more oriented toward welfare spending. Or in evaluating communications effects, one might administer pre- and postconvention interviews to a panel of voters, all of whom watched TV convention coverage, and note that level of interest in the campaign increased; conclusion: TV coverage of the nominating conventions was the factor that stimulated level of interest.

This design suffers from many threats to internal and external validity, but perhaps the most severe of these are history, maturation, statistical regression, and the interaction of testing and the experimental treatment. In the communications effects illustration, *history* constitutes a major source of uncontrolled variance; TV coverage of nominating conventions does focus a lot of attention on campaigns, but so do newspaper coverage and everyday conversation. Americans have become accustomed to the rhythm of major elections every four years; interests which wane in the off-years are whetted in presidential years. People who were only marginally interested previously now become politicized. One medium contributes heavily to politicization, but so many other historical factors also contribute that it is difficult to isolate TV coverage from the cumulative effects of all these sources. The entire milieu is politicized—so much so, that one might argue instead that heightened political interest has led to watching TV coverage of the conventions.

The effects of *maturation* as an uncontrolled source of variance can be seen in the welfare appropriation illustration. Legislatures and public agencies at times behave very similarly to organisms. There seem to be biological and psychological tendencies which grow and mature. In studying the politics of the budgetary process, one is struck by the fact that the best predictor of appropriations level in year n is the regression line connecting the appropriations in immediately preceding years. The truncated time-series of t_1 and t_2 may lead one to attribute the increase in appropriation to a change in partisan control, whereas it should properly be attributed to the normal maturation process we have come to know as incrementalism. A longer time-series would be needed to test whether maturation or partisan control is the more plausible hypothesis.

The Connecticut auto speeding crackdown illustrates the threat of *statistical regression artifacts*. Every measurement contains both true values and errors resulting from measurement itself. Measurement specialists have noted the recurring tendency for the more extreme error values observed on a pretest to regress toward mean values on the post-test. Often, ameliorative social policies are introduced immediately following the most extreme value for a time-series. When inflation gallops, a wage-price freeze is introduced. When unemployment is highest, public works appropriations are released. In Connecticut, when traffic deaths peaked, the crackdown was imposed. The so-called experimental treatment, in these instances, never occurred along the normal values; it occurred when an extreme value was noted. In evaluating the policy's success, we may well confound the effects of the policy with the tendency for behavior to return to its normal pattern. To control for statistical regression effects, we must use a longer time-series than simply t_1, t_2 (see Designs 10 and 11), and we must be alert to plausible rival hypotheses stemming from other historical factors. In evaluating the Connecticut auto crackdown, for example, Glass, and Campbell and Ross looked at weather conditions, automotive safety features, and traffic fatality rates for a longer time-series in Connecticut and several comparable states, and also studied police and court enforcement of speeding laws in preceding and subsequent years.[4]

Under certain circumstances, this design is plagued by the *interaction effects of testing and* X. When a subject becomes aware of how he is being tested, it becomes increasingly easy for him to alter his behavior or performance on subsequent tests. In I.Q. tests, simple familiarity with the testing process gained by having taken it once can lead to a higher score on a later test. Knowledge of a teacher's scoring criteria resulting from midterm exam experience is likely to change our study habits for the final exam. The pretest sensitizes the subject to the experimental treatment and thus enhances later performance. The measure becomes *reactive;* its reactivity interacts with the experimental treatment and becomes confounded with it. In the communications effects illustration, asking people about their level of interest in the campaign may have sensitized them to the fact that a campaign was indeed going on. This sensitivity becomes merged with the presumed experimental treatment—TV coverage—in such a way that one cannot tell which has contributed more to any change observed in the post-test. Under these circumstances, great inferential strength would be added either by using Design 4 or 5 or by deleting the premeasure and using Design 6.

In general, the cost of introducing some other design in order to control the many uncontrolled extraneous sources of variance is so minimal that one can hardly justify continued reliance on this design by political scientists.

3 / THE STATIC-GROUP COMPARISON

$$X\ O_1$$
$$O_{1'}$$

This design is especially common in the *ex post facto* analysis of survey and aggregate data. Two groups are compared at only one point in time. One group has experienced the experimental treatment (independent variable), whereas the other has not. The difference in scores is attributed to the experimental treatment; a test of significance is commonly used to see whether the observed difference is beyond what one might expect by "chance" (see Chapter 11).

Let us suppose we want to assess the effects of strong two-party competition on policy outputs. We divide the American states into two groups, one consisting of all states with strong two-party competition (X), the other consisting of states without strong two-party competition $(\widetilde{X})$. Then we compare per capita expenditures for various programs—e.g., education, transportation, pollution control, welfare, health. Or let us suppose we want to study the effects of residency requirements for the suffrage on voting turnout. We dichotomize the American states into those with long residency requirements (X) and short requirements $(\widetilde{X})$ and compare differences in rates of turnout. Similar designs might be used to measure the impact of age on conservatism, or religious affiliation on candidate preference.

The most severe problem for this design is *differential selection* to experimental and control groups. Assignment has not been random. Rather, the design is typically applied to natural state groups that do and don't have the independent variable present. While the two groups differ on the treatment variables, they may also differ in unknown ways on many other variables.

Randomization is an important concept in inferential research. If we assume a pool of cases relevant to our research problem, we must decide how to assign them to analysis groups. Random assignment would provide for an equal probability that any single case or combination of cases could be assigned to an experimental or a control group. Thus, even if the individual cases do differ in unknown ways on many other variables, the probability is reasonably high that they would cancel each other out on these other variables, so that nearly equal numbers of cases representing different values of the other variables should appear in each analysis group. When assignment is not based on randomization, we do not have the confidence of the laws of probability to tell us that we can probably forget about unknown differences on these other variables which might be confounded with the experimental treatment.

This can be better understood by returning to our illustrations. In the first illustration the American states in the two groups may have had substantially different economic bases or social problems. The difference in policy outputs may have resulted more from these economic factors than from the presence or absence of two-party competition—the test characteristic that happened to coincide with the economic factors. In the second illustration one might find no relation between long residency requirements and depressed voter turnout. Yet if the states were further divided by population mobility, one might find that long residency requirements depress turnout (by systematic disenfranchisement) in high-mobility states but have little effect on turnout in low-mobility states. In this illustration, differential selection masked some important relationships.

Thus, whenever this design is utilized the scholar must employ several *ex post facto* controls to test for the effects of initial differences in the two groups. This controlling process, called *elaboration,* does much to enhance the plausibility of an explanation but it can be used only if performance data on other theoretically relevant variables are available.

Often, *matching* procedures are used to enhance precision. It is reasoned that if we are to get at the precise effect of a variable, we should match a group that has been exposed to that variable (or possesses that property) with one that hasn't. Two types of matching are commonly employed: frequency distribution matching and precision matching. In *frequency distribution matching,* the analyst will select other variables besides the presumed causal variable (X), and will try to assure that the two groups, X and $\widetilde{X}$, are similar by showing similar distributions or similar means on these other variables. Thus, he might note roughly equivalent classroom means on age, sex, race, and family income of students in classrooms which have traditional hierarchical teacher-student relations and those using an open learning environment format; observed differences in educational achievement might then be related to the teaching format. Unfortunately, when means or other central tendency measures are used, the figures may actually hide differences in the shape of the distributions which, in combination with each other, may have "caused" the effect. Under these circumstances, precision matching is likely to be used.

In *precision matching* each *case* is matched to an identical case on all specified variables except the presumed causal variable. Thus, each nine-year-old black male from a middle-income family in the X situation would be matched to a nine-year-old black male from a middle-income family in the $\widetilde{X}$ situation, and so forth. Here, control over spurious findings is enhanced. Often, however, randomness is lost; many cases, particularly in *ex post facto* analysis, will have to be excluded from consideration because an identical case in the opposite group cannot be found. Furthermore, it is often difficult to anticipate beforehand on what additional variables cases should be matched so that the precise effect of the treatment variable can be ascertained. Matching sometimes occurs on theoretically uninteresting variables and thus little is added to precision. The resulting imprecision of measurement *on theoretically relevant variables,* the reduced sample size, and the non-random character of assignment to the comparison groups reduce the confidence we can place in findings from this design, even when we have done *ex post facto* elaboration.

When manipulation of the experimental variable is done *ex ante,* selection still remains a problem. But two related problems are also particularly acute with this design—*differential* sample *mortality,* and the *interaction of selection and X.* Consider, for example, a study designed to evaluate the effects of a human relations training program on middle-range civil servants. Based on a postmeasure only, we might decide to compare human sensitivity scores of a group of civil servants who went through the program with the scores of those who didn't. Typically, however, selection biases have operated to admit only those who were most likely to benefit from such programs. Even then, some of those selected find that various group dynamics training approaches are too unsettling and they drop out; few people, of course, drop out of the control group. Thus, not only is there differential mortality in the two groups, but mortality operates so as to enhance the interaction between selection and the experimental treatment. Those who complete the training program, simply as a result of design effects, are bound to show higher human sensitivity scores than those who did not take it. The training program may be judged a success. Yet mistakenly so. The precise effect of the treatment variable, if any, remains unmeasured. Design 4, on the other hand, would provide sufficient data because of its pretest; in many natural-state programs pretest information is available to the persistent searcher.

4 / THE CLASSIC EXPERIMENT: PRETEST–POST-TEST CONTROL GROUP DESIGN

$$R \; O_1 \; X \; O_2$$
$$R \; O_{1'} \quad O_{2'}$$

When social scientists conjure up images of the "true experimental design," they probably have this design in mind. Through randomized assignment to experimental and control groups, premeasurement and postmeasurement of both groups, and application of the experimental treatment only to the experimental group, the design provides impressive controls for virtually all internal sources of invalidity. The control, of course, is achieved through randomization; if, according to the laws of probability, the groups differ in no known way, they will respond identically to history, maturation, testing, and so on.

Let us suppose you live in a city where the public housing authority has customarily located new low-income housing units in the ghetto. The court, responding to complaints under the equal-protection clause, has ordered the housing authority to disperse housing to sites throughout the city. Several sites are chosen in a previously all-white ward. The alderman of that ward decides he will not try to fight the court order; instead he will try to educate his constituents about the need for the policy and try to overcome a great many inflammatory rumors aimed at arousing racial prejudices. He approaches you, as a social scientist teaching at the city university, and asks you to test a brochure he has designed. Before distributing it widely, the alderman wants to make certain it will have the desired effect.

You decide that a survey or field experiment in the ward is not feasible; because of the logistics of conducting interviews over an extended period of time, you do not have adequate control over a variety of threats to internal validity. Furthermore, you want to enhance sensitivity to the experimental treatment—the brochure—and decide that a control group is essential for comparison. Since yours is a commuter college and includes many people above the usual student age, you decide to use a sample of students in your large lecture section (1,000 students) who reside in all-white neighborhoods. Students are unaware of your sampling criterion. On the first day, you have carefully trained T.A.s administer to the sample a paper-and-pencil test with a battery of cognitive and attitudinal items all dealing with the general subjects of racial and socioeconomic prejudice, housing, and governmental action. On the second day you randomly assign half of the sample to one room, the other half to another room. The first group is asked to read a news article describing the court order to scatter housing sites; it is also asked to read the brochure designed by the alderman. The second group reads the news article but not the brochure. Each group is then given the paper-and-pencil test again. The change scores beween t_1 and t_2 for the two groups are compared, and any significant differences in information and attitude are attributed to the brochure. Throughout the experiment great care has been taken to provide both groups with identical situations, instructions, and so on. Satisfied that all threats to internal validity have been controlled, you report your findings to the alderman and he decides the brochure merits distribution to his constituents.

Unless the dynamics of the two groups have differed in some important way, probably all threats to *internal* validity have been controlled. Randomization has assured that; the pretest will also permit a control for any differences between the two groups on the dependent variable which might have existed before the experiment. If the differences were great, you might have used stratified random assignment to the two groups before the experimental treatment occurred. (Stratified random sampling is discussed in Chapter 4.)

The major problems with the classic experimental design, however, stem from *external* validity. One is never quite certain whether the findings from the experiment represent such a universal phenomenon that we can generalize our findings to other people or other situations. Typically, the most difficult problem is the interaction between *testing and the experimental treatment.* Certainly the pretest, on one day, of items dealing with information and attitudes on race and housing will have a reactive effect on the post-test on the next day. The subjects in both groups can readily see the relationship between the news report and the test. Furthermore the experimental group also sees the relationship of the test to the brochure. When the sample is thus sensitized and the sensitization interacts with the independent variable, can we then generalize back to any other group which has not been similarly sensitized by the pretest? One might decide to remove the sensitizing effect by lengthening the period between the pretest and the treatment and post-test to three or four weeks. To do so, however, would increase the likelihood of uncontrolled variance due to history or maturation; presumably because of randomized assignment these effects should be operating equally on both groups, but we are never quite sure. In no case should the increased time span come between treatment and post-test because this would increase the likelihood of interaction between X and history or maturation. Another way to deal with the problem is to have no pretest (as in Design 6) but to rely strictly on randomized assignment. Yet, as we will discuss later, this approach requires larger samples to generate confidence that there were no initial differences between the groups.

The experimental arrangements themselves have reactive effects. The experiment was artificial, atypical. The students, you point out, could respond favorably to the reasoned tone of the brochure; after all, few if any of them owned property in the "threatened" area; few sent children to the public schools in the area. Generally, the more artificial the setting, the greater the likelihood of socially desirable responses on the post-test (when the purpose of the experiment becomes more apparent to the subject). Artificiality may be overcome by designing an instrument where the subjects feel their decisions will have real consequences (discussed in Chapter 7) or by moving the experiment itself into the field. Another way to surmount the problem is to add combinations of other kinds of experimental treatments to other randomly selected groups in such a way that the effects of experimenting itself can be isolated from the effects of experimenting with the brochure. This may be done with hybrids of the Solomon four-group design (Design 5) and counterbalanced designs (Design 9). Any such additions, however, will make the experiment more costly.

While the logic of the classic experimental design is readily apparent, one must not forget the importance of appropriate statistical tests. Most commonly the t-test, a test for the statistical significance of differences, is used when the experimenter is interested in comparing the two sets of scores (see Chapter 11). As Campbell and Stanley point out, it is often misused. One should *not* calculate separate t-tests for the change scores in each group and—if the experimental group t is statistically significant and the control group t is not—conclude that the treatment had an effect. Rather, a single t based on comparison of the experimental group change score and the control group change score should be used. Analysis of covariance is frequently employed in this situation (see Chapter 12).

Perhaps because political scientists deal more with large collectivities and group interactions than with analytical traits of individuals, they have avoided the use of the classic experimental design. It is true that what one gains in sensitivity and control over plausible rival hypotheses stemming especially from design effects, one loses in generalizability. And when greater generalizability is sought, usually the cost of supplementary features to the basic design becomes prohibitive. In some respects this is a problem of under-developed theory. When a body of scientific theory is developed which will penetrate to rather enduring characteristics of individuals or group processes, less attention will be paid to generalizability and greater attention will be addressed to precise controls. If political science knowledge becomes cumulative, we should expect greater use of experimental designs in the future.

5 / THE SOLOMON FOUR-GROUP DESIGN

$$R \; O_1 \; X \; O_2$$
$$R \; O_{1'} \quad O_{2'}$$
$$R \quad X \; O_{2''}$$
$$R \quad\quad O_{2'''}$$

This design, along with other factorial designs (e.g., Design 9), is the strongest design available for overcoming threats to both internal and external validity. Unlike Design 4, it controls for the interaction of testing and X by removing two groups from the sensitizing pretest. Furthermore, the use of only a postmeasure on the fourth group is apt to provide a standard for assessing the reactive effects of the experiment itself.

In our previous illustration, the sample of students would now be divided into four randomly assigned groups, but two of them would not have been administered the pretest. Both situations for the pretest and for the experimental treatment would need to be identical and all situations for the post-test would need to be identical.

Despite these new controls, however, one is still faced with the generalizability problem resulting from the use of students. If warranted (tested) theory tells you that students would behave the same way as the constituents in the ward, the problem is moot. If such theory is lacking, the question is still appropriate. But the Solomon design certainly does permit generalizability to the universe from which the experimental sample was drawn.

The most appropriate statistical procedure for this design, as with Design 9, is analysis of variance; this procedure allows the analyst to compare more than two samples (see Chapter 12). Campbell and Stanley summarize the procedure.

Disregarding the pretests, except as another "treatment" coordinate with X, one can treat the post-test scores with a simple 2×2 analysis of variance design:

	No X	X
Pretested	$O_{2'}$	O_2
Unpretested	$O_{2'''}$	$O_{2''}$

From the column means, one estimates the main effect of X; from row means, the main effect of pretesting; and from cell means, the interaction of testing and X. If the main and interactive effects of pretesting are negligible, it may be desirable to perform an analysis of covariance on $0_2{}'$ versus 0_2, pretest scores being the covariate.[5]

While the Solomon four-group design is one of the most effective designs available, its major drawbacks for political scientists involve generalizability to real-life situations and cost.

6 / THE POST-TEST–ONLY CONTROL GROUP DESIGN

$$R \ X \ 0_1$$
$$R \quad 0_1{}'$$

If subjects are assigned to groups through randomization, and if such a procedure controls for extraneous sources of variance, why should we expect randomly assigned subjects to differ initially on the dependent variable? This consistent extension of the assumption which underlies randomized assignment has led experimenters to omit the pretest on the dependent variable. In so doing, the principal source of weakness in the classic experiment—sensitizing the subject to the experimental treatment—is presumably removed. The design resembles use of only the latter two groups in Design 5. Thus, it is a sensitive design, controlling for virtually all design effects, and it is an efficient and inexpensive procedure.

While it is true that the design removes the reactive effects of the pretest from both groups, one must still be cautious that the experimental treatment has not stimulated method effects which are confounded with substantive findings. If subjects in the experimental group become aware of the nature of the experimental treatment they may still alter their post-test response to conform to some self-fulfilling or self-denying expectations. *Experimentation always carries with it the problem of reactivity,* even in this powerful and simple design. Within the limits of ethical propriety, with all designs the scholar must find some means of disguising the nature of the experiment so that the experimental group does not link the treatment to post-test performance. Otherwise generalizations are to some degree still subject to threats of external invalidity.

Furthermore, the scholar must extend special effort to assure random assignment in this design. There is no second line of defense, such as a pretest, to control for initial differences in the two groups. When this design is employed, the scholar is obligated to report fully all assignment decisions he makes.

In Designs 4, 5, and 6 matching is not a substitute for randomization. Nevertheless, in an *ex post facto* manner, one may enhance the sensitivity of this design by control on a variety of variables measured in the post-test. Under these circumstances, covariance analysis becomes a powerful tool for the interpretation of data. Without such controls, however, the *t*-test described under Design 4 is appropriate.

7 / THE NONEQUIVALENT CONTROL GROUP DESIGN

$$O_1 \ X \ O_2$$
$$- - - - - -$$
$$O_{1'} \quad O_{2'}$$

The design may look to some as though it approximates the classic experiment; it is really closer to Design 2 but with the important addition of a control group. While adding strength to the design, the nature of the control group is also its principal weakness. Assignment to groups has not been based on randomization. Rather, assignment to the experimental group is based on exposure to or presence of the experimental treatment at a given point in the life of the subjects. Assignment to the control group comes by virtue of being similar to the experimental group but without the experimental treatment occurring. This design is customarily used with natural-state groups: classrooms, schools, public agencies, legislative bodies, states, nations, and so on.

Let us suppose we wanted to consider the effects of "proper" apportionment and malapportionment of state legislatures on the fate of legislation deemed favorable to urban areas. It has often been argued that urban underrepresentation has caused the lack of legislative responsiveness to urban problems. Once the one-man, one-vote rule is followed, and compact districts equal in size are created, the argument runs, the cities will get a fair shake.

Employing this design, we divide the universe of American state legislatures into those properly apportioned and those malapportioned. Those properly apportioned presumably have received the experimental treatment. Then the fate of bills deemed favorable to urban areas is examined, first, before proper apportionment and then after proper apportionment. In the control group, equivalent time periods are used for the pretest and post-test. As in Design 4, the change scores would then be compared.

Although this design, even without randomization, does provide controls over a wide variety of method effects left uncontrolled in Design 2, it does not control for a host of interaction effects. Especially acute is the interaction between selection and X. Those legislatures which are at some point reapportioned properly may very well be located in states where urban legislation receives the most favorable treatment anyway for economic reasons. If their pretest score is higher to begin with, we might be alerted to this rival explanation. But their pretest score may be depressed through some last dying gasp of control exerted by rural legislators immediately prior to reapportionment; the gain in favorability might as a result be inflated. The control group, not being at this stage, would not show the same wide gap. The strongest control for interaction between selection and X would come through the use of Design 11. If a number of measures are taken in the life history of both experimental and control groups, and the experimental treatment comes somewhere near the middle of the time-series, one can see whether the interaction of selection and X, or the interaction of selection and maturation, or the interaction of selection and history have accounted for observed differences. A longer time-series of tests prior to the experiment would show whether urban legislation suffers a particularly unfavorable fate immediately prior to reapportionment. On the other side of the treatment, it would show how long such maturational processes as rural domination of committee chairmanships can depress favorable treatment of urban legislation. Without the time-series data, one might look only at the post-test and conclude that reapportionment has no effect; yet it may take three or four sessions before rural forces lose their ability to bottle up legislation. The time-series, coupled with other information, would show whether historical events other than reapportionment have interacted with reapportionment to cause the effect. For example, it may be that those states that reapportioned happened to do so at a time when massive federal inducements to the solution of urban problems were offered (e.g., 90-10 matching grants); the experimental group may show a great gain in urban favorability but the control group may show a similar gain. Thus, using Design 7, we might conclude that reapportionment has no effect. If we used a longer time-series we might find more favorable urban legislation emerging in reapportioned states long after the federal inducement is phased out, while the control legislatures do not continue urban favorability.

Still another kind of selection-maturation-X-interaction problem stems from the extreme character of the comparison groups. Depending on the point in time selected, those states which have reapportioned may have some very atypical characteristics. Now the comparison group is no longer "average" because the atypical states have been removed; it becomes more atypical in the opposite direction. Nevertheless, on the post-test, natural processes may lead these two atypical groups more in the average direction. This is similar to the regression effects discussed earlier. Sensitivity to the full effects of legislative reapportionment is diminished because of regression effects. Curiously enough, control could be enhanced by calculating the mean change scores for *all* states and comparing this with the mean change scores for the reapportioned states. The control group in the small finite universe of 50 states, then, would include all states (both X and $\widetilde{X}$).

Design 7 is widely used in political science literature. It appears in studies ranging from the socialization effects of civics classrooms to the effects of external economic aid on national development. Where assignment to groups is done through careful matching on *theoretically relevant* extraneous variables, the design becomes increasingly powerful and practical. But there is still no substitute for random assignment; without it, interaction effects still remain the principal sources for plausible rival hypotheses.

8 / SEPARATE-SAMPLE PRETEST–POST-TEST DESIGN

$$R\ 0_1\ (X)$$
$$R\ \ \ \ X\ \ 0_2$$

This design, sometimes called the *successive cross-section design,* is widely used in conjunction with sample surveys, although it is not limited to survey data. A random sample of the relevant universe is administered some kind of test. Then a historical event or experimental manipulation occurs. Finally, the test is again administered but to a totally new random sampling of the universe. The great attraction of the design is its practicality; often one can fruitfully employ it with data already collected by someone else and stored at a social science data archive. Furthermore the design controls for most interaction effects; assuming large probability samples, it is far more powerful than Design 2 (or panel studies, where the *identical* respondents are interviewed at successive points in time) because it does not sensitize subjects to the experimental treatment or lead to reactive effects on the post-test.

The strength of the design, of course, comes partly through randomized selection of the groups. If assignment had been based on matching, many of the uncontrolled effects in Design 7 would be felt. In discussing the American soldier studies, for example, Stouffer points out that often a sample of soldiers in one setting was compared with a later sample of soldiers in another setting.[6] While they may have been matched on a number of criteria—such as rank, length of service, marital status, age—they may have been very different on a variable that interacted with the experimental treatment. In morale studies, soldiers in the United States were compared with soldiers stationed overseas; yet, as Stouffer notes, the overseas soldiers had to be in better emotional and physical health initially in order to draw overseas assignments. Often crucial criteria for matching are overlooked. Thus, one must be careful that the samples in successive cross-sectional studies are truly *randomly* drawn from the same universe.

The principal threats to this design concern internal validity: history, maturation, and frequently, instrumentation, instability, and mortality. Star and Hughes used this design to evaluate the effects of a publicity campaign in making people more supportive of the United Nations and its subsidiary agencies.[7] Sample surveys were taken in Cincinnati, the first addressed to a probability sample of residents before the publicity campaign occurred, and the second to a probability sample after the campaign. On both tests a variety of questions were asked about the goals of the UN, American relations with Communist countries, especially the Soviet Union, and internationalism in general. Such a natural-state experiment would seem to allow considerable generalizability. Yet between the pretest and post-test a lot more was happening in the cognitive life of Cincinnatians than just the publicity campaign.

Historical events—the consolidation of Communist control in Eastern European countries, evidences of Soviet activity elsewhere in the postwar world—were serving as cognitive filters to the favorable publicity about the UN. Latent ethnocentrism and distrust were *maturing* in Americans, including Cincinnati burghers. Since no pretest—post-test data were available *on the same people,* no control could be exerted over the effects of history and maturation. Ironically, while the authors might conclude that the campaign led to no startling increase in support for the UN, the lack of increase may not have been the result of the campaign but of other uncontrolled historical factors. Yet such a conclusion would be warranted *for this setting;* when certain historical conditions obtain, the publicity campaign does not lead to unusual attitudinal change.

Had the authors introduced a pretest, however, one could not be confident about its reactive and interactive effects. Under such circumstances, one of the many variants of Design 8 could provide effective controls for history and maturation: the addition of another randomly drawn post-test group, tested at the same time as the other post-test group, but not exposed to the experimental treatment. The design would now look like this:

$$R \; O_1 \; (X)$$
$$R \quad X \; O_2$$
$$R \qquad O_{2'}$$

By comparing scores of $O_{2'}$ with O_2 it would be possible to isolate historical and maturational factors from experimental effects. Randomization, according to the laws of probability, should assure that the two post-test groups are initially similar to the pretest group and thus the pretest can be used as the basis of a change score. Unfortunately, in natural-state experiments it is difficult to withhold the experimental treatment from any group. Thus, there is a tendency to partition the control group in an *ex post facto* manner, according to the respondent's own recall of whether or not he was exposed to the treatment. The result, while providing some control for history and maturation, generates groups which are no longer based on random selection. Thus, increased control over threats to internal validity will lead to decreased control over threats to external validity.

The design may be patched up in many other ways, such as administering a test at t_3 to yet another random sample exposed to the publicity campaign.

$$R \; O_1 \; (X)$$
$$R \quad X \; O_2$$
$$R \qquad \quad X \, O_3$$

Adding time-series data always increases the likelihood of control over history and maturation, but now one faces increasing problems with the cumulative effect of *multiple-treatment interference.* A publicity campaign sustained over a longer period of time is likely to have different results simply through the cumulative nature of stored-up effects.

Design 8, because it is so commonly tied to sample surveys, faces some other threats from method effects: instrumentation, stability, and differential mortality. Whenever interviews are used, not only the question but also the questioner is the instrument. Typically the skills and the work-related attitudes of interviewers vary from pretest to post-test. Generally they are less skilled but more eager to perform well on the pretest, whereas they are more skilled but perhaps more careless or less interested on the post-test. Thus, the calibration of the instrument differs as a function of interviewer moods. Observed change from t_1 to t_2 may be as much a result of changes in *instrumentation* as it is the result of the experimental treatment. This is especially true when the interviewer (or the laboratory assistant) gradually becomes aware of the purpose of the study.

The *stability* of measures, their reliability, is a problem for both experiments and surveys. The indicators used to exemplify each concept always generate some idiosyncratic error (unreliability). In this design, because pretest data *for the same group* have not been gathered, it is difficult to isolate the effect of unreliability between t_1 and t_2 from the effect of the experimental treatment. (This problem is discussed at greater length in Chapter 5.) Perhaps the best evidence for dismissing unreliability as a plausible rival hypothesis is a large body of performance data using this measure on similar groups. If it has proven reliable on similar groups in similar circumstances in the past, we are more likely to be confident of its reliability in the current study.

Differential mortality constitutes the final threat to the design. At t_1 perhaps 85% of the assigned interviews are completed. But when another randomly drawn group is interviewed at t_2, perhaps 80% of the assignments are completed. The two groups have experienced differential mortality. Even if 85% of the assignments had been completed at t_2 we cannot be certain that the same kinds of people have refused or been unreachable at t_1 and t_2. To answer that question, we will probably select a variety of demographic characteristics of each completed sample—e.g., age, sex, race, income—and try to show that the samples are virtually identical. Yet the variables on which we match the two samples may not be the crucial variables for the study. If the first interview was done in the winter and the second in the summer, matching on income may not be particularly useful. Different kinds of people in the $20,000 income class take vacations in the winter (and can't be reached) as opposed to those in the $20,000 income class who take vacations in the summer (and can't be reached). In the final analysis, whether or not differential mortality is a problem depends on the substantive issue. Yet it is usually more pronounced in magnitude with surveys than it is with laboratory experiments. (Still the former may have less initial selection bias and therefore permit greater possibility of generalizing results to the theoretically relevant universe.)

In any event, the practicality and the range of controls over external validity offered by this design make it attractive to many political scientists. So long as care is taken to add design features which will lessen various threats to internal validity, its continued use in our imperfect social science measurement world is warranted.

9 / COUNTERBALANCED DESIGNS (*factorial, Latin-square*)

	t_1	t_2	t_3	t_4
Group A	X_1O	X_2O	X_3O	X_4O
Group B	X_2O	X_4O	X_1O	X_3O
Group C	X_3O	X_1O	X_4O	X_2O
Group D	X_4O	X_3O	X_2O	X_1O

This design, though used widely in agricultural experiments, has been slow to find its way into social science literature. In its most common form—the Latin-square design presented above—it permits the scholar control in three principal areas: (1) different experimental treatments, (2) different occasions, and (3) different groups. The scholar is not limited to the controlled introduction of a single presumed causal variable; instead he can introduce several experimental treatments to different groups at different times and in different sequences. No pretest is required. One can readily see that the design controls for most threats to internal validity and still permits generalizability to many different situations. Furthermore, while the greatest control is achieved by random assignment to groups, the scholar can take natural-state groups differing in unknown ways and still achieve a high degree of control by devising additional Latin-squares. Thus, in the early agricultural experiments in Great Britain, soil plots did not need to have identical physical properties before an experimental treatment was introduced; differential sequencing of treatments to different plots at different points in time provided a high degree of control. Educational psychologists have noted a similar utility for this design in classroom settings; because of its counterbalanced nature, it is obviously superior to Design 7.[8] Experimental psychologists have also used it effectively.[9]

To measure the effect of each experimental treatment, one can turn the Latin-square so that each treatment forms a column. The observations for each are summed and compared. In like fashion, one can compare sums for groups (A, B, C, D) and sums for occasions (t_1, t_2, t_3, t_4). Therefore each source of variance, in addition to the experimental treatments, appears to be controlled. But as Campbell and Stanley note, one must still be alert to the fact that ". . . apparent differences among the effects of the X's could instead be a complex *interaction* [italics mine] effect between the group differences and the occasions." [10] For example, selection biases might interact with time sequences in such a way that an *experimental effect* is produced; the best control for this is to choose groups for treatment on a random basis. Where such an approximation of the true experimental design is not possible or is inappropriate—as with many natural-state groups—findings are likely to increase in plausibility when additional Latin-squares are devised which assign the groups to different sequences. As the number of different sequences to which a group is exposed increases, the likelihood of an observed effect being an artifact of interaction between selection biases and occasion decreases.

The design still suffers from its own complexity: by providing control over so many possible effects, it requires a substantial number of repeated observations. In human subjects especially, such observations may well have a cumulative effect. What is attributed to each experimental treatment may, in part, be the result of the complex experimental situation. Thus, generalizations stemming from the experiment may not necessarily hold for portions of the human population not exposed to the experiment.

There is some evidence that factorial and Latin-square designs will be utilized more by political scientists in the future. For example, Cook and Scioli suggest that a multivariate factorial design would be ideally suited for policy impact analysis of programs such as air pollution control and criminal and alcohol recidivism treatment.[11] In political psychology, designs similar to this have already proven useful. For example, Brown has utilized Q-methodology to study phenomena ranging from the personality traits of McCarthy activists in 1968, to the constellation of values characteristic of "civic cultures," to the radicalization process among individuals after the Kent State shootings.[12] In each, Brown, building on the work of William Stephenson, analyzes depth interviews or similar material for recurrent themes and mental patterns. Then he abstracts a very large series of statements and structures them into dimensions which appear to recur in the original material. A multidimensional matrix results. A sample of items for each cell is selected; these items together (usually 25 to 60) form a Q-sample, which is administered to the target sample of subjects. Each subject is presented with a shuffled deck of the items. Thus, the experimental treatments—namely, the preanalyzed dimensions which seem to structure thought on the topic—are administered to each subject in a random fashion. The data are later factor-analyzed, and the resultant factor loadings for each individual are linked to other characteristics which might serve to explain his mental patterning of the items. The important point in this approach is that the stimuli are presented to each respondent in a sequence that differs only by chance. Thus, it approximates features built into "true experiments" and utilizes the controls available in counterbalanced and other factorial designs.

There is great flexibility in the range of factorial and similar designs. They are attractive because of their control and practicality; one can still achieve many of the values of the experiment while using natural-state groups or unpretested individuals. They permit the examination of many possible causes and effects in the same general experiment. Perhaps their only weaknesses are their complexity (and sometimes attendant cost and inability of some computers to handle the resultant data) and the unmeasurable cumulative effect which comes from repeated experimental treatments.

10 / THE TIME-SERIES DESIGN

$$O_1 \, O_2 \, O_3 \, O_4 \, X \, O_5 \, O_6 \, O_7 \, O_8$$

This design, despite its lack of a control group, controls for a wide variety of sources of internal invalidity. It may be used in conjunction with laboratory experiments, surveys, or aggregate data. It calls for a lengthy series of repeated measurements before a presumed causal event occurs, followed by another lengthy series of measurements. The change between O_4 and O_5 is the principal focus for measuring the effects of the experimental treatment; nevertheless, the overall pattern of the series provides controls for the interpretation of the O_4–O_5 change. The fact that a lengthy pattern of performance data is available makes this design far more useful than Design 2; idiosyncratic extreme scores which might have occurred immediately next to the treatment are now apparent. Depending on the nature of the substantive problem and the data employed, sources of external invalidity may or may not constitute a threat. For example, if one seeks to generalize about migration patterns based on all relevant U.S. census data from 1820 to the present, most sources of external invalidity would be irrelevant. However, if one wanted to generalize findings from one state to the entire United States, then greater attention would need to be paid to these threats.

The principal threats to the design are history, and to some extent, instrumentation and the interaction of testing and X. In the Connecticut auto speeding crackdown studies described under Design 2, the authors noted that even when they lengthened their time-series to control for idiosyncratic scores, they lacked control for plausible rival hypotheses stemming from *history;* good weather conditions may have returned after 1955, or the highways may have been improved, or automobiles may have been outfitted with more safety devices. Within Design 10 itself there is nothing to control for the confounding of history with the presumed experimental treatment. This point will be illustrated shortly with election data.

Instrumentation and the *interaction of testing with the experimental treatment* may on occasion serve as major threats. If one is using census data, it is entirely plausible that changes in a time-series may be the result of either qualitatively inferior or improved data-gathering methods. Certainly this is true with crime statistics; a sudden "crime wave" may be simply a statistical artifact of changes in precinct recording procedures. As Campbell notes, O.W. Wilson's appointment as reform police superintendent in Chicago did not stimulate robbers and murderers to do their thing; instead the increase in reported larcenies and homicides came largely as a result of reforms in record-keeping.[13] If record-keepers become aware that certain kinds of data are important to the evaluation of a social policy, they may alter their methods of recording, either to improve the outlook or to make it more gloomy. At a certain point in time, gross national product may simply be a datum of limited importance; as it is exalted to the status of a key economic indicator, its measurement may be refined to include more and more economic transactions; the result is extensive growth in GNP through time—not as a result of economic policies but as a result of careful conceptualization and refinement in measurement.

To use another illustration, state education officials may be alarmed at rising truancy in the cities. State officials decide to use a carrot on local school officials as an inducement to get youths to attend school: the state aid formula will be based on the average number of children attending school each day, rather than the number of students enrolled. School attendance shows a sharp increase. State officials congratulate themselves. But the enterprising local principal knows that, formerly, any child who was absent from school for more than five hours a day was recorded as absent for the day; now any child who enters the school doors and reports to a classroom or homeroom, no matter for how long, is counted as present for the day. Changes in instrumentation sometime interact with the experimental treatment.

Conventions regarding the appropriate statistical tools for analyzing change scores in the time-series have been slow to develop. Tests of significance comparing observed change between O_4 and O_5 and change between O_1 and O_4 or O_1 and O_8 are sometimes deceptive. Based on summary figures, they fail to note patterns of variability in the time-series. Furthermore they are not sensitive to a time-lagged effect of the causal treatment. Perhaps inspection of the pattern supplemented by tests of significance still constitutes the strongest analytic technique. At the least, one should expect the greatest discontinuity in the prevailing pattern at the point of experimental treatment or shortly thereafter (if one expects time-lagged effect). Depending on the substantive issue, one might also expect the slope of the pattern to change. For example, the Connecticut auto speeding crackdown, if successful, should have led to a sharp decrease in the number of traffic fatalities in 1956; if continued successfully in later years, one should also expect the slope to be at a lesser angle or perhaps even non-monotonic. Inspection supplemented by statistical tests, of course, still will not control for other historical effects.

Despite these deficiencies Design 10 is a fairly powerful design which may be applied to many existing data bases at a minimum of cost. Its practicality and range of controls make it very attractive. Its major weakness is not so much with intrinsic effects as with extrinsic effects. Because it exerts so little control over history, scholars who use it are especially at the mercy of the state of theoretical development in their disciplines. Design 11 does introduce a control for history; in so doing, it allows the test of plausible rival hypotheses stemming from theory or good hunch. The exchange between Burnham, discussed below, and Rusk, discussed in the next design, illustrates this point.

Upon inspecting American electoral data from the mid-nineteenth century to the present, Burnham was struck by what he calls the decomposition of the electorate.[14] American people in the twentieth century are less likely to vote than were those in the nineteenth and their ties of loyalty to the two major parties are weaker; a larger proportion of the electorate is peripherally involved. Burnham bases these conclusions on a variety of indicators—estimated turnout, drop-off in participation from Presidential elections to Congressional elections, attrition in voting for lower offices on the ballot, split-ticket voting, and the amplitude of partisan swings from one office to another on the ballot—applied to election time-series. The design for analysis on each indicator is similar to Design 10. In interpreting the data he notes a sharp discontinuity and change in slope around the turn of the century. He suggests that the X responsible for the change was the "System of 1896." In that election a Populist-Democratic fusion failed to develop. Had it worked, it would have kept the discontented farmers and working class in the core electorate. Because it failed, he argues, it precipitated the takeover of the political system by the "American industrializing elite." Succeeding elections simply demonstrated the alienation of a large sector of the electorate; the New Deal, with its programs aimed at the hopes of small farmers and workingmen, stimulated their reentry into the core electorate, but never on the magnitude of the nineteenth century. While this interpretation is highly suggestive and insightful, neither the data used by Burnham nor his design permit careful investigation of the interpretation. The design leaves uncontrolled other historical events and thus may lead to an unwarranted sense of precision. While the pattern is there, the control for plausible rival hypotheses stemming from extrinsic factors is not. Design 11 provides for such control.

11 / THE MULTIPLE TIME-SERIES DESIGN

$$O_1 \; O_2 \; O_3 \; O_4 \; X \; O_5 \; O_6 \; O_7 \; O_8$$
$$\text{-------------}$$
$$O_{1'} \, O_{2'} \, O_{3'} \, O_{4'} \quad O_{5'} \, O_{6'} \, O_{7'} \, O_{8'}$$

This design still uses the extended time-series with an experimental treatment, but it also uses, as a control group, time-series for an apparently matched group which lacks exposure to X. Although assignment has not been based on randomization, comparison of the long time-series for each group will alert the scholar to possible differences and will permit control over most internal and external sources of invalidity.

Just as Design 10 had possible difficulty with instrumentation and the interaction of testing and X, so does Design 11. Because of the lack of randomized assignment, Design 11 also lacks control for the interaction of selection and X. It may be that unspecified differences in the control group have shown up when exposed to X and that these differences as well as X account for the change. For example, a disease affecting children at a certain age may be studied by examining the life histories of those who get it and those who don't. It may be found that those afflicted by it were exposed to certain bacteria at a point in their life while the unafflicted were not exprsed. What may go unnoticed is the fact that the exposed group differed *initially* from the apparently unexposed group in that they had a blood deficiency at birth. Thus, the design is best used over and over again, each time controlling for another plausible source of interaction between selection and X. Clues about such interactions stem extrinsically from theory and hunch. Let us illustrate the use of the design.

Rusk noted the deficiencies of Burnham's design and decided that changes in election structures constitute a plausible rival hypothesis to Burnham's economic interpretation of American electoral history.[15] At about the time Burnham's electorate was severely decomposing, Rusk notes, the Progressive movement was sweeping the country. Voting registration was required and stringent laws were introduced to control vote fraud perpetrated by political machines. The secret Australian ballot replaced the different colored party slates which were dropped in ballot boxes in full public view. In some states office-bloc ballots replaced the party slate and thus required that the voter mark his choice in each contest rather than select the slate of an entire party. These changes, Rusk argues, were likely to account for a substantial amount of the depression in turnout and decrease in party loyalty. In effect, then, he is offering a plausible rival hypothesis for the uncontrolled effects of history in Burnham's design. To measure the effects, particularly of ballot changes, Rusk uses several multiple time-series designs. For example, he compares mean split-ticket voting through time in states that adopted Australian ballots (X) and states that continued party-strip ballots $(\widetilde{X})$; the same is done with party-column and office-bloc ballots. Through such analysis he is able to show that much of the observed change on indicators of party loyalty can be explained by ballot form. Furthermore, this design allows him to show through time the effects of ballot change. Careful controls are exercised through the design; evidence regarding interaction of selection and X is still problematic. Nevertheless, Rusk's design permits him to offer structural effects as a more plausible explanation than economic effects. To be sure, his explanation does not necessarily destroy Burnham's interpretation; it is at a different level. But it does suggest considerable refinement; to be able to hold to Burnham's interpretation we must now design studies which show the relationship of industrializing elites to electoral mechanisms. Converse has turned to the problem and, through a variety of evidence, has argued that nativistic ethos rather than economic gain may constitute a more plausible explanation for the election law changes.[16]

Regardless of how the intellectual issue is resolved, the use of Design 11, supplemented by new data, has permitted greater and greater control over plausible explanations for an important historical phenomenon. A design unsuited to the level of explanation sought by Burnham has been replaced. As new data such as collective biographies are available, other research designs will permit the controversy to be resolved at new levels of explanation.

Multiple time-series is powerful and practical. It can be applied to many data bases. It permits control for most method effects. Finally, it can force the scholar to a more suitable level of explanation than he might have used with another design.

12 / THE EQUIVALENT TIME-SAMPLES DESIGN

$$X \; O_1 \; \tilde{X} \; O_2 \; X \; O_3 \; \tilde{X} \; O_4$$

This design is a combination of time-series and control group features. The group under analysis remains the same throughout. But its behavior is measured when the experimental treatment is present and when it is absent. The time periods for each test should be roughly equivalent; the presence or absence of the treatment can be introduced either randomly or alternately. The design is appropriate for many problems where content analysis is utilized.

For example, let us suppose we wanted to see whether internal insta- bility of a government leads to increased hostility toward external "scapegoat" nations. First, we decide on indicators of governmental stability; secondly, we select a country that has experienced a "normal" amount of governmental stability. Then, we choose time periods throughout its national history which are characterized by instability. We choose roughly equivalent time periods characterized by stability. Finally, we content-analyze national media accord- ing to predetermined criteria for measuring hostility toward scapegoat na- tions. Mean test scores for unstable periods are compared with mean test scores for stable periods. The difference in hostility scores will be attributed to X.

The design, by running through large periods of a nation's life, controls well for most sources of internal invalidity. Since the X's and $\tilde{X}$'s have been selected from roughly equivalent time periods and since no periodicity is likely to last throughout the nation's history, the time periods should expe- rience such factors as history, maturation, and the like in a similar manner.

The major threats to the design, however, come from external sources. Often it is difficult to generalize one's findings from this design to other instances of the phenomenon. Essentially, the design is a case study of one group. It must be supplemented by similar data from other groups. For example, if we have looked at the stability-scapegoat phenomenon in an "average" country, we should do the same in less than average countries. External validity is suspect because the comparison group is itself the control group in a different condition.

Furthermore, the full effect of *multiple-treatment interference* may not be isolated in the comparison of means. It may be that a rapid succession of instabilities in one time period may lead to a very large hostility score, but normal instability decreases hostility geometrically. While it is not a problem in the illustration we have outlined, laboratory or field experiments where the purpose of the experiment becomes known to the subjects may well constitute reactive arrrangements as well as engender multiple-treatment interference. The noted "Hawthorne effect" was the result of continuous attention given to experimental subjects, rather than the presence or absence of X. Where the purpose of the experiment becomes known to the subjects, the interaction of testing and X also threatens this design. Subjects can condition themselves to act a certain way when X is present and another way when it is absent, because "that's the way we're supposed to act."

In short, the design may provide fairly strong controls and is especially practical for *ex post facto* analysis of public record data. It exerts less powerful controls in its more artificial experimental applications.

13 / MIXED DESIGNS

The research designs modeled here are not the only useful ones. These models are simply reconstructions of what researchers commonly do. So long as general rules of logic are followed and the scholar designs means for controlling for method effects or other plausible rival hypotheses, a wide variety of other designs may be developed.

The scholar must always face up to the limitations of his data bases. While one might view the Solomon four-group design, Latin-squares, or multiple time-series as the most desirable designs for control, access to data always stands in the way. When data are recalcitrant, the scholar will use a design suited to the limitations of the data, but will also seek to supplement the basic design with other designs and data which will shed light on otherwise uncontrolled sources of variance.

The social scientist is not unlike the practicing physician or the criminal lawyer. He tries to diagnose as best he can what the facts are and what the relations are. But from there on, his case rests on "convincing" evidence. For the patient, proof comes in recovery through the regimen prescribed by the physician; for the judge or jury, conviction comes through confidence beyond a reasonable doubt that evidence and inferences offered by one lawyer are more plausible than those offered by another lawyer. Evidence is always interpreted through conventions, through rules of the game generally accepted by the discipline—be it physicians, jurists, or political scientists. Within the conventions we build the strongest case we can with the data we have; if we are dissatisfied with the data at hand, we search for new data to strengthen the case.

EXTRINSIC EFFECTS

Extrinsic effects are substantive factors other than those hypothesized by the scholar which have affected his outcomes. They are outside his proposed blueprint for relating independent variables to dependent variables; yet they should have been included in the blueprint because, in varying degrees, they have affected the results. They are substantive in that they are or should be embedded in theory surrounding the phenomenon under study. Our hypothesis may specify that juvenile delinquency is, to some extent, caused by broken homes; yet "broken homes" may simply be one indicator for a more generic cause of delinquency such as "absence of appropriate role model." Not to include other measures of "appropriate role model" would constitute failure to control for extrinsic effects.

Controlling for extrinsic effects, however, is a far more nebulous thing than controlling for intrinsic effects. It is not particularly difficult to isolate various method or design effects; the more experience we gain with scientific measurement, the greater our alertness to these effects. But extrinsic factors are what social science is all about. If we already had a body of completely tested deductive theory in a particular substantive area, we would not need to conduct much research in that area. But we don't. We feel our way along. We deduce hypotheses from existing theory, but we also make discoveries of unexpected relationships as we play with our data. Given imperfect knowledge, then, it is impossible to control for all extrinsic effects. To do so would be to construct and test a completely closed theory—something inimical to the very assumptions of science. Rather we use theory, data, and hunch to direct us to the test of as many plausible rival substantive hypotheses as our data base will permit.

In this respect, experimental designs and *ex post facto* analysis were at one time thought to have differing strengths and weaknesses. The experiment was thought to be a superb method for active manipulation of variables; it permitted careful control over most method effects; but it did not allow us to test the effects of more than a handful of variables on each other. *Ex post facto* designs were thought to move in the other direction: they usually started with an observed finding and asked which, of a multitude of variables, might have accounted for the finding and in what way. Typically *ex post facto* analysis was done on survey or aggregate data where a pool of relevant extrinsic variables was available. But direct introduction and manipulation of presumed causal variables were sacrificed.

The task is to marry the two. Fortunately, both experimentalists and *ex post facto* analysts are now moving in that direction. In experimental research, factorial designs supplemented by the analysis of variance and covariance are replacing the classic experiment and the *t*-test. Such machinery permits the experimenter to introduce and manipulate several independent variables rather than a single one. Variance and covariance allow him to partition out the strength of the effects of each independent variable on the dependent variable. Among scholars who customarily do *ex post facto* research, analysis of variance and multiple regression models are now being applied to aggregate data far more frequently. Three important changes in their style of research may be noted: (1) Greater attention is being paid *prior* to the collection of data to theory and concept explication. Variables are developed with greater rigor and relationships are spelled out *before* the fact. (2) Through *elaboration* with correlational analysis and significance tests, it is possible to move beyond the simple bivariate finding to explanation of the relationships in a large net of variables.[17] (3) Through multiple regression and stochastic process models, scholars are also exerting great control, after the fact, in delineating the strength of causal paths both among several substantive variables and among possible measurement artifacts (see Chapters 12, 13, and 14). In short, all of these designs are permitting the simultaneous control and test of expanding networks of variables. Cumulative developments in theory and powerful analytical models are bringing extrinsic variables under control—despite weaknesses in the initial design. Of course no variable can be controlled where performance data for it are lacking. Neither the expanded experimental designs nor newer analytical techniques can surmount the failure to specify a relevant variable in the problem-formulation stage.

The logic of the research design—its ability to generate tests of plausible rival hypotheses stemming from intrinsic and extrinsic factors—is naturally the most important consideration in a discussion of research design. But the scholar is not simply a logician; he is also a cost accountant and an engineer. He must find clever and efficient ways to sample, generate, and analyze data which will transform his blueprint into a viable structure. While such matters as sampling, data generation, and measurement models receive treatment in separate chapters, they are in the broadest sense all important aspects of research design. Decisions in each area stem from the optimal design for a problem, but they in turn modify the decision about an optimal design.

NOTES

1. Donald T. Campbell and Julian C. Stanley, *Experimental and Quasi-Experimental Designs for Research* (Chicago: Rand McNally & Company, 1963), p. 1.

2. Donald T. Campbell, "Reforms as Experiments," *American Psychologist,* 24 (April, 1969), 412. This section relies heavily on three pieces by Campbell: *Ibid.;* Campbell and Stanley, *Designs for Research;* and Campbell, "Factors Relevant to the Validity of Experiments in Social Settings," *Psychological Bulletin,* 54 (July 1957), 297–311. It is also influenced by Samuel A. Stouffer, "Some Observations on Study Design," *American Journal of Sociology,* 55 (January 1950), 356–59; B.J. Underwood, *Psychological Research* (New York: Appleton-Century-Crofts, 1957), Chapters 4 and 5; Leslie Kish, "Some Statistical Problems in Research Design," *American Sociological Review,* 24 (June 1959), 328–38; and Fred M. Kerlinger, *Foundations of Behavioral Research* (New York: Holt, Rinehart and Winston, Inc., 1964), Part 4.

3. See Harold Stein, ed., *Public Administration and Policy Development* (New York: Harcourt, Brace & World, Inc., 1952).

4. G.V. Glass, "Analysis of Data on the Connecticut Speeding Crackdown as a Time Series Quasi-Experiment," *Law and Society Review,* 3 (August, 1968), 55–76; D.T. Campbell and H.L. Ross, "The Connecticut Crackdown in Speeding: Time Series Data in Quasi-Experimental Analysis," *Law and Society Review,* 3 (August, 1968), 33–53.

5. Campbell and Stanley, *Designs for Research,* p. 25. We have altered their notation system in the quotation to conform to ours.

6. Stouffer, "Some Observations on Study Design."

7. Shirley A. Star and Helen M. Hughes, "Report on an Educational Campaign: The Cincinnati Plan for the United Nations," *American Journal of Sociology,* 55 (1950), 389–400.

8. See, for example, O. Kempthorne, *The Design and Analysis of Experiments* (New York: John Wiley & Sons, Inc., 1952); O. Kempthorne, "The Design and Analysis of Experiments with Some Reference to Educational Research," in R.O. Collier and S.M. Elam (eds.), *Research Design and Analysis* (Bloomington, Ind.: Phi Delta Kappa, 1961), pp. 97–133; R.A. Fisher, *The Design of Experiments* (London: Oliver & Boyd, Ltd., 1935).

9. Raymond B. Cattell, ed., *Handbook of Multivariate Experimental Psychology* (Chicago: Rand McNally & Company, 1966).

10. Campbell and Stanley, *Designs for Research,* p. 51.

11. Thomas J. Cook and Frank P. Scioli, Jr., "Policy Impact Analysis: A Suggested Research Strategy," in Thomas R. Dye (ed.), *The Measurement of Policy Impact* (Tallahassee: Political Research Institute, 1971), pp. 52–66.

12. Steven R. Brown, "On the Use of Variance Designs in Q-Methodology," *Psychological Record,* 20 (Spring 1970), 179–89; Steven R. Brown and Dani Thomas, "Public Response and Private Feeling: Reaction to the Kent State Situation," (paper presented to the annual meeting of the American Educational Research Association, New York, 1971); Steven R. Brown and John D. Ellithorpe, "Emotional Experience in Political Groups: The McCarthy Phenomenon," *American Political Science Review,* 64 (June 1970), 349–66.

13. Campbell, "Reforms as Experiments," pp. 414–15.

14. W. Dean Burnham, "The Changing Shape of the American Political Universe," *American Political Science Review,* 59 (March 1965), 7–28.

15. Jerrold G. Rusk, "The Effect of the Australian Ballot Reform on Split-Ticket Voting," *American Political Science Review,* 64 (December 1970), 1220–38.

16. Philip E. Converse, "Change in the American Electorate," in Angus Campbell and Philip E. Converse (eds.), *The Human Meaning of Social Change* (New York: Russell Sage Foundation, 1972), pp. 263–337.

17. For an extremely lucid introduction to *elaboration,* as practiced by Lazarsfeld and his students, see Morris Rosenberg, *The Logic of Survey Analysis* (New York: Basic Books, Inc., 1968), especially Chapters 8 and 9 and appendices.

Chapter 4

SELECTION OF DATA:
SAMPLING DECISIONS

Consider the following general hypothesis: the size of the minority population and the extent of racial integration in a country determine the proportion of governmental decision-making posts held by persons of minority racial background. What are the sampling implications of this hypothesis? Who or what should be studied? Since theoretical concerns are foremost in determining the objects and subjects of investigation, we must answer these questions by looking at the concepts employed in the hypothesis.

The principal determinant of where we should look for our subjects is the phrase "in a country." It suggests that (1) we want to generalize about behavior in countries (2) by looking at selected properties of these countries. Our first decision, then, is to determine whether the universe of all countries will be used or whether a sample of them is desirable. This, of course, requires that we define a "country" and can identify and enumerate all those units which have all the characteristics of "countries." Our second decision concerns the country properties that are of interest to us, *viz.*, the ones specified by the hypothesis.

One of the properties—size of the minority population—does not present undue difficulties. We probably will settle for data about the total country population and the total minority population and, for purposes of comparison, will calculate the minority proportion for each country. Nevertheless, since "size" could refer to the total minority population figure, we will still keep that information available. But our unit is most likely to be a national ratio involving a body count.

Another property—the proportion of governmental decision-making posts held by persons of minority racial background—is a little bit more difficult. We will have to decide what the governmental decision-making posts in each country are, enumerate them, count all minority people in them, and calculate their proportion. But since most countries are characterized by national, regional, and local governmental bodies, each with differing decisional responsibilities, this will be no easy task. Still, our unit for sampling purposes will be a national ratio involving a body count.

The third property—extent of racial integration—presents all sorts of difficulties. What do we mean by "racial integration?" Let's pose several alternative indicators: (1) the attitudes of minority and majority people toward each other; (2) the physical pattern of contact as described by proximity of housing occupancy; (3) the social pattern of contact as described by occupational, commercial, and recreational interaction; (4) the sharing of cultural values; or (5) formal adjudication aimed at enforcing compliance with integration goals.

If we use the first as an indicator of the extent of racial integration, we will probably gather survey data on integration-related attitudes from a representative national sample in each country; our units will be the proportion of individuals holding certain attitudes. If we use the second as an indicator, we are quite likely to divide up urbanized areas into neighborhoods, examine the proportion of dwelling units in each neighborhood occupied by the racial minority, and then develop a national summary index figure from these neighborhood data. The unit for cross-national comparison would be an index number based not on individual people but on household occupancy of dwelling units. If the third indicator is used, a whole battery of census, survey, and observational measures may be developed. The units for cross-national comparisons might well be composite indices ranging from observed contact rates within factories, commercial establishments, or groups, to rates of interpersonal contact based on questioning individuals. If the fourth indicator is used, one might perform a content analysis of cultural values in different media and then compare consumer patterns for these media among majority and minority persons. The resulting index would be a composite of media, values, and persons as the units. Finally if the fifth indicator were used, we might look at the proportion of the judicial docket devoted to integration suits. Here the units of cross-national comparison would not be individuals or groups but proceedings.

This complicated illustration shows that sampling decisions pervade the entire research process. Sampling plans are never determined primarily by sampling theory; rather, they are first and foremost the product of the substantive research concern. Furthermore, the solution of the sampling decision at one level of analysis—e.g., the country—in no way lessens the need for careful attention to sampling decisions at other levels of analysis—the individual, the household, the group, the establishment, the neighborhood, the region within the country. Finally, sampling in the social sciences is not confined to the selection of persons. Altogether too often we use people as subjects when we should use interactions, processes, documents, or other analytical or inanimate things. "People" do not exhaust our data base; nor is sampling theory applicable only to "people" used in surveys and experiments.

97

Universes and Samples

A *universe* (sometimes called a *population*) consists of all those units with a specified characteristic to which the scholar seeks, ultimately, to generalize his findings. In our illustration above, countries were the primary unit of analysis *to* which we wished to generalize, but selected characteristics of countries constituted the units *about* which we wished to generalize. That is a common procedure in sampling: we sample units and generalize to them, but we are concerned only with a specific characteristic possessed by each of the units. Thus, while we may wish to compare population mobility in the Common Market countries, we are actually examining the behavior of individual people of different citizenship as they move from one locale to another. The universe is generally thought of as both the unit and its specified characteristic.

The *unit,* of course, is the smallest single element which possesses the specified characteristic. If personal income is the object of generalization, then persons are the sampling units although we are talking about their income. If family income is the object of generalization, then families are the sampling units. If international hostilities are the object of generalization, then the interactions between and among national governments (presuming each of those terms is defined clearly) become the sampling units.

A *sample* is a partial universe selected in such a way that we can generalize about the entire universe by examining only some of its units. While one can readily see the efficiency introduced by sampling, he can also see that it is a risky business. In fact, the concepts of *risk* and *efficiency* pervade sampling theory. Since findings based on samples are only *estimates* of the whole from some of its parts, it is the purpose of sampling theory to tell us how much confidence we may place in these estimates.

If the scholar is not greatly concerned about efficiency he may decide "to bear no risks." In that case, he may use a census to provide data. A *census* involves a complete enumeration of all units in the universe. When a universe is known to contain very few units, the cost of gathering data about each unit is minimal. For example, if we wish to generalize only to a universe of American "war" Presidents, we probably would not rely on a sample. Yet the smaller our universe becomes—ultimately the single case study—the more we, as *social* scientists, lay ourselves open to charges that we are dealing with theoretically uninteresting questions.

Whether such charges are warranted can be determined only by looking at the purpose of the study. *Idiographic* research typically involves intensive analysis of a single case in a single time and space. *Nomothetic* research, on the other hand, usually involves the attempt to generalize extensively about a universe of units across time and space. Both are aimed at description and explanation. But idiographic research is usually confined to such enduring or primitive traits of the unit that sampling risk becomes irrelevant; such analytic studies are common in psychiatry, personality research, or history where careful attention is paid to discovery within the confines of the idiosyncratic case. Nomothetic research, however, is more characteristic of a science at the verification stage, where it is important to find out whether observed relationships in a few units really are operative across the entire universe of similar units. When any scientist is seeking to generalize his findings from a select number of units to a larger universe, it is appropriate to be concerned about the risk of such generalizations.

In still another way, it is very difficult to bear no risks. The scientist might rely on a census of a small universe as a way to avoid the need to estimate. But the selection of the entire universe is no protection whatsoever against errors which come from ill-formulated measurement. As we will point out shortly, sampling theory and measurement theory, while interrelated, make separate demands upon research. When the measuring instrument is biased in some manner, it is of little value whether a sample of two thousand out of a universe of two million or a census of 20 out of a universe of 20 is employed.

When taken in tandem, these points provide sobering considerations for the political scientist. If he selects all units of a small universe as his subjects he must ask: (1) whether the theoretical concerns for which such a universe is appropriate are of such import to the discipline that it is worth the research effort, (2) whether he can assiduously limit his generalizations to that universe rather than succumb to the temptation to give his findings greater generality, and (3) whether his measures of the target traits possessed by each unit have satisfied all relevant concerns stemming from measurement theory. On the other hand, if the political scientist selects a sample from a larger universe, he will have to meet all of these considerations plus one: a statement of the risk involved in putting confidence in findings from the sample. Sampling theory will help him perform this last task. Thus, both theoretical interests and sampling theory provide the criteria for determining (1) which subjects to select and (2) what consequences the selection process will have.

Criteria for Judging Sampling Plans

The following are optimal criteria by which the sampling plan of any piece of research may be judged:

1. The sampling plan must permit the researcher to generalize to the theoretically relevant universe.
2. The sampling plan should provide a known probability for the inclusion of any single unit (person, interaction, country, document, etc.) or set of units from the universe.
3. The sample should be sufficiently *large* to:

    a. Permit estimations about characteristics of the universe (totals, means, distributions, etc.) with a high degree of precision and confidence.

    b. Permit estimations of characteristics of the universe subclasses (black mean, white mean, age distribution of Republicans, etc.) as the sample is disaggregated for comparative analysis.

4. The sample should be sufficiently *small* to:

    a. Permit efficiency, i.e., take full advantage of sampling theory and previous knowledge of the universe, while still generating theoretically relevant data.

    b. Guarantee economy, i.e., stay within available financial resources but still get your money's worth.

    c. Insure speed in data collection, i.e., make good use of available data collectors so as to exclude extraneous sources of variance related to history and maturation.

Each of these criteria will be discussed at length.

1 / THEORETICAL CONCERNS

If the sample is designed to permit generalizations back to the theoretically relevant universe, the scholar must pay attention to four principal considerations: (1) whether the sample consists of units at the appropriate level of analysis; (2) whether the locus for drawing the sample is fruitful in the sense that the properties and mechanisms specified in the test theory are likely to be present or absent in a sufficiently large number of cases; (3) whether the locus for drawing the sample is relevant in the sense that it allows the researcher to test plausible rival hypotheses; and (4) whether the locus for drawing the sample is relevant in the sense that it permits control over time-order as specified in a causal hypothesis.

Levels of Analysis. The level of analysis is a knotty problem precipitated by the fact that we are concerned with properties of units, not just with units; furthermore, in the social sciences, wholes are often characterized by the properties of parts. When we study a nation, a city, a pressure group, an agency, or a legislative committee, we often describe it through the modal personal characteristics of its inhabitants or members, or through the patterned or recurring interactions of these individuals. In like manner, individuals may be described in reference to the larger collectivity, e.g., American citizens, voters in blue-collar suburbs, bureau chiefs in developing countries. Inanimate objects of inquiry such as newspaper articles or judicial proceedings may be described in similar fashion. The decomposition or reduction of larger units into smaller units and the reconstruction of a whole from its parts are common practices in the social sciences. Unfortunately, sampling theory is seldom addressed to this issue. Nevertheless, severe logical problems are created by data unmatched to the level of analysis specified by theory. The issue must be examined both under the heading of "sampling" and later under "data generation."

While nomenclature differs, discussions of the whole-part, superunit-subunit, macro-micro issue specify at least four ways by which a unit may be described.[1] When a higher level unit (superunit) is described only in reference to itself, the characteristics are called *global properties*. Global properties are properties that characterize the unit without requiring any further knowledge about smaller subunits of it. An agency is 12 years old; a nation is bounded by two specific bodies of water and a mountain range; a state legislature enacts a fair housing ordinance; or the AFL merges with the CIO. In each instance, the characteristic or action referred to is the property of that unit as a whole. The statement's meaning would be altered if we said, for example, "the agency chief has been with the agency for 19 months." We may be implying that the purpose of the agency changes with its leading personnel and therefore our global characteristic—age—is ill-suited for the theoretical concern. But to do so is to refocus theoretical and empirical concern. In fact, that often occurs when we decide that a global property is less useful than a property characteristic of a lower level of analysis.

When the smaller subunits of the larger unit are described by characteristics common to all but derived from any one of them, the properties are called *analytical properties*. For example, since age is a property of all humans, we can describe the age distribution within a census tract. Or, if we can construct attitudinal or personality traits and measure them across the population, we might be able to offer the conservatism-liberalism distribution within a state electorate. Newspaper editorials in a country may be characterized by their degree of friendliness toward the government, or court decisions during differing time periods may be placed on a continuum dealing with protection of the rights of the accused. In each case, the property—age, conservatism-liberalism, friendly editorials, protection of the rights of the accused—is capable of being possessed by the subunit—people, editorials, court decisions—within the superunit—tract, state, country, time periods of courts. Analytical properties are generally reported with the distribution of the property held by the smaller unit. But it is the larger unit that is meant to be characterized by the distribution.

When interactions between and among smaller units of the larger unit are described, these are usually called *relational* and *structural properties*. The distinction between relational and structural properties is not altogether clear in the illustrations of Lazarsfeld and Menzel, Galtung, or Eulau. For Eulau, it seems to depend on the degree to which interactions recur as patterned behavior; the more pronounced the pattern, the more likely that it is a structural property. For us, this is an empirical question which does not require separate labels. What is clear, however, is the fact that relational or structural properties refer to interactions. Neither the common properties of individual subunits nor the properties of the larger unit itself form the basis for a relational or structural property; it must be gotten by examining the interactions and the relationships of the lower-level units. "Reciprocity," for example, could occur among members of a legislative body who supported each other's pet bills; or reciprocity could refer to agreements between states who return apprehended criminals to the state of original jurisdiction. "Leadership" statuses may refer to those positions within any group from which an individual may legitimately exert influence over the direction of that group's decisional life; it implies a "followership" relationship as well.

Finally, *contextual properties* describe the lower-level unit by various regularities in the environment of the higher-level unit of which it is a member. "Residents of racially integrated neighborhoods," "graduates of cow colleges," "part-owner of an establishment frequented by known hoodlums," "member of a fundamentalistic sect"—all are descriptions of individuals by a characteristic of their larger environment. Contextual properties can refer to any global, analytical, or structural property of a larger unit. And it is proper to refer to the individual member—e.g., resident of a racially integrated neighborhood—by the characteristics of the higher-level unit of which he is a member. But one must be very cautious not to infer that every individual characterized by the contextual information shares equally the constellation of characteristics suggested by the trait. That a person is a resident of an integrated neighborhood does not mean that he favors integration of housing. A graduate of a cow college is not always an agricultural or engineering student. An individual in a precinct voting heavily for Wallace might still have voted for McGovern. In short, a contextual property does not predict uniformly well to the properties of any given lower-level unit of the higher-level collectivity.

Each type of property has consequences for the selection of a sampling plan and the development of data-generating techniques. Which kind of property to seek depends on the test theory.

Global properties are appropriate whenever the scholar seeks information only at the higher-level unit. Implied is a lack of concern with any characteristics of the component lower-level units; this consequently severely limits the kinds of questions that can be asked. But global properties are seldom sufficient for social science analysis. In our AFL-CIO merger example the scholar may address only the fairly manifest relationship that one organization as a whole has with another organization. Would he not also like to know whether the political activist thrust of the leaders of one body will blend well with the bread-and-butter thrust of the other body's leaders; whether the resulting state and local labor federations will be dominated by former AFL officials or CIO officials; and how jurisdictional disputes in plants will be resolved? These questions bring into play the relational properties between officials and members of both labor confederations rather than a global property of one of them. This means that the sampling plan will no longer be addressed solely to generalizability about labor confederations that have national merger stances toward other labor confederations. The sampling plan will now seek generalizability from the level of the constituent parts of each labor confederation. This may require distributional information about leaders and members in each confederation at the state and local level, and relational information about interactions across confederations.

If *analytical properties* are suggested by the test theory, both the super-unit and the subunits will need to be sampled. The subunit data will provide distributional characteristics for each superunit. If the suburb is the super-unit, we can examine the distributional pattern for the income of each family and can characterize suburbs as high income, middle income, and low income according to some generally accepted criterion. Then we can compare suburbs on some other theoretically relevant variable such as redistributional tax policy. The important point is this: if we seek generalizability back to the theoretically relevant universe, we must be concerned with the probability features of the sample at both levels.

With *relational* or *structural properties* the two-level sampling problem is not so easily resolved, because of the nature of data generation. Whereas individual and aggregate indicators drawn from published reports or survey research are likely to be adequate for the formulation of global and ana-lytical properties, relational or structural properties are based on interactions. Interactions do not inhere in either the superunit or the subunit, the col-lectivity or the individual. To study and categorize interactions we must usually make more complex inferences; typically it is necessary to ascribe meaning to interpersonal (or inter-subunit) contact, or to penetrate to the meaning attached to it by the actors themselves. Self-report data generated by a survey instrument may be useful for this. Survey questions may be ad-dressed either to the participants in the interaction or to knowledgeable in-formants. But we must recognize that the underlying sampling unit is no longer an individual; it is a *relationship* between, at a minimum, two individuals.

If we are trying to characterize the superunit by the *incidence* of various types of interactions within the superunit, the recall of the actors themselves may sometimes be reliable, sometimes unreliable. People participating in ongoing real-life situations do not keep running tallies of the frequency of interactions. It may be that observational data-generating techniques which involve constant monitoring of the life history of the actors—e.g., videotape, tailing—would be more suitable than recall data.

If we are trying to characterize the superunit by the *meaning* actors at-tach to various types of interactions within the superunit, the recall of actors is undoubtedly more essential. Motives and meaning are often difficult to infer from nonparticipatory observations of the incidence of interactions; it is usually desirable to modify such inferences with recall data from the actors.

In either situation, current sampling theory and tests of significance are seldom appropriate for interaction generalizations. It would make little sense using a survey of individuals, for example, to present a table with the distribu-tion of actors who recalled the occurrence of various types of events and then to employ significance tests to estimate the incidence of these events. Sampling theory was not designed to estimate the relationship between recollection and reality; that is an empirical psychological question. In fact for some events, such as the public outcomes of interactions, we don't need a random sample of the actors—only one trustworthy informant, or a reliable public document, or good hearing and eyesight. Even to consider sampling theory in this circumstance would be to add unnecessary encumbrances to the research process.

It is difficult to resolve the sampling issue involved in characterizing superunits by the relational and structural properties among their subunits. In the absence of any fixed maxims, scholars must simply be alert to the issue and must seek to provide public and "reasonable" arguments for the decisions they have reached in each individual project. At the same time, they must avoid the temptation to present a confidence estimate dealing with *interactions* when the estimate is based on numbers of *individuals*. The units are not the same.

Contextual analysis also requires two levels of sampling, one at the level of the superunit and the other at the level of constituent subunits. Data from the latter characterize each of the superunits. The use of contextual properties, however, has often led to a "fallacy of the wrong level." Commonly the research analyst will forget that contextual sampling allows him only to move up, to characterize a higher unit by data from a lower level. He cannot use the contextual properties of the higher level to test hypotheses about the lower level without running serious risks. Galtung illustrates this point nicely with crime data.[2] One can certainly note from crime statistics that American neighborhoods inhabited primarily by blacks generally have higher crime rates than neighborhoods inhabited primarily by whites. Thus a theory about neighborhoods and crime rates could make use of contextual data. But from such data one could *not* test a theory about the tendency of individual blacks or whites to commit crimes. The data are at the wrong level; for example, there may be more marginal whites in black neighborhoods, law enforcement may differ, and so forth. To test that theory, we must develop a sample where individual blacks, not collective neighborhoods, constitute the sampling unit. This so-called ecological fallacy has commonly appeared in early historical analyses of voting and census data, but scholars are now at work devising correlational models that will lessen the magnitude of error in making inferences downward from contextual data.[3]

As we have argued earlier, the test of a theory involves mustering up as much reinforcing evidence as one can accumulate. If the scholar can devise ways to formulate and test a theory with data from several levels—individual, locale, state, or nation; or individual, small group, association, confederation; or what have you—much inferential strength is added by the reinforcing evidence. Existing theory is often expanded, modified, or questioned as the scholar moves from one level of analysis to another. Greatest confidence comes when the implications of a theory can be recast and tested at several levels.

Availability of Cases. The second theoretical concern in sampling relates to the selection of a locus or research site where the properties and mechanisms of the test theory are present in the proper proportions. It would be folly to test a theory in a locus where the target behavior rarely occurs. The practical scholar will seek a locus where the properties and mechanisms occur in quite a few instances but are also absent in quite a few instances. Jones illustrates this point in his discussion of sampling plans.[4] If a scholar were interested in studying the relationship between parental permissiveness and student radicalism and he had a limited budget, he would be ill-advised to conduct the study on a campus where only 2% to 4% of its student body were radical. In a probability sample of 100 students, the odds are very slim that more than a handful of student radicals would be drawn. On the other hand, he would not want to conduct the study on a campus that was 85% to 90% radical; he would not turn up a sufficient sample of non-radicals for comparison with radicals. Furthermore, he must keep in mind that the other variable—parental permissiveness—may not be distributed predictably with radicalism. Thus, he must choose a campus or campuses which will generate samples where the *full range* of values on *both* variables is likely to be represented in reasonably large numbers. At times this may suggest that a representative sample is less desirable than a purposive or factorial sample, but this is discussed later in the chapter. It is, in essence, an issue of whether the scholar is seeking generalizability through representativeness, or understanding and new information through precise observation of target cases. Our suggestion is to try to combine both by looking for green pastures—where the phenomenon both is and isn't, in abundance.

Testing Rival Hypotheses. In developing a sampling plan, it is necessary to consider what rival hypotheses can or cannot be tested by virtue of the plan. To extend the previous illustration, let us pose an alternate explanation for student radicalism; instead of resulting primarily from parental permissiveness, student radicalism might be a response to arbitrary coercive actions by university authorities; or another rival hypothesis might relate student radicalism to arbitrary coercive actions by local law enforcement officials. In either case, a sampling plan which included adequate representation on the full range of values for the variables "radicalism" and "parental permissiveness" would still be inadequate if it failed to represent the full range of values on "arbitrary coercive acts" by "university authorities" or "local law enforcement officials." For all practical purposes, the test of plausible rival hypotheses would rule out a sample located only in one time and one place. In our illustration, it would require a campus where these coercive actions had occurred at certain times and had not occurred at other times, with data collected on samples of students during each time period. Or it would require samples from several campuses, some where these coercive actions were present in varying degrees, others where they were absent.

There is a strong tendency for social scientists to add to surveys questions which will permit tests of plausible rival hypotheses. But adding questions as an afterthought may be futile; they cannot salvage a sampling plan that does not produce adequate numbers of cases with properties suitable for the test of an alternate explanation. Here again is a striking illustration of the consequences of inadequate attention to theoretical concerns *before* data are collected.

Time-Ordering. Finally, explanations involve temporal sequence statements; to be a causal agent, a factor must be present sometime prior to the presumed effect. The logic of research designs permitting control over temporal sequence must be reflected in appropriate sampling plans. For example, in McClelland's theory of the developmental process in nations, industrialization and modernization occur as the result of dominant "achievement motives." [5] But it would be folly to study this process if the data on achievement motives were collected for the identical time period as the data on industrialization and modernization; the latter take time to develop; thus the fruits of achievement orientations are best measured with time-lagged data. As a result of this logic, McClelland measures achievement motives *twenty years prior* to the level of industrialization, which is thought to be its product.

For many questions that interest political scientists we cannot generate data on the independent variable at a point in time earlier than data on the dependent variable. Frequently, this is the case with sample surveys. Under these circumstances we are likely to constitute our independent variable from the respondents' (1) standard demographic characteristics, (2) recall of past behavior or attitudes, or (3) more general attitude from which a specific opinion is likely to be derivative. When the first approach is used, we often suffer from deceptive imprecision; as we pointed out in an earlier chapter, it is probably not race (which a person is born with and logically precedes educational performance), but a cluster of other properties the social environment associates with race which may lead to low achievement. When the second approach is used, depending on the subject of recall, a host of problems stemming from respondents' differential needs to stabilize the past with the present may distort and falsify responses. When the third approach is used, we must be able to demonstrate why the general attitude leads to the specific opinion and not vice versa. In each approach, the lesson is clear: careful attention must be devoted to possible sources of error in data, particularly survey data on variables which are thought to precede related variables, but which are gathered at the same point in time as the latter. Some of the error-isolating mechanisms discussed in Chapters 5 and 7 will help the researcher recognize the nature of the problem in any given study.

2 / PROBABILITY

A sample should permit the researcher to make statements about a larger universe by examining only some of its units. Risk is involved in making such statements. If the sample is not very representative of the universe, any statements resulting from it may be misleading. To get some notion of the risk involved in using a sample, we rely on probability theory. If I discovered, for example, that 61% of the voters sampled in 1972 favored the reelection of President Nixon, I would want to know what the odds are that this represented the true proportion of the total electorate that favored Nixon's reelection. Sampling theory cannot tell me what the *true* proportion for the universe is; true values require some knowledge of the measurement process as well. But it can specify a range around that observed value where most of the values from other samples would fall and it can tell me what degree of confidence I can have that my finding is unlikely to fall outside that range. Thus, probability theory specifies the *precision* and *confidence* to be attached to characteristics drawn from a sample.

No other sampling plan except a probability plan can allow the scholar to estimate precision and confidence. To be sure, some astute observers may, over long periods of time, get to know the behavior of their universes very well so they can provide intuitive estimates about sample values. While such guesses may indeed be right on the mark, they are not consistent with the maxim of a science that the process for making inferences from observations be public and replicable by other observers. Probability sampling *does* permit public, replicable estimates of the representativeness of any sample from a universe.

We have not insisted on *equal* probability. We have asked only for a *known* probability. Equal probability comes only when the conditions of *simple* random sampling are met: (1) when all units of the universe are identifiable and can be enumerated, (2) when each individual unit has the same probability of selection as any other unit, and (3) when each combination of units has the same probability of selection as any other combination of units. Seldom in the social sciences, however, do we have large universes easily identifiable and already listed, or universes where the selection of one or a combination of units is done completely independent of the selection of other units or combinations of units. Yet we can still draw probability samples and make adjustments in the odds—so long as the probability for the inclusion of any element can be known. Common probability designs include: *simple* random sampling, *interval* sampling, *stratified* sampling, *cluster* sampling, and a variety of *multistage* sampling plans. *Non*probability designs are generally based on the availability of sampled units and often require that the scholar fill a predetermined "quota" of units with specific characteristics from those available. Still other nonprobability designs are based on the judgment that the mechanisms specified in the theory or the information desired is especially likely to be found in those units sampled. The machinery for statistical inference discussed later in this book is not intended for use with either universe censuses or with nonprobability samples.

3 / SIZE

Foremost in determining how large a sample should be is the degree of precision and confidence required by the test theory. If all units in a universe were identical, we would need only one unit for purposes of generalization.

But the kinds of problems which interest us are those where a range of values describes each variable. Thus, we are likely to use universes which have at least some heterogeneity. The more heterogeneous the universe is on our target variables, the more risky it would be to generalize from one unit. If we sampled more units, we would be able to draw some conclusions about the universe—e.g., a mean, proportion, distribution. But these conclusions are likely to be drawn from different values on a variable; e.g., the mean is an *average* of the observed values in the sampled units. We want to know how *precise* the mean is, i.e., how much variability we might expect in it if we drew additional samples. We also want to know how much *confidence* we can put in that range of variability of means, i.e., we want to know what proportion of our observed means might fall outside the precision range we have specified.

We can readily see that sample size involves a relationship among variability, precision, and confidence. The relationship can be formalized as follows:

$$\sqrt{\text{sample size}} = (\text{variability}) \; (\text{confidence}) \; (1/\text{precision})$$

The point can be clarified with an illustration making use of a simple random sampling plan.

Let us suppose we had a universe of 100 counties within a state. We would like to know what proportion of the Democratic Party's county chairmen derive their principal livelihood from various types of employment. Unknown to us, the actual distribution is as follows:

government employment	50%
self-employment	35%
corporate employment	15%

Let us suppose we draw five different samples consisting of 10 county chairmen each. Table 4.1 presents a hypothetical distribution of the number of people within each employment category who are drawn in each sample.

First, we can note that the universe is very heterogeneous; it has three possible values and one of these is near 50%, as is illustrated by observations of 6, 5, and 4 out of 10. As any proportion approaches 50%, the sample is

TABLE 4.1

Employment of County Chairmen (Hypothetical)

EMPLOYMENT CATEGORY	SAMPLE DISTRIBUTIONS				
	#1	#2	#3	#4	#5
Government	6	5	4	5	6
Self	3	4	4	3	2
Corporate	1	1	2	2	2
Total	10	10	10	10	10

more heterogeneous; its greater variability will require larger sample sizes for the same degree of precision or confidence. The farther it moves from 50%, the smaller the sample needed.

Secondly, repeated samples did not provide identical distributions. To make an estimate of the universe proportion in each category, we must calculate the value for each proportion. This can be taken from the formula: [6]

$$p = \sum_{i=1}^{n} \frac{x_i}{n} \qquad (4.1)$$

where p is the estimate of the proportion, x_i is the number of times the target value occurs in the sample, and n is the sample size. Thus, for government employment in Sample 1 the estimated proportion is $(1 + 1 + 1 + 1 + 1 + 1)/10 = 60\%$. Likewise, for self-employment the estimated proportion is 30%, and for corporate employment it is 10%. None of the combinations of individual samples would have given us the proportions 50%, 35%, and 15%. Instead, the five samples together gave us a range of estimates around the "true value"; some proportions were directly on the mark, some close, some far, some high, some low. And so it goes with sampling. We do not know the true value, but even if we did we would seldom hit it directly.

In this condition of imperfect knowledge, we construct a *confidence interval* out of our observed values from each sample. The first step in calculating the confidence interval is to compute the *standard error* (*SE*) for each proportion. The standard error makes use of the logic of the standard distribution over areas of the normal bell-shaped curve (see Chapter 11), for indeed, values from repeated samples are likely to create such a curve. The appropriate formula is:

$$SE\,(p) = \sqrt{\left(1 - \frac{n}{N}\right)\left(\frac{pq}{n-1}\right)} \qquad (4.2)$$

where n is the sample size, N is the universe size, and n/N is therefore the sampling fraction; p is the observed proportion with the characteristic; and q is $1 - p$. The term $(1 - n/N)$ is necessary as a correction for small finite populations; it can normally be overlooked when the universe is very large. For Sample 1, the standard error for the government employment proportion estimate would be

$$\sqrt{\left(1 - \frac{10}{100}\right)\left(\frac{.60 \cdot .40}{10 - 1}\right)} = 15.5\%$$

for self employment it would be 14.5%; and for corporate employment, 9.5%. Again, different standard errors would be calculated for each sampled set of proportions.

By multiplying the standard error by differing areas under the normal bell-shaped curve, we can set the limits on our confidence interval. If we followed the normal convention of the 95 out of 100 level of confidence, we would multiply each standard error by 1.96. For Sample 1 we would have the following confidence intervals:

government employment	±30.4%
self-employment	±28.4%
corporate employment	±18.6%

The plus and minus notations indicate that we must both add and subtract that value to our observed value to get at the confidence interval. Thus, for government employment the confidence interval would range from 29.6% to 90.4%. This confidence interval figure would tell us that in only 5 out of 100 cases could we have obtained a proportion like 60% by chance. In 95 out of 100 cases we would have drawn samples within proportions of 29.6% and 90.4%. So we are quite confident that the true proportion (forgetting measurement error for the moment) of government employees among the county chairmen is not less than 29% and not greater than 90%. In like manner, we are quite confident that the true proportion of self-employed county chairmen is not less than 1.6% or greater than 58.4%; for corporate employed, it may be 0% but is not likely to be greater than 28.6%. The confidence intervals for each of the proportions in our five samples could be calculated in similar fashion; as it happened, each observation is within the confidence interval specified for other samples, but we should expect that to occur in all but 5 out of 100 samples for each proportion. Thus, the confidence interval constructed around an observed value embodies both the notions of precision and confidence.

By now the reader is probably dismayed by the low level of precision we have achieved with any single one of the five samples. Ranges from 30% to 90%, or practically 0% to nearly 60% surely are not very useful. Especially this is true when one considers that the purpose of most studies is to test the relationship between *two* or more variables; even if correlations between type of employment and some other variable were high, we could hardly attribute much significance to them because of the imprecision of our estimate.

We stated earlier that we want to generalize about the entire sample with a high degree of precision and confidence. Given our illustration and the relationship between sample size, variability, confidence, and precision, we could seek to manipulate these terms. We cannot reduce variability; that is simply the way the data are. We could increase precision by reducing confidence, perhaps to the 67-out-of-100 level, but that would be an illusory gain. The only option open to us is to increase sample size. Let us suppose that, instead of drawing five separate samples of 10 each, and then using only the observations from each sample to generalize about the universe, we had drawn an initial sample of 50 cases. For the sake of comparison with our original samples, we have simply summed the 50 cases; the new distribution, proportions, and standard errors are presented in Table 4.2. By in-

TABLE 4.2

Employment of County Chairmen

EMPLOYMENT CATEGORY	SAMPLE *n*	ESTIMATED PROPORTION	STANDARD ERROR
Government	26	52%	5.0%
Self	16	32	4.7
Corporate	8	16	3.7
Total	50	100%	—

creasing our sample size we now have greatly reduced our confidence intervals. At the same 95-out-of-100 level, we now have a confidence interval for government employees of $52\% \pm (1.96 \cdot 5.0\%)$; thus, we are quite confident that the true value (again forgetting measurement error) is between 42% and 62%. That is far more precise than a range from about 29% to about 90%. In a similar manner, the self-employed county chairmen true value is likely to be between 23% and 41%; for corporate employees, between 9% and 23%. The confidence is still high but the precision is probably now of a sufficient degree to permit significance tests on correlational data involving this variable and others.

We can still see that we would have been better off knowing the true value to begin with, or else conducting a census of the entire 100 county chairmen. In the latter case, as our sample size approached 100% we should have been able to increase the level of precision and/or confidence. For most research problems we do not know the true value beforehand; thus, we have to measure and estimate it either from samples or censuses. The term "estimation" may sound appropriate where samples are involved, but it may sound out of place with a census. It ought not. For whenever we do not know the true value and must measure it, we are subject to various kinds of measurement error.

If we think of the true value as a score uncontaminated by any human errors, we might conceptualize error as coming from two sources: sampling and measurement. In fact, the classic right triangle, where the square of the hypotenuse is equal to the sum of the squares of each leg, describes this relationship. It is seen in Figure 4.1. Ideally, if we want to reduce total error

FIGURE 4.1

Sources of Errors

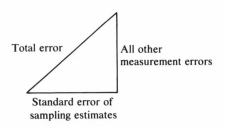

and reach the Nirvana of the "true value," we should seek to reduce error in both legs. If we could control both sampling error and measurement error at the same time, we would indeed reduce total error. Unfortunately, there is often a recalcitrant and almost compensatory relationship between the two legs. We may reduce sampling error but measurement error might increase, or vice versa. For example, I may have a high degree of accuracy in the measurement of variables through my intense depth interviews with 16 people. But I want to generalize my findings to a much larger universe. So I increase precision and confidence by drawing a probability sample of 1,000 people from the universe of 62 million to which I wish to generalize. But it is impossible for me to conduct depth interviews with all 1,000 people; I would not have good controls over extraneous sources of variance such as history or my own fatigue during this long time span. I decide to train other interviewers, each of whom will conduct about 16 depth interviews. While I now have history and fatigue controlled, I have weakened accuracy in measurement because of variable response to my staff members. What I have gained in precision and confidence, I have lost in accuracy. Frustrating? Indeed. The scholar seeks to use every ingenious strategem in his arsenal to reduce both sources of error at the same time. He will never be able to surmount this dilemma fully, but he can at least be aware of the consequences of error-control mechanisms for each source of error, try to effect reasonable trade-offs, and alert his readers to the most plausible sources of error.

There is still another difficulty in reducing sampling error. Few sampling plans can be carried out—even among the probability designs—which involve complete independence among units. According to simple random sampling assumptions, there should be no interaction among units, so that not only each unit, but each combination of units has a known probability of selection. There are two types of problems with the independence assumption. In the one, units once selected are seldom thrown back into the universe so that units drawn later would have the same probability of being chosen *in combination* with the earlier units. This is normally a trivial problem in large universes and is routinely violated in most probability plans addressed to such universes. Thus multistage samples used in voting studies and national public opinion polls usually delete cases, once interviewed, from being reinterviewed during that decade, unless reinterviewing is intended as in a panel design. When the universe is small, however, the scholar can meet probability assumptions only by returning the sample case to the universe for possible reselection. Here, too, the problem occurs only infrequently in political science research because of the tendency to avoid probability claims altogether in small samples. In either case, the formulae for estimating population parameters and standard errors *must* make adjustments for lack of independence. As we will discuss later, a multistage cluster sample, for example, may have two or three times more standard error than will a sample of similar size drawn according to simple random sampling criteria.

Finally, the same *relationship* between sample size, variability, confidence, and precision which obtains for generalizations from the total sample also obtains for generalizations from subclasses of the sample. But the subclasses are smaller; thus a sampling error estimate for the total sample cannot be applied to a table involving only a portion of the sample. New confidence intervals must be developed for this portion of the sample. For example, suppose that a scholar had developed standard errors and tested for the significance of observed differences in education and political participation for an entire sample. Now he would like to control for race, but from his original sample of 2,000 cases only 90 are blacks. He cannot use sampling error estimates from the total sample to apply to correlational data between education and participation in blacks alone. He must develop such estimates based on the 90 cases, not the 2,000 cases. The level of precision and confidence apply only to the sample included in the table under analysis. Failure to observe this maxim is one of the most common sources for misplaced confidence.

If the scholar intends to do subclass analysis, as is typical of social science research, the subclass sizes must be anticipated *before* the sample is drawn. Concern for precision and confidence in the elaboration of data and tests on many different variables may require an increase in sample sizes of certain groups before collecting data. The higher initial cost may be small relative to the cost of being stymied later in the interpretation of relationships. Although there are no official standards of what constitutes a satisfactory sample size for elaborating data into subsamples, Galtung has presented a very useful guideline, which is reproduced in Table 4.3. It depends

TABLE 4.3

*Minimum Number of Units of Analysis for an Average of
Ten Cases Per Cell (Twenty Cases in Parentheses)*

| | | r: NUMBER OF VALUES PER VARIABLE | | |
		2	3	4
n: NUMBER OF VARIABLES PER TABLE	1	20(40)	30(60)	40(80)
	2	40(80)	90(180)	160(320)
	3	80(160)	270(540)	640(1280)
	4	160(320)	810(1620)	2560(5120)

Reproduced from Johan Galtung, *Theory and Methods of Social Research* (New York: Columbia University Press, 1967), p. 60, by permission of the publisher.

on the number of values, r, per variable, and the number of variables, n, per table. It suggests the minimum sample size needed to permit elaborated analysis of data under the specified condition. If for example, we had four values for each of the three variables—political participation, education, and ethnicity—then our minimum sample size (assuming 10 cases per cell) would be 640. If only two variables were anticipated, 160 cases would be adequate—a staggering difference. It is no wonder that scholars who fail to anticipate complex multivariate relationships before data are collected are often frustrated when they analyze their data; frequently their sample *n*'s simply will not sustain the desired level of precision and confidence beyond simple bivariate relationships. Of course, social scientists depend upon outside sources of funding, especially for large surveys, and frequently these sources are too limited to permit the sample sizes required for refined estimates of subclass phenomena. Failure to convince donor agencies of the need for larger samples may inordinately delay progress in the disciplines, assuming that the project is of sufficient importance to justify greater outlays of capital.

Galtung's table is based on the assumption that the scholar knows little beforehand about the variability within his universe on certain variables. If, however, the researcher can anticipate homogeneity on certain variables and has sufficient information beforehand about each unit, sample size might be reduced accordingly. For example, if it is known that 85% of the universe have one value on a variable and the other 15% have another value, the researcher may proportionately undersample the number of units for the former and oversample the latter. Doing so may substantially reduce the total number of cases needed for elaborated analysis. Many varieties of stratified random sampling will permit such efficiencies in sample size.

4 / EFFICIENCY AND RELATED CONCERNS

Most of what we have said to this point has inclined toward *large* sample sizes. However, a strong argument can also be made for reducing sample sizes. The case for *small* sample sizes is based on both sampling theory and practicality. In general, sample sizes should be no larger than sampling theory requires, available financial resources can sustain, and available data collectors can cover in a limited time period.

First, sampling theory does not always require large samples. As we stressed, sample size depends on the level of precision and confidence desired as well as the variability in the universe. When the universe is homogeneous on a variable, there is certainly no reason to insist on many cases. This is doubly true when it is homogeneous across several variables. Since variability plays such an important role in determining sample sizes, the rule is simple: Draw many units when the units are heterogeneous on a variable but fewer units when they are homogeneous. Thus, in *optimum allocation disproportionate stratified random sampling* the same level of precision and confidence will be based on very different sampling fractions for each class. But to be able to follow this rule, the scholar must have all units of the universe classified into the relevant stratum. That requires fairly complete *a priori* information about the universe. Seldom is such information available outside of previous surveys of the same people, employees' dossiers, school children's records, or clients' files, and access to such private information is often restricted. Nevertheless, the scholar should always be alert to the ways in which sampling theory will allow him to *reduce* instead of increase sample size. Great efficiencies can result.

Secondly, economy often dictates a reduction in sample size. All scholars must learn to live within the constraints of their research budgets. Consequently, the project may have to be fielded with a sample size smaller than is optimally desired. Faced with this hard fact of life, the scholar would do well to examine whether he is seeking (1) new information or (2) generalizability from the study. If it is the former, then a sampling plan—perhaps nonprobability—which generates a large enough number of cases for precise *intensive* analysis may be desirable. It may not be possible to test the whole range of plausible rival hypotheses, but at least some of them can be examined and some insights gained. To recall our earlier illustration, if we want to test the relationship between parental permissiveness and student radicalism, a small purposive sample with adequate representation on these two variables would at least represent some contribution to knowledge. On the other hand, if relationships among a wide variety of heterogeneously distributed variables *and generalizability* are to be sought, the scholar must either seek economies in the mode of data generation or he simply cannot undertake the project with a substantially reduced sample size. In this case, either he will have to regard his findings as "suggestive for further study," or he might delay the research project until he can persuade additional foundations or agencies to ante up sufficient funds.

Finally, smaller sample sizes may be preferable to larger samples when the supply of qualified data-gatherers is insufficient to complete collection of data in a short time span. Again, we must keep in mind the relationship between sampling error, measurement error, and total error. If time-related sources of variance—e.g., history, maturation—are likely to alter scores on the variables at different points in time, the data should be collected as swiftly as possible. Given a limited supply of appropriately trained and supervised interviewers, observers, or coders, reducing the sample size may provide greater control over measurement error than is lost in sampling error. The same argument is applicable to instability in measurement resulting from the data collectors themselves. If the workloads of suitable interviewers, observers, or coders is too heavy, fatigue and carelessness may result. Accordingly, the scholar might reduce total error by reducing sample size.

Wise trade-offs between precision, confidence, and generalizability, on the one hand, and efficiency, economy, and dispatch, on the other, require substantial knowledge of sampling theory, a feel for the subject matter, experience in working with the data-collection staff, and a touch of foundationmanship. That is why social scientists who discuss "good" and "bad" sampling plans are quite willing to speak of the *art* of sampling, as well as the *science* of sampling.

Evaluation of Various Sampling Plans

1 / NONPROBABILITY DESIGNS

The distinctive feature of nonprobability sampling designs is that precise estimates about their representativeness cannot be made. The laws of probability do not apply because the selection process in these designs does not yield a known probability for the selection of any single unit or combination of units. These designs rely on either the availability of units or the judgments, however biased they may be, of the investigator or data collector. Nevertheless, not all nonprobability designs are ill-suited to the research purpose; given an early state of knowledge about a topic and the limited availability of funds and trained data collectors, predesigned availability and judgmental samples may be more desirable than probability samples.

Haphazard Sampling. This, the least useful of all designs, allows the investigator to select cases simply by whoever or whatever happens to be around at the site of data collection. If a straw poll on the election is being conducted, selection may depend on whether a person happens to be at the corner of State and Washington at 10 o'clock Friday morning, or in the Super Discount Plaza at 8 o'clock that night. If a content analysis of editorial assessments of the SALT agreements is at issue, selection may depend on the newspaper acquisition policies of the Tidewater Polytechnic University library where I do my research. If "knowledgeable" reaction to the President's economic policy is of concern, selection may depend on which taxicab drivers I have talked to on my three-day funding foray into Washington. While such unrefined approaches to sampling may grace the pages of less reliable newspapers or the student's first undergraduate attempt at a research paper, their limitations are so obvious that we need not spend time discussing them. Even if a straw poll has a good track record for predicting winners, its failure to explain *why* its sampling plan works makes it of limited scientific utility.

Predesigned Availability Sampling. All sampling plans depend to some extent on the availability of the unit. But this plan differs from haphazard sampling in that careful attention is directed to the selection of only certain kinds of units. Once the properties of the unit are specified, then whoever is available who meets those properties is selected. The three principal variants of predesigned availability plans may be called: (1) volunteer samples, (2) natural setting samples, and (3) quota samples.

In *volunteer samples,* the investigator is typically dealing with subject matter which is either sensitive or possibly objectionable to the general public, or it involves considerable inconvenience on their part. Because of the high likelihood that large sectors of a probability sample would refuse to cooperate, the investigator specifies the characteristics of the people to be studied, and solicits volunteers. In the Kinsey studies, for example, findings were based on people who volunteered information about their sexual behavior.

For psychological experiments, many universities will maintain a "subject pool" of volunteers; the investigator then selects from it the volunteers with characteristics appropriate for the experiment. Consumer research firms often conduct initial surveys of nationwide samples, gathering basic demographic and psychological information; then they will ask the respondents about their willingness to volunteer for specific product tests, and lists of volunteers with appropriate characteristics are made available to the firm's clients. Some university-based survey research organizations in similar fashion have established volunteer panels.

Natural setting samples exploit the research opportunities afforded by a captive audience. The investigator specifies types of people who would be suitable for the project and then searches around in public agencies, hospitals, schools and colleges, and industry for access to a large collectivity of such people. For university-based scholars, the most natural captive audience is the large introductory-course classroom.

Findings drawn from both volunteers and captive audiences may provide an inadequate base for generalizability. There is considerable reason to doubt that people who enter the Masters and Johnson clinic have sexual hangups and sexual satisfactions which represent a faithful replica of adult Americans. College students who serve as the basis for so many psychological generalizations are not necessarily representative of the general public, much less their own age cohort; many academicians who thought the McCarthy movement of 1968 represented the ideological voice of youth were astounded to find out that more young people, especially off the campus, preferred Governor Wallace to Senator McCarthy in that election. Whenever such sampling plans are used, the scholar must be extremely cautious not to generalize his findings beyond the limitations of the sample.

On the other hand, such samples are desirable for at least two reasons: (1) they are very practical, and (2) they provide important insights which can lay greater claim to knowledge the more primitive (particularly with mental traits) or universal the phenomenon under investigation. The financial outlay for collecting data on volunteers or captive audiences is minute compared to the cost, for example, of interviewing or conducting a series of experiments on a nationwide probability sample. Furthermore, many investigators are more concerned with documenting precisely the mechanisms involved in a phenomenon—e.g., conflict resolution, cognitive complexity—than they are with generalizing to the incidence and distribution of that phenomenon. Initially for them, predesigned availability samples represent sound scientific stewardship. Since any scientific discovery must stand the test of replication, the soundness of their work will be put to the test when later research is conducted on probability samples or on other predesigned availability samples which differ in theoretically relevant ways.

The third kind of predesigned availability plan—*quota samples*—can, under a very stringent set of circumstances, approximate a probability design. Because many sampling specialists consider that statement a heresy, we need to give special attention to the manner in which quota sampling is typically done and the conditions under which it approximates probability features. Those who use quota sampling usually seek both knowledge and generalizability. They proceed by classifying the population about which they wish to generalize according to several of its characteristics; next, they determine—usually from examination of recent census reports—what proportion of the population possesses each characteristic; then, they set the proportion of the sample which must have that characteristic; finally, each interviewer is given a predetermined quota of types of people to be interviewed. For example, one interviewer may need to fill a quota of 4 blue-collar white Catholic males in the $8,000-$15,000 income bracket, 2 nonemployed white wives of high-income Protestant professional men, 3 black males between the ages of 21 and 45, and so forth. Some research organizations will classify the population on only a few characteristics, some on many, and thus the complexity of the quota varies. Some organizations will require the exact proportion of cases with specified characteristics in the sample as is found in the population; others may undersample or oversample certain classes and then weight these accordingly at the analysis stage. In all instances, however, the sample under analysis is intended to be an exact replica of the population *on the characteristics selected.* And, until recently, in most instances the interviewer was free to choose whatever households he or she wished until the quota was filled.

From a probability standpoint, the weaknesses of the traditional approach to quota sampling are apparent. It is based on two sets of judgments: that of the investigator and that of the interviewer. Unknown and uncontrolled biases may result from these judgments. The investigator, in choosing population characteristics for quota-filling, may have selected characteristics irrelevant to the research problem. For example, union membership might have been a good predictor of candidate preference in 1960 but it may have ceased to be so by 1972, and thus no advantage is derived by having quotas of union members and non-union members in a 1972 election survey. But that is a problem with any design which seeks to control variance by stratification. The more important weakness with this approach to quota sampling is that the ultimate selection of respondents depends on the judgment of the interviewer. An efficient interviewer is likely to pick the most stereotyped neighborhoods or the most easily accessible individuals for the completion of quotas. If the quota calls for a black, the interviewer will avoid partially integrated neighborhoods in favor of a black ghetto; if it calls for a Roman Catholic, the interviewer will seek to fill the quota outside the Catholic parish after mass; if it calls for a blue-collar worker, the interviewer will hang out at an industrial bar until the quota is filled. In each case, there is no reason to believe that the available individuals who filled the quota are representative of the whole class of people who share that characteristic. If all the people who share the characteristic are homogeneous in their other attitudes and behaviors, the problem of biased selection is not severe. If they are heterogeneous, however, great uncontrolled risk is involved in quota sampling. At least with probability designs the magnitude of risk is known.

Nevertheless, quota sampling is the most common design utilized by commercial and some academic survey researchers. Even prestigious organizations such as Gallup and Harris relied on it for many surveys during their formative years. Many smaller organizations still do all their research from this design. Taking advantage of the ignorance of the client, some of these latter organizations have sold this design as though it presented a perfect replica of the population. Deceptive practices are so widespread, particularly in the political campaign–public relations field, that the Ethics Committee of the American Association for Public Opinion Research has prepared a set of guidelines, and many legislative bodies, including the U.S. Congress, have pending regulatory bills under consideration. The attraction of the design, of course, is its great economy and the accuracy of findings *when the selected characteristics serve as stable predictors of attitudes and behavior.*

Some of the reputable commercial firms and academic organizations, however, have recognized the weaknesses of quota sampling and have introduced certain controls which bring it closer to probability designs. Sudman refers to these newer design features as "probability sampling with quotas." [7] This approach to quota sampling requires selection of specific neighborhood sampling points and predesignated households, as in multistage probability designs (discussed later in this chapter). Further, the interviewer who is given a quota of types of people to be interviewed must follow a specific travel plan and conduct interviews at specified hours. If a quota type is not available at the predesignated household, the interviewer can fill the quota at another household so long as the travel plan and interviewing hour requirements are met. Sudman points out that, based on past performance records of similar people, it is possible to calculate a given type of respondent's probability of being available for the interview at a given hour. Together with the probability calculation for the selection of the respondent's neighborhood cluster, this does build in some probability features to the design. To be sure, probability of selection is now based on the *class* of the respondent, rather than on the *individual,* as in most probability designs. Comparing the results of standard multistage probability designs with callbacks and "probability sampling with quotas," Sudman notes that on all but a couple of variables, the distribution of characteristics for individuals selected by the two plans is nearly identical. The cost for this kind of quota sampling is higher, but it is still considerably less than the cost of standard probability designs.

In addition to its economy, perhaps the most attractive feature of this innovation in quota sampling is the reduced discretion of the interviewer. By specifying the neighborhood, household, travel plan, and interviewing hours, the investigator has removed many of the most likely sources of bias from quota sampling. Sudman advises that this modification of quota sampling should not replace standard probability designs because of the class-individual difference; nevertheless, it is a reasonable second-best plan when interviewing must be completed swiftly so that time is controlled, as in NORC's study of popular reaction to the Kennedy assassination. Unfortunately, the reported analyses of this approach utilized quota controls (on which availability probability calculations were made) limited to sex, age, and employment. As other characteristics are used for quota control purposes, it will be interesting to trace their effects on economy and dispatch. If further findings are consistent with early reports, probability sampling with quotas should become increasingly attractive as an alternative to probability designs.

Judgmental (Purposive) Sampling. Judgmental samples are commonly employed to document interactive processes within groups or communities. Where descriptive information is sought, the investigator may rely on knowledgeable informants. Or when sociometric information dealing with friendship or influence patterns within a group is sought, the investigator may begin with individuals who he thinks are most likely to know a good deal about these patterns, and use information supplied by them to select other individuals who are knowledgeable. When a sample of informants grows in this fashion it is sometimes called *snowball* sampling. Usually such a sample will eventually embrace data collection on all people who have been identified as part of the friendship or influence network.

Perhaps the most common type of judgmental sampling is done when the investigator selects a *typical* unit for a *case study*. Likely, the unit will be a superunit and the topic under investigation will involve interactive behaviors among the subunits. The investigator may select the typical unit based on lengthy experience studying such units; his expertise presumably will guide him to the typical case. Or, more likely, he will rely on measures of central tendency among distributions on a variety of relevant indicators to select the typical case. This latter strategy, which is more defensible from the standpoint of a *public* science, is well illustrated in Katz and Lazarsfeld's study of the two-step flow of influence.[8]

Lazarsfeld, in his early studies of voting choice, noted that mass media seemed to have little direct impact on candidate preference. Instead, media influence itself seemed to be mediated orally by opinion leaders in small face-to-face groups. To control for a variety of extraneous sources of variance, Katz and Lazarsfeld argued that a nationwide sample of communications effects on individuals would be ill-suited. They needed the ability to monitor precisely the content of media, and to investigate the mediation process in the small face-to-face groups in which each individual respondent was located. A study confined to a manageable community was thought most desirable. But to be able to generalize the process, once documented, to "communications effects" as a phenomenon generally, the authors sought a "typical" community. Furthermore, they knew a panel design would be required for the documentation of communications effects; available financial resources suggested a sample of no greater than 800 households. So that the sampling ratio would not be too large, they decided to limit their study to a community of approximately 60,000.

By a process not clearly documented, Katz and Lazarsfeld decided that the Middle West suffered from the least sectional peculiarities in the United States and thus they listed all cities in that region that currently had populations of 50,000 to 80,000. From the resulting list of 28 cities, 10 were pared because they were suburban satellites of a central city. The authors gathered a wide variety of data on the social characteristics of the population in the remaining 18 cities—e.g., sex, age, nativity, occupation, standard of living, commercial structure, magazine reading, education, stability, Thorndike "goodness" score, and political participation. An average for each indicator was determined and each community's deviation from the average was calculated. Then, grand averages based on clusters of characteristics were established. Finally, those communities deviating the most from these averages were eliminated. Three were left: Decatur, Illinois; Terre Haute, Indiana; and Springfield, Ohio. The grand average and occupational diversity scores for Decatur were nearest to the typical constellation of properties, so it was chosen. Once the superunit was selected, a probability design was employed to select households.

Judgmental sampling need not be arbitrary. In a public manner the analyst can present all the variables which were thought relevant for selection and then choose the most typical unit. If these variables are thought by the scientific community to be inappropriate, then other studies can be designed using other variables. Replication in an altered setting can help determine whether each of these judgmental designs was well-suited for the task. Of course, when judgmental sampling designs are utilized, it is impossible to estimate the generality of any given finding. On the other hand, the control gained over extraneous sources of variance may, at times, make judgmental samples far more attractive than any financially feasible probability designs.

2 / PROBABILITY DESIGNS

Simple Random Sampling. Our earlier discussion of probability and sample size was based on a simple random sampling illustration: therefore, it is not necessary to repeat here the procedures one follows in estimating the precision and confidence level for this design. In addition to the assumption of the statistical independence of units, the principal prerequisite for drawing a simple random sample is that a unique identifying number can be attached to each unit. Although the analogy is often used that simple random sampling is like listing each unit on a separate slip of paper and then drawing a sample of these slips out of a hat, few analysts will proceed in that fashion. Instead, they will assign a unique identifying number to each unit and consult a table of random numbers until a sufficient number of units is drawn. For example, if the universe consists of 2,000 units and 200 cases are to be drawn, the analyst will begin at any point in the table and draw the first 200 four-digit numbers of 2,000 or less. Use of the table of random numbers should guarantee the equal probability of selection of any unit or combination of units. In simple random sampling, the probability of drawing any given sample can be derived from the formula:

$$Pr = \frac{1}{C_n^N} \tag{4.3}$$

where C_n^N is the possible combinations resulting from a universe of size N and a sample of size n. In our illustration, the probability is

$$\frac{1}{\left(\dfrac{2000 \cdot 1999 \cdot 1998 \cdot \ldots \cdot 1801}{200 \cdot 199 \cdot 198 \cdot \ldots \cdot 1}\right)}$$

It is a simple matter to apply the formulae for means, proportions, and standard errors to determine the level of precision and confidence to be attached to the sample.

Simple random sampling requires very little advance knowledge about the characteristics of the universe, except that each unit is unique. Mechanically, it is one of the easiest to draw of the probability designs and involves the least complicated formulae for confidence and precision estimates. On the other hand, it would be inefficient to use it when information about universe characteristics would permit the analyst to stratify the sample.

Interval (Systematic) Sampling. Social scientists sometimes find it cumbersome and uneconomical to draw a simple random sample with the help of a table of random numbers. Instead they will draw an interval sample. An interval sample, in most cases, has all of the features of a simple random sample and is amenable to the same formulae for estimating precision and confidence.

In interval sampling the analyst must first know the size of his universe. Then he sets the size of sample he wants. The *selection interval, k,* is determined by dividing the universe size, N, by the sample size, n. A *random starting point* of value k or less can be selected from a table of random numbers. Then each sampling unit is drawn by adding the sampling interval to the random starting point or the previous value. To return to our earlier illustration, if the universe consists of 2,000 units and a sample of 200 is desired, $k = 10$. Suppose the random starting point is 6. Then, the analyst selects the units numbered 6, 16, 26, 36, . . . , 1996.

Particularly when large universes and large samples are involved, the procedure is very economical. Furthermore, if the units have been ordered according to some stratifying principle—e.g., beginning with the lowest age on up to the highest age—interval sampling will build in the variance reduction features of stratified sampling. In this case error estimates based on simple random sampling will be higher than in actuality they should be. In most instances there is no reason why interval sampling cannot replace simple random sampling.

Nevertheless, the social scientist must be alert for two similar confounding factors which reduce the utility of interval sampling: *periodicity* and, in time-series data, recurring *linear trends*. Periodicity is a threat when certain characteristics of the units happen recurringly to coincide with the selection interval. Two illustrations can sharpen this problem.

One of the authors once taught at a teachers' college where every student did practice teaching during his or her senior year. One spring afternoon a dismayed practice teacher dropped into the office and described a problem he had had that morning. He was directing a playground game where he expected boys and girls to differ systematically by sex in their abilities. Therefore he wanted each team mixed with equal numbers of boys and girls. He asked the children to line up—boy, girl, boy, girl, etc. Then he asked them to count off— 1, 2, 1, 2, . . .—and directed the 1's to come to one side and the 2's to go to the other. To his perplexity, he found one group contained all boys and the other group contained all girls! By having the numbering process coincide with the ordering process and making it the basis of selection, he had guaranteed periodicity. Not all aspiring elementary teachers suffer from the inability to think abstractly; this one even asked a short time later for a letter of recommendation to enter graduate school in political science!

Sometimes thorough knowledge of the subject matter is required before periodicity is discovered. Mueller and Schuessler describe an early empirical attempt to study social status in the United States.[9] In it, Hatch and Hatch sampled marriage announcements in the June issues of *The New York Times* Sunday edition from 1932 to 1942. Finding that only Protestant marriages were described, they concluded "the upper-upper social class of New York City was preponderantly Protestant." Rival hypotheses immediately suggest themselves: e.g., the *Times* has a religious bias. However, one rival hypothesis—namely, that the finding was a result of periodicity—quickly found substantiation. Cahnman pointed out that "Jewish marriages happen for ceremonial reasons not to be performed in June," and a sampling of *Times* issues at other points in time disclosed a proportionate number of Jewish marriages.

If the investigator is uncertain whether periodicity is a problem and would still like to use interval sampling, he can overcome the threat by using several different random starting points. For example, for units numbered 1 through 500 the starting point may be 6 and the intervals lead to cases 6, 16, 26, etc., but for units numbered 501 to 1,000 the starting point may be 2, leading to cases 502, 512, 522, etc., and so on through the universe. The additional cost of such a procedure is minimal, and it is highly unlikely that the same pattern of periodicity would recur for all or most alternated random starting points.

Stratified Random Sampling. When the values of each unit are known on some theoretically important variable, the most powerful and efficient probability design available would be some version of stratified random sampling. By portioning off the sample into various strata and drawing cases randomly from within each stratum, the analyst can either reduce sampling error or reduce the number of cases needed to attain a given level of precision and confidence. Sampling error, of course, increases with the heterogeneity of the universe. If the universe can somehow be channeled into homogeneous classes or strata, sampling error will be reduced *within* each stratum and increased *between* strata. Since the formulae which generate precision and confidence estimates ignore between-class variance, it is advantageous to reduce within-class variance by stratifying.

This point can be seen by examining Table 4.4, where the educational distribution for the Survey Research Center's 1964 Election Study is presented in selected classes. The table also displays the mean, standard deviation, and variance for (1) the total distribution, (2) the distribution when minimally stratified, and (3) the distribution when stratified into the maximum reasonable number of classes. Comparison of the variance columns under each condition illlustrates how a large initial variance can be reduced *within* classes by stratification (13.30 compared with 0, 3.31, 1.13, and 2.72, etc.). A comparison of means and variances under the stratified conditions indicates that most of the variance is now between classes, and therefore controlled for sampling purposes.

From Table 4.4 one can also see the effects skewed distributions within a class will have. When the grade school and high school classes were further maximally stratified by whether or not that level of school had been completed, the variance for completion went down to 0, as it should when only one interval composes a class, while the variance for not completing that level increased in each case over the minimally stratified case. Inspection of the raw data distribution might have suggested such a finding, because well over half of the cases in each instance are in the interval which has now been made a separate class. Where distributions within a class more closely approximate bimodality, further stratifying the class into two classes will reduce within-class variance. Where the distributions in the original class are highly skewed or normal, probably the gain in reduction of error will not be great enough to move from a minimally stratified sample to a maximally stratified sample.

To determine the overall variance in a stratified sample, we must calculate the separate variances for each stratum and weight each variance according to the proportion of the total population in that stratum. If the data in Table 4.4 had resulted from a proportionate stratified random sample, for example, the variance for the overall mean of the stratified sample could be calculated from the formula:

$$s_{\overline{X}}^2 = \Sigma W_i^2 s_{\overline{X}_i}^2 \tag{4.4}$$

TABLE 4.4

Distribution and Variance Estimates of SRC 1964 Adult U.S. Sample on Formal Education

LEVEL COMPLETED	NUMBER OF PEOPLE	MAXIMUM STRATIFICATION			MINIMUM STRATIFICATION			UNSTRATIFIED ESTIMATES		
		MEAN	STANDARD DEVIATION	VARIANCE (s^2)	MEAN	STANDARD DEVIATION	VARIANCE (s^2)	MEAN	STANDARD DEVIATION	VARIANCE (s^2)
None	9	0	0	0	0	0	0			
Some Grade School 1 — 6 2 — 10 3 — 17 4 — 25 5 — 23 6 — 45 7 — 56		5.24	2.49	4.99	6.68	1.82	3.31			
8 Completed Grade	197	8	0	0						
9 Some High School 10 11	87 * 120 * 104 *	10.05	1.43	2.04	11.25	1.06	1.13	11.15	3.65	13.30
12 Completed High	491 *	12	0	0						
Some College (14)	198	14	0	0						
Completed College or Law School (16)	137	16	0	0	15.77	1.65	2.72			
Advanced Degree (19) (M.A., Ph.D., M.D., etc.)	37	19	0	0						
DK, NA	9									
Total	1571									

* Includes about 20% in each class who also attended trade or vocational school beyond that grade.

Raw data source: Inter-University Consortium for Political Research, SRC 1964 Election Study Codebook, Variable 196.

where $s_{\overline{X}}^2$ equals the variance in the overall mean, W_i is the proportionate weight of each stratum, and $s_{\overline{X}_i}^2$ equals the estimated variance in the mean for each stratum. In our minimally stratified case:

$$s_{\overline{X}}^2 = (.006)^2 \, (0) + (.24)^2 \, (3.31) + (.51)^2 \, (1.13) + (.24)^2 \, (2.72)$$

$$= .64$$

The mean would be calculated from the formula:

$$\overline{X} = \sum_{i=1}^{k} W_i \overline{X}_i \qquad (4.5)$$

when $\overline{X}_i$ are the sample means for each of the k strata. In our illustration, again assuming a proportionate stratified random sample:

$$\overline{X} = (.006) \, (0) + (.24) \, (6.68) + (.51) \, (11.25) + (.24) \, (15.77)$$
$$= 11.12$$

The means for the unstratified sample and the stratified sample, given rounding error, are virtually identical. But the striking difference is in the level of precision and confidence which the variances generated by the two sampling plans sustain. The variance, assuming simple random sampling, would have been 13.30. The variance, assuming proportionate stratified random sampling, is now .64, a remarkable reduction in variance and control over sampling error. For the same sample size, far more precision and confidence are possible with some version of stratified random sampling.[10]

Throughout our illustration we have used *proportionate stratified random sampling*. In this plan the investigator must know beforehand in which stratum each case will fall on the stratification variable, and thereby can determine what proportion of the universe is in each stratum. Then, when he employs the same sampling fraction for random selection within each stratum, he will draw within each stratum a number of cases proportionate to that stratum's representation within the universe. This design has several attractive features: (1) as a stratified sample it is a highly efficient procedure, yielding less variance and permitting smaller sample sizes; (2) since the sample is proportionate to the universe within each stratum, the sample is highly representative; (3) since the sample is proportionate to the universe within each stratum, generalizations can be made about characteristics of the universe without the cumbersome procedure of weighting the values for each stratum and adding the weighted values together to get universe totals; and (4) since estimates of means, variances, and so on for each stratum are easily calculated, the design lends itself well to elaborated analysis of strata and subclasses. Unfortunately, like any stratified sampling procedure, the sample cannot be drawn without advance classification of each unit on the stratifying variable. Furthermore, when the proportion of cases within a stratum is very small, the variance may still be too high to permit elaborated analysis; or, when the stratum is highly homogeneous, it may be inefficient to have the proportionate number of cases drawn for that stratum—fewer cases would generate adequate control over variance. Because of these last two disadvantages with proportionate stratified random sampling, some other variants of this design have been developed.

In *disproportionate stratified random sampling* the investigator will proceed as above, but will employ different sampling fractions within each stratum. Thus, within a small stratum every tenth case may be drawn after the selection of a random starting point, whereas in a large stratum every fiftieth case may be drawn. By drawing the sample disproportionately, it may now be possible to generate sufficient cases for elaborated analysis and to reduce variance in the smaller classes to the level of the larger classes. But to yield correct estimates of characteristics for the entire sample, the investigator must weight each case before adding values together. For example, in the small stratum each case would count 1, whereas in the large stratum each case would now count 5. Weighting factors can range from an annoyance on a computer to an exceedingly difficult obstacle on a counter-sorter. Scholars who use archived data must be especially alert for the weight fields located on these data sets; one of the most common errors we have noted in supervising student research with data sets from the Inter-University Consortium for Political Research or the Roper Center results from the student's failure to apply weighting properly to generate distributions for the total sample.

The most efficient version of stratified sampling is called *optimum allocation disproportionate stratified random sampling*. It proceeds similarly to the disproportionate version, but the sampling fraction for each stratum is determined by the variance within that stratum. If the stratum is homogeneous, it does not matter whether it is a proportionately small or large part of the universe; a small sample in either situation will yield small variance. On the other hand, if the stratum is heterogeneous, a fairly large sample will have to be drawn from a large stratum and a disproportionately larger sample will have to be drawn from a small stratum to yield the same variance as the homogeneous stratum. Thus, the design clearly makes the most efficient use of sampling theory and advance knowledge of the universe. But therein lies its disadvantage as well. The investigator must have very complete information on the relevant stratifying variables before the sample is drawn. Such information is seldom available outside private records. Where such records are accessible and easily machine-manipulable, this design is powerful and economical.

A recurring issue with the two versions of disproportionate stratified sampling concerns which variable to use for stratification purposes in selecting the sample. The answer is obvious: select the variable which seems to explain the largest number of relationships. If education is expected to account for most political cultural values, stratify on education. Unfortunately, advance listings of units on these key variables are often unavailable. Furthermore, it is not uncommon to discover in the course of analysis that some other variable seems to be more important than the one on which the sample was stratified; the control over variance gained by disproportionate selection on the stratification variable may not be very useful in controlling variance on the newly discovered key variable; the distributions on each may be very different. Under these circumstances, perhaps the best strategy is to use the optimum allocation design primarily when a great deal is known about the topic and to rely on less powerful versions of proportionate and disproportionate sampling where theory is less fully developed.

Sometimes a procedure called *post-stratification* is used. In its most common form, the analyst will compare the results of a probability sample with available general characteristics of the universe, e.g., census reports. In those strata where the data collected on the sample turned up proportionately fewer or more cases than are found in the universe, the analyst may weight accordingly. Resulting totals are thought to provide more accurate estimates of universe distributions. For example, if a survey turns up 10 cases of young black males when the universe proportion might have called for 20 cases, the analyst will double the weight for each young black male. There is much confusion about the effects of post-stratification. Despite the contentions of some authors, we do not feel that it reduces the variance *within* any stratum; strictly speaking, that can be done only by stratification and random selection at the time the sample is drawn. Nevertheless, if there is no reason to believe that the 10 completed interviews are unrepresentative of the young black male stratum, then weighting their responses proportionate to their incidence in the universe is likely to improve the accuracy of generalizations from the total sample to the universe. Particularly on surveys, whenever a sizable sector of a stratum cannot be reached or refuses to be interviewed, the analyst must exercise great caution in the decision to post-stratify. It would be best to gather further information on the missing cases to show that the completed portion of the sample is unbiased.

Stratified sampling, because of its greater efficiency, is the most desirable of the probability plans. Wherever advance information about the universe permits it, stratified sampling will yield the greatest return in precision and confidence for research dollar invested by the scholar.

Cluster Sampling. Cluster sampling works in quite the opposite direction of stratified sampling. It yields higher sampling errors for the same sample size, but it may be the only reasonable alternative when little information about the universe is available and funds and staff are in short supply.

Cluster sampling is common when units are geographically dispersed. Units are grouped into clusters, not because they possess a common analytic trait as in stratified sampling, but because they happen to be close together geographically or on a listing sheet. Each cluster is then identified by a unique identifying number and a random sample of clusters is drawn. Each sampled cluster is expected to yield a predetermined number of cases, and these cases are usually drawn randomly from within each sampled cluster. For example, if 600 cases are to be sampled from a universe of 100,000, the universe may first be divided into 200 clusters, each consisting of approximately 500 contiguous cases; then perhaps 50 clusters will be drawn randomly and, within each sampled cluster, 12 cases will be drawn. One can readily see that at the second stage there is no equiprobability of selection for the individual units; units in clusters not drawn have a probability of 0.

Depending on how the clusters have been developed, cluster samples normally will yield higher sampling errors than simple random samples of the same size. Blalock has characterized the relationship as follows:

$$\frac{\sigma_{\bar{X}_C}^2}{\sigma_{\bar{X}_R}^2} = 1 + p_i\,(\bar{N} - 1) \tag{4.6}$$

where $\sigma_{\bar{X}_C}^2$ and $\sigma_{\bar{X}_R}^2$ are the respective variances for means of cluster samples and simple random samples, p_i is the population intraclass correlation, and N is the mean number of cases in each of the clusters.[11] The coefficient of intraclass correlation refers to the homogeneity of each cluster. The more homogeneous each cluster is, the larger the value of p_i; the more heterogeneous each cluster, the smaller p_i. As one can see, the greater the homogeneity and the larger the number of cases in each cluster, the higher the variance of the cluster sample. Thus, the more efficient cluster samples will be those which are more heterogeneous and have fewer cases in each cluster.

Unfortunately, there is a strong tendency for contiguous cases to be similar. This is particularly true where clustering has been done by geography; 12 neighbors are more likely to be homogeneous than are 12 individuals drawn from different neighborhoods. And if only 50 neighborhoods (clusters) are to be drawn, one can see intuitively that the odds of getting an unrepresentative sample are higher than if 600 individuals had been randomly drawn from all 200 neighborhoods. But to create heterogeneous clusters, each having only a small number of cases within it, defeats the principal purpose of cluster sampling—reduction in data-collection cost. Consequently, researchers who utilize cluster sampling must learn to live with higher variances than they might optimally desire. Many of them seek to reduce variance by developing a multistage sample, which introduces other probability features; some options will be discussed in a moment.

Nevertheless, besides cost, a major advantage of cluster sampling is the increased ability to characterize neighborhoods, as the size of each sample from a cluster increases. For many research purposes in the social sciences, the neighborhood is an important unit of analysis; cluster sampling could prove more useful than simple random sampling in these instances. For example, there are times when information about voters in each of several types of precincts would be more useful than information about voters in a specified income stratum, because of the documented tendency for voter choice to be highly affected by forces operating in the neighborhood independent of or in conjunction with socioeconomic status. Thus, cluster sampling should not be dismissed simply because it appears to be inefficient in reducing variance. Again, the purpose of the study must determine the sampling plan.

Multistage Sampling. A wide variety of multistage hybrids of probability designs exist. Perhaps the most common of these is used by large-scale survey research organizations in their nationwide studies. At different stages these designs typically build in features of simple random or interval sampling, various versions of stratified sampling, and cluster sampling.[12]

Initially the country, state, region, or other geographical superunit will be divided into counties. Often these counties are stratified by urban concentration: (1) all of the largest cities and their surrounding area, often coterminous with the U.S. Bureau of Census' Standard Metropolitan Statistical Areas; (2) small cities and towns, usually outside the SMSA's; and (3) the remaining rural counties. At this stage, counties may be sampled proportionately or disproportionately. Next, the sampled counties are divided into census tracts, enumeration districts, blocks, or some other geographical unit, and a specified number of these units are drawn randomly. Then all households within the selected geographical units are listed—by city directories, census output, field inspection, or supplemental sources—and a random sample of households is selected within each of the units. Finally, in those households all people over a specified age are listed, and depending on the composition of the household and the purpose of the study, a respondent is interviewed. A variety of respondent selection charts based on simulations of household composition have been devised, but the one developed by Kish has consistently yielded samples most representative of census data for various geographical units.[13] Nevertheless, if the investigator has reason to believe that household composition in the locale selected for his study differs from national characteristics, he should develop his own simulation, based on available census data for that locale, to guarantee representativeness in the selection of respondents.

As one might surmise, while any given individual has a known probability of selection even in such multistage designs, that probability is far from equal. Furthermore, depending on the nature of the clustering at various stages, the variance for sample estimates is likely to be considerably higher than would be derived from a simple random sample of the same size. Based on extensive experience with SRC's nationwide samples, Kish has suggested that the sampling error figure is usually two or three times larger for multistage area samples.[14] A simple random sample of 2,000 people might have a confidence interval of $\pm 2\%$, but a multistage sample of the same size might actually have a confidence interval of $\pm 4\%$ to $\pm 6\%$. The formulae for making estimates and calculating variance in multistage samples are extremely complex. Usually it requires a trained statistician to make such estimates. Whenever analyzing data supplied by a survey research center directly or through an archive, the investigator must insist on a full documentation of sampling procedures and a table of confidence limits. Without such information, the investigator would be unable to make decisions about the significance of many findings.

While multistage probability designs reduce the cost of data collection and may include features which reduce the high variance level of most cluster sampling plans, they require special skills, both in unit selection and in the analysis of resultant data. Some of the most crass violations of inferential sampling theory are found in political science literature based on multistage designs. Therefore, we advise care in using archived data based on such designs.

3 / MIXED DESIGNS

Since research purposes, sampling theory, and financial concerns all play such an important part in the choice of an appropriate sampling plan, it is not uncommon to find in the literature designs that mix probability and non-probability features. Particularly when structural and relational properties are required for analysis, mixed plans are useful. For example, in Lazarsfeld and Thielens' study of the effects of McCarthyism on academic freedom, instead of selecting college professors according to simple random sampling, they first selected types of campuses and then drew samples of professors sufficiently large to generalize about each campus.[15] Thus a contextual variable —"climate of opinion"—could be formulated from the resultant data. In Leege's study of control in the party convention nominating system, the county delegation was viewed as the principal locus for influence relationships.[16] Consequently, he developed typologies of counties, drew samples of each, and interviewed their county chairmen and other local knowledge-ables. Since delegation sizes ranged from 7 to 338 people, a sliding proportion of $5 + [(N-5)/10]$ delegates from each county was also interviewed. Resultant data permitted the formulation of variables describing decision-making, competition, cohesion, and control structure. These were then corroborated against delegation roll call data for the conventions, and against additional data gathered from interviews addressed to representative and judgmental samples of candidates for statewide nomination, state party officials, and reputed statewide "influentials."

The necessity of mixed sampling plans is illustrated in another design formulated by Leege for a manpower training program evaluation study conducted by Drotning, Lipsky, and others in Buffalo, New York.[17] The Manpower Division of the U.S. Department of Labor suggested that a simple random sample be drawn from all trainees in the JET program, an on-the-job training and adult basic education program aimed at hard-core "unemployables." The project directors, however, argued that while the success or failure of the program might depend on the characteristics and attitudes of the trainees themselves, they suspected that the nature of the work setting— the demands of the job, the attitudes and behaviors of personnel managers, on-line supervisors, union officials and shop stewards, and fellow workers— was far more important. Therefore, a sampling plan which could test both hypotheses and control for several extraneous sources of variance was devised. A sample consisting of one-half all the plants and shops with JET contracts in the Buffalo area was drawn; interviews were conducted with personnel directors and on-line supervisors or their equivalent; 215 employer units were involved. Next, a matched sample of 215 non-JET plants and shops was drawn; they possessed similar characteristics on a battery of manifest indicators (e.g., nature of enterprise, size, product) but they did not have any JET trainees; officials at levels similar to the first sample were interviewed. Third, the universe of local union presidents and appropriate stewards or business agents from plants and shops in the first two samples was interviewed. Fourth, a simple random sample, with a sampling fraction of one-in-five, of all JET trainees was selected and interviewed. Finally, based on a typology of work settings drawn from the first three sets of interviews, contextual samples of co-workers of JET trainees and workers at similar levels in non-JET industries were selected and interviewed. A minimum of three and a maximum of six co-workers were selected for each trainee or similar nontrainee setting. The sample design for this final stage rankled Department of Labor and Bureau of the Budget statisticians because it did not have a probability feature to it. They insisted on a simple random sample of workers in the Buffalo area. To us the odds of getting co-workers of JET trainees with their design were so minimal that it would have defeated the purpose of the study—to generalize about the effects of work contexts on the success of the trainees. Thus, at peril of losing continued financial support, we drew the contextual samples. Again, the samples permitted formulation of a variety of typologies at different levels of analysis.

The overriding factor which determines whether a sample is good or bad is the intellectual concern for which the research is undertaken. While it is essential to know and understand probability theory, it is most important to devise a sample which can generate data suitable for the exploration of a problem and the test of hypotheses. Tests of hypotheses are based on probability considerations, to be sure. But when resources are limited, sometimes more can be learned from a mixed design or a nonprobability plan.

NOTES

1. For relevant discussions see Paul F. Lazarsfeld and Herbert Menzel, "On the Relation between Individual and Collective Properties," in Amitai Etzioni (ed.), *Complex Organizations* (New York: Holt, Rinehart and Winston, Inc., 1961), pp. 422–40; Johan Galtung, *Theory and Methods of Social Research* (New York: Columbia University Press, 1967), pp. 40–48; Heinz Eulau, "The Legislative System and After: On Closing the Micro-Macro Gap," in Oliver Walter (ed.), *Political Scientists at Work* (Belmont, Calif.: Duxbury Press, 1971), pp. 171–92.

2. Galtung, *Theory and Methods*, pp. 45–46.

3. Mattei Dogan and Stein Rokkan, eds., *Quantitative Ecological Analysis in the Social Sciences* (Cambridge, Mass.: The M.I.T. Press, 1969).

4. E. Terrence Jones, *Conducting Political Research* (New York: Harper & Row, 1971), p. 24.

5. David C. McClelland, *The Achieving Society* (Princeton, N.J.: D. Van Nostrand Co., Inc., 1961).

6. We have presented only the formulae relevant for proportions. The reader is advised to consult standard sampling works for other formulae, particularly when we evaluate various probability designs. See Bernard Lazerwitz, "Sampling Theory and Procedures," in Hubert and Ann Blalock (eds.), *Methodology in Social Research* (New York: McGraw-Hill Book Company, 1968), pp. 278–328; Leslie Kish, *Survey Sampling* (New York: John Wiley & Sons, Inc., 1965), especially pp. 1–298; William G. Cochran, *Sampling Techniques* (New York: John Wiley & Sons, Inc., 1953); Morris H. Hansen et al., *Sample Survey Methods and Theory*, 2 volumes (New York: John Wiley & Sons, Inc., 1953); Frederick J. Stephan and Philip J. McCarthy, *Sampling Opinions* (New York: John Wiley & Sons, Inc., 1958).

7. Seymour Sudman, *Reducing the Cost of Surveys* (Chicago: Aldine-Atherton, Inc., 1967). See especially pp. 6–37.

8. Elihu Katz and Paul Lazarsfeld, *Personal Influence* (Glencoe: The Free Press, 1955). See especially Appendix A.

9. John H. Mueller and Karl F. Schuessler, *Statistical Reasoning in Sociology* (Boston: Houghton Mifflin Company, 1961), p. 355.

10. Unfortunately, prior information about the educational attainment of every U.S. adult is not available for sampling purposes. If it were, since educational attainment bears important relations to many political variables, tremendous precision and/or savings could be introduced by stratified random selection. SRC's sample for the 1964 study was, for obvious financial reasons, neither a simple random sample nor stratified by education. We have used their data only for illustration; the variance calculations presented here should not be used for actual calculations with the SRC's multistage sample.

11. Hubert M. Blalock, Jr., *Social Statistics* (New York: McGraw-Hill Book Company, 1960), p. 407.

12. For illustrations see Kish, *Survey Sampling,* or periodic reports on sample designs from the Survey Research Center (Michigan), the National Opinion Research Center (Chicago), the Public Opinion Survey Unit (Missouri), or other national, state, or regional survey organizations.

13. Leslie Kish, "A Procedure for Objective Respondent Selection Within the Household," *Journal of the American Statistical Association,* 44 (September 1949), 380–87. For other examples see Charles H. Backstrom and Gerald D. Hursh, *Survey Research* (Evanston: Northwestern University Press, 1963), pp. 50–58.

14. Leslie Kish, "Confidence Intervals for Clustered Samples," *American Sociological Review,* 22 (April 1957), 154–65.

15. Paul F. Lazarsfeld and Wagner Thielens, Jr., *The Academic Mind* (Glencoe: The Free Press, 1958).

16. David C. Leege, "Control in the Party Convention Nominating System," in James B. Kessler (ed.), *Empirical Studies in Indiana Politics* (Bloomington: Indiana University Press, 1970), pp. 200–26.

17. John E. Drotning, et al., *Interim Report on Jobs, Education, and Training* (Washington, D.C.: Office of Manpower Research, U.S. Department of Labor, October 1969).

Chapter 5

SELECTION AND DEVELOPMENT
OF DATA: MEASUREMENT
AND SCALE CONSTRUCTION

Both this chapter and the next are addressed to a common problem: how to move from the verbal definition of a concept to empirical indicators and composites of these indicators which will faithfully and usefully exemplify the concept. This chapter introduces a number of measurement concerns which can best· be understood in the context of relatively homogeneous items designed to form scales. It draws heavily from psychometric literature. The next chapter raises similar concerns but in the context of less homogeneous properties, indicators of which may be combined in a variety of ways to form indices or constructed typologies. That discussion is rooted more in econometric literature. It is no simple mechanical task to coordinate the operations designed to generate data with those conceptualized properties to which they are addressed. But various procedures designed to estimate reliability and validity and to permit standardized comparisons assist the scholar in dealing with measurement problems.

The Measurement Problem

Concepts are the stuff of the mind, the figments of fertile imaginations. They are meant to order objects or recurring events, selecting and abstracting aspects of events in such a way that men with sufficient curiosity can "get hold" of the events. Men can understand, or explain what happens, by examining posited relationships among concepts. Out of the confusing mass of particulars presented to us by our senses, concepts direct us to what we are to observe. A concept offers us a specific way of looking at phenomena.

Though concepts are sown by fertile minds, they often fall on fallow soil. In order to bear fruit, the concept must refer in fairly precise ways to something that can be observed, *measured*. The imagery about the concept must suggest some indicators by which we can tell whether the conceptualized behavior is present or absent, to what degree, and under what conditions. Furthermore, it must be something more than a private idea; many people must be able to share in the knowledge of the concept, to observe those aspects of events to which it refers, and to agree on what they have observed.

Anyone can conjure up an idea or a concept. One of the authors once knew a delightful inmate of a state hospital who called himself a retired floor man. That label immediately suggested a somewhat older person who had worked either in an industrial warehouse or a large department store and was on call whenever his services were required. But the imagery didn't fit; this inmate was 28 years old and had never held a job other than hawking newspapers. The concept "floor man" qualified by "retired" took on a different meaning, however, after an extended visit with him. He was retired because he was no longer on the outside, because he was in the back ward of the hospital where no one made any demands on him. He was a floor man because he was in the floor; the floor and he were one; people walked on him but that's what floors were for. (The inmate was the sole child of an elderly, unmarried black welfare recipient; he had never been more than a half-mile from his mother's South Side Chicago flat prior to his hospitalization.) In this case the imagery he held about "retired floor man" was quite different from the standard expectation others had; the task of measuring his congruence with the floor—of finding relevant and accurate recurring indicators of this—presents an unusual challenge to the curious observer.

However bizarre the illustration, political discourse is laced with such concepts: even if well-defined, they have empirical indicators that are difficult to measure in such a way that people generally agree they have been properly selected and properly measured. "Fascist regime" or "fascist state" has found its way into current campus parlance. In an earlier usage, the term "fascist regime" referred to a political order where the barons of industry, military, and established wealth tended to collude with an all-powerful leader. The leader was permitted to ignore guarantees of civil rights and liberties and to act swiftly and singularly in the name of an almost mystical "people" or "Volk." In current American usage it seems to refer to a military-industrial capitalist establishment which suspends the rights of free speech and assembly, exploits the poor, relies on coercion to maintain order, and depends on a mindless inarticulate middle class for electoral legitimacy. But what are the indicators of such a concept: the number of drug busts, penalties meted out for alleged courtroom misconduct, the socioeconomic and attitudinal characteristics of "middle-American" voters, the proportion of the national budget spent on defense, the allocation of defense contracts to certain industries and universities, the pronouncements of high public officials? How do we scale constitutional guarantees of civil rights and liberties so that we know when a regime may properly be called fascist? Should all rights and liberties be treated equally or should some be weighted? Will people agree on the use of these indicators?

When is a regime tending toward being democratic and when is it tending toward being fascist? This is both a conceptual and an operational problem. In fact, the problem of conceptual-operational coordination is *the* measurement problem. It is the problem of defining a concept in such a way that it is possible to get public, relevant, and accurate evidence on indicators which are useful for the examination of hypothetical statements employing the concept.

Strategies of Conceptual-Operational Coordination

Scholars have devised several strategies for dealing with problems of conceptual-operational coordination. We will examine these strategies, first as they focus on the relationship between concept and indicator, and second, on the relationships between indicators.

There seem to be two not-mutually-exclusive styles for handling the relationship between concept and indicators in the social sciences. In one, only limited explication of the concept is undertaken; the concept is defined almost completely by the operations which measure it. This may be referred to as the *strict operationalist, definitional operationalist,* or *empirical* strategy. Typically, the scholar using this strategy will begin with a general notion of a concept and move swiftly to select a large pool of indicators which may or may not define it. What the concept becomes is determined by the data collected in response to the indicators. A powerful statistical model such as factor analysis is applied to the indicators, and the numerically reduced factors that emerge are given labels. What distinguishes this strategy is not the use of factor analysis, but the fact that little attention is directed to meaning analysis before or after labeling the factors. The labels are the concepts. This inductive approach to conceptual-operational coordination unfortunately has few built-in correctives to (1) determine whether the sampling of indicators properly represents the range of definitions for the concept, or (2) permit theoretically based predictions to see whether people performing in various ways on the discovered factors are behaving as the theory in which the concept is embedded says they should.

The other approach, which Fiske and Pearson call the *rational* strategy, begins with careful explication of the concept.[1] First, the theoretical literature where the concept is used is examined for the meanings of the concept and for the "syntactical status of the concept's defining phrases." [2] For example, in his explication of the concept of power, Dahl notes that power always involves relational properties.[3] Jackson and Curtis, in their examination of social stratification, contend that the concept of social status implies the rank-ordering of people or aggregates.[4] Secondly, the relationship of the target concept to other concepts is extracted so that it may be possible to validate a measure of the target concept through measures of theoretically related concepts. At this point the scholar sets about formulating an instrument which will presumably provide reliable and valid measures of the target concept and companion concepts, and he uses empirical techniques to refine such measures. For example, in his work with the concept "amateur politician," Hofstetter developed 24 items abstracted from existing literature about the concept.[5] These items were thought to distinguish the perspectives *amateurs* held about party activism from the perspectives of *professionals*. But after an initial analysis of performance on the items by a sample of party regulars and insurgents in Columbus, Ohio, he discarded ten of the items for failure to discriminate between the perspectives of amateurs and professionals. Hofstetter then tested whether scores on his resulting 14-item two-dimensional measure of amateurism corresponded with theoretically based predictions. Such usage of the rational strategy should enhance the possibility of empirically grounded cumulative contributions to theory and it should provide, through the construct validation process, useful evidence about the correspondence between concept and measure.

Fiske and Pearson note two variants of the rational strategy. In one—the *global-rational*—the scholar proceeds as outlined above but assumes that the indicators he uses exhaust all aspects of the target concept. For example, some political scientists will ask the respondent for a self-classification of liberalism-conservatism and assume its validity without getting other indicators of it. Or, they may employ a set of political participation items which are unidimensional by scaling criteria but which do not exhaust the several possible dimensions of that concept, e.g., support dimension, protest dimension.

On the other hand, a scholar using the *separated-rational* strategy will proceed as outlined above but will assume from the outset that his concept, if abstract at all, will likely be multidimensional or *multifaceted*. He will then attempt to break down his concept into several aspects, develop homogeneous measures for each aspect, correlate aspects where possible, develop a total score, and examine the variance on the total score accounted for by each aspect. He may even use different operations to generate data for each aspect. He may, for example, divide political participation into several aspects and use direct observation to measure one, recall-type questions to measure another, and a picture-story-telling technique for still a third aspect.

Cataldo, Johnson, Kellstedt, and Milbrath were dissatisfied with earlier conceptualizations of political participation which omitted a wide range of protest activities commonly engaged in by blacks and city dwellers; they developed a card-sorting instrument based on a subdivision of political participation into two components called "conventional participation" and "protest activities." Supportive (allegiant) items were also included in the instrument, but the authors doubted whether these items would generate reliable performance data on actual participatory *behaviors*. Kellstedt's extensive attempts to develop participation scales through item analyses and factor analyses of performance data have produced three factors for the white sample, labeled "electoral activity," "protest", and "communication." [6] Similar, although not identical factors have emerged for blacks. Most of the variance, especially among blacks, is explained by the electoral activity and protest factors. Rioting was not closely associated with either of these two dimensions. This study witnesses to the utility of the separated-rational strategy: it moves the conceptualization and measurement of political participation beyond the unidimensional scale of the American voter studies and is particularly useful for studies of urban political behavior in the 1960's and 1970's.

The attraction of the separated-rational approach is that it protects against premature cloture on the conceptual domain of a measure, is more sensitive to the need for change in indicator selection as a result of changes in time and space, and is more likely to encourage multiple measurement of the same concept.

This last point leads to the manner in which scholars use indicators. There are perhaps four approaches to the use of indicators for a concept: (1) use of a single indicator, (2) use of multiple indicators of the same kind, (3) use of multiple indicators each based on different operations, and (4) use of multiple indicators—some of the same kind but others based on different operations.

Although political science literature is still replete with reported studies where a *single indicator* is used to exemplify a concept, few methodologists will argue in favor of this approach. Use of a single indicator is unadvisable for at least two reasons: (1) a concept, by its very nature and intent, is usually too abstract to be embodied by a single indicator, and (2) we have yet to reach the stage, and probably never will, where our measures will be so free of systematic and random error that we can confidently rely on single indicators. Regarding the former point, we can return to the illustration in Chapter 1: it is of little *theoretical* moment that Catholics in the United States tend to vote Democratic and Protestants, Republican. What is theoretically interesting is a statement that people of higher social status support the party which advocates conservative (status quo) policies, while people of lower social status support the party which advocates liberal (change-oriented) policies. Single indicators (Catholic, Protestant) would be ill-suited as measures of a theoretically important concept like social status. Or to return to the "social status," illustration, even when a single indicator such as occupation is used to exemplify social status, what makes that indicator useful is the ranking *system* which has been developed through the use of several other indicators—e.g., average income for that occupation, educational requisites, functional significance, and so on. It is not *occupation* that is being measured, but *occupational prestige*.

Regarding the second point—error-free measurement—values on a variable are a combination of the true value and measurement error. If only one indicator is used we have no way of estimating just how much *random* error is confounded with a value. When values on additional related indicators are available, and these values form a composite score, most of the random error confounded with each person's indicator score is likely to be cancelled out. If, for example, we rely solely on a respondent's self-classification on a question designed to measure social class, we have no way of knowing what frame of reference (or what conceptualization of social class) each respondent has. While directing the Public Opinion Survey Unit, Leege noticed an interview schedule where, in response to a self-classification measure with the options of upper-class, middle-class, working-class, and lower-class, a never-married jobless mother of 11 children from the Pruitt-Igoe urban renewal homes in St. Louis stated that she was upper class. When the interviewer probed for her reasons, the respondent stated: "I'm deeply religious and I have no bad habits." Without scores on other indicators of social class to correct for idiosyncratic responses on this question, she might well have been placed in the same stratum as the millionaire corporate official from McDonnell Aircraft who lived in suburban Ladue. To control for measurement error, additional indicators are usually needed.

Single indicators also commonly appear as outside criteria in the criterion-validation process. This too is an undesirable practice for dealing with *systematic* error. For example, a multiple-item test for conservatism may be used; to validate his use of the test the scholar may point out that high scorers were more likely to be members of the John Birch Society than low scorers. In this case, the use of a single outside criterion is suspect; all it may show is that the test is a good measure of propensity toward joining the John Birch Society but that may not be conceptually the same thing as "conservatism." Not only the measure of the concept itself, but also the criterion for validation should be based on multiple indicators.

But that raises the question: Are all multiple indicators of equal utility in guaranteeing the quality of measurement? To answer this question we need to examine each of the three approaches to multiple indicators. Scholars use *multiple indicators of the same kind* particularly in attitude and personality measurement. The subject or respondent is administered a battery of items designed to test for an underlying trait; the response to each item is an indicator, but these indicators are all of the same kind. They utilize the same stimulus—e.g., a statement followed by a request for "agreement" or "disagreement"—to generate a response. Responses to all items are then combined into a scale score. If the test is relatively homogeneous, one might be tempted to conclude that measurement error has been minimized; the subject may have responded to individual items in idiosyncratic ways but his total test score is fairly reliable. Such a conclusion does not take into account the possibility that scores have resulted from the test method itself; since all items were based on measurement operations of the same kind, we again have no external control for distinguishing error that is peculiar to test method from variance in true scores. To control for measurement method effects—even though we used several indicators of the same kind—we need to employ at least one measurement method of another kind. For example, if we argue that "people with a high rate of self-doubting run for political office," we might administer to a sample of candidates and noncandidates a series of tests where multiple items were designed to measure self-confidence, paranoid tendencies, and need-inviolacy. But we might also ask for clinical observations on the sample, or we might design a set of experimental games to measure the same traits. Results of the latter measurement methods would help us to estimate to what extent scores on the initial test were a function of the measurement method employed.

When *multiple indicators each based on different operations* are used, the scholar may be closer to an accurate estimate of the error of measurement. Nevertheless, he should not limit himself to a single indicator for each kind of measurement operation. For example, he may ask the respondent, a governmental employee, for a self-classification on a "cooperativeness index." The scholar may also observe the employee's behavior and rate him on cooperativeness. While the measuring operations appear to be different, the score may contain an error factor based on the employee's perception that the second measure is being taken and his desire to make the ratings consistent (and probably consistently high). Multiple related self-ratings from which a cooperativeness index is drawn plus *repeated* observations (but unknown to the employee) would enhance the likelihood of a true score unconfounded by the common obtrusive effect in the different measurement methods.

This leads us to the conclusion that *sound measurement is more likely to occur when multiple indicators, some of the same kind but others based on different operations, are used.* This is the position of *multiple operationalism.* One of the most articulate spokesmen for this position, the psychologist Campbell, argues:

> [O]ne of the greatest weaknesses in definitional operationism as a description of best scientific practice, was that it allowed no formal way of expressing the scientist's prepotent awareness of the imperfection of his measuring instruments and his prototypic activity of improving them. . . . It is thus on the grounds of self-critical hardheadedness that we face up to our unsatisfactory predicament; we have only *other invalid measures* against which to validate our tests; we have no "criterion" to check them against. A theory of the interaction of two theoretical parameters must be tested by imperfect exemplifications of each, and thus even if predictions are confirmed, the truth of the theory is merely "corroborated" not confirmed or proven. *In any one test, the outcome might have been due to the theoretically irrelevant components of the exemplification of either variable. In this predicament, great inferential strength is added when each theoretical parameter is exemplified in two or more ways, each mode being as independent as possible of the*

other as far as the theoretically irrelevant components are concerned [7] [italics mine].

The strategy we espouse for conceptual-operation coordination, then, is one where the concept is carefully explicated and differentiated to derive its location in a theoretical network of concepts. Measures of the concept in all its aspects are developed, as well as measures of other concepts in the theoretical network; the measures are refined through empirical operations using multiple indicators of the *same* kind and multiple operations of *different* kinds. Then, the entire predictive network surrounding the concept is subjected to empirical examination. Through such procedures, we argue, theory becomes cumulative and measurement error is less of a mystery. The next step is the classification and description of the machinery for handling measurement error.

Sources of Variance in Measures

The value an individual is assigned on a set of indicators is, to varying degrees, a reflection of his true value and a reflection of measurement error. Since repeated measurement of the individual with the same indicators, or measurement with a modified set of indicators for the same concept, is likely to yield different scores for the same individual, we must be alert to the many sources of variance in scores. In using a political participation index, for example, a highly participatory individual may get a modest score because he sat out a recent election to which the index was keyed. Or certain types of people may get low scores on an index which measures conventional forms of participation, but get higher scores on an index which includes items about rent strikes, street demonstrations, school board confrontations, and the like. Whenever variance in scores appears, we must be able to sort out the "true" score from error scores which are the result of: (1) the stimuli used to generate a score, (2) the person doing the measuring, and (3) the measurement occasion.

Following Helmstadter and others, we will group the many erroneous sources of variance in test scores into four classes: (1) *stable* or *systematic error* (questions of validity), (2) *unstable* or *random error* (questions of reliability), (3) *interpretative error* (questions about standardization or appropriate group norms for comparison, and (4) *personal error* (questions about objectivity).[8] Regardless of the mode of data collection—existing public records, responses to interviews and questionnaires, or observers' or raters' judgments—these sources of variance due to error in measurement require consideration; some modes of data collection, of course, minimize certain kinds of error but typically maximize others. Throughout the discussion, one must also keep in mind that error variance refers to the entire *process of making inferences* from operations to concepts and is not a property of the operation itself.

Stable or *systematic errors* occur because measurement is indirect, because we must infer from a set of indicators to a concept. They are the result of inadequate conceptual-operational coordination. The measure (again referring to all aspects of the measurement process) does not measure what we say it does. It may measure only a limited facet of the concept or it may actually measure some other characteristic which is associated with appropriate indicators of the concept. In the former case we would have to ask whether the entire conceptual domain is appropriately represented by the sample of indicators chosen to exemplify the concept. In the latter case we would ask whether some relatively stable characteristic which is associated highly with test performance—e.g., intelligence, information—may be confounded with the score. In his study of political attitudes and beliefs, for example, McClosky noted that high scorers on his conservatism scale were poorly educated and generally uninformed and that there was a tendency for people of lower social class to agree indiscriminately with the statements.[9] Finally, with regard to systematic errors, one might ask whether the operations uniformly lack clarity or are ambiguous to all people in the target group. As the earlier illustration suggests, self-classifications of social class require of the respondent unusual conceptual abilities, and, even among those capable of it, the frame of reference for comparison differs substantially. As a case in point, ask your classmates or colleagues to define what is meant by social class.

Unstable or *random errors* tend to result, not so much from problems with conceptual-operational coordination, but more from idiosyncratic, unpredictable, or accidental responses to the measurement stimuli or situation. Perhaps in interviewing situations, interviewers will stress different words to different respondents. The presence of one respondent's spouse in the room may alter certain responses to attitudinal questions. When coding of documentary data is done, one rater might work longer hours than another rater and, because of fatigue, not be as alert to subtle distinction in the documentary source. Sometimes typographical or recording errors exist in the original document. In their "Case of the Indians and the Teen-Age Widows," Coale and Stephan present a fascinating detective story of an attempt to track down a transposition error in a 1950 census report.[10] Random errors are usually specific errors that result from transient personal factors in the object of measurement, the measurer, or the measurement situation; the resultant error does not vary in a systematic way across all subjects in the sample. Inconsistencies appear which are not the predictable result of conceptual problems.

Interpretative errors typically occur when the scholar is deciding how to analyze his data. They stem from the difficulty of deciding what norm to use for comparison of performances by individuals or groups. In measures of social status, for example, should income be adjusted regionally by cost of living? The student who is offered a research assistantship of $3,200 for 12 hours' work per week at a university in the Boston metropolitan area wants to know how this compares with an assistantship of $3,000 for 14 hours' work per week in a small Midwestern university town. Is an "A" from Professor X in Administrative Theory the same as a "Pass" from Professor Y in Scope and Methods? Matthews and Prothro, for example, sought comparability between Southern whites and blacks on an index of political participation, but the index was based on data from the early 1960's before blacks were allowed to vote in many Southern locales.[11] Should the scores on the index be standardized so that they reflect a percentage of the total number of participatory acts in which one could legally engage? Should a lower score for blacks be considered the *conceptual* equivalent of a higher score for whites? If a scholar is examining internation conflict acts, should he compare raw scores of nations or should he adjust these scores by regional patterns of conflict? For example, the potential for conflict among small contiguous nations in the Middle East may be much greater than that between medium-sized nations in South America. Standardized scores such as percentages or per capita amounts are commonly used in political comparisons, but they depend on selection of appropriate norms.

Personal errors have to do with the perspectives and personal biases of personnel who actually perform the measurement. They are, of course, related to conceptual problems but typically result from conscious or unconscious decisions consistent with a measurement person's own biases but inconsistent with the shared perspective of all other measurement personnel on the project. For example, one rater may tend to emphasize central tendencies, that is, avoid extreme scores, while another rater may emphasize contrasts, that is, avoid placing objects on the middle ranges of a scale. Or a rater, in evaluating several different characteristics of an object, may indiscriminately carry over a rating from one characteristic to all the others. For example, one of the writers found that, in using a semantic differential with the word pairs "fair-unfair," "active-passive," "strong-weak," "moral-immoral," and "safe-dangerous" to evaluate candidates Johnson and Goldwater in 1964, respondents used as raters showed a tendency to carry over the same score on each of the first three pairs but to emphasize contrasts on the last two. Certain coders overuse favorite code categories to classify responses to open-ended questions. What is at stake here is the objectivity of some raters compared with the shared objectivity (intersubjectivity) of the rest.

It should be apparent that even though we have classified sources of error variance into four groups, in the actual measurement situation they are not mutually exclusive. Methodology texts in the past gave this impression; the machinery for estimating and controlling each group of errors was usually highly differentiated. We feel, however, that a procedure for dealing with measurement error should correspond with the customary steps in scale development. Therefore, we are eschewing comprehensive discussions of reliability (as a distinct set of considerations) and validity (as a distinct set of considerations) in favor of a presentation which follows customary research practice. This style of presentation will still permit full discussion of the issues, but at the same time it should help the reader understand how the sources of error are interrelated. Error estimation, like all stages of the research process, involves a hypothesis-testing approach. In essence, the scholar must formulate hypotheses which state that a given finding may be the result of a certain kind of method effect or an unsatisfactory selection of indicators for the concept. He or she then examines all available evidence to see whether these hypotheses are unfortunately sustained, or whether indeed confidence can be placed in his or her manner of explicating, defining, and measuring the concept. What has come to be known as "measurement validation" is part and parcel of the theory-building enterprise.

The Validation of Measures

Selection of Items. We have previously discussed two of the most important stages in the development of measuring scales: concept explication and selection of a strategy for conceptual-operational coordination. In Chapter 2 we suggested that meaning analysis at the level of usage in both theoretical literature and ordinary parlance be undertaken. The various meanings for the concept having been reviewed, the scholar settles on a definition which he feels will be useful, and translates this definition into indicators of empirically observable properties. Then, analysis of performance on these indicators is undertaken to see whether in fact the concept has been usefully exemplified by the indicators. In this chapter, we suggested that for most social science concepts a separated-rational strategy be utilized. Multiple indicators would be combined into a scale; if the concept was addressed only to a single unidimensional property, high homogeneity should be sought for the scale; however, if it was addressed to several related properties, as many abstract social science concepts are, high homogeneity should be sought among indicators for each aspect or dimension, but somewhat lower homogeneity should be sought for the entire multifaceted scale.

The initial stage following concept explication and definition involves selection of appropriate indicators. Since measuring instruments are intended to *discriminate* the degree of presence or absence of the property in the subject, it is usually desirable to select for a scale a battery of indicators that have differing degrees of difficulty. In political attitude research this is called *item difficulty*. Each item involves a different expectation about the proportion of people who will agree or disagree with it. For example, we may expect 80% of the American public to approve of government-supported medical care for the aged and 20% to oppose it. However, only 40% might approve of government-supported medical care for all people regardless of age or income, and 60% might oppose it. The items have differing difficulties—fewer people favor the one than favor the other. Item difficulty, however, is not limited to mental measurement. It can refer to self-reported behavior and rated observations of behavior as well. For example, on a political participation scale, running for office is more "difficult"—i.e., fewer people do it—than is voting for a candidate; typically in the United States, living next door to a family of a different race occurs less frequently than working in the same industrial plant. Thus, multiple indicators of roughly the same phenomenon—political participation, racial integration—are likely to have different performance distributions.

As can be seen from Thorndike's calculations reproduced in Figure 5.1, items which have greater homogeneity—i.e., the extreme items where a higher proportion of people agree or disagree—permit fewer discriminations. Thus, no scale should consist solely of extreme or highly skewed items. Ideally scales should consist of several items spread out between the 90–10 and 10–90 proportions of difficulty, with most anticipated proportions occurring in the middle ranges between 75% and 25%.

FIGURE 5.1

Number of Discriminations as a Function of Item Difficulty

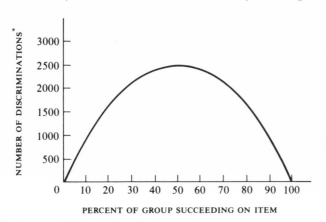

PERCENT OF GROUP SUCCEEDING ON ITEM

* Based on a sample of 100 persons.
Reproduced from Robert L. Thorndike, "The Analysis and Selection of Test Items," in Douglas N. Jackson and Samuel Messick (eds.), *Problems in Human Assessment* (New York: McGraw-Hill Book Company, 1967), p. 202, by permission of the publisher.

Of course, it is never possible to know with certainty beforehand how difficult each item will be. Educated hunches can be made by examining the distributions other scholars have gotten when using similar items in their research, or by conducting a pretest of the measuring instrument on a reasonably large sample (perhaps 50 to 60 cases).

145

Content Validity, Item Analysis, and Item Discrimination. The next stage in scale development is the initial attempt to sort through the battery of indicators utilized in order to see whether a reasonably homogeneous summary scale which seems to measure the same or related properties can be derived. For every concept, one might hypothesize, there is a wide variety of indicators which could exemplify it. Psychologists sometimes call this the *universe of content.* In any given measuring instrument only a sample of these indicators is used. Content validity is concerned with whether or not the sample of indicators used is an adequate representation of the concept, i.e., whether it measures all that the scholar means by the concept.[12] Content validity is especially a problem with complex or multifaceted concepts.

One common way to approach this problem is through *face validation.* The scholar inspects the indicators or items used to see whether they seem to exemplify the concept adequately. Unfortunately, seldom is the reader of his work clear whether this inspection was done according to strict logical criteria or whether it was based on a "feel" for the subject matter or just a hunch. Sometimes critiques of a piece of research are based solely on face grounds.[13]

To be sure, face criteria are important. Many things we measure can be exemplified in very manifest ways. It is reasonable to assume that the relationship between at least some indicators and a concept will, on the surface, be apparent to scholars who study the same phenomena. Certainly in the concept explication process a scholar will have derived insights about the range of indicators to use, and face inspection will suggest whether the full range is covered. Vague, ambiguous, and unclear indicators may be modified as the result of face inspection. Finally, face considerations may be important for public relations purposes; a scholar may lose access to certain groups or he may tax the patience of subjects who cannot find even a remote linkage between indicators and the concept under study.

Face validity, however, is never sufficient grounds for accepting or dismissing a measure. One must always ask for public, empirical evidence about performance on the indicators. Even the practice of using a panel of judges to assess the content of the indicators is not sufficient evidence of content validity. Hunchwork is helpful; logical analysis is vital; other peoples' judgments are reassuring; but empirical analysis is demanded.

Empirical analysis of content is likely to proceed in two stages: at the first stage the concept is broken into its different aspects and a *sampling* of indicators for each aspect is refined; at the second stage a *factorial model* is applied to the indicators for each aspect; what is common across all aspects and what is peculiar to each is abstracted.

Operations performed at the first stage usually involve *interitem analysis.* For each item or indicator which is to go into a total score, a frequency distribution is presented and this distribution serves as the basis for judgments about the suitable combination of indicators. The distribution on each of two items is compared; this can be done either by examining the scatterplot profile of the items or by calculating correlations between the two, preferably by doing both. If the raw values on the items measure the same thing, at the least, their profile should be *monotonic,* i.e., successful performance on a more difficult item should not be accompanied by unsuccessful performance on a less difficult item. But one should look for evidences of skewness and kurtosis. If a number of highly skewed items is observed, probably some of them should be dismissed from the scale; otherwise the scale will not have much ability to discriminate. In like manner, kurtosis—which describes a distribution more peaked than the normal curve—is evidence that the scale as a whole will not discriminate well. (The concepts of skewness and kurtosis are discussed in Chapter 9.) If the empirical distributions, based on item difficulty, follow the pattern predicted by the scholar, he is usually satisfied that these items are likely prospects for a scale.

Usually it is convenient to summarize the bivariate distribution of each pair of indicators through a correlation measure. Depending on the level of measurement involved, a phi coefficient, tetrachoric correlation coefficient, or a product-moment r is calculated (see Chapter 10 for discussions of these).

Often it is advisable to calculate the correlation between each item and some outside criterion which also presumably exemplifies the concept. If items are intended to represent the same concept they should predict well to behavior on an outside criterion, it is reasoned. Those items which survive these operations—that is, correlate highly with each other in a more or less homogeneous linear or monotonic distribution and correlate highly with the criterion variable—usually are taken to the next stage of item analysis; those which fail to survive are often dropped from possible inclusion on the scale or index.

The next stage—*item-test analysis*—resembles item-item analysis but at this point the pairs consist of performance on each item with performance *on the entire test* (i.e., the composite score of all items kept). It begins by plotting on the Y-axis the proportion of persons giving a specified response to each item, against these persons' scores on the entire scale, minus that item, on the X-axis. Again it is likely to be convenient to summarize this process through a correlation measure, and point biserial is commonly used for this purpose.

Another approach to item discrimination through item-test analysis involves analysis of variance. Decisions about keeping or dismissing items may be based on the following formula suggested by Green: [14]

$$\text{Critical Ratio} = \frac{M_{\text{high}} - M_{\text{low}}}{\sqrt{\dfrac{\sigma_{\text{high}}^2 + \sigma_{\text{low}}^2}{n}}} \tag{5.1}$$

where M_{high} refers to the mean score on the particular item of the highest decile or quartile on the entire scale, M_{low} is the mean score on the particular item for the lowest decile or quartile on the entire scale, σ^2 refers to the variance of each, and n refers to the number of respondents in the two groups.

As can be seen from any of the approaches, those items which do not display performance patterns consistent with patterns for the entire scale are likely candidates for dismissal. Again, however, if the concept is complex and multidimensional, one should be cautious about dismissing any items which, while failing to show consistency with the preponderant items which form the homogeneous core of the scale, still show consistency with several other "inconsistent" items. These latter items may well be tapping a different dimension of a multidimensional scale.

Because of the difficulty in deciding beforehand whether a scale for a concept should be multidimensional, many scholars will use a factorial model for the item discrimination and content validation task. Factor analysis (see discussion in Chapter 13) is especially helpful in discovering separate dimensions of a concept and the interrelationships among these dimensions. As Helmstadter notes, factor analysis will:

1. Ascertain the minimum number of traits or factors which will account for all the observed relationships among tests.
2. Determine the extent to which each such factor is measured by each of the tests included in the battery.
3. Develop equations by which it is possible to determine each person's score on the factor when given his score on each of the tests in the battery.[15]

Correlation matrices developed earlier for item-item analysis can easily be fed into a factor analytic model to permit judgments about the selection of items for the scale. However, in the use of factor analysis one must always be cautious to compare performance data with expectations drawn from the concept explication stage; otherwise, no criterion is available to judge whether an adequate number of indicators for each aspect of the concept have been utilized. Factor scores, based only on a portion of the initial battery of indicators, may have subtly redefined the concept.

This, of course, is a problem regardless of the empirical approach to item discrimination and content validation. The scholar must first *judge* whether a sufficient number of indicators for each dimension have been selected. Then when the test has been administered, he must examine the manner in which items discriminate among respondents and must discard certain vague or inconsistent items. Then again he must *judge* whether enough indicators for each dimension remain. If they do not, either the test must be done over again until an "adequate" number is achieved, or it must be made absolutely clear at the reporting stage how the concept has been limited by these operations, and hence, redefined. There is no magical formula to sound scale development. These initial stages rest heavily on judgments—first about what indicators to devise, then about what indicators to keep. Fortunately, the adequacy of those judgments will be submitted to later test: the evidence of whether judgments about item selection and item discrimination have been done well comes with the ultimate test of theory which occurs in construct validation. But before moving to that stage, the scholar is likely to engage in another set of consistency-evaluation operations known as reliability.

Reliability. Over the past two decades the notion of reliability has come to mean many things to many measurers. Such terms as accuracy, stability, homogeneity, equivalence, consistency, or generalizability have been used to describe it.[16] Subtle differences in meaning have led to constant tinkering with the mechanisms for estimating reliability. Since there seems to be a common core in the alternate conceptions of reliability as well as a good deal of redundancy in the various statistical formulations, we will try to deal with the common features but alert the reader to some of the peculiarities of different measures of reliability.

Reliability refers to *consistency*. It is concerned with whether (1) repeated use of the same indicators and (2) use of different indicators for the same concept will provide consistent scores for the individual (group, organization) being measured. As a measure of consistency, it estimates to what extent any index or scale is free of unstable or random errors, that is, errors resulting from varying observers, stimuli, or occasions.

Reliability is concerned with that aspect of "true" measurement that focuses especially on the operations performed. Validity, of course, is more concerned with the conceptual-operational coordination problem. Leaving aside the question of how well a set of indicators exemplifies a concept, reliability looks at the consistency among the selected indicators. It is based on the assumptions that scores for individuals will differ on each indicator and these differences will help to discriminate among individuals across the total set of indicators. But reliability involves an attempt to estimate what proportion of the observed differences is the result of true differences and what proportion is the result of idiosyncratic or unstable errors of measurement.

In formal terms the variance of observed scores (σ_X^2) equals the sum of the variance of true scores (σ_T^2) plus the variance of errors in measurement (σ_E^2):

$$\sigma_X^2 = \sigma_T^2 + \sigma_E^2 \qquad (5.2)$$

The coefficient of reliability ($r_{xx'}$) equals the ratio of the variance in true scores on all indicators used, to the variance in observed scores on all indicators used.

$$r_{xx'} = \frac{\sigma_T^2}{\sigma_X^2} \text{ or } \frac{\sigma_X^2 - \sigma_E^2}{\sigma_X^2} \qquad (5.3)$$

This coefficient provides an estimate of the consistency with which selected indicators measure a concept. It varies on the usual scale from 0 to 1.0, with values approaching 0 when all variance is due to error, and values approaching 1.0 when all variance is due to true differences in the target sample on the characteristic being measured. For example, a coefficient of reliability of .21 on eight indicators for the concept "political participation" would tell us that our selection of indicators did not provide for very consistent responses and that there was a lot of "noise" (error) in our measurement process. On the other hand, a coefficient of .76 would tell us that whatever we have measured (hopefully, political participation—that, of course, is ultimately a question of validity) has been fairly consistently measured by the indicators we have selected. Since reliability estimates are based on the performances of particular samples of subjects, they all have sampling distributions and confidence intervals.

Unfortunately the calculation of reliability coefficients is not as simple as the foregoing formalization might suggest. The reader will have surmised that we do not have "true variance" and "error variance" portioned off for us in the measurement process. Rather we have observed scores from which we can calculate observed variance. From the pattern of responses to the indicators we must *estimate* true and error variances. To be able to estimate each source of variance, we must apply statistical models, and it is here that subtle differences in the meaning and estimation of reliability show their effects.

The item discrimination and content validation operations discussed earlier might be considered the minimal versions of reliability estimates. We have noted that more than one indicator and more than one method of measuring are desirable. We have suggested that scores on all pairs of indicators should be plotted on a scattergram and that their intercorrelations should be calculated. Further, scores on each indicator should be plotted and correlated against scores for the entire set of indicators, minus that indicator. Finally, each indicator should be correlated with an outside criterion which is thought to exemplify the same concept. This last step is done to eliminate items that are homogeneous by interitem and item-test criteria but do not behave similarly to other items when related to outside criteria. Through such item-item and item-test analysis procedures some *initial* refinements of a scale or index may be made. Many authors go no further than this stage in their reliability estimation procedures. The homogeneity estimates which result from such operations, however, do not embrace all that is meant by the notion of reliability.

A useful reliability estimation procedure should allow us to assess the stability of scores on the same indicator through time and, when multiple indicators for a concept are used, allow us to assess the consistency of performance for each individual from one indicator to another. Ideally, the resulting coefficient should not be greatly affected by the number of items in the scale, the number of subjects in the sample, or the degree of difficulty of the items; at the same time, the estimation procedure should protect the analyst from confusing lack of homogeneity with "error" when it is actually caused by multidimensionality; finally, it should have a test of significance which allows the analyst to decide when a specific value of the coefficient will sustain a high level of confidence in the consistency of the scale.

Over the years at least two dozen reliability estimation procedures have been developed by psychometricians. Commonly a new procedure was devised in response to the apparent weaknesses of one or two other procedures. Until recently, no systematic attempt was made to examine the strengths and deficiencies of the most commonly used procedures *on the same data sets*. However, Rutherford and his associates are now reporting the results of Monte Carlo simulations: a variety of true distributions with specific assumptions about number of items, respondents, and so forth are manipulated, and the resulting reliability coefficients from each estimating procedure are calculated.[17] These reports merit continued close attention by all social scientists because of their normative impact on the selection of appropriate measurement models. In a moment we will summarize their most important findings, but first we need to discuss some of the other, more common procedures for reliability estimation.

1. Coefficient of Stability. This is a measure of consistency using the same indicators on the same sample of subjects over time. Assuming that real change has not occurred, a reliable set of indicators should generate the same score for individuals through time; random fluctuations from one testing session to another should not occur. To calculate the coefficient, a simple correlation (e.g., phi, tau, Pearsonian r) between t_1 and t_2 scores is used.

The limited utility of the coefficient of stability is obvious. It should be used only in the measurement of characteristics which, on the basis of other evidence, one can show to be relatively stable. Furthermore, there is abundant evidence of the reactive effects of many measuring instruments; thus the score at t_2 may reflect both a true score and an idiosyncratic reaction to the measuring instrument carried over from t_1. Unfortunately, the model for this coefficient does not contain within itself any controls for instability in the characteristic or the reactive effects of the measurement process. For example, in the participation study cited earlier, the authors wanted to know whether political participation increased as a result of community organizing in poverty areas. Their indicators of political participation were applied to a panel of respondents on two occasions, about a year and a half apart. By manipulating the test variable—that is, selecting separate samples of people in poverty areas and nonpoverty areas—presumably something could have been said about the effects of the test variable. Let us suppose a coefficient of stability had been applied to the participation indicators; a low score for poverty people and a high score for nonpoverty people would have been judged desirable, because one could argue that the experimental factor had measurable effects. Yet, it is conceivable that the measuring process, including the participation indicators, interacted differently with poverty and non-poverty people. It may have generated much random error for the former, little for the latter. To increase confidence about the reliability of the measure, then, additional evidence would have been needed—e.g., if they had applied the participation indicators to other panels in other studies, scores on a coefficient of stability would not have differed by social class. When stability coefficients are employed as tests of reliability, scholars usually use time periods that are relatively short (thus minimizing the likelihood of real changes on the characteristic), but not too short (thus minimizing the respondents' or subjects' specific recall of the earlier test). One is usually safe in assuming that the coefficient of stability is likely to *under*estimate the true test-retest consistency of a measure.

2. Parallel Forms. At one time, psychometricians commonly developed parallel forms of indicators containing two batteries of items for the same concept. Each form would be administered sometime during the same measuring occasion. Then the usual machinery for calculating reliability was employed. This approach is seldom used today. It is similar to the measures of equivalence, to be discussed in a moment, and never did adequately approximate test-retest stability features since the time that elapsed between administration of the two forms was so short.

3. Omnibus Internal Consistency Measures. Although consistency over time is an important consideration, most methods for estimating reliability deal with the extent to which all of the indicators in a composite score exemplify the same concept. Consistency from this standpoint means that the individual should perform the same way on each similar indicator. In short, the indicators or items on a scale all tap the same thing—they are homogeneous.

Interitem and item-test correlations, as discussed earlier, can provide estimates of reliability in this sense. But usually tests of homogeneity are more of an omnibus nature, that is, the entire set of indicators is subject to analysis in the estimate.

One of the most common tests of internal consistency is the *split-half reliability* test from which a *coefficient of equivalence* is generated. In it, the entire set of indicators is applied to the object. Then the battery of indicators is divided into two equivalent halves and the two halves are correlated. The process by which the equivalent halves are selected varies. If one is certain that each indicator should exemplify the concept in precisely the equivalent way, then he may simply assign even-numbered indicators to one half, odd to the other. But if the indicators are intended to tap the concept to varying extents, the scholar will make matching assignments to each half by degree of difficulty, item content, and item discrimination. The calculation of the coefficient of equivalence would follow the same procedure as for stability were it not for a correction needed for test length: the larger the number of equivalent indicators for the concept, the higher the reliability score. Thus, the Spearman-Brown correction formula is used to adjust for the effects of test length.[18] This formula has served as the basis for many other formulae commonly appearing in the literature which are designed to incorporate the same assumptions—e.g., the Guttman adaptation of Spearman-Brown.[19]

Another line of thinking has held that if a composite score is to be derived from truly homogeneous indicators, the procedure of dividing and correlating two equivalent halves is unnecessary. Any *random* sampling of half the items should have the same variance as the remainder of the items. This has led Cronbach to offer *coefficient alpha* as a measure of homogeneity.[20] It, too, commonly appears in the literature dealing with the measurement of political attitudes.

Another line of development in reliability estimation procedures was addressed to composite scale scores which were explicitly *cumulative*. Loevinger states the more stringent assumptions of homogeneity in this approach:

> The definition of perfectly homogeneous and perfectly heterogeneous tests can be restated in terms of probability. In a perfectly homogeneous test, when the items are arranged in the order of increasing difficulty, if any item is known to be passed, the probability is unity of passing any previous items. In a perfectly heterogeneous test, the probability of an individual passing a given item A is the same whether or not he is known already to have passed another item B.[21]

In the *psychometric* tradition, the Kuder-Richardson formula #20 has served as the point of orientation for the cumulative approach.[22] $K-R_{20}$ is probably the most common reliability coefficient appearing in the literature but several adaptations and improvements on it are also utilized—e.g., measures by Hoyt[23] and by Horst.[24] In effect, this estimation procedure requires unidimensionality. It assumes that no factor, save one, should account for test performance across the battery of items; anything else is attributed to errors of measurement.

Guttman used the same logic to develop the *scalogram* model. His procedures for estimating the internal consistency of the test, called *reproducibility,* were thought to be highly attractive.[25] They involved calculating the ratio of "scale type" observations—i.e., following perfect predictability (see Loevinger's definition)—to the total number of observations. Unfortunately it has been repeatedly shown that Guttman's estimation procedures are greatly affected by item difficulty, the number of items, and the homogeneity-producing operations used in the preliminary interitem scale-building analysis (especially through the Edwards procedures[26]). Because the resulting coefficient is so difficult to interpret, few measurement specialists would advise its continued use, despite its continued appearance in political science literature. Several corrections for these deficiencies have been proposed, particularly by Loevinger[27] and Green,[28] and their estimation procedures are far more promising.

Rutherford and his associates have argued convincingly for the Horst correction formula for $K-R_{20}$ and Green's Index of Consistency-B, as the optimal procedures for estimating reliability.[29] In the Horst version of $K-R_{20}$ the estimating procedure corrects for items of different difficulty; and, of course, from the standpoint of discrimination, it is desirable to have several such items. The resulting coefficient provides an adjustment for the maximum variance possible, given item distributions, and usually yields a higher value (and more accurate estimate) than $K-R_{20}$ when item difficulties are dispersed.

Since the scalogram model is more common in political science literature, it is desirable to present Green's Index of Consistency-B in full.

Green's Index of Consistency—B *

All items must be dichotomous. In the mathematical notation we will let k be the number of items, N be the number of respondents, i be a subscript referring to item i (where the items are in any arbitrary order), and g be a subscript referring to item g in rank order.

Step 1. Designate the positive response to each item by referring to the item content. The positive response designations should be consistent with the investigator's hypothesis concerning the dimension being scaled.

Step 2. For each item tabulate n_i, the number of respondents who gave the positive response to the item.

Step 3. Arrange the items in rank order according to their popularities, (n_i/N), with the *least* popular item getting rank k, and the *most* popular item getting rank 1. If there are any ties, adopt an arbitrary order.

Step 4. Tabulate $n_{g+1,\overline{g}}$ for $g = 1, 2, \ldots, k-1$. This is the number of respondents who gave the positive response to item $g+1$ and the negative response to item g. If it is easier to tabulate $n_{g+1,g}$ or $n_{\overline{g+1},g}$, then the following identities can be used:

$$n_{i\overline{j}} = n_i - n_{ij}$$

$$n_{\overline{i}j} = n_{i\overline{j}} + n_j - n_i$$

Step 5. Use . . . the following . . . for estimating the rep [reproducibility].

B. Tabulate $n_{g+2,\overline{g}}$ for $g = 1, 2, \ldots, k-2$. This is the number of respondents who gave the positive response to item $g+2$ *and* the negative response to item g. Estimate the rep from the formula

$$\text{Rep}_B = 1 - \frac{1}{Nk} \sum_{g=1}^{k-1} n_{g+1,\overline{g}} - \frac{1}{N^2k} \sum_{g=2}^{k-2} n_{g+2,\overline{g}}\, n_{g+1,\overline{g-1}}$$

The standard error of . . . Rep_B is approximately given by

$$\hat{\sigma}_{\text{Rep}} \frac{(1-\text{Rep})\,(\text{Rep})}{Nk}$$

Step 6. (*Optional*) Estimate the rep that would be expected by chance if the items had their observed popularities but were mutually independent. The rep of independent items is estimated by the formula

$$\text{Rep}_I = 1 - \frac{1}{N^2k} \sum_{g=1}^{k-1} n_{g+1}n_{\overline{g}} - \frac{1}{N^4k} \sum_{g=2}^{k-2} n_{g+2}n_{g+1}\, n_{\overline{g}}n_{\overline{g-1}}$$

(Note that $n_{\overline{g}} = N - n_g$.)

---

* Reprinted from Bert F. Green, "A Method of Scalogram Analysis Using Summary Statistics," *Psychometrika,* 21 (March 1956), 80–81, by permission of the publisher.

Compute the *Index of Consistency*,

$$I = \frac{\text{Rep} - \text{Rep}_I}{1 - \text{Rep}_I}$$

The index I will be unity if the items are perfectly scalable and has an expected value of zero when the items are independent. If the items show some negative correlation in the sample, I will be negative. If desired, label the set of items "scalable" if I is greater than .50.

Step 7. Give each respondent a scale score that is the number of items to which he gave the positive response.

Rutherford argues that the Goodman z-score is the most useful of the available tests of significance for Green's measure.[30] The Green index comes very close to satisfying all the criteria for estimating the reliability of a scale, as specified earlier. Rutherford also suggests that the analyst may determine whether a low value on the Green index indicates either low reliability or the presence of multidimensionality, by comparing the Green index score with Loevinger's index of homogeneity: " . . . if the Green (index) is below 0.10 and the Loevinger (index) is between 0.10 and 0.40, there is a high likelihood that the scale under question is a low error multi-dimensional set of items."[31]

Although it is still too early to evaluate fully the impact of the work of Rutherford and his associates, available evidence indicates that the two recommended measures should receive closer attention by all social scientists. Unfortunately, they are seldom found as measures of internal consistency in political science literature.

4. Variance Components Approaches. In recent years psychometricians have turned more to variance components models for estimating reliability. To be sure, virtually all of the post-Kuder-Richardson procedures have relied on the logic of analysis of variance. But several of the recent proposals would permit the isolation of different sources of error variance. These are usually incorporated in the many versions of *ANOVA* computer subroutines.

We would suggest the following model as a modification and extension of Cronbach's work.[32] Let us suppose any scale scores are made up of several components of variance. Then let the following general formula isolate the effects of each:

$$X_{poi} = M + (M_p - M) + (M_o - M) + (M_i - M) + \text{residual} \qquad (5.4)$$

where X_{poi} is the observed score for person p as measured by observer o on indicator (or test method) i;

M_p is the mean of all scores for person p with all observers on all indicators, that is, his average score;

M_o is the mean of all scores for all persons on all indicators for observer o;

M_i is the mean of all scores for all persons by all observers on indicator (or test method) i;

and M is the grand mean of all scores for all persons over all observers on all indicators;

then the observed score will be the sum of all these separate components as well as the residual figure which measures interaction among all sources of variance, p, o, i.

For purposes of calculation, standard analysis of variance computational procedures may be used to calculate the variance of each term. We seek to maximize variance of persons (M_p). We seek to minimize error variance, that is, we want low figures on M_o, M_i, and the residual or interaction effects. The coefficient of reliability would be our familiar $\sigma_{Mp}^2 / \sigma_{Xpoi}^2$. Thus, this formalization provides for the estimation of reliability but it also permits us to judge how much unstable or random error can be attributed to each non-person source of error: stimulus, observer, and interaction. If one of these sources of error variance can be controlled—e.g., a single interviewer or rater may conduct all interviews or ratings for the sample in the identical way—then the controlled source of variance may be dropped from the model—e.g., M_o. Or, other terms may be substituted when they become an identifiable source of variance—e.g., t_1, t_2.

Of course full utilization of this model would be an expensive and cumbersome routine, but within the next half-decade we expect computer-assisted offshoots of *ANOVA* to be refined in such a way that use of the model may be more feasible. In isolating different sources of error, the model illustrates the application of the hypothesis-testing paradigm to a finding; in effect, it tests with precision plausible rival hypotheses stemming from method effects.

The Interpretation of Reliability Coefficients. Once the scholar has calculated a coefficient of reliability for his measure, he must ask the question: So what? The answer to this interpretive question leads us into two important concerns: (1) the comparative evaluation of reliability coefficients and (2) the relationship of reliability to our central problem—validity.

It would simplify the political scientist's task if there were a threshold —say .75—which, if satisfied, would serve as *prima facie* evidence of the reliability of a set of items. But there is no such magic in hard-nosed measurement. One reason is that *different models for calculating reliability by their very nature produce coefficients in different ranges.* For example, we should expect a lower coefficient of stability when the test-retest time span is lengthened. Coefficients of stability, for most reported measurements in political science, are lower than coefficients of homogeneity. Interitem coefficients are, by algebraic necessity, lower than item-test and omnibus internal consistency coefficients. Robinson, for example, calls attention to the fact that "Factor loadings . . . of .60 and .70 would generate inter-item correlations on the order of .36 and .49 respectively." Because of the peculiarities of Guttman (cumulative) scaling, the coefficient of reproducibility is almost always so high as to tell little about the internal homogeneity of the measure. Robinson reports an experience where " . . . a scale having an average inter-item correlation of .35 can have more homogeneity than a scale with a Coefficient of Reproducibility of .91." [33]

We know also that many reliability coefficients are affected by both item difficulty and test length; thus as Scott, and Loevinger before him, noted, it is desirable to norm the reliability measure in some way by the maximum and minimum possible coefficient which can be attained.[34] We know, finally, that group homogeneity affects the reliability coefficient. Helmstadter describes this curious artifact of the model used to estimate reliability:

> . . . by definition, reliability, as the ratio of true score variance to observed score variance, is a relative measure. Suppose that the actual amount of error in the test remains the same, but the observed variation in score changes considerably (as might well happen if a scholastic ability test were administered first to a group of high school students and then to a population of college graduates). From the formula
>
> $$r_{xx'} = 1 - \frac{\sigma_e^2}{\sigma_x^2}$$
>
> it is apparent that the decrease in observed variance resulting from the restriction in range of ability would sharply increase the second term of the expression and reduce the reliability by a considerable amount.[35]

For this reason, tables with standard errors of measurement based on repeated use of a measure are developed. These tables should be keyed to the kind of group tested. For example, we should expect the coefficient of reliability on a conservatism test to be higher when administered to a sample of the general public than when administered to a sample of homogeneous political science graduate students.

The lesson is obvious: do not compare different reliability coefficients without knowledge of their separate derivations. While certain internal consistency and stability models will remain popular (and important), the scholar should always seek at least two kinds of evidence about the reliability of a measure: (1) the kinds of data from which interitem correlation matrices could be developed and (2) the kinds of data which will allow for an omnibus measure, hopefully one where analysis of error variance can permit the apportionment of error to each source. Once these kinds of data are available, the reader himself can estimate, by whatever general or specific model of reliability he chooses to employ, the best reliability coefficient. He can then compare *comparable* measures of reliability on competing exemplifications of the same concept. If, for example, measures of alienation have been developed by several scholars, he can decide on the basis of these kinds of evidence which way of measuring alienation is best suited to his intellectual problem.

No discussion of the interpretation of reliability can overlook its impact on validity. To some, high reliability is taken as instant proof of validity.

Rozeboom facetiously calls reliability "the poor man's validity coefficient." [36] Some people will say that an increase in reliability will usually generate an increase in validity. We are not that optimistic. In fact, there may be times when an increase in the reliability coefficient will signal a decrease in validity. After all, indicators may be homogeneous but still not measure what they were intended to measure. At best, we would contend, *the reliability of a measure sets the upper limit of its validity* but it does *not* provide a faithful prediction of how closely a given measure approximates that limit.

Regarding the relationship of the reliability coefficient to the validity coefficient, Cronbach argues: "An inaccurate test cannot be a good predictor. The error portion of the test score will not correlate with any criterion; consequently, the greater the error variance the lower the validity coefficient." [37] With this we have little quarrel. To this statement is often added a corollary: if reliability is low, try to increase it so that validity can increase. While this is generally a good piece of advice, we must, however, be very cautious about operations designed to increase reliability (and hopefully validity).

One way to increase the reliability of a measure is to *clarify the indicators to both the observer and the observed*. For example, if raters or coders are being used, the scholar must make certain that his instructions to them provide for a common, unequivocal frame of reference. If interviewing is being done, he must make certain that the questions are unambiguous and that they deal with something at least minimally salient to the respondent. If public statistical records are being used, the scholar may very well lobby with the data-collecting governmental agency in an effort to upgrade consistency from collector to collector. All these operations are, of course, highly desirable in controlling both for personal error and random error. But in the process, the concept itself may subtly be redefined or narrowed in a manner unnoticed by the scholar; the possibilities of serendipitous findings may be somewhat reduced. In the case of interview or questionnaire data, the process of presenting clear, concise, and pertinent questions may increase reliability by controlling for idiosyncratic response to ambiguity, but it may also decrease validity by systematically increasing falsifiability. Fiske notes that reliability can be increased by letting a subject know what the consequences of his performance on a test will be, and to some degree, letting him know what the test is intended to measure.[38] But Cook and Selltiz warn that the likelihood of falsifiability is highest on those direct test methods where it is clear to the subject just what is being measured.[39] One way out of this dilemma is to utilize more than one measuring method for the same concept; if the direct method with high reliability and an indirect method (with probably lower reliability) generate mutually reinforcing findings, then the scholar can be fairly confident about the initial measure. If not, he then seeks to find out what kind of systematic bias has been introduced by his effort to increase reliability. In any case, this process of clarification is likely to have salutory effects on the scholar's handling of conceptual-operational coordination.

Another way to increase reliability is to *add more indicators of the same kind*. If an attitude scale is being developed, for example, add more items designed to tap the attitude. If judicial votes are being used, examine more of the court's decisions in a specific substantive area. We know according to the Spearman-Brown prophecy formula that the coefficient of homogeneity is likely to increase.

Still another approach to increasing reliability is to *perform internal consistency* or *item discrimination tests* on each indicator. If several high scorers on the total test receive a low score on a single item, whereas most of the target group scores high on that item, then the item is ambiguous or fails to measure the same thing as the other items. Such items or indicators can then be discarded.

These approaches not only increase reliability by expanding the base for inference and maximizing internal consistency, but they also appear to increase validity. The concept itself, however, may be subtly redefined by these operations. This is particularly true if the concept has many facets (as we argued most theoretically important concepts have). If a concept is multi-faceted, an increased reliability coefficient may simply reflect the fact that, in adding indicators of the same kind, one facet has been heavily represented by the new indicators and the resultant homogeneity has overcome the heterogeneity implicit in using all the facets exemplified by the original sampling of indicators. Or, in weeding out items which fail to discriminate well, the resultant homogeneity coefficient may reflect the fact that only one dimension of the concept is now represented whereas originally most of its dimensions were.

This unfortunate relationship between validity and attempts to increase reliability has been called the *attenuation paradox*. Again the solution to the dilemma involves careful explication of the concept and refinement of proposed measures for it. If the concept itself is not very complex and it describes a fairly stable characteristic, homogeneity is a desirable property of a measure. If the characteristic changes greatly under new historical conditions, then a more valid measure may be one with less homogeneity. For example, if a scholar were measuring radicalism among college students, the items that were discarded for failure to discriminate well in, say, 1964 might very well become the homogeneous core of a scale in 1971; what was the extreme left at one point may become the right extreme later; goals may remain stable but appropriate actions, with the cross-cutting attitudinal dimensions underlying them, shift frequently. If the concept is complex, the scholar should most certainly not require a high homogeneity coefficient. Rather he should require high homogeneity on each separate dimension and a more modest level of homogeneity when scores on all the dimensions are thrown together. Though reliability may be more seductive, it must always be the servant, not the master of validity.

Validity. Validity refers to whether or not a given measuring process has really measured the phenomenon for which it was designed. Since concepts are abstractions and since we get at them through indirect means, we must have some way of judging the trustworthiness of our inferences from indicators back to concepts. Have the instruments we devised and our entire strategy for making inferences provided us with relevant evidence?

There are many ways of answering this question. In his study of political attitudes, mentioned earlier, McClosky used a panel of graduate students as an outside criterion of validity; he also used scale-building devices to assess the representativeness of the sample of items employed to exemplify the concept; finally, he promised that as other variables from his study could be analyzed, he would place his measures for the concept into a theoretical network to see how well performance on related measures could be predicted. For Hofstetter, these latter two approaches to validation were central; from the "theory sketch" about amateur politicians and professional politicians, he predicted certain traits and attitudes they would or would not have and then examined the pattern of correlations between these characteristics and activists' expectations about political parties. He added a "known-groups" approach as another piece of evidence about the validity of his measuring instrument and strategy. The fact that each of these scholars performed a variety of operations to assess validity illustrates an important point: although we typically speak of three kinds of validity—*content, criterion,* and *construct*—in practice they are likely to overlap, and operations for one kind of validity will also be employed for another kind.[40] Content validation was discussed earlier; we will now examine the other two validation strategies which culminate the measurement process.

Criterion validation is probably the most common kind of evidence offered in political science literature for the validity of a measure. It is derived by looking at the relationship between performance on the scale or battery of indicators and scores on some outside criterion. Usually a high correlation between the two sets of scores is taken as evidence of the validity of the initial measure. But, as Campbell pointed out, it may only demonstrate the high correlation between two *invalid* measures or, we might add, it may involve us in an operational tautology.

The difficulty in criterion validation lies in the selection of an appropriate criterion. Whether the criterion is a future activity—as in *predictive validity* —or one which is measured at the same time as the initial measure—as in *concurrent validity*—is primarily a practical consideration. For example, while one would like to have predictive evidence about the validity of a measure of vote intention, the secret ballot may force him to settle for some concurrent measure. In fact, voter validation studies are not easy to conduct. Often precinct records indicating which voters turned out are less reliable than recall data from questionnaires. In one study, the findings were never published because of the widespread and unpredictable deviation between the individual voter records and the vote totals in the precinct. Sample mortality is also a major problem. A study designed to measure the effects of school integration on the success of black and white students may develop a measure of predicted success; its validation would come through observation of the same sample of school children perhaps at age 24. But anyone having met the frustrations of urban school research will know that turnover of pupils in a single elementary school may be as high as 100% over a two-year period. It is difficult to keep track of people. Nevertheless, an important piece of evidence about any measure is how well it predicts to a later behavior. How well can a measure of riot propensity predict the likelihood of participation in urban riots? How well can a measure of attraction to demogogic appeals predict candidate preference? One can readily see that answers to these questions involve measures of both the *concept* and the *criterion* in theoretical questions; in short, predictive validity forces us into construct validity if we are to have a modicum of confidence in the criterion employed.

When time-span, instrumentation, or sampling limitations do not permit predictive validation, concurrent evidence is likely to be offered. But here again the selection of the criterion is crucial. One might be tempted to offer evidence for the validity of a conservatism measure by noting that more Republicans than Democrats scored high on the measure. Yet in New York, conservatives may be in the Conservative Party; or Conservatives and Liberals may endorse the Democratic candidate. A Republican in Atlanta may regard his party as being more liberal than the Democratic Party. If party identification is not a satisfactory outside criterion, one might then note that John Birch Society members had higher scores on the conservatism scale than nonmembers of that organization. But maybe active members of the Presbyterian Church or the Kiwanis Club or the Urban League also had higher scores. In short, the score may be associated with "joining," not just with joining the John Birch Society. Because of the criterion problems in concurrent validation, again we are forced into further analysis of a construct validation nature.

There are many kinds of criteria used to validate measures: (1) *known groups,* (2) *judges' ratings,* (3) *known traits,* and (4) *stereotypes and self-classifications.* Ideally, diverse evidence must be provided to show that a confounding source of error has not been present in the criterion. If the *known groups* procedure is used, it must be shown that group membership itself is not correlated with test performance. If *judges' ratings* are used, it must be shown that the judges are not simply reinforcing a bias that is peculiar to the investigator and the judges but not shared widely in the area of investigation. If the *known traits* technique is used, the investigator is already approximating some theoretically based predictions useful in construct validity and it makes sense to move the rest of the way into a careful examination of the theory in which the concept is embedded. Finally, if *stereotypes and self-classification* are used, the investigator will have to show that his earlier administration of the measure did not have a reactive effect on the criterion or vice versa. Thus, the validity coefficient does not of itself provide adequate evidence about validity.

Like many reliability coefficients, the validity coefficient is not difficult to calculate. It is simply the correlation between the test scores and the scores on a criterion. The correlational machinery used depends on the level of measurement for each variable, but commonly the product-moment, the rank-order family, biserial, or others will appear.

The validity coefficient, like the coefficient of reliability, should not be regarded as a *true* value. Rather, it is an *estimate* of the true value. As an estimate, it has a distribution and a standard error. Scores on the initial measure and the criterion, derived from additional samples, will form the distribution and provide data for calculation of the size of the standard error. Such information is especially important when the initial measure is used for screening purposes or for making public policy recommendations. If, for example, test scores are used in the selection of personnel for a governmental agency, the standard error of the test's validity will give some notion of the confidence one may place in individual rankings and will provide guidance on where to set the threshold for "passing" the test.[41]

Because the validity coefficient provides only an estimate, it is extremely important to *cross-validate* the test or measure. Where concurrent evidence has been provided, typically cross-validation involves gathering performance data on the test and the criterion for another sample of the target group. The second and successive coefficients provide a corrective for over- or underestimation in the original coefficient. Cross-validation may involve the use of additional indicators for the criterion in the second and successive samples. When that is done, one can expect the value of the coefficient to fluctuate; nevertheless, the true value is more likely to be approximated when additional indicators of the criterion are employed. But this procedure again moves us away from criterion validation to the concerns of construct validation.

Presumably, in criterion validation we are seeking high correlations between the measure and the criterion. What happens if the correlation coefficient is rather modest? The scholar may conclude any of the following: (1) the original measure (including instrument, occasion, etc.) was not valid; (2) the criterion was not suitable, that is, not valid; or (3) other kinds of errors in measurement have been made somewhere along the line. Reliability data and a careful check of computational procedures may determine whether the third is in fact the case. But unfortunately, criterion validation does not have within it the capability of determining which of the first two is the appropriate judgment. For more of that kind of evidence we must go the rest of the way into construct validation.

Construct validation is central to the process of social inquiry. It involves examining the entire theoretical network in which the concept is embedded. Other approaches to validation deal particularly with the operations or the criterion. But as Rutherford notes, ". . . many scientific concepts have no pure criterion groups or no single pure criterion variables."[42] It is to the theoretical network that construct validation turns.

The notion of construct validity is usually traced to the work of an

American Psychological Association committee and then to an article by Cronbach and Meehl; [43] it has been developed further by them and many others over the past two decades. Helmstadter summarizes it as follows:

> . . . the logical process of construct validation requires: First, setting forth the proposition that this test measures trait A; next inserting this proposition into present theory about trait A; third, working through the theory to predict behavior characteristics which should be related to test scores and those which should show *no* relation to test scores if the test truly measures trait A as presently conceived; and finally securing data which will empirically or experimentally confirm or reject the hypothesis.[44]

Construct validation may differ in its comprehensiveness. For example, it may be applied to a *theory sketch,* that is, an initial imagery or a loose set of expectations about the relationship of the target concept to other low-level concepts. This is all Hofstetter claims about his use of construct validation on the amateur politician. Or, it may be applied to the *nomological network,* that is, the formal theoretical network from which predictions involving the concept and other related concepts are generated. Used in this latter sense, we might validate measures for concepts found in, for example, a theory of political development, and in that very process, be confirming propositions stemming from the theory. Construct validation is less appropriately applied to the process of dimensional analysis for a specific trait or concept; therein lies the difference between it and factorial approaches to content validity. Although such evidence may be useful, construct validation is intended for a higher level of generality.

Regardless of the comprehensiveness of the application, construct validation requires both converging and discriminating evidence about the indicators. Some indicators, according to theoretical prediction, should *converge,* that is, show high positive or negative correlations. We might expect alienated people, for example, to have high scores on indicators designed to measure social estrangement. We would not expect them to have high scores on a test designed to tap something theoretically unrelated to alienation, such as mechanical aptitude. Thus we must also employ indicators which, according to theoretical prediction, *discriminate,* that is, have little or no correlation. Finally, we must use indicators of relatively stable characteristics which may be confounded with our test scores on the target concept and related concept: intelligence, social desirability, acquiescence, and other response sets. In construct validation the theory, the indicators, and the measuring methods are all on trial. According to Cronbach and Meehl, if the theoretical predictions are not substantiated, any of the following options will require investigation:

1. The test does not measure the construct variable.
2. The theoretical network which generated the hypothesis is incorrect.
3. The experimental design failed to test the hypothesis properly.[45]

Since multiple options exist, the scholar using construct validation will seek evidence from several sources as a way of determining which of these is most likely. Some of these sources, many of which were discussed earlier, are as follows: group differences, changes in performance through time, changes in performance through controlled use of different indicators, changes in performance through controlled use of different methods of measurement, or changes related to factors in the test-taking situation—e.g., response sets, social desirability, salience—which may be confounded with scores.

One approach exemplifies more than any of the others what is meant by construct validation. Devised by Campbell and Fiske, it uses correlational analysis in a *multitrait-multimethod matrix*.[46] Since the purpose of construct validation is to validate measures by asking, according to theoretical prediction, which measures should converge and which should discriminate, and since hardheaded measurement admits that a single method of measuring a concept is not likely to be adequate, the multitrait-multimethod matrix is designed to incorporate these principles.

Let us suppose that we have separate measures of three concepts, *a, b,* and *c,* all of which are theoretically closely related to each other, and we are mainly interested in *a;* further we have a measure of another concept, *d,* which is theoretically unrelated to *a;* in addition we have measure *e,* a trait we suspect may be confounded with *a;* finally, we have data from three distinct ways of measuring the concepts or traits—let us say, interview responses, judges' ratings, and responses to experiments in a small group laboratory. Or, if the scholar can work only with the survey method, he might use different questioning techniques: e.g., open-ended, agree-disagree items, rating scales, card sorts. We should have the following expectations: (1) If the various methods or techniques of measuring *a* are all tapping *a* adequately, they should show a high intercorrelation. (2) Regardless of the method used for tapping the concepts, the intercorrelation of scores among *a, b,* and *c* should all be higher than the intercorrelation of *a* with *d* or *a* with *e*. The matrix, then, permits controls to be placed on method effects as well as substantively based predictions; if, for example, the second method of measuring *a* correlated more highly with the second method of measuring *e* than it did with the other methods of measuring *b,* we would suspect that there is a systematic error (a source of invalidity) introduced by using that method. The matrix, of course, can become very complex as the number of concepts employed in the theoretical network increases and the number of measuring methods producing available data on each concept increases.

In part because of the difficulty of interpreting such large correlation matrices, Jackson has devised a factor analytic model which is also consistent with the principles of the multitrait-multimethod matrix;[47] it is, perhaps, too early to assess its full utility. In Chapter 13, on factor analysis, we also discuss a regression model recently devised by Costner for a similar purpose. Regardless of the mechanism—correlational analysis, factor analysis, or regression analysis—one can readily see how reliability and validity come together in this approach to construct validation. The homogeneity and relevance of various exemplifications of the concept are combined in a matrix whose contours are determined by theory and method.

The multitrait-multimethod approach to construct validation is a terribly demanding model of measurement. Campbell and Fiske found that only a very few of the most frequently used personality tests met their expectations. Robinson could produce no attitude scale that did. At this point in our measuring experience, we would be rather pleased by validity coefficients in the .20–.30 range in the matrix. We are only beginning to refine measures for many of the key concepts in political science and it is to be expected that much of the variance is the result of the measuring method. But more careful attention to problems of conceptual-operational coordination and greater cumulative experience with concept explication and instrument refinement should permit a more optimistic projection for the future. In the meantime, of course, evidence of any kind which bears on construct validation should be offered.

Standardization

The hallmark of interpretation is comparison. To be able to compare objects meaningfully, one must have variables and a metric common to the objects. The old saw that "you can't add apples and oranges" means very little, for some genius quickly points out that sweetness or vitamin content or nutritional value are common to both and he will devise a metric for the measurement of each. The metric will provide "sweetness" scores for a sample of apples and for a sample of oranges. If we had sweetness scores only for the apples we wouldn't really know how to interpret their meaning. What does a "6" on a sweetness index mean? We could, of course, compare some kinds of apples with others. Then, we would have a criterion for judging. Or we could go back to the original comparison between apples and oranges. There again we have specified the criterion—the sample of apples and oranges we have used. But if we find apples to be sweeter than oranges, we cannot say from our study that apples are a sweet fruit; we have not constructed our metric with fruit in mind.

So it is in political measurement. We cannot say that a country is warlike unless we specify: (1) the acts which may be taken as warlike, (2) the sample of countries used for deciding whether a country is warlike, and (3) the nature of the metric designed for comparisons on warlikeness. While questions of reliability and validity are implicit, another problem, that of interpretability or standardization is also involved. If the United States gets a score of 84, what does it mean? It may mean that the United States is more warlike than Australia and Guinea, which had lower scores. But maybe China was excluded from the sample and maybe its score would have been 91. But still, what does that mean? Does the scale go from 0 to 100 or does it go from 72 to 145? Is the difference between 84 and 91 equivalent to a difference between 91 and 98? In short, what are the appropriate group norms for comparison? What is the appropriate way to standardize the metric?

These questions are usually answered in one of two ways: scores are criterion-referenced or they are norm-referenced. When a score is *criterion-referenced,* Cronbach explains, ". . . provision is made for translating the test score into a statement about the behavior to be expected of a person with that score." [48] Thus if a person scored 96 verbal, 91 quantitative, and 94 advanced political science on the Graduate Record Exam, a department may predict that the odds are 95 out of 100 that he or she will be able to successfully complete the Ph.D. requirements in a five-year time period. Such predictions are likely to be based on an expectancy table which has incorporated past experience with GRE scores and graduate performance. Or, to use another example, if a person says he is a strong Democrat who is greatly interested in the outcome of a campaign and has a favorable reaction to his party's candidate and always votes in elections, then the odds are high that he will vote for his party's candidate in this election. The score on the metric, then, is interpreted by the associated behaviors we can expect.

When a score is *norm-referenced,* according to Cronbach, ". . . the translated score tells where the person stands in some population of persons who have taken the test." [49] A 760 on the GRE verbal doesn't tell us much unless we know something about the test; but when the 760 is standardized to 97, it tells us that 96% of the people who took the test that day scored below the candidate and 3% scored above him. When we are evaluating election turnout in Western democracies, and we note that 42 million people went to the polls in 1970 in one country while 28 million voted in another, it doesn't tell us much. But if we say 42 out of 63 million eligible people (or 67%) voted in one country while 28 out of 32 million (or 87.5%) voted in the other, then we can say that relative turnout is greater in the latter. We have supplied a norm—the eligible electorate—by which to interpret country scores.

Norms may be calculated in many ways. The most common, of course, is the *percentage distribution.* Observed scores are given a percent value by dividing them into the highest possible score. While appearing to be straightforward, such "standardized" scores can be very deceptive; for example, if observed scores fall in only one portion of the total range, a percentage gives a very insensitive norm. Let us say that there are 100 indicators of a trait in a test, and everybody in the sample scores between 77 and 94. If we want to make comparisons among the people, we may want to impose a norm on the distribution which tells us the average scores and the deviations from the average. This we do, of course, with the *normal distribution.* From it we compute *standard deviations* (See Chapter 9); these will tell us how far from the "average" scores a given person, group, or nation departs, and how likely it is that scores like this observed score will occur due to chance factors in measurement. Many other techniques have been used to produce standardized norms, and these are discussed later in the context of specific statistical models.

As we note in Chapter 6, standardization becomes especially problematic when one wishes to combine multiple indicators of different kinds into an index, but it is also a problem with scale items. Usually it is essential to standardize the scores on each indicator through the same procedure; that is, if normalization is used on one it should be used on all.

The reader of scholarly literature is often faced with judgments about interpretability; the scholar who wants to use in his research a measure devised by another scholar faces these same questions. At a minimum, the following questions about test norms should be answered:

1. Is the author's sample representative of the population he generalizes to and the population I want to generalize to?
2. Is his sample divided into appropriate subgroups for comparison and are norms offered for these subgroups?
3. Are there enough cases within these subgroups to permit trustworthy comparison of group norms?
4. Is the model for standardizing scores appropriate to the target concept and the kinds of indicators employed?

While only some of these questions impinge on reliability and validity, all of them are central to an assessment of the adequacy and utility of a measure. It does us little good to refine consistent and relevant measures if we do not know how to interpret observed findings across a variety of populations. All comprise the measurement task.

NOTES

1. Donald W. Fiske and Pamela H. Pearson, "Theory and Techniques of Personality Measurement," *Annual Review of Psychology*, 21 (1970), 49–86.
2. Richard G. Dumont and William J. Wilson, "Aspects of Concept Formation, Explication, and Theory Construction in Sociology," *American Sociological Review*, 32 (December, 1967), 985–95.
3. Robert A. Dahl, "The Concept of Power," *Behavioral Science*, 2 (July 1957), 201–15.
4. Elton F. Jackson and Richard F. Curtis, "Conceptualization and Measurement in the Study of Social Stratification," in Hubert M. and Ann B. Blalock (eds.), *Methodology in Social Research* (New York: McGraw-Hill Book Company, 1968), pp. 112–49.
5. C. Richard Hofstetter, "The Amateur Politician: A Problem in Construct Validation," *Midwest Journal of Political Science*, 15 (February 1971), 31–56.
6. Lyman A. Kellstedt, "Dimensions of Political Participation" (mimeographed paper presented at MUCIA Conference on Requirements and Consequences of Political Participation for Development Policies, Chicago, 1970).
7. Donald T. Campbell, "Definitional Versus Multiple Operationism," *et al.*, 2 (Summer 1969), 14–17.
8. G. C. Helmstadter, *Principles of Psychological Measurement* (New York:

Appleton-Century-Crofts, 1964), pp. 35ff. See also Claire Selltiz et al., *Research Methods in Social Relations*, rev. ed. (New York: Holt, Rinehart and Winston, Inc., 1961), pp. 149ff; Lee J. Cronbach, *Essentials of Psychological Testing*, 3rd ed. (New York: Harper & Row, 1970), especially pp. 173–79.

9. Herbert McClosky, "Conservatism and Personality," *American Political Science Review*, 52 (March 1958), 27–45.

10. Ansley J. Coale and Frederick F. Stephan, "The Case of the Indians and the Teen-Age Widows," *Journal of the American Statistical Association*, 57 (June 1962), 338–47.

11. Donald R. Matthews and James W. Prothro, *Negroes and the New Southern Politics* (New York: Harcourt, Brace & World, Inc., 1966).

12. For a useful discussion of content validity see Helmstadter, *Principles of Psychological Measurement*, pp. 89–111.

13. See, for example, the exchange of letters between Lentner and McClosky in the *American Political Science Review*, 58 (December 1964), 963–65.

14. Bert Green, "Attitude Measurement," in Gardner Lindzey (ed.), *Handbook of Social Psychology*, Vol. 1 (Reading, Mass.: Addison-Wesley Publishing Co., Inc., 1954).

15. Helmstadter, *Principles of Psychological Measurement*, p. 93, by permission of the publisher. (Copyright © 1964 Meredith Publishing Company.)

16. Every standard research methods textbook, particularly those in psychological measurement, offers extended discussion of the notion of reliability. It is difficult to trace the parentage of ideas presented here; in fact, some may represent mutations. While we do not agree with all perspectives presented by the authors, we have found the following useful: Cronbach, *Essentials of Psychological Testing*, pp. 151–93; Selltiz et al., *Research Methods*, pp. 166–86; Helmstadter, *Principles of Psychological Measurement*, pp. 58–86; William W. Rozeboom, *Foundations of the Theory of Prediction* (Homewood, Ill.: Dorsey Press, 1966), pp. 375–426; Julian C. Stanley, "Reliability," in Robert L. Thorndike (ed.), *Educational Measurement*, 2nd ed. (Washington, D.C.: American Council on Education, 1971), pp. 356–442; and various articles cited later in our discussion.

17. Brent M. Rutherford, "Dilemmas in Construct Validation: An Integration of Measurement Criteria in Political Science" (paper delivered at Annual Meeting of the Midwest Political Science Association, Chicago, 1970); Brent M. Rutherford, "True Variance Estimation: Comparing Scalogram and Psychometric Models by Monte Carlo Simulation of Respondent Behavior" (paper presented at Annual Meeting of the American Political Science Association, Chicago, 1972); Brent M. Rutherford, Donald G. Morrison, and Donald T. Campbell, *Measurement Models for the Social Sciences* (Chicago: Aldine-Atherton, forthcoming); Brent M. Rutherford and Donald T. Campbell, "Sensitivity and Bias of Scalogram Indices and Tests of Significance," mimeographed (Eugene, Oregon, 1970).

18. Charles Spearman, "Coefficient of Correlation Calculated from Faulty Data," *British Journal of Psychology*, 3 (1910), 271–95.

19. Louis Guttman, "A Basis for Analysing Test-Retest Stability," *Psychometrika*, 10 (1945), 255–82.

20. Lee J. Cronbach, "Coefficient Alpha and the Internal Structure of Tests," *Psychometrika*, 16 (1951), 297–334.

21. Jane Loevinger, "A Systematic Approach to the Construction and Evaluation of Tests of Ability," *Psychological Monographs*, 61 (1947), 29.

22. G.F. Kuder and M.W. Richardson, "The Theory of Estimation of Test Reliability," *Psychometrika*, 2 (1937), 151–60.

23. C. Hoyt, "Test Reliability Estimated by Analysis of Variance," *Psychometrika*, 6 (1941), 153–60.

24. Paul Horst, "Correcting for Kuder-Richardson Reliability for Dispersion of Item Difficulties," *Psychological Bulletin*, 50 (1953), 371–74.

25. See especially chapters by Louis Guttman in Samuel Stouffer et al., *The American Soldier: Measurement and Prediction*, Vol. 4 (Princeton, N.J.: Princeton University Press, 1950).

26. Allen Edwards, *Techniques of Attitude Scale Construction* (New York: Appleton-Century-Crofts, 1957).

27. Loevinger, "A Systematic Approach."

28. Bert F. Green, "A Method of Scalogram Analysis Using Summary Statistics," *Psychometrika*, 21 (March 1956), 79–88.

29. Rutherford and Campbell, "Sensitivity and Bias."

30. Leo A. Goodman, "Simple Statistical Methods for Scalogram Analysis," *Psychometrika*, 24 (March 1959), 29–43.

31. Rutherford and Campbell, "Sensitivity and Bias," p. 28.

32. Cronbach, *Essentials of Psychological Testing*, especially pp. 158–60.

33. John P. Robinson, "Reliability and Validity of Attitude Measures in Sample Surveys," mimeographed (Institute for Social Research, Ann Arbor, 1969).

34. William A. Scott, "Measures of Test Homogeneity," *Educational and Psychological Measurement*, 20 (1960), 751–57.

35. Helmstadter, *Principles of Psychological Measurement*, p. 76.

36. Rozeboom, *Foundations of the Theory of Prediction*, p. 375.

37. Cronbach, *Essentials of Psychological Testing*, p. 171.

38. Donald W. Fiske, "Some Hypotheses Concerning Test Adequacy," *Educational and Psychological Measurement*, 26 (Spring 1966), 69–88.

39. Stuart W. Cook and Claire Selltiz, "A Multiple-Indicator Approach to Attitude Measurement," *Psychological Bulletin*, 62 (1964), 36–55.

40. Our discussion of validity can again be traced to the standard textbook and journal sources cited earlier. In addition to articles which will be cited later, the following have been especially useful: "Technical Recommendations for Psychological Tests and Diagnostic Techniques," Supplement to *Psychological Bulletin*, 51, No. 2, Part 2 (March 1954); Donald T. Campbell, "Recommendations for APA Test Standards Regarding Construct, Trait, or Discriminant Validity," *American Psychologist*, 15 (1960), 546–53, which we have employed heavily in our discussion of construct validity; *Standards for Educational and Psychological Tests and Manuals* (Washington, D.C.: American Psychological Association, 1966); and Rutherford, "Dilemmas in Construct Validation."

41. For a discussion of the use of validity coefficients for screening purposes, see Lee J. Cronbach and Goldine Gleser, *Psychological Tests and Personnel Decisions*, 2nd ed. (Urbana: University of Illinois Press, 1965).

42. Rutherford, "Dilemmas in Construct Validation," p. 20.

43. Lee J. Cronbach and Paul E. Meehl, "Construct Validity in Psychological Tests," *Psychological Bulletin*, 52 (1955), 281–302.

44. Helmstadter, *Principles of Psychological Measurement*, p. 135.

45. Cronbach and Meehl, "Construct Validity in Psychological Tests," p. 295.

46. Donald T. Campbell and Donald W. Fiske, "Convergent and Discriminant Validation by the Multitrait-Multimethod Matrix," *Psychological Bulletin*, 56 (1959), 81–104.

47. Douglas N. Jackson, "Multimethod Factor Analysis in the Evaluation of Convergent and Discriminant Validity," *Psychological Bulletin*, 72 (1969), 30–49.

48. Cronbach, *Essentials of Psychological Testing*, p. 84.

49. *Ibid.*

Chapter 6

SELECTION AND DEVELOPMENT OF DATA: DEFINITIONS AND INDEX CONSTRUCTION

At the heart of social science inquiry is the correspondence between concept and measurement. Correspondence emerges out of a delicate interplay between verbal manipulation and measurement adjustment. In this chapter we will be concerned with verbal manipulations that result in formal constructs and with measurement only as it directly relates to such constructs. Formal constructs will include definitions, indexes, and measures. Of special concern are formal constructs displaying algebraic properties, their clarification and utility, and their sensitivity to data transformations.

Simple Definitions

In any language, conventional meanings are assumed to be known and it would be highly inconvenient to define the most primitive words in the natural language. It seems reasonable to assume, for example, that the phrase, "the number of people in the world," is understood, and that we would not need to specify the meaning of "number," "people," or "world." In fact it will probably be more convenient to shorten the phrase through a definition:

World Population = the number of people in the world

World population is *defined* as the number of people in the world. To *measure* world population, one must count the number of people in the world. In the cardinal number system this means that the counting begins at zero and that a "one" is added each time a different person is observed, until such time that all persons have been observed. Important to note in the above equation is that no new measure has been created, only a "new" concept that shortens the expression.

Suppose that we are interested in the number of people in the world who are taking coursework from an educational institution. We would probably need to come to an agreement over what qualified as an educational institution, but given resolution of that difference, we might agree upon the following definition:

$$\text{World Student Population} = \text{the number of people in the world who are taking coursework from an educational institution}$$

Further evaluation might lead to a distinction between full-time and part-time student populations. Any such qualification would be inserted in both sides of the equation. Here again, counting the number of people taking coursework will measure whatever is suggested by either side of the equation. It is from simple definitions of this sort that more complex constructs are developed.

Defining through Compared Quantities

The most common definition of this nature appears in the form of a proportion. Pursuing the above examples, we may say that

$$\text{World Student Population Proportion} = \frac{\text{World Student Population}}{\text{World Population}}$$

This is a definition because the proportion of students in the world population can be measured by reference only to the right-hand term. The left-hand term is an abbreviation that assumes knowledge of the word "proportion." From the above equation, a third expression can be developed,

$$\frac{\text{World Student Population}}{\text{World Student Population} + \text{World Nonstudent Population}}$$

which suggests a basic assumption that all people may be separated into one of two categories, students and nonstudents.

A proportion may range from 0 to 1, whereas, by convention, a *percent* may range from 0 to 100. A proportion is converted to a percent through multiplying by 100. Thus we may define the world student population percent as

$$100 \times \frac{\text{World Student Population}}{\text{World Population}}$$

The distinction between a proportion and a percent is trivial enough that many writers ignore it by referring to any decimal fraction as a percent or percentage—that is, assuming the denominator contains the elements of the numerator (the numerator must be a subset of the denominator).

Slightly more complex definitions are expressed in what may be called *ratios*. The simplest ratios involve only one unit of measurement. Let the world teacher population equal the number of people in the world who are teaching courses in an educational institution. A new definition follows:

$$\text{World Teacher-Student Ratio} = \frac{\text{World Teacher Population}}{\text{World Student Population}}$$

or

$$\text{World Student-Teacher Ratio} = \frac{\text{World Student Population}}{\text{World Teacher Population}}$$

The unit of measurement is the individual. Individuals are counted according to their attributes, student or teacher, excluding those who are neither. A ratio simply expresses the relative size of two numbers, such as 45 to 1, or 2 to 7. We might observe here that teachers and students are not mutually exclusive categories unless it is determined empirically which is each person's primary activity.

A large number of definitions include more than one unit of measurement. Most prominent in this group are those definitions that relate a monetary quantity to a given number of people, such as per capita gross national product or per capita personal income. An example related to the previous definitions could read:

$$\text{World Per Capita Educational Expenditures} = \frac{\text{World Educational Expenditures}}{\text{World Population}}$$

Of course the various currencies of the world would be arithmetically converted to a single one so that expenditure estimates are more comparable. A slightly different but related definition could read:

$$\text{World Per Student Educational Expenditures} = \frac{\text{World Educational Expenditures}}{\text{World Student Population}}$$

All of the above definitions, expressed as ratios, may be viewed as *averages,* or *means,* and could be described as the average number of students per teacher, or the average amount of expenditures per student, as the case may be. The *distribution* of students and expenditures may be highly unequal. Naturally, there are many other units of measurement incorporated into ratios, such as hours, miles, number of buildings, newspapers, radios, automobiles, and so on. For example, one could divide educational expenditures by the number of hours of classroom contact. With slight adjustment, any of the above equations could be applied at the national, state, or local level.

Simple Indexing through Compared Quantities

In a strict sense, an index is never simple. If X is an index to Y, then X may be only one of several indexes to Y, most of which might be unidentified. The term "index" seems to imply that, in the above case, there are theoretically true values of Y, and, to some extent, the values of X correspond to the theoretical values of Y. Frequently, Y is a broad concept, like modernization, political development, or public welfare effort. These concepts embody enormous flexibility of interpretation. To illustrate, let us take the concept of world educational effort. We can propose the following indexes to this concept:

1. World Student Population Proportion
2. World Teacher-Student Ratio
3. World Per Capita Educational Expenditures
4. World Per Student Educational Expenditures

Any of the above, it can be argued, would yield information related to educational effort; yet, none of the above would be wholly satisfactory.

Faced with the above problem of selection, the analyst might be tempted to say: "For my purposes, world educational effort will be *defined* by world per capita educational expenditures." The critic can then appropriately ask why the "effort" concept is at all necessary. We feel that the critic is correct. Let the analyst call per capita expenditures an index to effort, or else let the analyst drop the term "effort." There are many indexes to effort.

But what are the true theoretical values associated with world educational effort? How *are* they derived? Actually, in many cases there is no reason to think that the true values can be derived, since the "true" values will depend upon how people are willing to use the concept and the connotations they give it. The problem would be much easier if we could agree that the true values are found, for example, from the following ratio:

$$\frac{\text{World Educational Expenditures}}{\text{Gross World Product}}$$

This in essence would be a definition, implying the calculation of two monetary measures. Dividing one into the other gives the world educational effort.

173

Now it could be determined empirically which of the earlier indexes best approximates world educational effort. The scores derived from the Expenditure-Product Ratio may be compared to the scores produced by the proposed indexes.

Let us assume for the moment that the Expenditure-Product Ratio is the agreed-upon definition of educational effort. Intuitively, the ratio modifies performance by capacity to perform, which is perhaps what many people would mean by "effort." If for the year 1970 the scores for all indexes and the defining ratio were calculated, those scores by themselves would provide no basis for selecting among the indexes; the scores would need to be calculated for each of several years, or, alternatively, they would need to be calculated for each of several subunits of the world. In either case, the procedures will require a method of summarizing and assessing the relationships between sets of scores, that is, between the set produced by the Expenditure-Product Ratio and each of the sets yielded by the indexes.

The steps of comparison lead to regression and correlation analysis, a subject covered in more detail in later chapters. Briefly, the relationship between the defining ratio and an index is expressed through a regression equation,

$$Y'_i = a + bX^e_i$$

where X_i is an index value, the superscript e is an exponent (noted only if e does not equal 1), b is a slope coefficient serving to convert the X units of measurement to Y units of measurement, a is a constant giving the value of Y' when X_i is zero, and Y'_i is an estimated value of Y produced by the right-hand terms where Y_i represents the actual score given by the Expenditure-Product Ratio. Roughly, the regression equation represents a characteristic line or curve drawn through plotted points on a graph. A correlation coefficient will indicate the extent to which the plotted points can be accurately represented by a regression line or curve. Two sets of scores are said to be highly correlated if the Y-prime estimated values are very close to the actual values of Y. Thus the index yielding the highest correlation with the defining ratio would be selected, in most instances, as the best index.

The selection of an index by comparing index values with defined values can have only one purpose: to find a more convenient empirical instrument. It may be very expensive and not always possible to acquire the information necessary to use the definitional construct. A more accessible index can serve more practical needs for prediction and assessment. An index may also be less subject to low-quality reporting either periodically or within various subunits of the population. In some countries, for example, population estimates can be much more accurate than monetary estimates, or, as is often the case, monetary estimates are not made available. Of course it may be that the analyst is not at all interested in selecting an index, but rather in examining the theoretical relationships among all of the variables previously listed in the education example. An ensuing *multivariate* statistical analysis would be more appropriate.

Complex Indexes

The construction of an index, simple or complex, implies at most the approximation of theoretically true values. In our example, it was assumed that the true values of educational effort are derived from the Expenditure-Product Ratio. Several simple indexes for approximating those values were considered. Experience might show, however, that taken individually the indexes are poor approximations, but that in a collective form the true values are estimated with greater accuracy. It may be found, for example, that when the proportion of students in the population and the teacher-student ratio are combined in some way, a substantially improved index is created. Exactly how to combine the two indexes, however, presents us with a difficult problem.

To understand how difficult the problem is, we can consider several rival formulae for estimating the true values:

Let Y' = Estimated value of expenditure-product ratio
Y^u = Unconverted estimated value of expenditure-product ratio
P = Total population
S = Number of students
T = Number of teachers
b = slope
a = constant

$$(1) \quad Y' = a + b_1\left(\frac{S}{P}\right) + b_2\left(\frac{T}{S}\right)$$

$$(2) \quad Y^u = \frac{S}{P} + \frac{T}{S}$$

$$(3) \quad Y^u = \frac{S}{P} \times \frac{T}{P}$$

$$(4) \quad Y^u = \sqrt{\frac{S}{P} \times \frac{T}{P}}$$

$$(5) \quad Y^u = \frac{S}{P} \times \left(\frac{T}{S}\right)^2$$

The first equation represents what would result from a direct application of linear regression analysis. It should be clear that such an equation cannot be calculated without a set of known Y values. The formula for calculating the slope, b, includes Y. The remaining formulae give unconverted values, that is, Y^u is calculated before consulting the actual values of Y. To determine the extent to which one of the latter formulae produces correspondence with the Expenditure-Product Ratio, several values of Y^u must be compared with several actual values of Y, such that $Y' = a + bY^u$. The process would be repeated for the remaining complex indexes in order to determine which one gives the closest approximations of Y. The determination is made by comparing the predicted values of Y, symbolized Y', with the actual values of Y for each of the constructs.

For those familiar with multiple regression analysis (Chapter 12), complex indexes as illustrated by formulae (2) through (5) are likely to appear too much a product of guesswork. If the Y values are known, each of the four equations can be improved upon through regression analysis. Given the least squares criterion, and allowing logarithmic transformations to meet the linearity assumption, we find that

$$(3) \quad Y' = a + b_1\log\left(\frac{S}{P}\right) + b_2\log\left(\frac{T}{P}\right)$$

$$(4) \quad Y' = a + (\tfrac{1}{2})b_1\log\left(\frac{S}{P}\right) + (\tfrac{1}{2})b_2\log\left(\frac{T}{P}\right)$$

$$(5) \quad Y' = a + b_1\log\left(\frac{S}{P}\right) + 2b_2\log\left(\frac{T}{S}\right)$$

are superior expressions of indexes (3), (4), and (5) and their relationship to Y values. Equation (2) is expressed more amply in Equation (1).

With this caveat on complex indexes of the plain variety, let it be said, however, that they are probably closer to the intuition of most people. It is very unlikely that the above equations would be tested without a preliminary formulation similar to the unconverted constructs. Furthermore, if the Y values have not yet been discovered or observed, only the unconverted constructs will give answers. The selection of an index would need to be highly subjective. It seems that most constructs called indexes are selected without knowledge of the theoretically true values.

It is when the true values have never been ascertained that confusion can arise. It is often difficult to distinguish between an index and a definition. As a general rule, *when the type of data base employed for or implied by a construct is not the type of data base that would be used under ideal conditions, the construct is called an index.* An index, however, must be distinguished from a *sample estimate,* which is derived from the ideal data base, and merely offers a probabilistic way of reducing the quantity of observation. An index construct, in other words, falls short of incorporating the ideal variables. In many interviewing studies, for example, recollections of behavior are recorded, whereas it would have been desirable to have observed the actual behavior. Observing the actual behavior could have been highly impractical. For example, to ask every legislator with whom he interacted over an issue is a practical inquiry. But try to observe all such interactions first-hand—impossible without a task force of observers. Constructs developed from recollections, then, are only indexes to past behavior. In the simplest of cases we might say that the frequency of interaction (over issue X) is defined by the number of people the person interacted with, which is in turn indexed by the number of people with whom the person recalled interacting. The index is a guess. It might even be better to square the value produced. Perhaps the more that people interact, the greater the proportion of names they forget. Alternative formulae are in ample supply.[1]

The study of the exercise of influence offers another example. In a sizable organization it would be a monumental task to observe who causes whom to do what. The formal organization chart might provide one index. An interview study of "reputations for influence," counting the number of times members get named as influential, could provide another index. It is not really clear, however, that we are able to execute the ideal research, regardless of the resources available to us. Is there any ideal way to measure the degree of influence people have exercised, possess, or will exercise? If the technique is discoverable but not yet known, indexes will need to suffice.[2]

A so-called index construct sometimes constitutes part of the full definition of a concept. For example, "reputations for influence" may be part of the full definition of "influence." In other cases it is not clear when so-called index constructs are part of the full definition. Several authors, for example, have created indexes to party competition in elections. These indexes have been developed from voting and office-holding data, covering a period of years, to describe territorial units of government. Most notably, such indexes have been applied to the American states. In the state government setting, where third parties seldom offer a serious challenge, the indexes to party election competition have been constructed from the following kinds of information: [3]

1. Percent of votes won by majority party for the governor and other statewide offices.
2. Percent of elections for statewide office won by the majority party.
3. Percent of elections won by a party that lost the previous election for the same office.
4. Percent of senate and house seats won by majority party.

All such percents are averaged over a number of years. If by party competition the authors have in mind the balance between the degree of campaign activity generated by each of the two major parties, then constructs derived from the above described data are appropriately called indexes. Campaign effort does not always yield success. But suppose that a direct measurement procedure was developed, and that in each of two states the Democratic Party engaged in 50% of the campaign activity. In the first state the Democrats won 50% of the votes, elections, and seats; in the second state they won only 25% of each. Are we willing to abide by the direct measure and say that the two states are equally competitive? Do they have the same degree of party election competition? If not, the so-called index may then be part of the definition.

When it is difficult to determine whether a construct is a partial definition or a separate index, a clarification would be helpful (rather than earth-shaking). In general practice, the use of the term "index" implies that the analyst is merely dissatisfied with the correspondence between the construct and the concept employed.

Definitions, Indexes, and Measures: A Clarification

To distinguish between definitions, indexes, and measures, it is necessary to separate measurement procedures from the concepts that are related to them. To do this, we can examine the equation

$$(A,a) = (B,b)$$

where A and B are concepts, and a and b represent measurement procedures that define the respective concepts. The expression (B,b) is a *measure* of (A,a) if it always produces (save slight random measurement error) the same value. However, (B,b) is an *index* of (A,a) if its resulting values are only rough approximations. If there is no measurement procedure directly associated with A, such that

$$A = (B,b)$$

then (B,b) is a definition. More interesting definitions, indexes, and measures would involve additional concepts and measurement procedures in the same equation. In all cases, definitions do not include measurement procedures on the left-hand side of the equation. A *partial definition* can be represented by

$$A = (B,b) + (U,u)$$

where either U and u are unknowns, or U is a concept with an unknown measurement procedure.

Complex Definitions

The great variety of definitional constructs that appear in the literature would be nearly impossible to capture in a single work. In this section we will il-lustrate two definitions of broad concepts and one definitional system. The first two illustrations embody definitions of political development and degree of democracy, and yield what can be called "concept-dependent" constructs. The third example derives from a set of data on international trade.

In 1963 Philips Cutright "operationally defined" political development, a long-standing concept, through a set of measurement procedures applied to 21 years of experience for each of 77 countries. The construct employed may be restated as follows: [4]

Degree of Political Development

> = 2 (number of years minority parties occupied at least 30% of seats in parliament)
>
> = (number of years minority parties occupied less than 30% of seats in parliament)
>
> = (number of years ruled by chief executive elected popularly over opposition candidates, or selected by parliament in which minority parties occupied at least 30% of seats)
>
> = ½ (number of years ruled by chief executive selected by other non-hereditary means where also at least 30% of parliament seats are occupied by minority parties)

The construct yields country scores ranging from 0 to 63. The author labeled the construct an "index," whereas by our earlier criteria we would call it a partial definition. There are no true values associated with the concept "degree of political development." A second analyst might define political development by the proportion of government budget devoted to health, education, and welfare (i.e., people-oriented programs).

McCrone and Cnudde, in a reanalysis of the Cutright data, decided to narrow the concept, arguing that Cutright was essentially examining *democratic* political development.[5] Other types of political development are not tapped by the construct. Another author, Neubauer, was almost equally dissatisfied by the more narrow formulation. In his view the concept should be changed to "degree of democraticness," or at most, "degree of democratic development." Even here, Neubauer would totally revise the construct, arguing that it lacks sensitivity to differences within the most "developed" group of countries and within the least "developed" group of countries, serving in the end to distinguish only between the two groups. Neubauer's index to democratic development includes an averaging of several indicators: the percent of adult population eligible to vote, the distortion between the number of votes won and the number of legislative seats won by political parties, the number of newspapers and the total newspaper circulation in capitol cities, and the degree of election competition as evidenced by office-sharing and voting divisions. He finds that for the 23 relatively advanced countries in his sample the composite index values correspond very poorly to the relative values derived from the Cutright construct.[6]

Briefly, the above arguments represent a debate over definition. Use

179

of the term "index" expresses simply a lack of complete satisfaction with a formulation, and not the existence of true numeric values. What is clear is that the Cutright and Neubauer constructs should be given different conceptual names. We can suggest that the Cutright construct roughly defines the degree to which countries have legitimate political opposition, and that the Neubauer construct might define the degree of democratic leadership selection. It seems self-evident that the way in which leaders are selected is a political matter, but it would also appear that there are other factors that make up the democraticness of a political system, namely, in the selection of policies that are not foreclosed by the selection of leaders.

A somewhat different perspective on the same problem is acquired by beginning with the question of who can win or lose on any issue under any institutional circumstances or within any particular domain of a political system. Can the degree of democracy be defined within any decision-making arena? Rae implies that it is theoretically possible through the following construct: [7]

$$Q = \frac{n + D_{\min} - L_{\max}}{n + 1}$$

For our purposes here we can let

Q = the degree of democracy
n = the number of people within a domain
$D_{\min}$ = the minimum number of people who can win on an issue
$L_{\max}$ = the maximum number of people who can lose on an issue

A legislature with 101 members, for instance, operating by the rules that every member must vote and that 51 concurring votes are necessary to prevail in the passage or defeat of a bill, will yield

$$Q = \frac{101 + 51 - 50}{101 + 1} = 1$$

In Rae's terms, the legislature would be operating as a "pure democracy," at least within its own organizational boundaries. Bicameral legislatures necessarily fall short of "pure" democracy.

Again it is clear that the above formulation is a definition, related to what is often called procedural democracy. The definition can be applied readily to electoral and policy-making processes. Since most societies are characterized by a variety of decision-making institutions and practices, a given society will more than likely receive several separately derived Q values. How such values could be combined to characterize a whole system is a new question, one that has no obvious answer. The construct need not be limited to the written rules of a system, but may be applied to what has actually happened in past decision-making. For example, what is the minimum percent of people who have won a national election? The empirical problem is immense, since leaders also achieve office through semi-elections, pseudo-elections, and nonelections. The counting of noses in a comparable manner requires a translation device of incredible genius. Nevertheless, for a portion of the world, the Rae construct might acquire operational clarity, and depending upon one's preferences, either the Rae construct or the Neubauer construct could be called, appropriately, an index of the other. Otherwise, they are separate definitional constructs.

The above definitional constructs have the utility of giving precise elaboration to what many consider important concepts for political research. Conversely, it is often the case that an important set of information can be conveyed to its fullest only through the imposition of a set of concepts. Most typically, the concepts are generated to give the meaning of certain arithmetic manipulations. The arithmetic may be complex and tedious, as in factor analysis, or fairly easy to understand. In either case, the arithmetic is represented by algebraic statements. Here we will take one grass roots example to demonstrate how a system of definitions can highlight an information pool. The data are country-by-country import and export figures, reported yearly in dollars by the International Monetary Fund and made available in both machine-readable tapes and library reference volumes. Each reporting country (some do not report) is listed with its dollar trade in imports and exports with every other reporting country. The only other information set will be the gross national product of each country, the estimates of which are reported periodically by the United Nations.

The problem begins with a hunch that trade relationships might provide an important barometer of international behavior, well beyond the immediate economic advantages of the transactions. While trade relationships are in part a result of calculated economic efficiencies, they also reflect political alliances and hostilities (e.g., the lack of trade between Cuba and the United States). In addition, trade patterns may be indicative of future political relationships between countries. Political leaders may adjust their policies in response to the success or failure of prior trade agreements and transactions. Furthermore, countries that rely heavily on trade, as distinguished from those that do not, may behave differently in the resolution of international political questions. Given these possibilities, the immediate task is to create an inventory of constructs that may, in later analysis, reveal the significance of international trade.

We may begin by designating two countries, i and j, whose attributes are expressed in dollars as follows:

P_i = Gross national product of country i
P_j = Gross national product of country j
A_i = Total imports and exports of country i
A_j = Total imports and exports of country j
a_{ij} = Trade between countries i and j

Trade between the two countries may be calculated by summing the value of goods each has exported to the other. From the above information we can first ask how extensively a country trades in relation to its gross national product. In direct language the resulting construct can be called a trade-GNP ratio, for which there are three applications:

$$\frac{A_i}{P_i}, \quad \frac{A_j}{P_j}, \quad \frac{A_i + A_j}{P_i + P_j}$$

The third construct is the ratio for the two countries taken together.

Given the amount of trade negotiated by country i, how much does it depend on country j, and vice versa? Let

Trade dependency of i on $j = \dfrac{a_{ij}}{A_i}$, or, proportion of i trade with j

Trade dependency of j on $i = \dfrac{a_{ij}}{A_j}$, or, proportion of j trade with i

If the two countries do not trade, the construct will yield a value of 0. If they trade only with each other, it will yield a value of 1. What is the economic value of this dependency in relation to the country's GNP? We can state that:

Economic value of dependency to $i = \dfrac{a_{ij}}{P_i}$

Economic value of dependency to $j = \dfrac{a_{ij}}{P_j}$

If the two countries are dependent upon each other, we can be more abstract by saying that they are also interdependent, as follows:

Trade interdependency between i and $j = \dfrac{a_{ij}}{\frac{1}{2}(A_i + A_j)}$

This construct has more utility when several pairs of countries are compared. Likewise, the economic value of the interdependency:

Economic value of interdependency $= \dfrac{a_{ij}}{\frac{1}{2}(P_i + P_j)}$

The above equations provide a set of basic definitions for treating the data. It should be noted that it becomes increasingly awkward to adhere to descriptive phrases that elucidate the algebraic relationships involved. The trade-GNP ratios and the proportion of one country's trade with another are fairly straightforward, and perhaps even the ratio of one country's trade with another to the former's GNP is clear enough without a guiding concept. It is possible, however, that the concepts of dependency and economic value aid in understanding what the equations imply. The need for a guiding concept, such as interdependency, is more apparent for the relationship expressed by $a_{ij}/1/2(A_i + A_j)$. The construct must be distinguished from

$$\frac{a_{ij}}{A_i \text{ or } A_j, \text{ whichever is less}}$$

such that the denominator connotes the possible amount of trade between the two countries given each country's total trade. In this case we have a ratio of actual trade to possible trade for a given year. The value would be identical to one of the two dependency constructs.

Further inquiry might necessitate a construct that will show the difference in the extent to which two countries are dependent upon each other for the trade they transact. The comparison might be expressed as

$$\text{Trade dependency imbalance} = \frac{a_{ij}}{A_i} - \frac{a_{ij}}{A_j}$$

If there is no imbalance, the construct will yield a value of 0. One might even find it useful to formulate the notion of imbalance in economic dependency through the construct

$$\frac{a_{ij}}{P_i} - \frac{a_{ij}}{P_j}$$

Of course there are other forms of economic dependency not reflected necessarily in trade, generally under the heading of foreign investment. The construct could be called an index, pending the collection of the elusive foreign investment data.

Composite Constructs and Standard Scores

Many constructs such as those relating to political development, discussed earlier, incorporate the summing of two or more separately derived scores. These shall be called *composite constructs*. When these separately derived scores fall consistently within some well-known range, say between 0 and 1 or between 0 and 100, their summation is more readily interpretable. The addition of percent of Democrat vote for two statewide offices, for example, is easy to comprehend, and the total can be divided, without ambiguity, by 2. When a composite construct contains scores that come from different measurement procedures, it may be necessary to standardize the results. For example, if a communication construct sums the per capita newspaper consumption and the number of radios per capita, the resulting total seems a bit artificial. Dividing by 2 does not help. Or even further, add the number of telephones per capita and the number of television sets per capita to the newspaper and radio scores and then divide by 4.

Since the scores in the above example yield artificial totals or averages, it may be convenient to standardize each measure such that all four have the same mean and standard deviation. *Any* distribution of values can be transformed to exhibit a particular mean and particular standard deviation without either the loss or distortion of information. This means that two variables that have vastly different ranges of values can be made more comparable. The procedure requires finding the *mean* and *standard deviation* of the original distribution of values for each measure. Then one must arbitrarily determine what the new common mean and common standard deviation will be. Typically, analysts will choose a mean of 0, 50, or 500, depending largely upon personal preference. Typically they will choose respective standard deviations of 1, 10, or 100.

Let us take a mean of zero and standard deviation of 1. Given that the standard deviation of the original distribution,

$$s = \frac{\Sigma (X_i - \overline{X})^2}{N}$$

the standard score for any X_i value is calculated from the following equation:

$$z = \frac{X_i - \overline{X}}{s}$$

For example, if the standard deviation of the original distribution is .10 around a mean of .60, we may convert two individual values of .35 and .54 to standard scores as follows:

$$z_1 = \frac{.35 - .60}{.10} = \frac{-.25}{.10} = -2.5$$

$$z_2 = \frac{.54 - .60}{.10} = \frac{-.06}{.10} = -.60$$

The new mean of all z scores will be 0 and the standard deviation will be 1.0.

The full equation for calculating standard scores is

$$z = M' + \frac{S'(X_i - \overline{X})}{s}$$

where M' is the desired mean and S' is the desired standard deviation. Thus, if a mean of 50 and standard deviation of 10 were preferred,

$$z_1 = 50 + \frac{10(-.25)}{.10} = 25$$

$$z_2 = 50 + \frac{10(-.06)}{.10} = 44$$

To demonstrate that the transformations do not distort the relative scores in the original data, we may take a third value of .70. The standard scores in each case will yield

$$z_3 = \frac{.70 - .60}{.10} = 1.0$$

$$z_3 = 50 + \frac{10(.70 - .60)}{.10} = 60$$

It can now be observed that

$$X_3 - X_2 = .70 - .54 = .16$$
$$z_3 - z_2 = 1.0 - (-.60) = 1.6$$
$$Z_3 - Z_2 = 60 - 44 = 16$$
$$X_2 - X_1 = .54 - .35 = .19$$
$$z_2 - z_1 = -.60 - (-2.5) = 1.9$$
$$Z_2 - Z_1 = 44 - 25 = 19$$

The ratio of distances between X_i, z_i, and Z_i scores is identical. Because the relative distances between values are preserved, the transformation is called *linear*.

While linear transformations will not affect the relative distances between scores on any single distribution, they will affect the relative distances between *composite* scores derived from the transformed values. For example, if in each of several countries the raw figures for telephones per capita and radios per capita are summed and then compared to the summed transformed values of each measure, the totals for each procedure will not exhibit the same relative distances. In relation to each other, the countries will not receive the same relative total values from the transformed data as they did from the orginal data. This distinction is particularly important if the totals are to be correlated subsequently with other variables. It may be that the summed raw values correlate more closely with other variables than do the summed transformed values. Standard scores do not necessarily improve the explanatory power of a construct, and they are to be used with this caution in mind. The best procedure is to try both to determine which yields the stronger relationships with other variables.

A second standardizing procedure in widespread use generates what may

FIGURE 6.1
Normal Curve Distribution

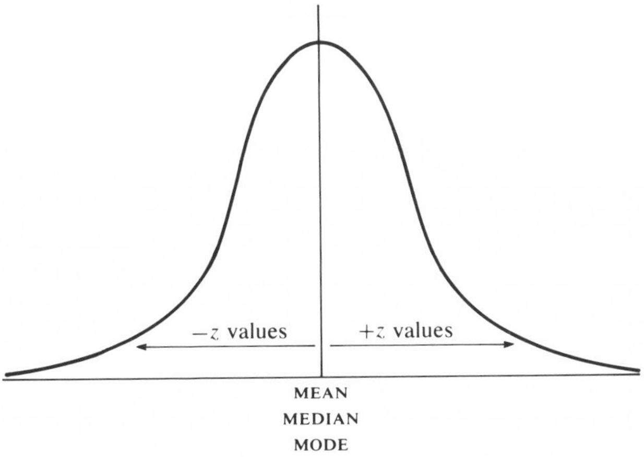

MEAN
MEDIAN
MODE

be called *normalized z scores*. The purpose of the procedure is to produce an approximate normal curve distribution out of data that are not normally distributed. As illustrated in Figure 6.1, a normal curve is symmetrical and unimodal with its maximum height at the mean. It represents a mathematical function for events that occur by chance. The standard normal curve has a mean of 0 and a standard deviation of unity, or 1.0. The z values are linear distances from the mean. The standard deviation is a z value. For every z distance from the mean there is associated a particular height of the curve and a particular area between the mean and the z distance. For example, approximately 34% of the area falls between the mean and a standard deviation (or z value) of 1.0. Thus the normalized z scores are created to fit a very precisely defined distribution. This is called a *nonlinear* transformation, since the relative distances between the raw values are not preserved.

The first step in creating normalized scores requires converting the data to percentile ranks, a process that keeps the observations in the same relative order but eliminates the measured distances. The percentile ranks are calculated most easily from the equation

$$PR = \frac{100}{N}\left(cf - \frac{f}{2}\right)$$

where cf is the cumulative frequency or the number of scores below and equal to a given score that has a frequency of f. The mean percentile rank is obviously 50, since percentiles range from 0 to 100. The mean percentile is then subtracted from PR and the result is interpreted as the area of normal curve between the mean and some yet undetermined z value. The z value is found by consulting a table of areas under the normal curve which specifies the value for any given area. Thus if PR minus the mean equals +20, 20% of the area falls between the mean and the PR value. Finding .20 in the interior of a normal curve table (Table A) yields a z value of .52. Again the mean of z values is 0, the standard deviation is 1.0 and such values are seldom higher than 3.0, or less than –3.0.

Some analysts prefer to work with *T*-scores. *T*-scores are normally distributed around a mean of 50 instead of 0. *T* is directly calculated from z as follows:

$$T = 50 + 10z$$

The calculation of *T* eliminates negative values and sets the standard deviation at 10, and the scores generally range between 20 and 80. Neubauer, for example, in creating his index of democratic performance, utilized *T*-scores to arrive at a composite construct.[8]

The reasons for developing normalized scores vary. There is a sound reason for doing so when the analyst is certain that the true distribution is normal. It must then be concluded that the measurement instrument or procedure contains a bias. For example, it is possible that past attitude surveys have demonstrated that people are normally distributed along a particular opinion dimension. A new questionnaire instrument may yield a skewed distribution. Perhaps the opinion items were not controversial enough, or perhaps the range of response choice was inadequate. There are other cases where one may suspect that the reporting function systematically biases a distribution. Crime statistics, for example, reflect how willing people are in various areas to report crimes and how conscientiously public officials record and detect crimes. Incidence rates of any sort depend in part upon how well-equipped a community or society is to record the events. In such cases, normalized scores may be a better representation of the true values.

A less persuasive but possible reason for normalizing scores relates to the status of statistical reasoning, which has progressed in several areas under the assumption that the input data are normally distributed. If it is found that normalized distributions yield more appealing multivariate models and more accurate predictions of real events, then it may be that the measurement procedures need to be improved. In any case, to normalize a distribution in the above way is to guess that the raw data are inaccurate and that the normalized scores are more accurate in portraying the relative distances between values. Generally, if the transformation produces a higher correlation with a second variable, it is considered helpful. Further discussion of transformations will be pursued in Chapter 10. There *are* ways to make *direct* mathematical transformations to approximately normal curves without losing the original values in the process.

NOTES

1. This example may be unfortunate. One could argue that memory is nothing but a sample of experience, and recorded recollections nothing but a sample of memory. Thus one would be calculating a subsample estimate of a sample.

2. Robert A. Dahl, *Modern Political Analysis* (Englewood Cliffs, N.J.: Prentice-Hall, Inc., 1963).

3. Richard E. Dawson and James A. Robinson, "Inter-Party Competition, Economic Variables, and Welfare Policies in the American States," *Journal of Politics,* 25 (1963), 265–89; Richard I. Hofferbert, "Classification of American State Party Systems," *Journal of Politics,* 26 (1964), 550–67. See also the classification by Austin Ranney, "Parties in State Politics," in Jacob and Vines (eds.), *Politics in the American States* (Boston: Little, Brown and Company, 1965), pp. 61–100; and an earlier article by Joseph A. Schlesinger, "A Two-Dimensional Scheme for Classifying the States According to Degree of Inter-Party Competition," *American Political Science Review,* 49 (1955), 1120–28.

4. Phillips Cutright, "National Political Development: Measurement and Analysis," *American Sociological Review,* 28 (April 1963), 253–64.

5. Donald F. McCrone and Charles F. Cnudde, "Toward A Communicative Theory of Democratic Political Development: A Causal Model," *American Political Science Review,* 61 (March 1967), 72–79.

6. Deane E. Neubauer, "Some Conditions of Democracy," *American Political Science Review,* 61 (December 1967), 1002–9.

7. Douglas Rae, "Political Democracy as a Property of Political Institutions," *American Political Science Review,* 65 (March 1971), 111–19.

8. Neubauer, "Some Conditions of Democracy." See his footnote 8.

Chapter 7

GENERATION OF DATA: METHODS AND TECHNIQUES

There is a classic early English observation of unknown origin, which runs something like this: "The government are keen on all manner of statistic. They furnish reports on every commerce of man and animal. But truth doth not abound in them, for the numbers come from the village watchman who putteth down whatsoever he damn pleaseth." Apparently problems of generating trustworthy data are not of recent origin.

Sound measurement is not simply a matter of careful concept explication, followed by selection of a statistical model which will minimize error. The quality of data is inextricably tied to the methods and techniques used for generating data. No amount of sophistication with statistical manipulation can fully overcome deficiencies inherent in data generated by an inappropriate instrument.

Political scientists in the past have relied heavily on two sources for data: (1) published governmental documents and (2) the large-scale survey. But scholars currently have available to them a wide variety of instruments for generating data. Data generated by each instrument have characteristic strengths and weaknesses. Our hope is that the following discussion will help political scientists to avoid overreliance on certain methods or techniques and to match, as much as feasible, the data-generating instrument to the intellectual problem at hand.

Types of Data

Earlier in our discussion of sampling we pointed out that, while we were sampling individual units, we were typically not concerned with the unit as a whole but with selected properties of the unit. Data generation is the science and art of acquiring information about the selected properties of units. Any of four types of information about sampled units are likely to be of interest:

(1) behavior, (2) knowledge, (3) meaning, and (4) location. Our discussion here should be read in the context of our earlier discussion of levels of analysis where we talked about global, analytical, relational, and contextual properties. In many instances it can apply to both the level of the individual and the level of the group.

Behavioral data may be collected about the individual, the group, or complex events. In generating behavioral data the scholar is especially concerned with the detailed documentation of an occurrence. If the individual is the target of inquiry, the investigator must observe the behavior directly, or devise a mechanism for generating reliable self-reports. Where interactions between persons or within groups are of interest, the scholar must decide what kinds of observations or which actors' reports of behavior are sufficient to generate trustworthy information about the interaction. Complex events, as used here, refer to interactions among actors who represent larger units —e.g., nations, parties, associations. Often they are studied by sampling published documentary sources, private communiques, or diaries. Where access is not an obstacle, however, they may also be analyzed through direct observation by the investigator or self-reports by the actors. Because of the level of analysis problem, complex events are among the most difficult about which to acquire appropriate information. Generally, direct observation is the optimal method of data collection on behavior but accessibility and temporality may force the scholar to rely on the self-reports and recollections of the actors or the reports of other observers.

Knowledge generally refers to the level of information possessed by subjects. It is particularly of interest in studies where the cognition level of persons is theoretically relevant. But knowledge could also refer to adaptive and instrumental capabilities possessed by individuals, or within groups, nations, or cultures. When either the person or the larger group is the target of inquiry, the investigator examines performance (behavior) in a task-oriented situation. He may ask a person questions, for example, that have a right and wrong answer, which can serve as a criterion for cognition level attained. Studies that tap instrumental capabilities usually require direct observation of performance on both verbal and nonverbal acts. For example, the public administration specialist might study group problem-solving skills in an agency by designing a structured laboratory or field experiment; the community organization specialist might join a neighborhood association and, through a combination of direct observation and trusted informants' reports, determine how the group achieves its goal. Sometimes behavioral "footprints" such as documents, reports, and diaries are used to infer the level of information possessed by subjects.

Meaning data are perhaps the most difficult pieces of information to obtain. They deal with the intentions or meaning that individuals or groups attach to their mental and physical behaviors, and with their interpretations of their physical and social environments. Sometimes meaning resides solely in an individual actor; usually a large part of it is socially shared by participants in an activity. When individuals are examined, a variety of observational and self-report instruments may be used to tap personality, attitude, opinion, motivation, or goal orientation. Typically self-report data involving verbal acts have been favored by investigators. When shared social meaning is the target of inquiry, both strategies have been used, but observation of behavior tends to predominate. In either case, complex inferences are necessary to tap the meaning that people attach to their relationship to other objects or social processes. It is much easier to observe a legislator's vote than to infer why he voted that way.

Locational data place the actors in some personal, social, or environmental context. *Personal* location generally requires a listing of personally held attributes of the unit; for an individual this may refer to sex, race, age, ethnicity, or other standard demographic items which appear on interview schedules or can be easily observed. *Social* location refers to properties which are better understood in relationship to social objects; for an individual this might involve marital status, family composition, organizational affiliations or memberships, social class, and so forth. Some properties such as education might be either personal or social locational variables, depending on both the perspective of the investigator and the characteristics of a society; in a fixed class structure with limited mobility, education might be regarded as a personal location, whereas in a society with high mobility, education often involves manipulation of the social environment. *Physical* and *environmental* locational data for the individual typically involve a contextual classification based on such factors as nature of dwelling unit, neighborhood characteristics, degree of urbanism, region, or whatever. While personal and social locational data are usually collected by observation or self-report, environmental locational data often involve the use of documentary sources before or after data collection about the individual. In similar fashion, larger organized or unorganized aggregates—associations, countries, etc.—may be characterized by locational data; these usually involve reliance on documentary sources.

For a variety of reasons—completeness, particularity, accuracy, accessibility, expense, etc.—the type of data desired will affect the selection of an appropriate data-generating instrument. These factors will be included in the discussion when we evaluate specific methods and techniques. But the point here is that the scholar must decide *before* collecting data what type of content is most suitable for his intellectual question.

Extent of Information

A second general consideration in the selection of a data-generating instrument is the extent of information required about each unit. This ranges on a continuum from *wholistic* data, on one end, to *particularistic* or abstracted data, on the other. The investigator must determine how many properties on each unit are desirable for the intellectual problem. If only a few characteristics are to be abstracted, he may settle for a very particularistic instrument. If it is necessary to view each unit as a uniquely interacting system of parts or if it is not clear beforehand just which parts are desirable for hypothesis testing, a wholistic instrument may be preferable. If wholistic information about the individual is desired, the investigator may use life histories or biographies, film, or some other tailing device whereby observation is sustained over a long period of time. If particularistic information is thought to be adequate, the investigator may devise an experiment whereby only two or three variables are manipulated, or develop a self-report instrument such as an interview schedule or questionnaire with multiple measures for only a few properties.

The decision regarding the extent of information required is based on several criteria: (1) the state of theory development about the phenomenon, (2) the need for serendipity, (3) the degree of efficiency required, and (4) the importance of reliability and validity of information. If not much is known about the phenomenon, it is desirable to conduct exploratory research with fairly wholistic information. As more becomes known, it is possible to develop testable hypotheses dealing with the relationships among a small number of controllable variables; at this point a particularistic instrument is preferred. Thus expense of data collection is minimized. So that unanticipated relationships are not excluded, it may be desirable to return to a wholistic instrument at a later time. If theory is to be developed, to be tested with precision, and to be expanded into a larger network, wholistic and particularistic instruments must complement each other.

Finally, these instruments are subject to different sources of systematic and random error. A wholistic data-generating instrument such as tailing, tape recording, or filming may be obtrusive and thus have a reactive effect on the individual; a politician dealing with a sensitive matter will say one thing "off the record" and another on tape, or an ordinary citizen acts unnaturally on first exposure to videotape. Through time, however, the reactive effect may be overcome; those who use videotape argue that, if the interaction situation under filming is salient to the individual, he will soon ignore the presence of the camera. Particularistic instruments that include direct measures of attitudes, for example, may also have a reactive effect; for that reason, a variety of indirect or disguised tests and experimental situations have been developed. The evaluation of specific strategies for data collection is discussed in the next section.

The Forms of Data Collection

Social scientists have used many schemes to categorize the principal forms of data collection. We prefer to evaluate families of methods and techniques through a scheme first devised by Cook and Selltiz to deal with attitude measurement; [1] the utility of their classification is increasingly becoming recognized, as can be seen in Summers' excellent collection of readings and Phillips' suggestive critique of survey methods. [2] It can be modified and adapted to the many intellectual problems outside attitude measurement with which political scientists deal. The scheme allows assessment of the sources of error within common groupings of instruments.

From our variance components model of reliability it was shown that true variance and error variance must be separated; further, different components of error variance that stem from persons, observers, situations, or interactions between any of these must be isolated. In selecting an appropriate data-generating instrument, the scholar should be alert for the following kinds of error:

1. Error stemming from persons:
   A. *Evaluation apprehension:* anxiety that a person feels when aware of being tested.
   B. *Subject role:* the subject's desire to behave as he or she thinks the investigator wants, so that the test hypothesis will be substantiated.
   C. *Response sets* such as acquiescence or opposition ("yea-saying" or "nay-saying"), choosing of socially desirable answers, or systematic selection of alternatives occupying a certain location on the instrument.
2. Error stemming from observers, interviewers, or related sources:
   A. *Expectancy effects:* in some unknown manner—tone of voice, manifestation of nervousness, etc.—the investigator tipping off the subject to behave, verbally or physically, consistent with the hypothesis.
   B. *Changes in instrument calibration:* through time the investigator unknowingly altering the administration of the instrument through familiarity with it, fatigue, boredom, etc.
   C. *Changes in the data matrix:* while the format in which data are embedded appears similar through time, undocumented changes in classification principles or recording practices, or unknown erosion effects on the artifacts confounding apparent substantive change with a method effect.
3. Error stemming from physical settings and situations:
   A. The *process of measurement* itself serving as a change agent with lasting effects.
   B. *Inaccessibility* of some populations and *instability* of other samples through time.
   C. *Idiosyncratic situational factors* generating positive or negative effects on either subject or investigator, such as persons other than the subject present in the situation, visual and aural attractiveness of the setting, interaction of subject's and investigator's physical and emotional attributes.

There was a time, particularly in the history of psychological measurement, when social science disciplines tended to discard an instrument totally if it was discovered that its use led to characteristic errors. Then a new instrument was used until it met the same unfortunate demise. It is now recognized that every method and technique will generate scores laden with some error. Because error is generic to virtually all data-collection instruments, careful research dictates (1) pinpointing the most common errors resulting from each method or technique, (2) controlling for errors where possible, and (3) generating data by at least two methods or techniques, different in the extent to which they suffer from the same potential sources of error.

Self-Report

Clearly the dominant family of methods and techniques for data collection in the social sciences involves respondents' or subjects' self-reports of behavior, knowledge, meaning, and location. Commonly an interview schedule or questionnaire is used to generate self-report data, but such footprints as autobiographies, letters, recorded conversations, and diaries are also employed. Webb and associates and Phillips report that nearly 90% of all published research in disciplines such as social psychology and sociology has been based on self-report interviews and questionnaires.[3] While the percentage is undoubtedly not that high in political science, self-report is still a dominant strategy for data collection; furthermore, many important governmental reports and most of the files stored by social science data archives had their origins in a questionnaire. Ironically, then, most studies dealing with behavior and interactions are based, not on direct observation of that behavior, but on the actors' self-reports; most of what we know about both nonverbal and verbal political acts has been generated through instruments that require an oral or written verbal act removed in time from the original act. Although there are many advantages to the use of self-report instruments, seldom are independent controls utilized to assess their characteristic errors.

1 / INTERVIEW SCHEDULES AND QUESTIONNAIRES

In this strategy the investigator presents the subject with a question, usually fairly direct, designed to stimulate a verbal response about the topic; then either the investigator or the subject records the response. The principal recording devices are the interview schedule and the questionnaire. An *interview schedule* or *protocol* is administered and recorded by the researcher, whereas a *questionnaire* is administered and recorded by the respondent.

Surveys using either instrument have a variety of advantages. Perhaps their principal strength is that data thus generated (1) are easily formatted in a standardized manner, (2) are amenable to quantitative analysis, and (3) if sufficient attention has been paid to sample selection, permit generalizations with high degrees of precision and confidence across known populations. Few of the other forms of data collection can make such claims. Furthermore, survey instruments also provide relatively efficient access to such "private" behaviors as the respondent's past, internal mental operations like motives and attitudes, and actions not normally performed in public. Where aggregate data do not already exist in archives or published documents, surveys through samples can be performed more cheaply and usually more reliably than through censuses. Finally, many forms of data collection, particularly those relying on existing records, often are devoid of crucial variables for a new intellectual concern; it is difficult to add these variables later to the files of individuals or to attribute to the individual a contextual characteristic of the physical or social environment in which he is located. In designing a survey instrument to generate new data, however, the scholar can anticipate the kinds of information required for each individual and can make the data file as wholistic or particularistic as his skill and the respondent's patience will permit.

From the standpoint of cost and efficiency, questionnaires are very attractive. Questionnaires can be mailed to far-off places and, particularly in low-budget research, can permit generalization to a much less narrowly confined population. Mail-out questionnaires, however, suffer from three major weaknesses: (1) lack of control over the administration setting, (2) inflexibility of the instrument, and (3) nonreturns. The investigator has limited knowledge about who has actually completed the questionnaire and in what mood; responses may have been dashed off hurriedly—usually with very terse comments—or delegated to another, less knowledgeable person. Of course when a response requires collective discussion or consultation of records, the more relaxed pace of questionnaire completion is to be preferred to the social pressure which forces immediate response to an interviewer's questions. Questionnaires are inflexible in that it is impossible for the investigator to elaborate on a question beyond what appears on the instrument; when an interviewer sees that a respondent has difficulty comprehending a question or has a different frame of reference, within predefined limits he can clarify the question; a paper-and-pencil questionnaire can be clarified only by return mail or telephone. Finally, sample sizes and permissible generalizations are likely to be heavily distorted by nonresponse. Only with unusual groups, careful attention to auspices, short instruments, persistent and repeated exhortations to complete the instrument, and special incentives is the investigator likely to get a completion rate of more than 25% to 40%. He must then conduct additional research to prove that his nonrespondents differ from his respondents on no important variables.

One way to avoid the weaknesses of mail-out questionnaires is to administer the questionnaire to captive audiences. The investigator thus controls the setting, may occasionally clarify questions, and gains maximum returns. But seldom are captive audiences as representative of theoretically relevant populations as those reached by direct mailings. To enhance representativeness, usually considerable additional cost is involved. Finally, the group dynamics of the captive audiences must be controlled so that they do not vary from one audience to another.

While questionnaires are well-suited to particularistic research, survey interviews can be designed to yield more wholistic information. They are generally more expensive per unit, but the rate of return with call-backs is normally over 80%. From one standpoint, interview data are more reliable and valid than questionnaire data: ambiguities can be clarified by the interviewer. Furthermore, a well-trained interviewer will record marginal notes of all comments the respondent makes, including those indicating difficulty in responding to the question. Serendipitous discoveries and careful question refinement are thus more likely to occur from interviews than from questionnaires. The temporal sequence in the asking of questions is also under the control of the interviewer. However, the use of interview schedules introduces a potentially obtrusive party to the data-collection process—the interviewer. Interviews are themselves social interaction situations, and responses to questions are composed partly of recollections of behavior, meaning, and so on and partly of reactions to the immediate situation. The respondent is thrust into an uncustomary role and may rely on a number of socially protective devices.

A number of rapport-building procedures relating to the characteristics and training of the interviewer have been devised. These are elaborated on in many interviewers' manuals of large survey research centers.[4] Current research indicates that, depending on the subject matter of the interview, the race, sex, age, and socioeconomic and educational status of the interviewer should be matched to those of the respondent.[5] The auspices surrounding sponsorship of survey interviews can also affect the interaction situation. On their Census of Core-Area Businesses in Buffalo, New York, the study director, Andreasen, and the director of Buffalo's Survey Research Center, Leege, spent nearly two months gaining the approval of black leaders to conduct the project, even though it was in large part black-originated. A black field director was employed and well over half of the interviewers were black. Anticipating cooperation problems with Polish-Americans in the area, the Center hired the brother of a popular Polish politician as a field coordinator. Response rates from both ethnic groups were nearly 100%. The only difficulty was unanticipated: a Jewish interviewer failed to complete several of her assignments because she spoke Yiddish with a German accent and many of her Russian-born Jewish respondents resented the nationality difference. The lesson of the Buffalo experience was enhanced several months later when a sociology professor, acting independently of the Survey Research Center, undertook a survey on the Polish East Side; he neglected to gain community endorsement, and the same popular Polish political leader publicly denounced the project (although its content was less controversial than that of the earlier project); response rates for his interviewers plummeted to 25%.

TABLE 7.1

Illustrations of Question Structure

OPEN-ENDED	FORCED CHOICE OR FIXED ALTERNATIVE	
Nondirective Q. How are you getting along these days? Q. What do you think are the most important problems American people face today?	*Fixed alternative (cognition)* Q. Please indicate which functions, to the best of your knowledge, are presently located in the Department of Community Affairs? (CIRCLE ONE FOR EACH)	*Fixed alternative (meaning)* Q. We're interested in people's feelings about Lyndon Johnson's actions and policies as President of the United States. Thinking back on the past few months, would you say that you are *very satisfied, moderately satisfied, moderately dissatisfied,* or *very dissatisfied* with President Johnson's actions and policies?
Fixed topic, nondirective Q. Is there anything in particular about Mr. Nixon that might make you want to vote for him? Q. What things do you like best about living in this neighborhood?	1. Administration of "701" Local Planning Assistance. (Yes) (No) (Don't Know) 2. Administration of state grants-in-aid for housing and urban renewal. (Yes) (No) (Don't Know) 3. Review of all statutes affecting local governments. (Yes) (No) (Don't Know)	1. very satisfied 2. moderately satisfied 3. moderately dissatisfied 4. very dissatisfied 5. don't know
Focused interview, funnel questions Q. How do candidates for nomination seek to persuade your county delegation to support them? How many months before the convention do candidates begin approaching you? How frequently does the same candidate or his assistants contact you? Is it more important for candidates to ask for your support or to work directly on all convention delegates? Does your county delegation endorse candidates? For what level of office? When does this usually occur? What impact do endorsements have on individual members of the delegation? Does the delegation vote as a bloc? Is there any way to discipline delegates who don't vote for candidates your delegation has endorsed?	4. Provision of technical and advisory assistance in police and fire services. (Yes) (No) (Don't Know) 5. Development of regional (multicounty) planning commissions. (Yes) (No) (Don't Know) *Rating Scales* Q. Here is a list of descriptive words. You will notice that each pair of words is made up of opposites and then there are spaces between them. I'm going to give you some names of persons and I'd like you to tell me which position between	*Checklist* Q. Some people tell us that they like to have various ways of protecting their house from a burglary. How about you? Do you have any of the following? (PLEASE CHECK THOSE YOU HAVE) 1. special locks or bolts on doors ____ 2. special lighting outside ____ 3. burglar alarm ____ 4. telephone in bedroom ____ 5. watchdog ____ 6. timer on inside lights ____ 7. gun ____

TABLE 7.1 (continued)

Illustrations of Question Structure

OPEN-ENDED	FORCED CHOICE OR FIXED ALTERNATIVE	
Q. A few months ago a report came out on smoking and its effects on health. It was put out by the Federal Government. Do you remember reading or hearing anything about it? (IF "YES") As far as you can remember, what did the report say about the effects of smoking? What else? Did the report, as you remember it, have any effect on your own smoking? What? Do you think the parts of the report linking smoking to lung cancer are true or false? How is that?	these words best describes your feelings about that person. First, George McGovern: very sort of neutral sort of very Active ___ ___ ___ ___ ___ Passive Weak ___ ___ ___ ___ ___ Strong Fair ___ ___ ___ ___ ___ Unfair Dangerous ___ ___ ___ ___ ___ Safe Moral ___ ___ ___ ___ ___ Immoral	*Items forming scales* Q. Here are some statements that people have sometimes made to us. There are no right or wrong answers here; we're just wondering whether you would *agree* or *disagree* with each statement as we read it. 1. It is contrary to my moral principles to participate in a war that requires my bearing arms against other people. A D 2. Waging nuclear war would be worse than living under Communism. A D 3. Pacifism is simply not a practical philosophy in the world today. A D
Partially fixed, partially open Q. Generally speaking, do you usually think of yourself as a Republican, a Democrat, an Independent, or what? (IF R or D) Would you call yourself a strong (R,D) or a not very strong (R,D)? (IF I) Do you think of yourself as closer to the Republican or Democratic party? Was there ever a time when you thought of yourself as a (NAME OPPOSITE PARTY)? (IF YES) When did you change? Why was that?	Q. Please choose the position closest to your feeling about each statement: A. Effective leadership consists of getting others to use the methods you have found successful. disagree 1 2 3 4 5 6 7 agree B. Experience is not essential to good leadership. disagree 1 2 3 4 5 6 7 agree	*Rankings* Q. On which of the following committees do you feel your colleagues would most prefer to serve? (RANK "1" FOR FIRST CHOICE, "2" FOR SECOND, ETC.) A. Education ___ B. Judiciary ___ C. Commerce ___ D. Appropriations ___ E. Labor ___ F. Public Works ___
Q. Which of the following do you feel we should do in Vietnam? 1. Pull out of Vietnam entirely. 2. Keep our soldiers fighting in South	*Paired comparisons* Q. Here are descriptions of different kinds of people who want to get elected to the U.S. Senate. From each pair of statements choose the one you like best.	

TABLE 7.1 (continued)
Illustrations of Question Structure

OPEN-ENDED	FORCED CHOICE OR FIXED ALTERNATIVE	
Vietnam but limit all military action to the South.	A. 1. A man who has always been active in a party organization.	G. Health and Welfare ———
3. Keep up the bombing of North Vietnam until our POW's are returned.	or	H. Agriculture ———
4. Invade North Vietnam with our ground troops.	2. A businessman who is running for office for the first time.	I. Taxation ———
5. Other (please specify) ———	B. 1. A former astronaut who seems like a swell guy but has never held office.	J. Environmental Resources ———
———	or	
———	2. An aging man who has served in the Senate for three terms.	
	C. 1. A woman long active in civic causes in this state.	
	or	
	2. A man who served in the President's Cabinet before moving to the state a couple of years ago.	

2 / QUESTION STYLE

Interview schedules and questionnaires can be devised with varying degrees of structure ranging from *open-ended* questions to *forced-choice* or *fixed-alternative* questions. Table 7.1 illustrates several formats for each with questions drawn from a variety of instruments.

Open-ended questions, particularly in personal interviews, are usually followed by probes. Much of the art and science of interviewing involves learning how to administer probes. In the *nondirective* or Rogerian (after Carl Rogers) *interview,* the probe is quite neutral but aimed at getting the respondent to clarify ambiguities or elaborate on his earlier response. Commonly on interview schedules the need to probe is suggested by the follow-up question, "How is that?" But a variety of neutral probing strategies are available. Table 7.2 lists some of these.

TABLE 7.2

Illustrations of Probing Strategies

ACCEPTABLE NEUTRAL PROBES WHICH CAN BE EMPLOYED BY INTERVIEWER
1. What do you have in mind when you say that?
2. Can you give me an example of that?
3. How do you mean that?
4. I don't quite understand what you mean.
5. Can you explain that a little more fully?
6. Why do you feel that way?
7. Why do you think that is so?
8. Which figure do you think comes closest?
9. Do you have any other reason for feeling as you do?

Please note that Question 9 mentioned above differs from the others. Questions 1 through 8 ask, in effect, for *clarification* of answers already given, or for additional information. Question 9 asks for *expansion.*

Remember to ask for further information only after answers already given are completely comprehensive and lucid.

OTHER PROBING TECHNIQUES
1. Repeating the respondent's reply with a neutral probe at the end.
2. An expectant pause with a questioning look after the respondent has made a brief answer.
3. Brief assenting comments, such as "yes," "I see," "uh-huh," or "that's interesting." (These comments should be made in a rather hesitant or inquiring tone to encourage further answers.)

Reproduced from the Public Opinion Survey Unit's *Interviewer's Manual* (Columbia: Research Center, School of Business and Public Administration, University of Missouri, 1967), Section 2, pp. 16–17.

When a focused interview is used, the interviewer has more leeway in selecting previous comments of the respondent, trying to pattern them in an explanatory manner, and then confronting the respondent with the resulting probe. To some extent, the interviewer may be leading the respondent in the focused interview, but leading probes should occur only very near to the end of the session and as a way of testing out new insights gained from the interview. Otherwise probing in this type of interview should be relatively neutral, while still narrowing the topic from the general to the particulars. Probing is ideally suited to the interaction situation of the interview; one can usually not expect much richness of detail from probes that are appended to open-ended questions on questionnaires.

Open-ended instruments are especially useful when not much is known about an intellectual problem, when wholistic information is needed, and especially when the respondent's own frame of reference is required. Certainly when meaning analysis is undertaken (e.g., attitudes, motivations), the early stages of research will require self-reports based on open-ended questions. In the very process of providing meaning data, open-ended instruments can also generate information about knowledge level. Probing often allows the investigator to discover the extent to which an attitude or opinion is informed by knowledge. Furthermore, if good rapport develops in the interview, the respondent is quite likely to drop his guard and offer all manner of information which would not likely be offered in the crisp, mechanical response to fixed-alternative items; under these circumstances reliability and validity will be enhanced.

As with all wholistic strategies, however, open-ended instruments involve considerable cost and the resultant data are cumbersome to analyze. If intensive analysis of each case is desired, sample sizes will need to be reduced and generalizability may suffer. If extensive analysis is desired, the rich data files for each must be quantified, usually through content analysis and coding. Where large samples are used, a staff of coders must be trained and supervised, and an additional source of error is introduced. There have been recent experiments with field coding of open-ended questions by the actual interviewer, based on the assumption that an additional staff of coders may at times be unnecessary; it is argued that the interviewer knows best what the respondent meant by a certain response, use of words, or tone of voice. But such procedures minimize the investigator's own involvement in the data, perhaps prematurely reduce otherwise wholistic information, and decrease the likelihood of serendipitous findings. More experiments—balancing theoretical concerns, controlling measurement error, and maintaining efficiency—are desirable before the field-coding procedure is likely to be widely adopted in scholarly circles.

Fixed-alternative questions are generally better suited to particularistic information collection and are commonly employed when a reasonably advanced stage of theory development has been achieved. They are well suited to questionnaires, although most interview schedules will also have a large percentage of this type of question. Forced-choice and fixed-alternative questions are obviously efficient in the sense that they force the respondent to focus on one rigidly structured problem, and the resulting responses already follow a standard format and are easily quantified. If the instrument is properly designed, coders can be bypassed altogether, and keypunch operators can transcribe responses directly, or a machine-scoring system such as FOSDIC may be utilized. (Even when such economies are realized, the investigator should always scan the completed questionnaires for respondents' marginal notations.) But efficiency usually has a cost in terms of reliability and validity.

Fixed-alternative questions, as many authors have pointed out, require a frame of reference common to all respondents, a known range of logically and empirically possible responses, and clearly defined choice points along this range. Each alternative should represent one of these choice points. Furthermore, particularly when fixed-alternative questions are used in meaning analysis, the respondent may be forced into offering an opinion or attitudinal response where none previously existed; cognitive filter questions are often required to control for this kind of error. Generally, it is suggested that fixed-alternative questions are useful for locational and behavioral variables, and for knowledge variables where there is an objectively true-false response as a criterion external to the respondent, e.g., the first fixed-alternative cognition question in Table 7.1. While careful attention must be devoted to inferences from self-report data on any type of question, special care must accompany inferences from fixed-alternative responses on meaning data. Psychometricians are well along in that task, and it is to those special problems with fixed-alternative items that we now turn.

3 / SCALING DEVICES

Two of the most common forms of fixed-alternative questions are *batteries of items intended to form scales* and *rating scales*. In the former, propensities toward an attitudinal object or the existence of a personality trait are inferred from the pattern of responses to several items whose manifest relationship to the object or trait is not altogether unknown to most respondents. Most subjects are test-wise enough that they can decipher roughly what the investigator is measuring with these items. Generally it is held that such batteries constitute indirect measures; that may be true insofar as the total pattern that emerges from responses, yet on many of the items the respondent suspects what is at stake and can adjust the presentation of self according to his or her inclination. Thus, we prefer to discuss these scales under *direct* self-reports. Rating scales are usually even more direct in that the object or trait to be measured is usually mentioned explicitly and the respondents' feelings are focused on it. Both of these uses of fixed-alternative questions are attractive in that they do not confront the respondent as overtly as a very direct question on the topic might. An interviewer cannot readily ask a respondent, "Are you an authoritarian?" (although if he is then ordered off the porch by a bellowing voice, he may have a fairly reliable indicator of authoritarianism). But a series of items or rating tasks which engage the respondent apparently on the periphery of the question may gain fuller cooperation. Furthermore, the respondent may be unable to understand and communicate fully the dimensions of his feelings, and these tasks may help him to crystallize those feelings.

The most widely used scale construction procedures among political scientists involve variants of *Thurstone equal-appearing interval scaling, Likert summated scaling,* and *Guttman cumulative scaling.* Since these procedures are described in virtually every research methods textbook, we will not enter an extensive discussion of them.[6] We have, however, reproduced Miller's useful summary of the steps commonly followed in developing these scales.[7] This summary is presented in Table 7.3 along with a partial illustration of each type of scale.

While each scaling procedure has strengths and weaknesses, available evidence indicates that simple summated scoring (i.e., variants of the Likert procedure) is the most desirable procedure for dealing with items which might form scales. Extensive comparisons between Thurstone scaling and Likert scaling have been undertaken over the last three decades; summarizing these studies, Seiler and Hough conclude that the Likert method of scoring generally leads to a higher reliability coefficient.[8] Furthermore, they point out that typically 20 or 25 Likert items are needed to yield a .90 reliability coefficient, but about 50 Thurstone items are required to achieve that level. While they suggest that evidence about the length of time needed to develop a scale is inconclusive, many authors argue for the simplicity of Likert scale construction. Rutherford's Monte Carlo simulations of "true score" data indicate that summated scoring models are superior to Guttman scalogram models, as well.[9] With appropriate item discrimination techniques, summated scoring models yield better fits to true scores and they generate scale scores far more easily than do scalogram models. In suggesting the general superiority of summated scaling models, we are most certainly *not* implying that scales developed from Thurstone and Guttman procedures are automatically less useful. Error stems from many sources, and reliability is not the same thing as validity. Thus, many existing Thurstone and Guttman scales may be superior to Likert scales because of their greater adequacy of content.

Rating scales are widely used both to generate self-report data and in the observation of overt behavior. (We will defer some of our discussion of rating scales until we describe observer errors.) Rating scales used for self-reports can tap any of the four areas of content, but most frequently they apply to meaning; the investigator wants to uncover a person's self-assessment or his feelings about an external object. A variety of formats are used in rating instruments.

Graphic rating scales, illustrated in Table 7.1 (questions about McGovern and about leadership), usually involve a numbered continuum with brief descriptions above several choice points. The respondent is asked to check his or her own position on the scale. Sometimes pictorial devices can be used to bring the rating task within the ordinary life experience of the respondent and to make it more engaging. For example, in recent election studies the Survey Research Center devised a feeling thermometer to gauge the respondent's proximity to certain groups. By comparing the responses each individual makes to several groups, it is possible to get *comparative ratings* of proximity or affinity. One of the most widely employed models for comparative ratings is the Bogardus social distance scale; it is easily adapted to proximity judgments about a wide variety of groups and behaviors.[10]

Any rating scale requires full documentation about its measurement qualities before it is widely utilized. Scholars who develop such scales must pay special attention to the selection of end points for a continuum, making certain that they represent polar opposites and exhaust the range of choices. The continuum used in each question or item should ideally be unidimensional, so as to reduce ambiguity in interpreting responses; nevertheless, the *battery* of questions is not subject to this same limitation since many multidimensional scaling and factorial models are available for the analysis of such data. Finally, as with all scales, the objects of classification should be at least minimally salient to the respondent or subject.

One rating technique whose application to political phenomena has become widespread over recent years and whose measurement qualities are beginning to be well documented is the *semantic differential.* Devised by Osgood and associates,[11] this instrument asks respondents to rate an object along a seven-point continuum (+ 3 through 0 through − 3) between pairs of polar adjectives (e.g., fast-slow, big-little, nice-awful). While many adjective pairs are used, investigators generally find that ratings factor along three dimensions: evaluation, potency, and activity; these dimensions constitute the profile of the object. In a recent review of research to date with the semantic differential, Heise points to the high reliability scores and the convergent-discriminant validation capabilities realized through use of this instrument.[12] Objects are positioned on the same metric, and comparability and cumulative findings are enhanced. Furthermore, the instrument is remarkably easy to design, administer, and score. It can be used either in interviews or on questionnaires. Heise suggests, however, that little research has been devoted to social desirability effects and suspects that scores on the evaluation factor may be biased. As more experience is gained with the semantic differential, political scientists should be in a position to judge whether it merits the widespread acceptance accorded Likert and Guttman scaling procedures.

Two other self-report procedures are finding their way into the armamentarium of political scientists: Q-methodology and variants of paired comparisons (e.g., magnitude estimation). Described under "Counterbalanced Designs" in Chapter 3, *Q-methodology* offers one attractive solution to the problem of validity in the measurement of complex attitudinal constructs. It is a self-report procedure *par excellence,* since individual respondents are

TABLE 7.3
Procedures for the Construction of Certain Scales

THURSTONE EQUAL-APPEARING INTERVAL SCALE	LIKERT-TYPE SUMMATED SCALE	GUTTMAN-TYPE CUMULATIVE SCALE
Nature: This scale consists of a number of items whose position on the scale has been determined previously by a ranking operation performed by judges. The subject selects the responses which best describe how he feels.	*Nature:* This is a summated scale consisting of a series of items to which the subject responds. The respondent indicates his agreement or disagreement with each item on an intensity scale. The Likert technique produces an ordinal scale which generally requires non-parametric statistics.	*Nature:* The Guttman technique attempts to determine the unidimensionality of a scale. Only items meeting the criterion of reproducibility are acceptable as scalable. If a scale is unidimensional, then a person who has a more favorable attitude than another should respond to each statement with equal or greater favorableness than the other.
Utility: This scale approximates an interval level of measurement. This means that the distance between any two numbers on the scale is of known size. Parametric and non-parametric statistics may be applied.	*Utility:* This scale is highly reliable when it comes to a rough ordering of people with regard to a particular attitude or attitude complex. The score includes a measure of intensity as expressed on each statement.	*Utility:* Each score corresponds to a highly similar response pattern or scale type. It is one of the few scales where the score can be used to predict the response pattern to all statements.
Construction:	*Construction:*	*Construction:*
1. The investigator gathers several hundred statements conceived to be related to the attitude being investigated.	1. The investigator assembles a large number of items considered relevant to the attitude being investigated and either clearly favorable or unfavorable.	1. Select statements that are felt to apply to the measurable objective.
2. A large number of judges (50–300) independently classify the statements in eleven groups ranging from most favorable to neutral to least favorable.	2. These items are administered to a group of subjects representative of those with whom the questionnaire is to be used.	2. Test statements on a sample population.
3. The scale value of a statement is computed as the median position to which it is assigned by the group of judges.	3. The responses to the various items are scored in such a way that a response indicative of the most favorable attitude is given the highest score.	3. Discard statements with more than 80% agreement or disagreement.
4. Statements which have too broad a spread are discarded as ambiguous or irrelevant.	4. Each individual's total score is computed by adding his item scores.	4. Order respondents from most favorable responses to fewest favorable responses. Order from top to bottom.
5. The scale is formed by selecting items which are evenly spread along the scale from one extreme to the other.	5. The responses are analyzed to determine which items differentiate most clearly between the highest and lowest quartiles of total scores.	5. Order statements from most favorable responses to fewest favorable responses. Order from left to right.
	6. The items which differentiate best (at least six) are used to form a scale.	6. Discard statements that fail to discriminate between favorable respondents and unfavorable respondents.

TABLE 7.3 (continued)

Procedures for the Construction of Certain Scales

THURSTONE EQUAL-APPEARING INTERVAL SCALE	LIKERT-TYPE SUMMATED SCALE	GUTTMAN-TYPE CUMULATIVE SCALE
Illustration:	*Illustration:*	7. Calculate coefficients of reproducibility.
Scale Item ("Agree"-"Disagree" Value with each)	Format for each item is: Strongly Agree 1 2 3 4 5 6 7 Strongly Disagree	a. Calculate the number of errors (favorable responses that do not fit pattern)
7.2 1. Capital punishment may be wrong but is the best preventative to crime.	1. "The Establishment" unfairly controls every aspect of our lives; we can never be free until we get rid of it.	b. Reproducibility $= 1 - \dfrac{\text{Number of errors}}{\text{Number of responses}}$
10.4 4. Any person, man or woman, young or old, who commits murder should pay with his own life.	6. The solutions for contemporary problems lie in striking at their roots, no matter how much destruction might occur.	c. If reproducibility equals .90, a unidimensional scale is said to exist.
1.5 14. We can't call ourselves civilized as long as we have capital punishment.	13. Radicals of the left are as much a threat to the rights of the individual as are the radicals of the right.	9. Score each respondent by the number of favorable responses.
3.4 15. Life imprisonment is more effective than capital punishment.	28. Police should not hesitate to use force to maintain order.	*Illustration:* Format for each item is "Agree"-"Disagree"
[Selected from a 24-item attitude toward capital punishment scale in L.L. Thurstone, *Motion Pictures and Attitudes of Children* (Chicago: University of Chicago Press, 1932).]	[Selected from a 62-item New-Left scale devised by Richard Christie and associates; reprinted in J.P. Robinson and P.R. Shaver, *Measures of Social Psychological Attitudes* (Ann Arbor: Institute for Social Research, 1969), pp. 386–91.]	1. It isn't so important to vote when you know your party doesn't have a chance to win. 2. A good many local elections aren't important enough to bother with. [Selected from a 4-item citizen duty scale in A. Campbell et al., *The Voter Decides* (Evanston: Row, Peterson, 1954), pp. 194–99.]

Reproduced from Delbert Miller, *Handbook of Research Design and Social Measurement*, 2nd ed. (New York: McKay, 1970), pp. 91–94 (exclusive of illustrations). Copyright © 1964, 1970, by David McKay, Inc. Reprinted by permission of the publisher.

giving their own mental structure to the items included in the card sort. It is partially prestructured in that the investigator determines the content of the 25 to 60 statements to be sorted. Yet typically it is a multimethod strategy for scale development; statements are derived from content analysis of media or documents, depth interviews, and "R-method" instruments (e.g., Guttman, Likert, Thurstone), and then submitted to the individual for patterning. The instrument stresses a wholistic rather than a particularistic model of attitude measurement; the individual's score is determined not by deviations from group norms on several attitude scales but by his unique juxtaposition of statement preferences to form factors. Reliability estimates based on item analysis are bypassed, and content validation through judges is unnecessary. The large number of statements typically used and the presentation of shuffled cards randomizes idiosyncratic error related to temporal sequence in the administration of the instrument. Unfortunately, only small judgmental samples can be employed because of current limitations of computer processing capacities. Yet those who have successfully undertaken research through Q-methodology argue that Q isolates primitive traits which should precede (and sometimes render unnecessary) the formation of other types of scales. In short, it is an important method of discovery and logically precedes methods of verification or tests of the generalizability hypothesis. Q has many of the desirable features of a wholistic instrument, while at the same time permitting immediate quantified comparisons along a standard metric. Error from such sources as interviewers is minimized, and from coders outside the investigator, nonexistent. Card-sorting tasks are easily administered and seem to engage respondents.[13]

The method of *paired comparisons,* also originated by Thurstone, is especially useful for proximity estimates while controlling for acquiescence and other response sets.[14] Respondents are asked to select the more favorable of two statements, and the task is repeated across several pairs of statements; an illustration of the method is found in Table 7.1. Each decision, of course, involves a forced choice between one or the other stimulus, and each pair of stimuli is composed of statements drawn from a pool of opposites. Scoring procedures differ, but usually statements that fail to discriminate well are excluded and a simple summation of scores favorable to one of the opposing stimuli is calculated. Neal and Seeman's powerlessness scale[15] and Schuman and Harding's prejudice and rationality scale[16] illustrate two variants of this approach.

Magnitude estimation is similar to paired comparisons in form, but the paired stimuli do not need to appear as manifestly different and the scoring procedure is likely to produce a more precise fit to an underlying continuum. Instead of choosing between two stimuli, the respondent is asked to give a quantitative estimate of how close he perceives one stimulus to be to the other. Then one of the stimuli is given a value and it serves as a standard for the respondent's judgments of other stimuli. Modeled after Stevens' work in psychophysics, it is gaining acceptance in the social sciences.[17]

Research to date augurs well for the measurement qualities of variants on paired-comparison data-collection techniques. They are efficiently devised and administered and require only small numbers of stimuli to generate a wide range of decisions with many choice points (N^2). By careful attention to positive and negative wording and location on the instrument, response sets can be controlled. In most instances scholars utilizing these instruments have presented fairly convincing evidence of reliability and validity. Shinn also argues strongly for the utility of magnitude estimation in generating social indicators.[18] Since paired-comparison procedures can be adapted to multi-dimensional scaling and factorial models, it is possible to measure target populations' preferences among a wide variety of alternatives and to determine how well they feel these preferences are met by governmental performance.

4 / COMMON TYPES OF ERROR

Regardless of whether the investigator utilizes open-ended questions or various fixed-alternative techniques, he must give careful attention to *biases in wording*. Robinson illustrates this neatly with five possible wordings for the same question, running from extremely poor to good wording:

"You do feel the United Nations is doing a good job, don't you?"
"Do you feel the United Nations is doing a good job? Yes or no?"
"Do you agree or disagree with this statement: 'The United Nations is doing a good job'?"
"Do you think the United Nations is doing a good job or a poor job?"
"Some people say that the United Nations has done a good job, while other people say that it has not done a good job.. How do you feel?" [19]

Naturally, as Robinson notes, support for the UN would diminish with the wording of each question from the first to the fifth. Yet the last version would yield the most reliable and valid data; it does not force the respondent into either category (How do you feel?), yet makes either choice socially desirable (Some people say . . . while other people say. . . .).

Matters of bias in question wording are often discoverable upon inspection. However, more serious difficulties exist with most members of the self-report family of data-collection methods. These difficulties can be traced to a common source; as Cook and Selltiz point out, in a self-report instrument:

The purpose of the instrument is obvious to the respondent; the implications of his answers are apparent to him; he can consciously control his responses.[20]

That is why evaluation apprehension, subject role, and response sets are common sources of error in self-report instruments. The investigator must use a number of devices designed to control for these errors.

Some of these devices are aimed at *social desirability* response sets, situations where respondents or subjects seek to present their most favorable image to the data collector. Social desirability errors are usually uncovered by noting inconsistencies in responses; they may be minimized by assuring the respondent of anonymity, stressing the disinterested position of the researcher, or wording questions so that a socially undesirable response is treated as ordinary. It is interesting to note that in voter validation studies, the over-report of actual voting has ranged from 6.9% to 40%; consistently the lowest and most accurate figure is recorded by the Survey Research Center (Michigan), which uses question phraseology most sympathetic to nonvoters: "In talking to people about the election we find that a lot of people weren't able to vote because they weren't registered or they were sick or they just didn't have time. How about you, did you vote this time or did something keep you from voting?" [21] Another strategy for controlling social desirability response sets is to employ forced-choice paired comparisons where both alternatives on some pairs are more or less matched on social desirability yet still differ on the attitude or trait under consideration—for example, "Children get into trouble because their parents punish them too much" or "The trouble with most children nowadays is that their parents are too easy with them." A final approach to minimizing social desirability errors is to confound the respondent by giving conflicting signals about which topic is under study. Selltiz and associates describe Seeman's 1947 study of the attitudes of whites toward Negroes.[22] Seeman presented subjects with vignettes describing a variety of situations which appeared to be aimed at tapping attitudes toward male-female relationships. But the experimental design called for dividing the subjects into two groups, one receiving a picture where the couple described in the vignettes was white, the other group receiving a picture of a black couple. He was seeking to measure racial attitudes, but for the group receiving the picture of a white couple, at least, there was little reason to believe he was not measuring attitudes toward sexual conduct. Although the outcome of the study was inconclusive regarding racial attitudes, it does illustrate a clever strategy for confounding the respondent. Such procedures raise both ethical and methodological considerations, and they require very careful controls to partial out true effects and interaction effects. They also move us beyond strictly self-report instruments to indirect and disguised forms of data collection.

A second kind of distortion of true scores common in self-report instruments involves problems of either *acquiescence* or *oppositional mentality* (yea-saying and nay-saying). Some subjects either become subservient or oppositional to the perceived goals of the study, or, because of apathy, indulgence, or lack of interest, respond in a positive or negative manner regardless of question content. This type of response set can be discovered by examining each respondent's pattern of responses to see whether they are all in the same direction regardless of the direction of wording. It presumes that the investigator has either alternated or randomized the directionality of wording, so that a positive position on the object in question would sometimes require selection of an "agree" category, sometimes a "disagree" category. Writing item reversals is not a simple mechanical task of adding or deleting negatives (not, non-, un-, dis-) or of selecting the obverse of a term. Confusing double negatives can result and subtle changes of meaning can occur. Considerable effort and testing on both judges and sample populations are required to produce meaning that is truly the reverse of the original statement.

Besides alternation of wording, fortunately, the researcher may employ forced-choice, rating, or partially structured open-ended response formats. Two alternatives for forced choice may be used: (1) a single statement is made and the respondent must choose between either of two words, phrases, or clauses to complete the statement—e.g., "The main reason people go on welfare is that (they are lazy and won't work) (they are victims of an unfair economic system)"; or (2) paired statements are worded in the same direction, yet represent opposite points of view, and the respondent must choose one from each pair—e.g., "Clergymen should spend most of their time preaching the Gospel so that people will accept Christ as their Savior," or "Clergymen should spend most of their time working on social and moral issues so that we can transform this country." A variety of rating tasks such as Q-methodology or card sorting—where some items are worded positively, some negatively, and where they are presented to the respondent randomly—also move the respondent outside an acquiescence-prone format. Finally, the use of tasks related indirectly to the object under consideration—such as sentence completion, storytelling—and skillful open-ended interviewing may render this type of response set harmless.

Despite the widespread concern about acquiescence and oppositional mentality in measurement circles, Rorer reminds us that it is not always necessary to isolate these kinds of dispositions from presumed "true" responses;[23] if the measure is intended to predict to behavior in another situation where the respondent is likely to manifest the same disposition, it would be unnecessary to control for acquiescence or oppositional mentality. Again, the substantive concern determines whether a potential source of measurement error requires control; some sources of measurement error are themselves theoretically interesting and contribute to the purpose of the study.

A final kind of response set common especially to fixed-alternative self-report instruments has to do with *distributional errors*. These can also be discovered by examining each subject's pattern of responses to see whether it appears to be primarily a response to question format. Some people may customarily choose the first or last alternative read to them by the interviewer. On a questionnaire, a response that always occupies the same position—first, last, middle, etc.—may be selected. For lack of interest or fear of disapproval, a respondent may customarily choose a moderate response and avoid the extremes; or another respondent may "choose a forceful role" in the interview and always select the extremes. Control over distributional errors can be enhanced by presenting the respondent with paired comparisons where one statement is a control object and the other deals with the object under study, and then calculating the discrepancy score. For example, if anti-Semitism is under study, get scores for the respondent's reaction to people other than Jews as well, and use the discrepancy as an adjusted individual score. This might require gathering data on both interpersonal trust or faith-in-people items, as well as anti-Semitism items, or a social distance scale may be useful. Another strategy would be to select items known to represent widely ranging points on a continuum, and then to present the respondent with several response categories instead of simply "agree-disagree" for each item. A final strategy is to measure the salience of the object to the individual. Respondents are most likely to commit distributional errors where the object is of little interest to them.

5 / CONTENT ANALYSIS OF DOCUMENTS

One final mode for the generation of self-report data requires special treatment: namely, published and private written records such as memoirs, autobiographies, articles, letters, and diaries. All four types of content can be derived from these sources. They differ from other self-report instruments in that they are not typically generated in direct response to an investigator's stimulus. Rather, they exist because of reasons internal to the subject and, as artifacts, they are amenable to later examination by an investigator. Since these are footprints of the past, it is usually argued that they do not suffer from threats to reliability and validity which stem from the obtrusive nature of an investigator's stimulus. While that is true, one cannot argue that these forms of self-report are automatically more accurate and credible than other self-report data. The individuals who initially recorded these bits of information about themselves may have had a variety of intentions; it may have been to keep an accurate record of events, feelings, and reactions so that it could guide future actions; it may have been to protect an individual's place in history through a favorable slant on events. Whenever memoirs of famous governmental leaders are published, the public is skeptical about the credibility of their contents. When a recent American President's recollections first hit the market, an apocryphal story circulated around the country: He wandered into a bookstore and couldn't seem to locate a copy of his memoirs on the shelves or tables. He asked the clerk where it was, and she rejoined that he was looking for it in the wrong section of the store. It was located on the fiction shelves!

Artifacts of this kind, once located, must be analyzed in some manner by an investigator. If many records are involved, typically *content analysis* is used to render the data in a quantified format. Regardless of the number of records, inferences from the artifacts cannot be avoided. Hence, the use of published and private footprints still requires supporting evidence about the degree to which the investigator has followed scientific maxims.

In any type of content analysis procedure, whether quantitative or qualitative, there must be a careful definition of concepts, the establishment of categories and units for processes, actions, and actors, and a specification of how judgments are to be made in the classification of pieces of information. Also the authenticity of the documents must be carefully assessed. The survival of a footprint is not sufficient evidence for its reliability and authenticity, witness famous scientific hoaxes such as Piltdown Man. Finally, if a staff of coders is used to analyze the content of documents, evidence must be provided about the extent of their agreement in classification decisions. In most forms of content analysis an intercoder reliability coefficient is calculated for each variable.

There are many unobtrusive ways to generate data from self-reports. Regardless of the method or technique used, the investigator is obligated to isolate the likely sources of error, to indicate the mechanisms used to control these errors, and to adjust claims about confidence in findings to reflect the removal of error. Self-report instruments are likely to dominate data collection in political science for many years. With increased sensitivity to error and the use of other families of data-collecting devices not prone to the same errors, we can learn to evaluate the quality of data files.

Observation of Overt Behavior

While the observation of overt behavior includes a large family of instruments and strategies, those who use this approach come from two very different methodological backgrounds. This can be seen in the situs for data collection—the experimental laboratory as opposed to "the field." It can also be seen in the degree of structure involved in observation: rigid control over particularistic variables as opposed to very flexible exploration of an unfolding body of insights over time. Essentially, this is the difference between the *experimental method* and *analytic induction*.[24]

The *experimental method* is primarily a process of counting outcomes, after initial counts have been taken and specific treatments within rigidly controlled conditions over short durations have been introduced. It is quantitative research and makes use of a variety of statistical models for the precise calculation of variance and imputation of causal relationships. Observation of overt behavior is a characteristic strategy for providing data on the effects of experimental treatments; sometimes other strategies such as self-reports are used. This approach is used primarily as a method of verification and is applied most frequently to individual behavior, although sometimes it deals with collective interactions in small groups.

Analytic induction is usually associated with field observation. Proponents of this approach typically begin with roughly formulated hypotheses, immerse themselves very deeply in the phenomenon under study—experiencing it as much as possible over long durations—use a variety of observational techniques to collect data, and redefine the problem based on new insights gained from personal experience and available data. The approach to data is flexible—sometimes involving observation of interactions, sometimes questioning informants, sometimes examining organizational records, life histories, or other behavioral footprints. More often than not, the investigator seeks to become an active long-term participant in the interactions under study and utilizes his active involvement as a means of gaining both access and insight. Field observational techniques seldom are concerned with individual-level generalizations; instead they are focused on larger or more permanently interacting groups such as organizations and communities. Findings are difficult to quantify, and appropriate statistical applications are only beginning to be devised. This approach is considered primarily a method of discovery through intensive analysis; since, in effect, it generates case study data, interpretations must be compared with data from other case studies if generalizations to group-level phenomena are sought.

Rancorous controversy has characterized relationships between the proponents of each observational school; we feel that much of that controversy has failed to examine the different theoretical concerns of each method, the state of existing knowledge, and the practicality of certain research situs and collection techniques. Both have strengths and weaknesses which affect the reliability and validity of inferences drawn from them. Although all four types of data content may be generated through them, their most important uses are to document behavior and permit inferences about meaning.

Laboratory situs for observational research usually involve purposefully contrived situations. As a result, structured instruments are normally used for the recording of observations. Often not only the investigator but also a panel of observers or judges will view the behavior and rate it within predetermined recording categories. Raters are not present within most experimental groups; instead they observe externally through one-way mirrors, or they study filmed or videotaped replays of the experiment. The filming or taping device is also customarily hidden from the view of the laboratory subjects. The investigator or an accomplice often locates himself within the subject group to administer the experimental treatment, but his involvement is of short duration and has less of the affective commitment of the typical participant observer.

There is generally little quarrel with the quality of observational records of overt behavior; that is simply a task of giving observers sufficient access to see and hear what is going on; most filming devices capture that adequately. Error is more likely to occur with the *classification* of behavior on the rating instrument. As with self-report rating instruments, judges' ratings are likely to suffer from characteristic errors. Table 7.4, drawn from Helmstadter, summarizes these.[25]

The Bales Interaction Process Analysis rating system [26] is perhaps the most widely known structured observational scheme among political scientists; however, a wide variety of observer rating instruments have been developed.[27] Many of these have been applied in studies of group dynamics, leadership, problem-solving, and therapeutic treatment; research with these

TABLE 7.4
Types of Error in Observer Ratings

1. *Leniency:*	"a tendency for raters to be . . . overgenerous."
2. *Halo Effect:*	"a tendency on the part of raters to obscure intraindividual differences by rating a given individual in the same way on all behaviors whether the characteristics tend to go together or not."
3. *Proximity:*	"a tendency for a judge to describe behaviors which appear close together on the printed rating sheet more nearly alike than they do behaviors which are physically separated by some distance."
4. *Logical Consistency:*	"a tendency for raters to rate a person similarly on characteristics which the rater feels should [logically] go together."
5. *Contrast:*	a tendency "to place others on a scale in contrast to [the rater's] own characteristics."
6. *Central Tendency:*	a tendency for "raters . . . to avoid extreme positions on a rating scale."
7. *Limited Contact:*	a tendency for some raters to observe the subject for too brief a time before making the rating.

schemes is common in industrial psychology and organizational administration. A variety of instruments were devised by scholars at the Research Center for Group Dynamics and are grounded in Lewinian field theory. Still others are utilized by anthropologists for field observation of primitive societies and by cognitive and developmental psychologists in the study of children and classroom learning. Outside of studies in organizational behavior, research based on structured schemes for rating observed behavior has been slow to find its way into political science literature.

Raters do not constitute the principal source of error in laboratory experiments; if they did it would be possible to control error solely by rater training, and inter-rater reliability coefficients alone would be satisfactory estimates of validity. As with all research strategies, the manner in which the investigator has structured the experiment and the resulting reaction of the subjects to the experiment itself constitute the more worrisome sources of error. Laboratory experiments do not usually involve situations where it is so manifestly clear to the subject what is being tested (as in self-report instruments). But the laboratory setting is contrived and the subject knows that *something* is being tested. Simply by virtue of the artificiality of the situation, the subject is likely to make some adjustments in "normal" role and to display some evaluation apprehension. Both behavior and possible inferences about meaning will be affected.

Cook and Selltiz suggest that any of three strategies be employed to control for subject-situation interaction error: (1) use of standardized situations with real-life consequences for the subject, (2) use of subject role-playing in a fast-paced scenario, or (3) use of sociometric choice devices with real-life consequences for the subject.[28] Particularly where the observation of behavior is designed to permit inferences about attitudes, the investigator must make the situation as real as possible and usually not allow the subject time to determine mentally either the most ego-protective or socially desirable behavioral response.

In the first instance, for example, an investigator may call subjects into a laboratory setting, ask for a good deal of locational and attitudinal information from each, and then perform what appears to be an experiment on them. He then dismisses them one by one, having a short debriefing session with each and paying them a token amount. But actually he is concerned with attitudes toward unionization, which he hasn't attempted to measure. So he has placed an accomplice in the busy outside hallway, in a location apparently unrelated to the laboratory. The accomplice stops each subject, shows pictures of stoop labor, workers' camps, strike activity, and efforts to organize migrant farm workers, and solicits a small financial contribution to the lettuce boycott effort—the *real* experiment. The solicitation in this sequence of events is unlikely to seem artificial to the subjects and carries real-life consequences —a commitment of money.

When role-playing is employed, the situation is clearly staged and is understood to be artificial by the subject. But the investigator, who plays one of the roles, must devise decisional junctures unanticipated by the subject and must generate a swift response from him. The purpose is to catch the subject with his guard down so that he hasn't time to think out an atypical role.

Sociometric choice situations with real-life consequences make it appear to the subject that his choices will have significant consequences. The famous "popcorn box poll" could be brought to the campus and students could buy the box bearing the picture of their preferred presidential candidate. But as students say, "that's sandbox politics." Instead a faculty member might structure two mock political conventions where students are promised widespread publicity and where they know that local political leaders have been asked to monitor convention-related activities so that they can recruit capable young people to serve as delegates to the parties' national nominating conventions. In a sense, that could be regarded as an experiment with various possibilities of control, but in a more important sense it is viewed as a real-life situation with consequences. Many similar studies have been or could be done where race-related attitudes are the object of inquiry—e.g., selection of college roommates, grade school playmates, classroom seatmates, housing project neighbors.

The purpose of each of these strategies is to reduce the artificiality of a laboratory experiment. The assumption is that it is more difficult to disguise one's true feelings and resultant behavior when one hasn't time to think about an appropriate disguise or when he must live with the consequences. Data thus generated are probably more likely to be reliable and valid than data generated in a typical laboratory situation. However, a price is paid in the possible loss of control over some variables. In the first instance, some subjects may have known beforehand that they would be paid for participation in the "experiment" and may have already planned how they would spend the money. Then, when the real experiment occurred, they may well have been sympathetic enough to unionization to refuse to buy lettuce but simply may not have been able to afford a financial contribution as well. Any inference of meaning from behavior is subject to confounding factors; conceivably, what is gained in validity through control of evaluation apprehension and subject role may be lost by inadequate control over some other extraneous source of variance. Again, the best strategy would involve multiple methods for data generation—e.g., a self-report of attitudes toward unionization embedded in a host of other attitude items, a laboratory experiment involving role-playing situations dealing with unionization as well as a host of other public policy matters, and finally, the "unrelated" hallway solicitation.

Just as it is not always necessary to control for social desirability and acquiescence, so it may be unnecessary to isolate a subject's attempt to present a socially desirable role behavior. That is a question answered only by looking at the theoretical concern of the project. Because humans are such role-playing animals and because the presentation of self differs in many social situations, the investigator must ask whether it makes sense to speak of a stable "true" behavior which reflects a stable "true" attitude or whether these behaviors and attitudes are likely to shift in different settings. If the latter is the case, the socially desirable behavior for a specific setting may indeed be the true behavior and reflect the true attitude *in that setting*.

Field observation, in its intent, is no less scientific than experimental laboratory observation. In fact, it is based on an assumption that renders the "experiment" inappropriate to the problem at hand. It assumes that wholistic information is required to understand the phenomenon. Since not enough is known beforehand, the investigator immerses himself deeply in it, personally experiences it, and uses every data source available, but particularly personal observation, to interpret it. He views field observation as a flexible, nonstandardized device well suited to discovery and serendipitous insights. It is likely to provide access to more "private" things, since establishment of daily contact through time is calculated to build trusting relationships. Since subjects are likely to behave more normally under these conditions, the field investigator feels he can make more valid inferences about their motives and norms.

But a price is paid: (1) data thus generated are often not amenable to quantification; verification of generalizing hypotheses often requires additional case studies; (2) field observation through time can become expensive—investigator(s)' salary, travel, and so on—certainly far more expensive than short-duration experiments (but at least the highest paid talent is being used, directly); and (3) the investigator, as an interacting affective human being, begins to have a personal stake in the life of the group or community, and events may take on a meaning different to him than to most of the other actors.

Regarding this final point, many phenomenologists would argue that the nature of observer bias is the very strength of analytic induction through participant observation. Every observer sees events through his or her own perspective. Only by immersing oneself sufficiently to have a stake in outcomes, they argue, can the observer share the perspective of other actors in the group under study. Thus, the issue is not bias, but *informed* bias. The disinterested scientist uses his noninvolvement as a professional ego-protective device; in so doing, he is viewed by other actors as different—as obtrusive— and he is unlikely to penetrate the meaning of their interactions. The fully immersed participant observer is neither obtrusive nor surrounded by ego-protective devices different from the other actors; because he cares about what is going on, he learns to understand what is going on. We find merit in this point of view, but feel that it probably misses the point where bias is most likely to occur—at the reporting stage. Just as great men alter their memoirs to be accorded a favorable place in history, field observers show a tendency to fashion reports of their interactions so that they come off as perceptive, accepted, and respected members of the target group. Nobody likes to admit he is a rube. Because of the reporting bias, it may be desirable to have other investigators return to the group later and ask knowledgeable informants for their reports and assessments of interactions in which the initial investigator engaged.

Many recording devices—field notes, audio tape, film and videotape, or structured rating instruments—are used by field observers. Recording devices often change through the life of the project. Initially, the investigator must expend considerable effort explaining the auspices of the project and seeking cooperation. He commonly starts at the top of the status structure in the group and moves downward in his effort to gain access and approval. His initial forays into the group must appear routine, as reasonable "fact-gathering" enterprises.[29] As acceptance grows through time, he is likely to ask more penetrating questions about events crucial to the group and may be able to use a variety of recording devices unobtrusively.

Gold has described four roles commonly utilized by field observers: (1) *complete participant,* where the observer engages naturally in social situations common to the group and his research purposes remain unknown to them; (2) *participant as observer,* where involvement and interaction are as natural as possible, but the observer's research purposes are known to the group; (3) *observer as participant,* where rather formal observation of short duration is undertaken, and the observer's interaction with the group is limited to the formal observation situation; and (4) *complete observer,* where the observer tries as much as possible to have no interaction whatsoever with the group and, in fact, to remain unknown and obscure so that they are unaware they are being observed.[30]

There are, of course, sensitive ethical issues involved in field observation whenever the identity and purpose of the investigator are withheld from the target group. First, the interpersonal trust which has permitted the investigator to have unique access to the meaning of private events has been developed for exploitative reasons. Many investigators argue for the legitimacy of their behavior because they have continued friendships developed in the field and have endeavored to protect the identity of their subjects. Secondly, the observer often seeks to stimulate a specific behavioral outcome so that he can observe other social processes precipitating that outcome. During the campus protests of the late 1960's many of us questioned the ethics of a few scholars who deliberately stimulated a course of action and then analyzed it as a social process; did their behavior differ ethically from that of infiltrators from the local police department who encouraged violent action or drug use among students and then tipped off their accomplices so that arrests could be made? In these circumstances, the humans who are manipulated can be irreparably hurt. While there is no question that much has been learned about social process and social organization through studies such as Whyte's *Street Corner Society,* Liebow's *Tally's Corner,* Festinger and associates' *When Prophecy Fails,* Caudill's *The Psychiatric Hospital as a Small Society,* Blau and Scott's bureaucracy studies described in *Formal Organizations,* and Gans' *The Urban Villagers,* each of the investigators has had to solve or to rationalize away the ethical dilemmas of participant observation.

Participant observers also rely heavily on the reports of informants. An informant who is knowledgeable and trustworthy can not only report events but also provide crucial insights into the meaning of social behavior. Dean and associates have presented some thoughtful suggestions about useful kinds of informants.[31] Anthropologists have frequent recourse to informants, but some of the most insightful work of journalists—such as *The Kingdom and the Power,* Gay Talese's study of *The New York Times*—also relies heavily on informants. Recently the National Opinion Research Center sought support for a "permanent community sample" with informant features to it. Information and assessments on such policy questions as school integration, taxation, and fluoridation would be provided at regular intervals by a small number of knowledgeable informants located in a sample of American cities.

Since the field observer utilizes many techniques for data collection, and since their structure, systematic character, and trustworthiness differ widely, the plausibility of findings can be enhanced by the use of a data quality control rating scheme. First proposed by the anthropologist Naroll, a potentially useful accounting scheme for field observation has been refined by McCall.[32] Table 7.5 presents the scheme, as abstracted from McCall's discussion. Within each category the number or proportion of times the source of contamination is present can be calculated and a standardized metric for assessing data quality developed. The overall quality indices could be generated as the mean score on each source of contamination, and ranges of quality could be established. Although crude and presenting only rough approximations, quality profiles developed for each substantive point could serve as useful estimates in assessing the plausibility of findings in a variety of field studies addressed to similar intellectual problems. Their principal utility, as McCall points out,

TABLE 7.5

McCall's Data Quality Control Accounting Scheme for Field Studies

CATEGORY OF POTENTIAL CONTAMINATION	(across all substantive points)	
	MEAN OF DATA QUALITY VALUES	RANGE OF DATA QUALITY VALUES

OBSERVATIONAL DATA:

   A. *Reactive Effects,* i.e., extent to which observer's presence has affected observed behavior.
   B. *Ethnocentrism,* i.e., extent to which observer's frame of reference as a foreigner caused incomplete or inaccurate observation and interpretation.
   C. *Going Native,* i.e., extent to which observer's sympathetic overidentification with the subject culture renders him unable to reflect on and analyze behaviors according to more general external criteria.

   OBSERVATIONAL QUALITY INDEX

INTERVIEW OR INFORMANT DATA:

   D. *Knowledgeability,* i.e., whether the respondent or informant has complete first-hand knowledge of the topic under question.
   E. *Reportorial Ability,* i.e., whether he can recall in sufficiently expressed detail all aspects of the topic under question.
   F. *Reactive Effects of the Interview Situation,* i.e., whether either evaluation apprehension or subject role has caused the interviewee to modify his report in some way.
   G. *Ulterior Motives,* i.e., whether the interviewee was trying to distort his report to expose or cover something or to slant an evaluation of another individual or social process.
   H. *Bars to Spontaneity,* i.e., whether concern for others present in the situation or possible loss of anonymity limited the richness of information supplied by the interviewee.
   I. *Idiosyncratic Factors,* i.e., whether transient personal characteristics of the interviewee— mood, fatigue, fear, inebriated state, etc.— modified his testimony.

   INTERVIEW OR INFORMANT QUALITY INDEX

OVERALL DATA QUALITY INDEX

is in alerting the investigator *at the collection stage* to the need for additional data of improved quality from different sources.

One final type of observational technique has gained admirers within the social science fraternity—*unobtrusive measures.*[33] Our previous discussion has already touched on some of these measures. In general, they are fairly direct nonlaboratory observations of behavior or behavioral artifacts where the cooperation of the subject is not sought and he remains unaware that systematic observation is occurring. For example, instead of asking re-spondents for self-reports of their feelings following the funeral of slain civil rights leader Dr. Martin Luther King, Sawyer counted the incidence of black and white drivers turning on their headlights in three racially different South Side Chicago locations.[34] The behavior of blacks differed very little by neigh-borhood; half or more of them drove with headlights on. The behavior of whites differed considerably; in a predominantly black neighborhood about as many whites as blacks drove with headlights on; in a nearby predominantly white neighborhood, only a small percentage of whites had their headlights on. From these unobtrusive observational data, Sawyer could infer a public salute to King by sympathetic sorrowers, but he also inferred from the widely varying behavior of whites that apparently empathic behavior varies with fear of physical harm in neighborhoods of differing racial composition. The num-ber of "soul brother" signs appearing in the windows of white merchants during black ghetto riots might also be taken as substantiation for the latter inference.

The range of unobtrusive methods seems to be limited only by the clev-erness of the investigator. The frequency of replacement of worn-out floor tiles in front of each display case can gauge the popularity of exhibitions at a museum; inferences from such data can be made to prevailing cultural values. Discarded liquor bottles in trash cans may tell more about the level of alcohol consumption or entertainment patterns in a neighborhood than can self-report interviews. Signs of wear on certain pages of a paperback novel floating around a men's residence hall can direct the reader to sexually excit-ing passages without his asking anybody. In many cities the race of those sitting and those standing on a subway train heading for the central business district can tell the investigator whether suburbs are confined to whites and the inner city is confined to blacks and browns; those who get on near the point of origin get the seats—and keep them.

In each instance the data generation process is so "natural" that it is likely to remain unknown to the subjects. But in each instance, inferences must be made from the behavior to meaning. Where, on the basis of past research, the behavior is known to be directly related to the motive, norm, or attitude object, inferences can be made with some certainty. Unfortunately, however, unobtrusive measures typically leave a number of extraneous sources of variance uncontrolled, and other evidence must be sought to deter-mine which of many hypotheses is most plausible. In the Sawyer study we were unable to determine conclusively whether whites acted out of sympathy or fear. Additional evidence was needed. But that is no different than the vali-dational process surrounding inferences from any instrument. Unobtrusive measures have as their most attractive features minimal cost and a high degree of control over errors stemming from the obtrusive nature of most data-collection situations.

Denzin suggests several types of relatively unobtrusive observations which may provide fruitful sources of data.[35] First, the observer may study the *body* and *physical signs.* Dress, hair styles, and physical trappings have always provided clues about the nature of social stratification in a society. In colonial days male elites wore powdered wigs and shaved (the bigger the wig, the more important the man—hence, the term "bigwig"); backwoodsmen wore flannel, hides, and beards—and smelled unwashed. In the mid-60's, dress and hair style were a tip-off to involvement in what was then called "the Movement." Nowadays they mean little, but new differentiating physical trappings are likely to develop.

Second, the observer may study *expressive movements* of the eyes, mouth, face, or limbs. When we want to interpret interactions, to decide how others are receiving us, we tend to study their face and look at their eyes. Although cultures differ on the extent to which feelings are spontaneously shown, we usually examine the face for little "uncontrollable" clues about mental states; eyes become distant or warm, narrowed or open, and so on. Camera men sometimes focus on the fingers, the feet and legs, or the hindquarters; anxiety, impatience, or boredom are often expressed by finger-drumming, foot-bobbing, or fidgeting in one's seat. The speed with which people walk tells something about the pace of life in their communities; a swaggering gait or halting footsteps tell something about how people view themselves.

Third, the observer may study *physical locations.* Seating patterns in public conveyences or facilities may suggest something about residential segregation as a community value and racial discrimination as a personal attitude. In decision-making groups, adversaries often choose opposing sides of the room, unless a conscious decision is made to "infiltrate the enemy's ranks."

Fourth, an observer may study *language behavior.* Dialect not only permits some stereotyping of behavior and attitudes, but it also predicts the responses of others to the individual in question. People don't have to be told John Kennedy came from Boston, Lyndon Johnson from Southwest Texas, and Mayor Daley from Chicago; they have only had to listen to them speak—and at the same time tap a number of stereotypes about the speaker's region. Firmness of voice is often a tip-off to emotional states.

Finally, the observer may study *time samples.* A person may not be able to articulate his values, but how he spends his time—particularly when he has decisional control over free time—speaks clearly about those values. Recently a 12-nation comparative study of time samples was undertaken by scholars at the Institute for Social Research; the study should permit inferences about the range of values and dominant values in each country.[36]

Certainly many other studies of behavioral footprints can permit inferences about meaning. A comparison of graffiti in public places is not an unusual way to get a feel for a locale. If the public bathrooms at the University of Illinois at Chicago Circle are filled with colorful invective about local politicians and ethnic groups, while the bathrooms at the University of Michigan contain injunctions about the war, racism, and drugs, something can be inferred about the political cultures of each campus. Wherever unobtrusive footprints are utilized, the investigator must uncover documentary information about the quality of the data-preserving matrix, just as he would with aggregate election returns, legislative roll calls, or archived survey data. It may be, for example, that the janitors enjoy ethnic invective on one campus but are disgusted by it and erase it on another. Thus, a record may be differentially destroyed.

Regardless of the mode of data collection—experimental observation, field observation, or unobtrusive observational measures—observation is subject to errors. As with all collection modes, the plausibility of inferences from observational data is strengthened by corroborating evidence supplied through instruments not subject to the same sources of error.

Indirect Measures Involving Partially Structured Stimuli or Disguised Behavioral Tasks

Self-report and direct observation are the two principal families of data-collection methods and techniques in the social sciences. In varying degrees, indirect measures represent a hybrid of both families. Indirect measures are purposely designed to generate behavior and meaning data from subjects who will not recognize what it is that is under investigation and therefore will not alter their behavior and attitudes accordingly. To engage in extensive discussion of indirect instruments would be redundant; we have already provided evaluative criteria and judgments which may be extended to this hybrid. We will, however, provide some illustrations.

The family of indirect tests, as Kidder and Campbell point out, all involve a façade.[37] Stimuli or tasks are presented which divert the subject's attention from the true purpose of the test. Unlike unobtrusive measures, the tests are fabricated, artificial; like unobtrusive measures, although not to the same degree, the tests protect against some of the more severe errors stemming from evaluation apprehension and subject role. Because a façade is used, the subject often does not recognize a need to play a different role and, when speeded tests are utilized to describe others' roles, he often falls back on his own customary reactions.

Projective tests, particularly of attitudes and personality, make no attempt to hide the attitudinal object but make the subject believe he is interpreting the situation or describing someone else's feelings. Pictorial devices such as the Thematic Apperception Test and the Rorschach Test are widely used in clinical psychology, but their interpretation requires considerable training by a skilled practitioner; also, they are never used as a single criterion for assigning a trait score, but always in conjunction with other measures. Perhaps for these reasons, few political scientists have employed such devices; Warner, Van Riper, and associates' study of the career federal executive did employ projective tests, but they added a practicing psychologist to their staff so that data would less likely be misinterpreted.[38] Other projective devices include figure drawing, storytelling, and sentence completion. The utility of these devices for the measurement of political phenomena—e.g., attitudes toward racial minorities, social stratification, ethnocentrism, intergroup conflict, leadership—has been widely attested by the research efforts of social psychologists.

Disguised behavioral tasks usually require the subject to perform some objective mental or physical task where functioning is likely to be unwittingly affected by dispositions toward an object. Devices here include logical reasoning, memory, judgment, perception, and the like. Again, both Kidder and Campbell, and Cook and Selltiz describe a wide variety of illustrations touching on political phenomena. Two relatively recent studies also deserve mention. In one, Schooler decided to measure ethnocentric attitudes through a judgment device for rating the quality of products by country of origin.[39] Using an experimental design in a survey research setting, Schooler selected three small products which were of manifestly different quality. Then a list of several countries was drawn up where "the product was made." Following a factorial design treatment scheme which matched products (good quality, average, mediocre) with alternating countries of origin, interviewers asked respondents to rate each product along several semantic differential dimensions. Schooler was able to generate both substantively interesting findings about ethnocentrism and methodologically interesting findings about the disguised test. In the other study, which comes very close to being an unobtrusive measure, Milgram utilized the "lost letter" technique.[40] He scattered a number of pre-addressed, pre-stamped letters at locations known to be frequented by specific types of individuals. The objective task, of course, was for one of these individuals to pick up any or all of the letters, note that they were ready for mailing but apparently lost, and drop them in a postal box. Rate of return is taken as a measure of traits associated with different kinds of individuals. Return rate was higher, for example, from sites near "liberal" denominational houses of worship than from those at fundamentalistic churches. There is great flexibility in the lost letter technique, in that both the character of the group to which each letter is addressed (e.g., NAACP, American Independent Party, Chamber of Commerce, Young People's Socialist League, McGovern for President Committee) and the location where they are dropped can be manipulated experimentally.

Indirect tests, just as unobtrusive measures, require special attention to construct and criterion validation. Since controls over many extraneous sources of variance do not exist, a large body of cross-validational evidence must be amassed to justify the use of these devices. To present correlations with self-report data is not very convincing, because the principal argument for using indirect measures is that they overcome errors typical of self-report instruments. Where an extraneous source of variance is left uncontrolled, the investigator must take steps, if possible, to control it. In the lost letter technique, for example, an observer may be stationed near the drop to make certain the wind has not scattered the letters to other locations or that individuals visibly external to the target group have not picked up the letters. Experience with each indirect instrument under altered conditions will provide an assessment of its strengths and weaknesses.

Physiological Reactions

Political scientists are at the threshold of exploring instruments designed to measure physiological reactions to political objects. Only recently have panels on biology and politics appeared with regularity at professional meetings; reported research is not extensive. We anticipate increasing attention to measurement possibilities in this area, not unlike current developments in biopsychology.

Psychophysiological techniques are based on the knowledge that physiological reactions are not amenable to the subject's conscious control in the same degree as are verbal statements. The autonomic nervous system helps the body adjust to external conditions which might produce states such as fear or excitement. Psychophysiological techniques seek to monitor surface manifestations of the autonomic nervous system's regulatory mechanisms— e.g., galvanic skin response, vascular constriction, heart rate, pupillary dilation and constriction, salivation, and blinking. A common difficulty with this approach as Cook and Selltiz point out, is that it can measure the *extent* of arousal but not the *direction* of feeling.[41] Research is currently addressed to this problem by altering experimental treatments known to produce pleasure and displeasure and then monitoring the body signs.[42]

The approach is grounded in learning theory. Through experience, the mind learns to react to various objects in characteristic ways; to respond appropriately, bodily functions are triggered. Under conditions of perceived threat, for example, the heart is likely to beat faster, blood vessels constrict, adrenaline is secreted (increasing blood sugar and the energy supply), and so forth.

Wahlke and Lodge have suggested that traditional self-report and observational instruments have done an adequate job measuring people's overt reactions to political objects and the mental processes by which they rationalize their relationship to the political world. They argue, however, that these methods

> . . . cannot deal effectively with preverbal, non-rationalized beliefs, feelings, loyalties, which anchor the individual's self concept and serve as crucial links between the individual and the political system. These loyalties and identifications are not simply (and even primarily) conscious, deliberately formulated intellectual calculations which the individual can accept,

223

reject, or hold in abeyance at will. Rather they are complex sets of strong affective attractions and repulsions which link the individual . . . [to various political communities].[43]

Instead, they feel that measures which can tap internal indicators of these affective loyalties—*viz.*, psychophysiological measures—should be used. In their own experiments with politically threatening stimuli, they find that while these indicators do not signal large changes in the internal regulatory system, there nevertheless is some change and it is often in a direction opposite to that which the respondent tries to verbalize. In short, self-reports of reactions to political threat are commonly laden with self-protective distortions of a subject's true feelings. Wahlke and Lodge further stress that responses are likely to be situation-specific, varying with the salience of the situation, and that "nonartificial" situations must be devised for valid hypothesis-testing inferences. Unfortunately, the monitoring devices do not lend themselves well to nonlaboratory use.

In still another way, psychophysiological measures are important. They can provide multioperational evidence about measurement error. Just as Wahlke and Lodge were able to document discrepancies between self-report data and physiological reactions, so Clark and Tifft were able to assess the accuracy of questionnaire items dealing with "deviant behavior" through, first, suggesting the prospect of a polygraph (lie detector) test and then administering a polygraph.[44] Substantial numbers of changes in responses were recorded as a result of this multimethod control for social desirability.

Finally, as the field of psychopharmacology increases in importance, political scientists will be likely to rely more on physiological measures. While discussions of this issue bear overtones of Brave New World alarmism, specialists in mental health are turning increasingly to drug-induced control of mental states judged "harmful" to the individual. Pauling, in a thought-provoking article, suggests that properties of certain vitamins administered in various dosages could alter mental states.[45] These pharmacological capabilities raise the specter of "biological engineering" well beyond genetic selection procedures. As the issue is discussed, political scientists will need to be consulted about the consequences both for a political order and for human freedom (the enduring concerns of political theorists) posed by drug-induced states. Both sound theory and careful measurement will be required, and ethical issues are bound to pervade the research process.

• • •

The proliferation and development of new methods of research in the social sciences has significantly enhanced the prospects for increased understanding of political behavior. Almost any theoretical concern can be pursued through some explicit form of inquiry. While every form of inquiry is subject to error, a variety of techniques is now available for isolating and reducing error. Especially through multioperational strategies for data collection, a new level of verification can be achieved. Confidence in explanations can grow only through vigorous attempts to confront the same theoretical concern with data generated through alternate means. Scientific progress is unlikely in a monomethod discipline.

NOTES

1. Stuart W. Cook and Claire Selltiz, "A Multiple Indicator Approach to Attitude Measurement," *Psychological Bulletin*, 62 (1964), 36–55.

2. Gene F. Summers, ed., *Attitude Measurement* (Chicago: Rand McNally & Company, 1970); Derek L. Phillips, *Knowledge From What?* (Chicago: Rand McNally & Company, 1971).

3. Eugene J. Webb, D.T. Campbell, R.D. Schwartz, and L. Sechrest, *Unobtrusive Measures: Nonreactive Research in the Social Sciences* (Chicago: Rand McNally & Company, 1966), Chapter 1; Phillips, *Knowledge From What?* p. 3.

4. See Survey Research Center, *Interviewer's Manual* (Ann Arbor: Institute for Social Research, University of Michigan, 1969); Public Opinion Survey Unit, *Interviewer's Manual* (Columbia: Research Center, School of Business and Public Administration, University of Missouri, 1967); Eve Weinberg, *Interviewing for NORC* (Chicago: National Opinion Research Center, 1972). See also several important textbooks addressed to interviewing: Robert L. Kahn and Charles F. Cannell, *The Dynamics of Interviewing* (New York: John Wiley & Sons, Inc., 1957); Stephen Richardson, Barbara S. Dohrenwend, and David Klein, *Interviewing: Its Forms and Functions* (New York: Basic Books, Inc., 1965); Raymond L. Gorden, *Interviewing: Strategy, Techniques, and Tactics* (Homewood, Ill.: Dorsey Press, 1969).

5. An excellent summary of findings is located in Louis Hawkins and Jo Ann Coble, "The Problem of Response Error in Interviews," in John B. Lansing et al., *Working Papers on Survey Research in Poverty Areas* (Ann Arbor: Institute for Social Research, University of Michigan, 1971), pp. 60–97; and Charles H. Baer, "Interviewing Black Respondents: A Mississippi Delta Example," mimeographed (Williams College, Williamstown, Mass., 1972).

6. Research methods textbooks commonly consulted by political scientists all include discussions of these procedures, but outside the original sources the most thorough and perceptive discussions we have found are: Bert F. Green, "Attitude Measurement," in Gardner Lindzey (ed.), *Handbook of Social Psychology*, Vol. 1 (Reading, Mass: Addison-Wesley Publishing Co., Inc., 1954), pp. 335–69; Harry S. Upshaw, "Attitude Measurement," in Hubert and Ann Blalock (eds.), *Methodology in Social Research* (New York: McGraw-Hill Book Company, 1968), pp. 60–111; and Johan Galtung, *Theory and Methods of Social Research* (New York: Columbia University Press, 1967), pp. 240–70.

7. Delbert C. Miller, *Handbook of Research Design and Social Measurement*, 2nd ed. (New York: David McKay Co., Inc., 1970), pp. 91–94.

8. Lauren H. Seiler and Richard L. Hough, "Empirical Comparisons of the Thurstone and Likert Techniques," in Gene F. Summers (ed.), *Attitude Measurement* (Chicago: Rand McNally & Company, 1971), pp. 159–73.

9. Brent M. Rutherford, "True Variance Estimation: Comparing Scalogram and Psychometric Models by Monte Carlo Simulation of Respondent Behavior" (paper presented to the Annual Meeting of the American Political Science Association, Chicago, 1971).

10. For a summary of research and scoring directions, see Emory S. Bogardus, *Social Distance* (Yellow Springs, Ohio: Antioch Press, 1959). An interesting adaptation is found in Merton Stommen et al., *A Study of Generations* (Minneapolis: Augsburg Publishing House, 1972).

11. C.E. Osgood, G.J. Suci, and P.H. Tannenbaum, *The Measurement of Meaning* (Urbana: University of Illinois Press, 1957). See also J. Snider and C.E. Osgood, *The Semantic Differential: A Sourcebook* (Chicago: Aldine-Atherton, Inc., 1968).

12. David R. Heise, "The Semantic Differential and Attitude Research," in Summers, *Attitude Measurement*, pp. 235–53.

13. For interesting applications of Q-methodology to political phenomena, see those articles by S.R. Brown cited in earlier chapters, and William C. Stephenson, *The Play Theory of Mass Communication* (Chicago: University of Chicago Press, 1967). Experiences with other card-sorting instruments which do not make the full set of assumptions of Q-methodology are reported in Everett C. Cataldo et al., "Card Sorting as a Technique for Survey Interviewing," *Public Opinion Quarterly,* 34 (Summer 1970), 203–15; Robert G. Lehnen, "Assessing Reliability in Sample Surveys," *Public Opinion Quarterly,* 35 (Winter 1971–72), 578–92.

14. See L.L. Thurstone and E.J. Chave, *The Measurement of Attitude* (Chicago: University of Chicago Press, 1929).

15. Arthur G. Neal and Melvin Seeman, "Organizations and Powerlessness: A Test of the Mediation Hypothesis," *American Sociological Review,* 29 (April 1964), 216–26.

16. H. Schuman and J. Harding, "Prejudice and the Norm of Rationality," *Sociometry,* 27 (1964), 353–71.

17. Thorsten Sellin and Marvin Wolfgang, *The Measurement of Delinquency* (New York: John Wiley & Sons, Inc., 1964); Allen M. Shinn, Jr., *The Application of Psychophysical Scaling Techniques to the Measurement of Political Variables* (Chapel Hill: Institute for Research in Social Science, University of North Carolina, 1969); R.L. Hamblin, *Foundations of a New Social Science* (Indianapolis: The Bobbs-Merrill Co., Inc., 1972).

18. Allen M. Shinn, Jr., "Measuring the Utility of Housing: Demonstrating a Methodological Approach," *Social Science Quarterly,* 52 (June 1971), 88–102; Allen M. Shinn, Jr., "Magnitude Estimation: Some Applications to Social Indicators," (paper presented to the Annual Meeting of the American Political Science Association, Chicago, 1971).

19. John P. Robinson, "Reliability and Validity of Attitude Measures in Surveys," mimeographed (Institute for Social Research, Ann Arbor, Mich., 1969), p. 2.

20. Cook and Selltiz, "Multiple Indicator Approach," p. 40. The discussion in the next several paragraphs has been stimulated greatly by this excellent article.

21. *1964 Election Study* (5473), Inter-University Consortium for Political Research Codebook, Variable #0286.

22. Claire Selltiz et al., *Research Methods in Social Relations,* rev. ed. (New York: Holt, Rinehart and Winston, Inc., 1961), pp. 306–8; the original source is Melvin Seeman, "Moral Judgment: A Study in Racial Frames of Reference," *American Sociological Review,* 12 (1947), 404–11.

23. L. Rorer, "The Great Response Style Myth," *Psychological Bulletin,* 63 (1965), 129–56.

24. Most aspects of the experimental method have been previously explicated in Chapter 3. For further discussion of analytic induction, see Florian Znaniecki, *The Method of Sociology* (New York: Farrar and Robinson, 1934); Donald R. Cressey, *Other People's Money* (New York: The Free Press, 1953); Barney Glaser and Anselm Strauss, *The Discovery of Grounded Theory* (Chicago: Aldine-Atherton, Inc., 1967); Howard S. Becker et al., *Boys in White* (Chicago: University of Chicago Press, 1961); W.S. Robinson, "The Logical Structure of Analytic Induction," *American Sociological Review,* 16 (1951), 812–18; Ralph H. Turner, "The Quest for Universals in Sociological Research," *American Sociological Review,* 18 (1953), 604–11.

25. G.C. Helmstadter, *Principles of Psychological Measurement* (New York: Appleton-Century-Crofts, 1964), pp. 191–93.

26. Robert F. Bales, *Interaction Process Analysis* (Reading, Mass.: Addison-Wesley Publishing Co., Inc., 1950).

27. See Paul McReynolds, ed., *Advances in Psychological Assessment,* 2 volumes (Palo Alto, Calif.: Science and Behavior Books, 1968), especially Chapters 2 and 12; Thomas W. Madron, *Small Group Methods and the Study of Politics* (Evanston: Northwestern University Press, 1969); Dorwin Cartwright and Alvin Zander, eds., *Group Dynamics* (New York: Harper & Row, 1953); A. Paul Hare, *Handbook of Small Group Research* (New York: The Free Press, 1962); P. Mussen, ed., *Handbook of Research Methods in Child Development* (New York: John Wiley & Sons, Inc., 1960).

28. Cook and Selltiz, "Multiple Indicator Approach," pp. 43–46.

29. Several useful guides for field observation procedures are available. See John P. Dean et al., "Observation and Interviewing," in John T. Doby (ed.), *Introduction to Social Research*, 2nd ed. (New York: Appleton-Century-Crofts, 1967), pp. 274–306; and the excellent collection of materials on problems of field observation in George J. McCall and J.L. Simmons, eds., *Issues in Field Observation* (Reading, Mass.: Addison-Wesley Publishing Co., Inc., 1969).

30. Raymond L. Gold, "Roles in Sociological Field Observations," *Social Forces,* 36 (March 1958), 217–23.

31. Dean et al., "Observation and Interviewing," pp. 284–86.

32. George J. McCall, "Data Quality Control," in McCall and Simmons, *Issues in Field Observation*, pp. 128–41; see also Raoul Naroll, *Data Quality Control* (New York: The Free Press, 1962).

33. The term became part of most social scientists' vocabularies through the publication of Webb et al., *Unobtrusive Measures*. Other useful discussions of these methods are found in Lee Sechrest, "Nonreactive Assessment of Attitudes," in E. Willems and H.L. Rausch (eds.), *Naturalistic Viewpoints in Psychological Research* (New York: Holt, Rinehart and Winston, Inc., 1969), pp. 147–61; and Eugene J. Webb and Jerry R. Salanick, "Supplementing the Self-Report in Attitude Research," in Summers, *Attitude Measurement*, pp. 317–27.

34. Jack Sawyer's study is described in Webb and Salanick, "Supplementing the Self-Report," p. 317.

35. Norman K. Denzin, *The Research Act* (Chicago: Aldine-Atherton, Inc., 1970), pp. 269–84.

36. See John P. Robinson et al., "Everyday Life in Twelve Countries," in Angus Campbell and Philip E. Converse (eds.), *The Human Meaning of Social Change* (New York: Russell Sage Foundation, 1972).

37. Louise H. Kidder and Donald T. Campbell, "The Indirect Testing of Social Attitudes," in Summers, *Attitude Measurement*, pp. 333–85.

38. Lloyd Warner et al., *The American Federal Executive* (New Haven: Yale University Press, 1963).

39. Robert Schooler, "Bias Phenomena Attendant to the Marketing of Foreign Goods in the U.S.," *Journal of International Business Studies*, 2 (Spring 1971), pp. 71–80.

40. Stanley Milgram, "Four Studies Using the Lost Letter Technique" (address given at American Psychological Association annual meetings, New York, September 1966).

41. Cook and Selltiz, "Multiple Indicator Approach," p. 53.

42. See useful reviews by Daniel J. Mueller, "Physiological Techniques of Attitude Measurement," in Summers, *Attitude Measurement*, pp. 534–52; and John Wahlke and Milton Lodge, "Psychophysiological Measures of Change in Political Attitudes" (paper delivered at the Annual Meeting of the Midwest Political Science Association, Chicago, 1971).

43. Wahlke and Lodge, "Psychophysiological Measures," p. 2

44. John P. Clark and Larry L. Tifft, "Polygraph and Interview Validation of Self-Reported Deviant Behavior," *American Sociological Review*, 31 (1966), 516–23.

45. Linus Pauling, "Orthomolecular Psychiatry," *Science*, 160 (April 1968), 265–71.

PART
III

Statistical Evaluation

Chapter 8

MECHANICS OF COMPUTERIZED DATA-PROCESSING: FILE DEVELOPMENT AND FORTRAN PROGRAMMING

Data-processing is sometimes regarded as a set of mechanical operations to be relegated to technicians who have less intellectual interest in a research project than the principal investigator has. As a result, some scholars will avoid familiarizing themselves with these operations, leaving them to research assistants, coders, keypunchers, and computer applications personnel. This division of labor, while timesaving, is unfortunate because it removes the investigator from error-monitoring procedures at another important point of the research process.

Data-processing is the intermediate stage between data generation and data analysis. Properly understood, it involves crucial decisions about the transformation of the data matrix, for to be able to process data efficiently the scholar must usually reduce it to numeric symbols and transfer these symbols onto a machine-readable medium. The massive data-manipulation tasks for which computers are so well suited will reflect errors made in the reduction and transfer of data. Computers are among the dumbest beasts of burden known to man; uninstructed, they cannot correct the human errors programmed into their memories.

In earlier chapters we dealt with problems of measurement, scaling, and index construction—all data-reduction processes. We also suggested some of the likely sources of error in rating and content analysis decisions—both important in the coding process. In this chapter we will focus on the mechanical operations involved in the preparation of data for processing and in the performing of some simple programming tasks.

Guidelines for Data Preparation

Guidelines for the preparation of data involve a mixture of scientific maxims, common sense, and past experience with intramural processing facilities and extramural data archives.

The first guideline is that coding or data-reduction should be as empirical as possible. Whenever coding is done, some data are likely to be thrown away; the purpose of data-reduction is to sort out and keep only those pieces of information which are essential for analysis. Nevertheless, as data analysis proceeds, the investigator often changes his or her mind about what is essential—on some variables greater precision is needed; on others the requirements of serendipity will argue for maintaining the richness of the original body of information. Thus, for example, a level of measurement, once attained in the original information, should not be sacrificed in order to condense the data file. For example, the investigator may ask a respondent for actual age—normally a two-digit interval-level variable; in coding, he should not reduce that variable to ordinal categories—e.g., under 18, 18–24, 25–30, etc.—nor to nominal classes—e.g., young, old. Space in modern computerized processing systems is cheap. The loss of flexibility in analysis is not worth the reduction in the precision of the measure. This guideline would also suggest that both the scores on each indicator or item and the summary score on the index or scale should be transferred onto the data file; without the former, important data for the assessment of scale properties would be lost. Finally, it is not unrealistic to expect that within the next decade much of the response to open-ended questions will be transferred onto data files in their original alpha-text format; increased memory capacities of computers, refinements in string manipulation languages such as COMIT and SNOBOL, and key-word tabulation subroutines will facilitate efficient analysis of data in nearly its original state. The attractiveness of this final option will increase as more people besides the original investigator conduct secondary analyses on data files. In this era of large-scale social science data archives, the intellectual questions asked of a data file change from analyst to analyst; that is why data should retain as much of their original empirical flavor as is practical.

The second guideline is that information should be preserved in a readily accessible form. If large bodies of related information are reduced into two-, three-, or four-column fields on a punch card or magnetic tape, each column should be structured for its *analytical* convenience. In a three-digit code identifying the American states, for example, the first digit could be a regional code and the latter two could refer to an alphabetical ordering of the states in the region. A multiple-column code for cities could be structured by size. A two-digit master code for occupations could group similar occupations in the first column and use the second column for specific variants of each. The same rule applies to content analysis of open-ended responses or documents. By structuring code categories in this manner, the investigator can determine what level of specificity of information is needed for hypothesis testing and can efficiently select the combination of appropriate columns for analysis.

Third, as much as possible, coding should follow more-or-less standard conventions and formats used by large research organizations. Some of these conventions are set by the limitations of computer hardware and software. For example, although the "+" and "−" punches are available in each column, code categories should be restricted to 0 through 9 because of resulting sign complications in computation. When numeric punches are used, multiple punching of columns must be avoided; one and only one punch should appear in a column. Still other conventions are based on what appears reasonable; the inherent order in data can be preserved by using a smaller number such as 1 for lesser magnitudes and a larger number such as 5 for greater magnitudes. Commonly the 1 punch is positive (strongest agreement) and the 5 punch is negative (strongest disagreement); 0 is used for "none" or "inapplicable," 8 for "don't know," and 9 for "not ascertained." If other research organizations' master codes for commonly examined variables—e.g., occupation—are suitable for an investigator's purposes, he should not develop an idiosyncratic code for that variable. Cross-file analysis, particularly of archived data, is greatly facilitated by the use of standard conventions in coding.

Fourth, code categories must be logically correct. They must exhaust the logically and empirically possible values for a variable. Furthermore, each category must be mutually exclusive; each piece of information should have one and only one value on the variable.

A fifth guideline concerns who should code and transfer data. The general rule is that the more people making autonomous decisions at the different stages of data preparation, the higher the probability of error. Ideally, subjects should transform information about themselves into a machine-readable format. That can be done with questionnaires and machine-scored answer sheets, but many kinds of theoretical concerns do not lend themselves to self-report questionnaires; furthermore, many subjects are confused by such answer sheets and mark categories they had not intended to select. Thus, a more realistic rule is one which builds in error-control devices at each stage of data preparation: if coders are employed, the investigator reviews a sample of their decisions, more than one coder scores each instrument, and intercoder reliability coefficients are calculated. If keypunchers are employed to transfer information from code sheets to punch cards, the cards are punched by one operator and verified by another.

The final rule, which is closely related, concerns the cleaning of data once it is transformed into a machine-readable file. The investigator should utilize a battery of computer checks which can identify erroneous entries in the data file. Especially useful in this respect is a program which will set the value limits for each variable and identify all cases that are outside the value limits; for example, suppose values 0 through 4 are used for a variable; if a

9 appears, the computer will identify that case. The case can then be pulled, corrected, and repunched. Unfortunately, errors internal to the value range which have slipped through both intercoder reliability checking and card verifying are not identified by the wild-punch program. Another program can be employed, however, which can perform logical consistency checks based on contingent variables. As an example, if a respondent is 20 years old in 1972 when the survey is taken, he should have a 0 value (inapplicable) on the question which asks who he voted for in the 1968 election; any other entry would be erroneous. Thus, wherever contingent relationships exist among variables an additional defense against mechanical error is possible.

Attention to file preparation and error control will greatly facilitate primary and secondary analysis of data within the scholarly world. But in addition to the application of these few simple guidelines, the investigator would be well served by a rudimentary knowledge of computer programming.

Computers and Programming

A computer program is, in practice, a set of instructions, usually punched on cards. The set of instructions can be called the program deck. Generally the program deck precedes a deck of data cards, in order that it may inform the computer to perform a set of operations on the data cards. Large sets of data are usually recorded on a magnetic tape first to avoid the cumbersome handling of cards and to save operating time on the computer. Conceptually, however, one may always think of computer programs as if they were operating on data cards, or on card images recorded on tapes. There are many computer languages within which programs can be written, including FORTRAN IV, SIMSCRIPT, IPL-V, LISP, ALGOL, COBOL, and a variety of special purpose languages. In the United States, FORTRAN IV is available in almost every university computing center, and this chapter will present the elementary steps in learning how it is used.

FORTRAN IV is halfway between a machine language and a software program package. A *machine language* is rarely used by anyone but staff members of a computing facility and need not concern the social science user. It is used primarily for the efficient allocation of tasks within the electronic components of the computer. A *software program package* is usually written in a program language, such as FORTRAN, and has been refined to the point that the user can simply call upon the various subprograms with very few instructions. Of the two widely distributed social science packages— SPSS and OSIRIS—the first is written in FORTRAN and the second in a combination of FORTRAN and machine language. FORTRAN IV does not offer the same options in every computing center. Consequently, a program that works on one computer may require certain adjustments before it will run properly on a second computer. In this chapter, however, we will present only parts of the language we judge to be nearly universal. Even so, one must remember that each computer center requires a certain number of control cards to use any language in its reservoir. The contents of these cards are extraordinarily easy to satisfy, and most of them will be pre-punched by the center and stored in an obvious place, facilitating the user's desire to finish the business at hand. When a program is implemented, the cards must be arranged into the groups illustrated in Figure 8.1, from front to rear. If the data are on tape, of course, there will not be a data card group.

FIGURE 8.1
Programming Card Setup

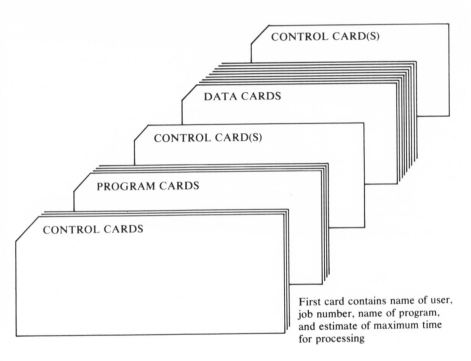

CONTROL CARD(S)

DATA CARDS

CONTROL CARD(S)

PROGRAM CARDS

CONTROL CARDS

First card contains name of user, job number, name of program, and estimate of maximum time for processing

The *data cards* normally have only numbers punched on them, and one number per column. A large number, like an election return, would take up as many columns as there are digits. A code for nine different occupations would take up only one column. The *program cards* will have a variety of characters punched on them—numeric, alphabetic, and special signs. If you examine a punch card, you will note that there are no letters or special signs printed on the punching locations of the card. The computer can distinguish letters and signs from numbers because letters and signs yield columns with double or triple punches, whereas a number will yield only one punched-out location in a column. It is a routine matter (for systems programmers) to create a coding system such that every character can be distinguished from every other character by the use of no more than three punches in a column. A computer program is made up of a set of program statements. For convenience, we will assume that there is one program statement per program card.

The question that seems to perplex most learners, and one that inhibits learning if not answered, is: How, in fact, does the computer "interpret" all of these numbers and statements? How is it possible? The underlying principle is disarmingly simple. It may be illustrated by showing how ordinary numbers are translated into electrical current. The first step involves the translation of decimal numbers into binary numbers. The decimal system has ten digits, 0 through 9, whereas, the binary system has two digits, 0 through 1. The decimal numbers may be translated into binary numbers as follows:

DECIMAL		BINARY	DECIMAL		BINARY
0	=	0	7	=	111 *
1	=	1	8	=	1000 *
2	=	10 *	9	=	1001 *
3	=	11 *	10	=	1010 *
4	=	100 *	11	=	1011 *
5	=	101 *	12	=	1100 *
6	=	110 *	And so on.		

* i.e., next highest number.

Every decimal number has a corresponding binary number. There is actually a special program called the *compiler,* stored either on a tape or on disc, that makes the above translation of all data and programming language. As mentioned, an alphabetic character gives a double-punched column (two of the above decimal numbers are punched); thus, in binary code it is represented by a combination of two of the above binary numbers. Now suppose that we let 0 = "off" and 1 = "on." This is the second step in the translation. The whole sets of data and program language are translated into series of "off" and "on" signals. If one were to place tiny light bulbs at every location and the computer were to stand still at the appropriate point, the patterns of off-and-on would represent the information input. It is then an engineering task to wire and organize the computer to perform processes that are performed with binary numbers. An engineer could carry this explanation further and give it greater precision, but this rough sketch should take the mystery out of computer processing for most social scientists.

FORTRAN NOTATION

A program is written on a sheet of paper, supplied by most computer centers, before it is punched on cards, and it is important that the characters on a keypunch are followed when writing the program. Furthermore, there are certain changes required by machine limitations. In programming there are no lower case letters, only capital letters; and subscripts and exponents appear on the same level as all other characters. The following conventions need to be learned:

FORTRAN	EXAMPLES
letters of alphabet – – – – A through Z	
add – – – – +	$A + B$
subtract – – – – –	$A - B$
divide – – – – /	A / B
multiply – – – – * (asterisk)	$A * B$
exponentiate : A^2, A^k – – – – **	$A ** 2$, $A ** K$
subscripts: B_3, B_n – – – – ( )	$B (3)$, $B (N)$

decimal point and period – – – – .

comma – – – – ,

equals – – – – .EQ.	
does not equal – – – – .NE.	
is less than – – – – .LT.	(these are
is greater than – – – – .GT.	logical operators)
is less than or equal to – – – – .LE.	
greater than or equal to – – – – .GE.	

and – – – – .AND.

or – – – – .ØR.

Set A equal to B – – – – A = B

Set A equal to 3 – – – – A = 3

Set A equal to $\frac{B - C}{B + C}$ – – – – $A = (B - C)/(B + C)$ (these are actual program statements)

Increase A by 1.0 – – – – A = A + 1

Let S = square root of A – – – – S = SQRT (A)

Algebraic statements are only an example of the great variety of statements that can be used in FORTRAN, and they are used here only because they are so easy to grasp. It is important to remember that the equal sign (=) always sets the left-hand term equal to the right-hand quantity, and that each letter that defines a variable in such statements refers to a specific quantity. We will see how the logical operators are used very shortly.

FORTRAN is in part an algebra, and to use its algebra one must recognize that there are two types of algebraic names: integer names and real names. Integer names begin with one of six letters: I, J, K, L, M, or N. The other letters are used for real names. Algebraic names may have as many as six letters. It is only the first letter in the name that makes a difference. An *integer* name specifies that the numbers to which the name refers do not have decimal points. *Real* names indicate that the numbers do have decimal points, even if the quantity to the right of the decimal is 0. Examples of each include:

INTEGER NAMES	REAL NAMES
K	D
KZ	DK
IDENT	DEMØ
K (I)	G (I)
KD (L)	GL (L)

Note that two of the variables in each list are subscripted. Subscripts must have integer names as they do in common practice, but of course the name of the subscript array can be either integer or real. As illustrated before, subscripts can also be numbers. This flexibility of naming makes it possible for the programmer to use names that reflect the variable used, and the names can help identify what the program is doing. It is advisable to keep the names short, however, to minimize the amount of program writing and punching. Excessive use of long names also makes the program difficult to read. Generally, *real* names are used when it is expected that the program will involve many divisions (e.g., percentages) or square roots or when the data on punch cards contain decimal points (a messy practice).

There are three *functions* among the many available in FORTRAN that are almost indispensable, SQRT, IFIX and FLOAT. The first was illustrated in the notation list. To understand the second, suppose you wanted to instruct the computer to drop the decimal point from quantity X and call it K so that 99.9 will be 999. The program statement would read: K = IFIX(X). Or suppose you wanted to place a decimal point after a quantity called K and call the new quantity X in order that 534 will read 534. in the new version. Then: X = FLOAT(K).

Note that the quantity to be transformed must be enclosed in parentheses. These function statements are very important because FORTRAN does not allow the mixing of integer and real variable names to perform direct arithmetic operations, unless the functions are employed; that is, one cannot write: A = K + B where K is integer and B is real, but one can write: A = FLOAT(K) + B

It is also not legitimate to mix an integer number with a real number, an integer number with a real name, or an integer name with a real number. The following are *not* permissible:

A = 8 + 4.2   A = A + 1
A = 8   K = K + 1.
K = 4.2

The following *are* permissible:

$$A = 8. + 4.2 \qquad A = A + 1$$
$$K = 42 \qquad K = K + 1$$

FORTRAN STATEMENTS

Up to this point only algebraic statements have been illustrated. Important to remember is that all FORTRAN statements tell the computer to do something. There are no idle statements. A = B does not mean "I think that A equals B"; algebraic statements issue the instructions "set equal to." The remaining statements necessary to write most programs may be described as:

GROUP A	EXAMPLES	MEANING
The READ statement	READ (6,11) I,K ******	From tape channel 6, read card with variables I and K, according to FØRMAT statement 11.
The WRITE statement	WRITE (5,12) IS,N ******	From tape channel 5, print values of IS and N, according to FØRMAT statement 12.
The FØRMAT statement	FØRMAT (4X,I1, I1)	Skip first 4 columns and locate 2 variables in columns 5 and 6.
	FØRMAT (4X,I1, F2.1)	Skip first 4 columns and locate integer variable in column 5, and real variable in columns 6 and 7, with last digit to the right of the decimal point.
The GØ TØ statement	GØ TØ 35	Go to statement numbered 35.
The logical IF statement	IF (J.EQ.2) I = 1	If J equals 2, set I equal to 1.
Logical IF statement	IF (J.NE.1) GØ TØ 35	If J does not equal 1, go to statement numbered 35.
The STØP statement	STØP	Stop program processing.

239

GROUP B	EXAMPLES	MEANING
The DØ statement	DØ 19 I = 1, 20	Execute statements to follow up through statement 19, 20 times. First time through, I = 1; second time, I = 2, etc.
The DIMENSIØN statement	DIMENSIØN A (30), K (50, 50)	Set aside in computer memory. 30 by 1 vector and a 50 by 50 matrix.
The CØNTINUE statement	CØNTINUE	Continue to next statement or signal return to DØ statement.

The examples do not have much meaning out of context, and here serve only as a reference to the style of statement. Almost any program can be written with the use of (1) algebraic statements, (2) the three function statements, and (3) Group A statements. Group B statements are not absolutely necessary; however, they increase the efficiency of programming to the extent that, in practice, without them programming wouldn't be worth the effort. But since they require slightly more advanced programming, we can do without them temporarily. When FORTRAN statements are written on a sheet of paper, a slash through the letter "O" is necessary to distinguish it from a zero at the keypunching stage. The asterisks under portions of the READ and WRITE statements have been inserted to indicate that you will need to consult your local computing center to find out the exact form they require or recommend.

PROBLEM TYPES

There are two basic types of problems: sorting problems and calculation problems. Of course, most research problems will contain both sorting and calculation processes, but in the beginning it is helpful to distinguish the two types. A *sorting* problem involves the construction of a frequency table. A *calculation* problem involves the application of formulae. To illustrate, let us assume that we have a data deck of 20 cards, one for each of 20 legislators, and that for the moment we are interested in three variables: party affiliation, primary private occupation, and number of terms served. From these three variables, we wish to calculate a frequency table showing the relationship between party affiliation and primary occupation, and the average number of terms served by the entire group. The data cards have the following punches in them:

Columns	8	12	25
Variable Names	IP	IO	T
Card 1.	1	1	3
Card 2.	1	3	2
Card 3.	1	2	5
Card 4.	2	4	8
Card 5.	1	3	6
Card 6.	1	4	5
Card 7.	2	4	1
Card 8.	1	4	1
Card 9.	2	2	4
Card 10.	2	2	2
Card 11.	2	2	9
Card 12.	1	4	7
Card 13.	2	1	5
Card 14.	2	1	6
Card 15.	1	4	4
Card 16.	2	1	2
Card 17.	2	1	3
Card 18.	2	4	2
Card 19.	1	2	4
Card 20.	1	4	6

Of course the cards would have other data recorded on them, but we are ignoring all columns but 8, 12 and 25. Note that the variable names for columns 8 and 12 are *integer,* and that the variable name for column 25 is *real.* Our problem is to write two separate programs, one to produce the average number of legislative terms, and one to produce the frequency table. Before proceeding, calculate the average and the frequency table by hand. Better yet, punch the data on cards and use the local counter-sorter machine to produce the frequency table. These steps will help the person new to data-processing understand the program. Columns 8 and 12 are punched according to the codes:

COLUMN 8	COLUMN 12	
Democrat −− 1	Business −− 1	Labor −− 3
Republican −− 2	Farm −− 2	Professional −− 4

The procedures should produce:

1. Average number of terms = 85/20 = 4.25

2. Frequency table =

		B	F	L		
		1	2	3	4	
D	1	1	2	2	5	10
R	2	4	3	0	3	10
		5	5	2	8	20

PROGRAM I: THE AVERAGE

Since a program is a series of statements punched on successive cards, one might expect that a program is executed by following the instruction on each card in succession. Basically, this is correct. However, it is possible to instruct the computer to jump over a statement or to go back to a previous statement, and certain statements require a reference to another statement in the program. This communication within the program is accomplished through the use of statement numbers. A programming sheet for FORTRAN is designed in the following way:

1. The first five columns are reserved for statement numbers.
2. The sixth column is used only when a program statement takes up more than one card.
3. A program statement begins in column 7 and may continue through column 72.
4. The last 8 columns are superfluous (and will be ignored by the computer).

As an example, we might find in a program:

IF (K.GT.100) GØ TØ 12

.

.

.

12 STØP

(Interpretation: If K is greater than 100, Go to statement 12 and stop.)

In general, we may assert that statement numbers *must* be used in READ and WRITE statements, in GØ TØ statements, and in DØ statements.

Returning to the legislators example, we are ready to calculate the average number of terms. In this program we are going to need to set up two so-called counters, one that will update the total number of terms each time a data card is read, and one that will keep tabs on the number of data cards (or legislators) that are processed. Call the first counter S and the second C, such that the first two program statements are:

$$S = 0.$$
$$C = 0.$$

Next we will want to read a data card with a READ statement, and we will want to come back to this READ statement 19 more times to read the remaining data cards. Thus, we will need to identify the READ statement with a statement number, say, number 3. The READ statement fulfills the command: Read a card, name the variable and identify the statement number of the FØRMAT statement which, in turn, will tell the computer where to find the variable on the card. Typically, the READ statement will also identify a tape channel for the local computing center. The tape channel is the first number in parentheses, and the FØRMAT statement number is the second. The next two statements in the program are:

$$3 \text{ READ } (6, 12) \text{ T}$$
$$12 \text{ FØRMAT } (24X, F1.0)$$

In other words, read off tape channel 6 a card image with a variable given the real name T, and consult FØRMAT statement 12. The FØRMAT statement instructs the computer to skip the first 24 columns on the card, 24X, and find a real variable. For our purposes, there are three specifications in a FØRMAT statement: X, F, and I. X is used to skip columns; F is used to identify real variables. The first number following F signifies the number of columns encompassed by the variable (or how many digits in the quantity). The number after the decimal point signifies how many of the digits are to the right of the decimal. A few READ statement examples are given in Table 8.1. The I specification, not needed here, is used to identify integer variables. I is always followed by a whole number indicating the number of columns taken up by the variable, such as I5 or I3. The specifications must be separated by commas. In this example, the computer will take the number 3 from the 25th column of the first card and give it a decimal point.

The machine has read a card and identified a variable. Now it needs to count. In FORTRAN, counting is done in the following way:

$$C = C + 1.$$
$$S = S + T$$

These are the next two statements: Note that each time a card is read, C will increase by 1.0, since the statement commands the machine to set C equal to $C + 1$ each time. S will increase by the magnitude of T in each case (the number of terms the legislator has served). The job is now completed for the first data card. As long as C is less than 20, we will want to go back to the READ statement for another card. Thus:

$$\text{IF } (C.LT.20.) \text{ GØ TØ } 3$$

TABLE 8.1

The F FØRMAT Specification

	NUMBER ON CARD IMAGE	F	NUMBER STORED IN COMPUTER
Format for Reading from Card Images	99	F2.0	99.
	99	F2.1	9.9
	99	F2.2	.99
	56789	F5.2	567.89
	.99	F3.2	
	9.99	F4.2	(No other F legal unless
	−.99	F4.2	zeros precede number)

	NUMBER STORED IN COMPUTER	F	NUMBER PRINTED OUT
Format for Writing from Computer Storage	−99.	F4.0	−99.
	99.	F4.0	99.
	99.	F6.0	99.
	99.999	F4.0	99.
	99.999	F6.0	99.
	99.999	F6.2	99.99 *
	99.999	F7.3	99.999
	99.999	F9.3	99.999
	99.999	F6.3	error
	.999	F5.3	.999
	.999	F3.3	error
	.999	F3.1	.9 *

* Computer does not round, but deletes places to the right of decimal when cut in F specification.

When finally C is not less than 20., the computer will go on to the next statement, *which is what always happens when the IF-paren quantity is not satisfied.* The next statement is:

$$AVE = S/C$$

Having obtained the average, we may now write out the result along with S and C and then stop the program.

WRITE (5,13) C,S,AVE

13 FØRMAT (10X,F5.0,F5.0,F10.5)

STØP

The results will come out on a print-out sheet, and this should be kept in mind when designing the FØRMAT statement. Whenever a *real* number is printed out, the F specification must allow for the decimal point and the sign (+ or −). F2.0 will not print 85; F3.0 will not print 85; but F4.0 will. F5.0 will print the number and leave one blank space at the left. Thus, the number following F in the specification must always be at least two larger than the expected number of digits to the left of the decimal. See Table 8.1 for examples.

Eleven program statements are necessary to calculate the average, a sizable task for only 20 cards, but essentially the same program could be used for 3,000 cards. Only the WRITE FØRMAT and IF statements would require changes.

PROGRAM II: SORTING, LONG AND SHORT

This section will include a long version to produce the party-occupation frequency matrix, one that is easy to comprehend, and then a much more efficient version that is more difficult to grasp. A person new to programming will probably need to write one or two of the longer variety before moving on to the more efficient style (unless he or she is a frequent user of matrix subscripts). Before proceeding, we should mention that it is usually best to write a program that nowhere specifies the number of cards in the data deck. Programs are often run on different subsets of cards, and furthermore, the analyst may be incorrect in specifying the number, especially when the data decks are large. Better to let the machine do the work. Thus, in this next program we will set up a technique that will work for most problems and at the same time indicate when the program has finished processing card images.

Long Version. As in the previous program, this program requires setting a number of counters to zero, one for each cell in the 2×4 table that will illustrate the relationship between party affiliation and primary occupation. In this program we will use *integer* names, since decimal fractions are not anticipated. We can also set up a counter to count the number of cards processed. The first nine statements are:

$$
\begin{array}{ll}
\text{IA} = 0 & \text{IX} = 0 \\
\text{IB} = 0 & \text{IY} = 0 \\
\text{IC} = 0 & \text{IZ} = 0 \\
\text{ID} = 0 & \text{I} = 0 \\
\text{IW} = 0 &
\end{array}
$$

(Each of these nine statements must be punched on a separate card.)

Now we wish to read a card and name the variables in columns 8 and 12:

```
4  READ (6,8) J,K
8  FØRMAT (7X,I1,3X,I1)
   IF (J.EQ.9) GØ TØ 100
   I = I + 1
```

The I specification is the proper specification in the FØRMAT statement for integer variables. The letters in the FØRMAT statement are never confused with, and are isolated from, the letters used elsewhere in the program. For example, the counter, I, will not interfere with the specification. The IF statement asks whether the value of J is 9. We know that in column 8 there are only 1 and 2 punches, for Democrat and Republican, respectively. Why 9? A dummy card has been placed at the end of the data deck with a 9-punch in column 8. This device will indicate that all of the actual data cards have been processed, and that we are ready to do the final calculations and print out the results, beginning with statement number 100 as indicated by the GØ TØ command. If J does not equal 9, the computer moves down to the next statement, I = I + 1, counting the data card.

Now we wish to distinguish between Democrats and Republicans, and then, if the person is a Democrat, determine his or her occupation. If the person is a Republican, we will go down farther into the program and determine the Republican's occupation:

```
    IF (J.NE.1) GØ TØ 50
    IF (K.EQ.1) IA = IA + 1
    IF (K.EQ.2) IB = IB + 1
    IF (K.EQ.3) IC = IC + 1
    IF (K.EQ.4) ID = ID + 1
    GØ TØ 4

50  IF (K.EQ.1) IW = IW + 1
    IF (K.EQ.2) IX = IX + 1
    IF (K.EQ.3) IY = IY + 1
    IF (K.EQ.4) IZ = IZ + 1
    GØ TØ 4
```

	K			
	1	2	3	4
J = 1	1A	1B	1C	1D
J = 2	1W	1X	1Y	IZ

When the IF statements virtually pin down the combination of numbers in columns 8 and 12 of the card, the appropriate counter is augmented by 1, and the computer is sent back to the READ statement. The process continues until the dummy card is reached, whereby it goes to the statement numbered 100. Now we wish to calculate the column and row totals for the table to the right of the above programming:

```
100   IDEM = IA + IB + IC + ID
      IREP = IW + IX + IY + IZ
      IBUS = IA + IW
      IFAR = IB + IX
      ILAB = IC + IY
      IPRØ = ID + IZ

  1 WRITE(5,9)IA,IB,IC,ID,IDEM,IW,IX,IY,IZ,IREP,IBUS,IFAR
    2 ILAB,IPRØ,I
  9 FØRMAT (10X,5I10/10X,5I10/10X,5I10)
    STØP
```

In the WRITE statement, the variables must be listed in the order in which they are going to be printed. In the FØRMAT statement, the slash

246

(/) is used to skip down to the next line before printing more results. The slash can replace the comma that would otherwise be required. A new efficiency is also introduced. It is not necessary to list every I specification. 5I10 is the same as I10, I10, I10, I10, I10. I is allowed 10 printing columns to leave space between the numbers. The numbers will appear at the right of the allowed space. If *real* numbers were being printed, one could use, for example, 5F10.2 instead of F10.2, F10.2, F10.2, F10.2, F10.2.

This program has required 33 statements. The larger the table size (not number of cases), the greater the number of statements required. A 9 × 9 table would require an enormous amount of programming. However, this program will work as well for 10,000 cards as it will for 20 cards.

SHORT VERSION

In this program subscripts will be employed. In FORTRAN, subscripted variables must appear in a DIMENSIØN statement. The DIMENSIØN statement specifies the maximum value of each subscript, and sets aside the appropriate number of locations in the computer. It is the first statement in the program:

DIMENSIØN M (2,4), IPAR (2), IØCC (4)

This DIMENSIØN statement sets aside one matrix and two vectors—the matrix for the cells of the table and the vectors for the row and column totals of the table. We must still set all of these locations to zero, and for this we use the DØ statement:

DØ 19 I = 1,2
DØ 18 J = 1,4
IPAR (I) = 0
IØCC (J) = 0
M (I,J) = 0
18 CØNTINUE
19 CØNTINUE
I = 0

In English the first DØ statement translates:

Go down through statement 19 twice, the first time letting I = 1, and the second time letting I = 2.

The second DØ statement reads:

Go down through statement 18 four times, the first time letting J = 1, the second time letting J = 2, the third time letting J = 3, and the fourth time letting J = 4.

In total, the matrix and two vector names will each be processed eight times. The first time through, I and J will both be equal to 1, the second time I = 1 and J = 2, and respectively, the remaining combinations of 1 – 3, 1 – 4, 2 – 1, 2 – 2, 2 – 3, 2 – 4 will be covered. The CØNTINUE statements signify the end of the DØ loops. One must understand that in reading across a table, the cells are referenced in standard mathematics in a precise way, so that:

$$
\begin{array}{cccc}
1,1 & 1,2 & 1,3 & 1,4 \\
2,1 & 2,2 & 2,3 & 2,4 \\
3,1 & 3,2 & 3,3 & 3,4 \\
4,1 & 4,2 & 4,3 & 4,4
\end{array}
$$

The DØ statement is vital to efficient programming. See the Appendix to this chapter for examples. The next four statements are the same as in the previous program:

```
4 READ (6,8) J,K
8 FØRMAT (7X,I1,3X,I1)
  IF (J.EQ.9) GØ TØ 100
  I = I + 1
```

The next four statements provide for the counting in the appropriate cells, row totals, and column totals in the table.

```
M (J,K) = M (J,K) + 1
IPAR (J) = IPAR (J) + 1
IØCC (K) = IØCC (K) + 1
GØ TØ 4
```

Note that the integer names for the two variables are used as subscripts for the matrix and the two vectors. After adding 1 to the appropriate locations, the computer is sent back to the READ statement. Finally, when the dummy card is reached, it goes to statement number 100:

```
100   WRITE (5,9) (M (1,K),K = 1,4),IPAR (1),(M (2,K),K = 1,4),
   2 IPAR (2), (IØCC (K),K = 1,4),I
  9   FØRMAT (10X,5I10/10X,5I10/10X,5I10)
      STØP
```

The FØRMAT statement is the same as before; however, the WRITE statement utilizes a way of printing out subscripted variables. The statement is too long to punch on one program card, so a second card with a 2-punch in column 6, a column that has not been used before, indicates a continuation of the statement. (M(1,K),K = 1,4) asks that the values corresponding to cells 1,1 1,2 1,3 1,4 be printed, and then the number of Democrats IPAR(1).

This is a bit shorter than listing each cell individually, especially with larger tables. For larger matrices, it is more efficient to use a statement like the following:

WRITE (5,9) ((M (J,K),K = 1,4),IPAR (J),J = 1,2), (IØCC (K),K = 1,4),I

The new programmer will need to engage in a bit of trial and error with these WRITE statements, but once mastered, they save a great deal of time.

This program required 21 statements, as opposed to 33 statements in the previous program. In contrast, this program would require the same number of statements for a 9×9 matrix, whereas the earlier program would expand to well over 150 statements.

FURTHER PROGRAMMING

The basic learning argument here is that if one is able to write with facility the three types of programming illustrated, more complicated problems will be well within the reach of the programmer's skill. A side benefit will be the ability to communicate clearly with programming specialists. As Kenneth Janda suggests, communicating with a programmer without knowing any programming is like communicating with a statistician without knowing any statistics.[1] This chapter, of course, is not a substitute for a FORTRAN reference manual, a requirement for any programmer.[2]

One problem that stumps most beginning programmers is: How is it possible to read through a deck of data cards, perform calculations on each one, and then return to the original data once again in the same program? For example, the average number of legislative terms was calculated in the first program by keeping a running count as the computer scanned over the cards. But suppose one wished to know the sum of the squared deviations from the average, usually written $\Sigma(X_i - \bar{X})^2$? The program did not save the original information. The X_i values were lost in calculating the average or mean, $\bar{X}$.

To save large amounts of data, it is imperative to use subscripts. Therefore, a DIMENSIØN statement is required, and more than likely DØ statements will be needed. Following are two examples of the technique for saving data in computer memory:

```
    DIMENSIØN T (20)
    DØ 19 I = 1,20            (This is for one column of data read
    READ (6,12) T (I)            from 20 cards.)
12  FØRMAT (24X,F1.0)
19  CØNTINUE
    S = 0
    D = 0                     (This is the remainder of the
    DØ 20 I = 1,20               program.)
    S = S + T (I)
```

```
20 CØNTINUE
   AVE = S/20.
   DØ 21 I= 1,20                      (These statements calculate the sum
   D = D + ((T (I) – AVE)**2)            of squared deviations.)
21 CØNTINUE
   WRITE (5,13) C,S,AVE,D
13 FØRMAT (10X,2F5.0,2F12.5)
   STØP

   DIMENSIØN N (500,2)                (This reads 2 columns, 8 and 12, from
   DØ 40 I = 1,500                     an unknown number of cards, up to
   READ (6,8) (N (I,J),J = 1,2)        500. The last card is a dummy card;
 8 FØRMAT (7X,I1,3X,I1)                thus NC will equal the number of
   IF (N (I,1).EQ.9) GØ TØ 41          data cards.)
40 CØNTINUE
41 NC = I – 1
   .
   .
```

Extremely long programs are usually segmented into a *main* program and several SUBRØUTINES. The main program governs the sequence in which the SUBRØUTINES are utilized, and often the sequence depends on a particular result in one or more SUBRØUTINES. It is our judgment that programmers who do enough programming to find a need for segmenting programs will be able to do it with the help of a reference manual.

Appendix

A. *Statement numbers:*
   1. A given statement number should appear no more than once in the first five columns in a deck of program cards.
   2. Any whole number may be used as long as it does not exceed 99999.
   3. The last digit of a statement number must be in column 5.
   4. Statement numbers appear in the body of a program in all READ, WRITE, GØ TØ, and DØ statements.

B. *The DØ statement:*
   1. The DØ statement governs a range of statements, from the DØ assertion down to the statement specified in the DØ assertion.
   2. It is not permissible to start from outside the range and GØ TØ a statement in the middle of the range.
   3. In the beginning it is best to make a CØNTINUE statement the

last statement in a DØ range; however, the DØ statement number can also be assigned to the last executable statement, such as an algebraic statement or IF statement.

4. It is permissible to have a DØ range *within* a second DØ range, which is, in turn, within a third DØ range, which is, in turn, within a fourth DØ range—referred to as the nesting of DØ loops.

5. Below are some common uses of the DØ statement:

   a. Sum the whole numbers from 1 through 20:
      ```
      K = 0
      DØ 5 I = 1,20
      K = K + I
      5 CØNTINUE
      ```

   b. Find the case with a value of 10 on variable N:
      ```
      DØ 5 I = 1,200
      IF (N (I).EQ.10) GØ TØ 8
      5 CØNTINUE
      8 . . . . .
      ```

   c. Assign rank order values to 100 X-scores and record in Y vector, assuming there may be some tied ranks (a tough problem for nonspecialists):
      ```
      DØ 6 K = 1,100
      A = 0.
      Q = 1.
      DØ 5 I = 1,100
      IF (I.EQ.K) GØ TØ 5
      IF (X (K).EQ.X (I)) Q = Q + 1.
      IF (X (K).LT.X (I)) A = A + 1.
      5 CØNTINUE
      Y (K) = A + Q - ((Q - 1.)/2.)
      6 CØNTINUE
      ```

6. It is frequently desirable to skip over the remaining statements within the range of a DØ statement when certain conditions are found, yet at the same time return to the beginning of the range to increase the value of the index. To accomplish this, GØ TØ the CØNTINUE statement, and do *not* send the computer directly back to the DØ assertion. See example "c" above.

7. A DØ index cannot begin with 0.

C. *The FØRMAT statement:*

1. Perhaps the most frequent error in programming results from failing to line up the FØRMAT specifications in exact accordance with the columns on the data card.

2. Do not specify the columns following those assigned to the last variable read.

3. If there is more than one data card per person or unit of study,

the set may be read as one card "image." For two cards, each having 40 variables of two-column fields, the statement will be:

FØRMAT (40I2/40I2)

The slash allows all 80 variables from the two cards to be read as one image, or one unit record.

4. Consult a manual for an explanation of specifications other than X, I, and F.

D. *The READ and WRITE statements:*
1. Consult the local computing center to determine the appropriate form at the beginning of these statements. Tape channels are specified in different ways.
2. If you are reading data directly from a tape, consult the computing center for the appropriate program setup.
3. A program may have several **READ** and several **WRITE** statements.
4. A blank or unpunched column in a data card, if read, is read as if it had a zero-punch.

E. *Subscripts:*
1. A subscript value cannot be zero.
2. A variable name with two subscripts [e.g., A (I,J)] is a matrix, and with only one subscript it is a vector.
3. Subscripts must have integer names.
4. Subscripted variables must be DIMENSIØNED.
5. Usually all subscripted variable names can be accounted for in the same DIMENSIØN statement.

F. *The logical IF statement:*
1. Permitted:

IF (I.EQ.3.AND.K.EQ.3) GØ TØ 8

IF (I.EQ.3.ØR.I.EQ.2) GØ TØ 8

2. Not permitted:

IF (I.AND.K.EQ.3) GØ TØ 8

IF (I.EQ.3.ØR.2) GØ TØ 8

3. The periods must always appear before and after a logical operator. If the decimal fraction .23 follows the operator EQ, it should read .EQ. .23 in the statement.

G. *General comments:*
1. The FØRTRAN compiler will detect almost all grammatical and logical flow errors; however, a hand check of at least one or two of the printed results should be made. Dividing incorrectly by 2. rather than 3. will not be detected.

2. Of the more common errors are unanticipated attempts to divide by zero or into zero. Avoid this problem with IF statements.
3. Reading data from tape is as easy as reading them from cards.
4. Before ordering a tape from a remote center, check local computing center requirements.

NOTES

1. *Data Processing*, 2nd ed. (Evanston: Northwestern University Press, 1969), p. 107. See his Chapter 4 for supplementary reading.

2. It is advisable to purchase the manuals recommended by your computing center. See also Daniel McCracken, *A Guide to FORTRAN IV Programming* (New York: John Wiley & Sons, Inc., 1965).

Chapter 9

FREQUENCY DISTRIBUTIONS: HYPOTHETICAL AND OBSERVED

Applied statistics is essentially the science of assembling and summarizing data. The subject begins with very elementary questions about how various classes of data are distributed. In common language, we are concerned with the distribution of educational opportunity, the distribution of government spending among different programs, and so on. The large amounts of information available at almost all levels of social analysis force the comprehension of social events to be, in part, dependent on statistical ways of describing such events. This chapter sensitizes the reader to the language for describing the *frequency distribution* of a single variable, and the difference between *hypothetical* and *real* distributions.

Statistical Conversation

A frequency distribution is commonly represented by a bar graph, or a curve that connects the midpoints at the top of the bars in the bar graph when the categories are too numerous. Most of the conversation about the shape of the area produced by a frequency distribution relates to variables that have a clear dimension, low to high, whereby the categories used for graphic display such as in a bar graph have an inherent order. The conversation embodies a terminology that is not always precise, but serves to make rough distinctions between different kinds of distributions. Most commonly, distributions are referred to as symmetrical or asymmetrical, and as unimodal, bimodal or multimodal. By *symmetrical* it is meant that at some point a vertical line can be drawn through the area under the curve so that each side of the line has roughly the same shape and same amount of area. If the distribution is perfectly symmetrical, the vertical line will pass through the *mean* value and *median* value of the distribution. Distributions of raw data are almost never perfectly symmetrical.

If a distribution is roughly symmetrical, it may be *unimodal,* meaning that it exhibits one prominent peak, or it may exhibit two or more peaks, as do *bimodal* and *multimodal* curves, respectively. The distribution may even be *rectangular* or *flat,* meaning that approximately the same number of cases fall in each category. If the distribution is unimodal, it may have a very high peak, sometimes called *leptokurtic,* it may have a rather broad and flattened peak, sometimes called *platykurtic,* or it may be *normal,* meaning that it corresponds rather closely to a well-known probability distribution. Figure 9.1 illustrates a variety of curves that are roughly symmetrical.

FIGURE 9.1
Symmetrical Distributions

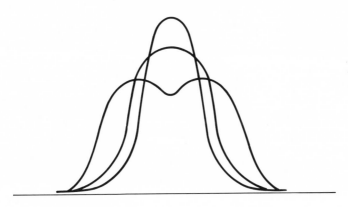

FIGURE 9.2
Asymmetrical Distributions

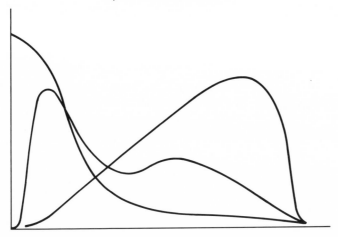

Asymmetrical curves can also be unimodal, bimodal or multimodal. An asymmetrical curve is either *skewed to the left* or *skewed to the right,* regardless of the number of observable modes. Examples are shown in Figure 9.2. It is not possible to draw a vertical line through an asymmetrical distribution such that the area on one side of the line is a rough mirror image of its counterpart.

The above italicized terms are the basic linguistic tools for discussing frequency distributions. They provide shortcut ways of evaluating distributions. The shape of the distribution is an important factor in the application and interpretation of statistical formulae. Most statistical inference is affected by distributional characteristics; therefore, it is important to go beyond this preliminary stage. Generally, distributional characteristics are divided into measures of central tendency and measures of dispersion. The characteristics of *cumulative* frequency distributions can also be considered.

Measures of Central Tendency

The mean, the median, and the mode are the three primary measures of central tendency. The *mode* is the category in a frequency distribution that contains the most cases. The *median* is the value in a frequency distribution that divides the cases in two. There will be 50% of the cases to the left of the median and 50% to the right. The *mean* is calculated by summing all of the values in a distribution and then dividing by the number of cases.

To illustrate, we may take the per capita total state expenditures for each of the contiguous 48 states. As in Table 9.1, the states can be ordered according to the expenditure values. By statistical convention, the number of cases, or number of states in this example, is symbolized by N (the lower case n is used for samples). A single value is symbolized as X_i, where i in this example may range from 1 to 48. We may note that $N = 48$, and that for Nevada, $X_i = 277.06$. To sum all of the X_i values, the following notation is used:

$$\sum_{i=1}^{N=48} X_i = 8706.11$$

where the large sigma means "sum," the note below the sigma gives the first value of i, and the N above the sigma gives the last value of i, which in this example is 48. By convention, when all of the values in a distribution are summed, the notation may be abbreviated to read:

$$\Sigma X_i = 8706.11$$

The mean is found by summing all of the values and dividing by N, so that

$$\frac{\Sigma X_i}{N} = \frac{8706.11}{48} = 181.38$$

Because the mean is employed so often in statistical work, the symbol used to designate the values, in this case X, can serve to connote the mean by placing a bar over it. Thus $\overline{X}$ is the mean. Any symbol may refer to the values, such as X, Y, or Z. Once selected, that symbol with a bar over it refers to the mean of the distribution. The mean,

$$\overline{X} = \frac{\Sigma\, X_i}{N} = 181.38$$

In Table 9.1 the mean value falls between the listed values for Connecticut and West Virginia, or the 21st and 22nd states as they are ordered. The median value will fall between New York and Rhode Island, or the 24th and 25th states. The median is the midpoint between the two values for these states. The states are first ranked; then, using the ranks to locate the median, it is necessary to calculate:

$$\frac{N}{2} + .5$$

With 48 states, the median rank is 24.5. Since no state has this rank, the corresponding value must be interpolated so that it is halfway between the adjacent values. Thus,

Median $= 169.71 + \frac{1}{2}\,(176.46 - 169.71) = 173.08$

The median is substantially less than the mean (over 8 units), a fact that indicates that the frequency distribution is not symmetrical.

The frequency distribution is more readily observed by creating a set of categories of equal length along the per capita expenditure continuum. As a general rule, we would suggest that the number of categories not exceed $N/4$; otherwise, it may be difficult to observe the pattern. The procedure requires first a decision as to the number of desired categories, symbolized C. The *length* of the interval for each category in most problems may be calculated from the equation:

$$L = \frac{X_{max} - X_{min}}{C - 1} \tag{9.1}$$

where X_{max} is the maximum observed value of X, and X_{min} is the minimum observed value of X. If in our example we desire 11 categories to display the frequency distribution,

$$L = \frac{283.69 - 110.47}{11 - 1} = \frac{173.22}{10} = 17.322$$

To apply the interval length to the data, a starting point must be selected, usually either the mean or one-half an interval below the lowest value. Using the second alternative, the frequency distribution in Table 9.2 is constructed.

This table illustrates that the distribution is skewed. The range of the modal category, 153.775-171.097, includes neither the mean nor the median. In general, we may conclude that when a distribution is asymmetrical, *typically,*

TABLE 9.1
State Expenditures Per Capita, 1962

STATES	X_i	
1. Wyoming	283.69	
2. Nevada	277.06	
3. Vermont	255.10	
4. Louisiana	251.74	
5. Washington	249.62	
6. Delaware	246.53	
7. New Mexico	238.68	
8. Oregon	221.18	
9. California	218.30	
10. North Dakota	214.29	
11. Kentucky	209.25	
12. Utah	208.60	
13. Arizona	205.45	
14. Oklahoma	203.64	
15. Montana	196.43	
16. Michigan	195.87	
17. Colorado	192.13	
18. Idaho	188.46	
19. South Dakota	186.57	
20. Minnesota	182.76	
21. Connecticut	182.12	
	Mean = $\overline{X}$	181.38
22. West Virginia	180.73	
23. Maryland	179.28	
24. New York	176.46	
	Median	173.08
25. Rhode Island	169.71	
26. Wisconsin	168.92	
27. Mississippi	168.34	
28. Alabama	164.19	
29. Maine	163.19	
30. Iowa	161.25	
31. Kansas	160.06	
32. Massachusetts	159.58	
33. North Carolina	157.52	
34. Georgia	156.20	
35. Arkansas	155.14	
36. New Hampshire	151.71	
37. Pennsylvania	145.92	
38. Indiana	144.87	
39. Tennessee	142.97	
40. South Carolina	141.80	
41. Virginia	141.56	
42. Missouri	140.61	
43. Texas	137.21	
44. Florida	135.79	
45. Illinois	131.33	
46. Ohio	130.34	
47. Nebraska	125.49	
48. New Jersey	110.47	
$N = 48$	$S_i = 8706.11$	

Data appear in Ira Sharkansky, *Spending in the American States* (Chicago: Rand McNally & Company, 1968), pp. 101–2; they have been rearranged for this purpose.

TABLE 9.2

Frequency Distribution, State Expenditures Per Capita, 1962

INTERVAL (Size of Interval: 17.322)		FREQUENCY
275.029 – (292.351)		2—
257.707 – 275.029		0
240.385 – 257.707		4——
223.063 – 240.385		1–
205.741 – 223.063		5————
188.419 – 205.741		6————
171.097 – 188.419		6————
153.775 – 171.097	Mode	11—————————
136.453 – 153.775		8———————
119.131 – 136.453		4——
(101.809) – 119.131		1–

and only typically, the mean, median, and mode will give substantially different values. This should not lead one to conclude, however, that the degree to which they differ is an appropriate measure of asymmetry. In fact highly asymmetrical distributions can be contrived to yield the same mean, median, and mode. Comparing the three measures of central tendency will reveal relatively little about a distribution. A more fruitful line of inquiry will incorporate appropriate measures of dispersion. In developing measures of dispersion, it will be helpful to consider the different types of data that may be summarized by both measures of central tendency and measures of dispersion.

Dispersion in Nominal Classifications

A nominal classification is usually created for the immediate purpose of observing the frequencies with which people or things fall into different categories. Occupations, religions, and types of government or policy are common illustrations of this kind. The categories can be rearranged in any order. There is no underlying dimension that necessitates that one category precede or follow any other category. For display purposes, a bar graph is almost always given, with the categories listed either alphabetically or according to the number of observations that fall into each category. Distributions in nominal classifications must be treated in a special way; they cannot be treated like income distributions, test scores on an examination, voting percentages, and other dimensional arrays.

To describe dispersion in nominal classifications, one must ordinarily have a reason. For example, one may wish to know whether over a period of 20 years the occupational backgrounds of elected public officials have become more or less widely distributed among various categories. Or perhaps a legislature has implemented a committee reorganization, and now one wishes to know whether the quantity of bills assigned to the committees is more or less equitable than before. In these two examples, we may state that there is *no* dispersion if:

1. All public officials have the same occupational background;
2. All bills are assigned to a single committee.

By the same token, there is *total* dispersion if:

1. An equal number of public officials come from each of several occupational categories;
2. Each committee receives the same number of bills.

For both practical and statistical reasons, of course, we would want to describe exactly how much dispersion characterizes the distributions. The measure introduced here will be called the *nominal coefficient of dispersion*. It ranges between 0 and 1–0 indicating no dispersion, and 1, total dispersion. The coefficient may be expressed verbally as follows:

$$CD = 1 - \frac{\text{Summed absolute deviation from average frequency}}{\text{Maximum absolute deviation from average frequency}}$$

The entire formula reads:

$$CD = 1 - \frac{\sum \left| \frac{N}{C} - f_i \right|}{2 \left(N - \frac{N}{C} \right)} \tag{9.2}$$

where N = the total number of cases in the distribution;

C = the number of categories;

f_i = the number of cases in a particular category;

| | connotes that the absolute differences in the contained expression are summed (ignore resulting minus signs).

To illustrate the calculations, we can first take a hypothetical example, and then consider a set of actual data.

In the hypothetical case we have five occupational categories into which 50 state legislators are classified. The frequencies exhibit the following distribution:

1. Lawyers	20
2. Farmers	15
3. Business managers and owners	10
4. Sales and office clerks	2
5. Laborers	3
	$\overline{50} = N$

Since there are five categories, $C = 5$ and $N/C = 10$. There are five values of f_i: 20, 15, 10, 2, and 3. The numerator in the right-hand term of the formula requires that we sum the absolute differences between N/C and each value of f_i, such that

$$
\begin{aligned}
20 - 10 &= 10 \\
15 - 10 &= 5 \\
10 - 10 &= 0 \\
2 - 10 &= 8 \\
3 - 10 &= \underline{7} \\
30 &= \Sigma |N/C - f_i|
\end{aligned}
$$

Substituting in the formula, we have:

$$
CD = 1 - \frac{30}{2\,(50 - 10)} = 1 - .375 = .625
$$

Switching to the second example, we may note that the formula allows one to compare the dispersion in sets of data that have been categorized differently. The data in Table 9.3 are drawn from legislative records before and after a major committee reduction and reorganization in a state legislature. Considering only the number of bills assigned to each committee in two different legislative sessions, the coefficient of dispersion indicates that the reorganization had the effect of distributing the workload more evenly among the standing committees. The coefficient increases from .48 to .57.

The reader might consider in regard to these examples how inadequate the *mode* is in describing the distributions. The mode is useful only if there are two or three categories or when there is very little dispersion. Most statistics texts avoid the discussion of dispersion for nominal classifications. This is probably due in part to historical circumstances, whereby statistical reasoning grew out of the need to summarize the relationships between variables having metric qualities and out of the need to make direct estimates of sampling error. The equation for the coefficient of dispersion is not very useful for advanced statistical analysis.

Generally, it is suggested that the shape of a distribution for a nominal classification can be best portrayed visually by ordering the categories according to frequency count, beginning with the category containing the fewest cases, and ending with the one containing the most cases. The next step is to draw a bar for each category that represents in altitude its frequency. Draw a horizontal line across the bar chart at the mean or average altitude. The vertical distances between the horizontal line and the tops of the bars provide the basis for measuring dispersion. It should be understood that if the frequency distribution produces a perfect rectangle, total dispersion exists. Given these procedures, the rectangle is the only symmetrical distribution possible. In a sense, the coefficient of dispersion is a measure of symmetry, and $1 - CD$ could be a measure of asymmetry.

TABLE 9.3

Measuring the Effect of a Committee Reorganization
on the Distribution of Legislative Bills

(Nominal Coefficient of Dispersion)

1959	NUMBER OF ASSIGNED BILLS		1961
Lake County	1	17	Lake County
Agriculture	6	9	Marion County
Aviation	2	5	Agriculture
Banks-Trust Co.-Savings Assoc.	9	0	Appointments and Claims
Benevolent & Penal Institutions	25	13	Benevolent & Penal Institutions
Cities and Towns	28	29	Cities and Towns
City of Indianapolis	7	3	Corporations
Claims-Salaries-Expenditures	1	48	County & Township Business
Congressional Apportionment	0	27	Education
Corporations	10	11	Elections
County & Township Business	43	7	Financial Institutions
Education	30	7	Insurance
Elections	6	0	Interstate Cooperation
Employing Assistants and Debt	0	78	Judiciary A
Federal Relations	2	18	Judiciary B
Finance	27	6	Labor
Insurance	8	7	Legislative Apportionment
Interstate Cooperation	1	1	Legislative Procedures
Joint Rules	0	5	Military Affairs & Memorials
Judiciary A	68	12	Resources and Conservation
Judiciary B	7	28	Courts and Criminal Code
Labor	17	19	Public Health
Legislative Apportionment	3	17	Public Policy
Manufacturers	1	9	Public Safety
Military-Veterans Affairs	3	5	Roads
Mines and Mining	0	0	Rules
Resources and Conservation	20	5	Transportation
Courts and Criminal Code	19	50	Finance
Bill Phraseology	0	6	Welfare and Social Security
Public Health	22	$442 = N$	$C = 29$
Public Policy	29		
Public Printing	0		
Public Safety	26		
Railroads	1		
Roads	19		
Rules	0		
Social Security	5		
War Memorials	0		
Supervision of Journal	0		
$C = 39$	$466 = N$		

$$CD = 1 - \frac{356.8}{2(442 - 15.2)}$$

$$= 1 - .43$$

$$= .57$$

$$CD = 1 - \frac{455.8}{2(446 - 11.4)}$$

$$= 1 - .52$$

$$= .48$$

There is one other closely related statistic that may be employed as a measure of dispersion in nominal classifications. It is called the *Gini Index of Inequality*. The calculations are more complex and it will be introduced later in this chapter. It will be shown that the *Gini Index* value can be treated as an estimate of dispersion.

Dispersion in Dimensional Variables

In social science work it is the general practice to divide dimensional variables into two types—ordinal and interval—according to the way in which numbers are assigned in the process of measurement. For ordinal variables the numbers are meant to be ranks and nothing more. For interval variables the assigned numbers connote exact distances. Underlying this distinction is the notion that there are different types of measurement scales. A brief review of these scales will help place statistical interpretation in perspective.

Ratio scales, more common to the physical sciences, have the most sophisticated mathematical properties. On such scales, absolute zero is known, and the distances between numbers on the scales are interpreted literally. Length is based on a ratio scale. The distance between 1 meter and 2 meters is the same as the distance between 3 meters and 4 meters. Since we know where zero is, we can say that 2 meters divided by 4 meters equals 4 meters divided by 8 meters. Money can be treated the same way.

Interval scales do not have a known zero value, but as in ratio scales, the distances between numbers are exactly specified by those numbers. The Fahrenheit temperature scale, for example, uses an artificial zero. It would not be appropriate to say that 10 degrees is to 20 degrees what 40 degrees is to 80 degrees. The distances between 10 and 20 degrees and between 70 and 80 degrees, however, are identical. If the location of absolute zero is *not* known on a scale, the actual points on the scale cannot be assigned absolute quantities. For example, either of the two sets of numbers below might be the true values if zero has not been located:

	Mean					
	.	.	.	.	.	.
(1) *True Values?*	1	2	3	4	5	6
(2) *True Values?*	201	202	203	204	205	206

Even though $2 - 1 = 202 - 201 = 4 - 3 = 204 - 203$, and the mean falls at the same point on the scale, the lack of a zero origin makes it inappropriate to use the numbers in ratios, such as 1/2 and 201/202 or 2/4 and 202/204.

Ordinal scales lack the property of "known" distances between the numbers employed. In these scales the numbers convey order and not distance. So if we were to rank presidential candidates by personal appeal, we do not necessarily mean that each, in turn, is equidistant from the next in appeal. In fact, the following might be more true:

	High Appeal						Low Appeal
	.	. .	.	.	. .		.
Candidates:	A	B C D	E		F G		H
Ranks:	1	2 3 4	5		6 7		8

Observe that addition and subtraction of such numbers could be highly misleading, but that the median rank of 4.5 would be an appropriate division of the eight cases. The mean requires addition, and although identical to the median in this example, its calculation is not warranted.

It is also possible that an ordinal scale will have an absolute zero origin, but this would have no impact on statistical application at the present time.

In social science statistical application, variables having ratio or interval scales are treated in the same way, that is, as if they were interval scales. Thus, when texts refer to nominal, ordinal, and interval variables, they are reflecting the general guidelines along which statistical formulae have been developed. Measures of central tendency and dispersion have been divided into these three categories so as not to violate the meaning of numbers generated by the measurement procedure. Later we shall see that statistical correlations and tests are divided up according to the types of variables that are compared.

Measurement of dispersion in ordinal variables is informative primarily when there are many tied ranks. It has been our observation that ordinal scales or variables appearing in the literature of political science tend to be one of two extremes: either the distribution will exhibit almost no tied ranks (or none) or it will exhibit a great number of tied ranks. The reason for this relates to the ways in which ordinal scales are created. Frequently the analyst will have crudely devised numeric estimates, say relating to a characteristic of countries. The analyst is more certain that the countries have been ordered correctly than he is of the precise numeric estimates, and therefore he converts the scale to an ordinal one by ranking the countries accordingly. Obviously, there will be very few tied ranks in a typical conversion of this sort. The contrasting occasion arises when the data warrant only a very roughly segmented dimension, such as high, medium, and low, or very favorable, favorable, neutral, unfavorable, and very unfavorable.

In a more precise way, ordinal scales or variables can be clarified by stating the ratio of the number of cases to the number of unique ranks, or

$$\frac{N}{\text{Number of Ranks}}$$

where at least one case is assigned to each rank. Thus, when the value of the ratio is near 1.0, the distribution is nearly rectangular and needs no special technique for describing dispersion. As the value of the ratio increases, so does the latitude for different kinds of distributions and the need for a measure of dispersion. The most common ordinal measures of dispersion are called the *interquartile range* and the *interdecile range*. The first measure gives the range of ranks covered by the middle 50% of the cases, excluding the top 25% and the bottom 25%. The second measure gives the range of ranks corresponding to the middle 80% of the cases. The measures are seldom used, but would be appropriate, for example, in summarizing dispersion based on the results of Likert or Guttman attitude items. The scores from these attitude scaling techniques are sometimes treated as interval numbers, but probably the inferences in such analyses are more valid when the scores are treated as numeric ranks. There is substantial evidence that the distribution of scores, and thereby the distances between scores, is influenced by the structure of the stimuli that evoke responses (see discussion of "alternate wordings" in Chapter 7).

To illustrate the measures, we take two hypothetical sets of data, let us say, gathered from 100 respondents in each of two studies of different administrative agencies. The respondents are each assigned a rank from 0 to 16, based on their responses to four Likert scale items relating to the degree to which they think the agency is accomplishing its goals. The distribution is as follows:

RANKS (OR SCORES)	STUDY A (NO. OF RESPONDENTS)	STUDY B (NO. OF RESPONDENTS)
0	4	1
1	6	1
2	12	2
3	13	5
4	20	3
5	10	6
6	8	11
7	6	12
8	3	20
9	4	13
10	3	8
11	1	6
12	4	4
13	2	2
14	1	3
15	2	2
16	1	1
	100	100

Quartiles, deciles, percentiles and the median are all calculated by the same procedure, since they may all be expressed in percentiles. Note that the

median = the 50th percentile;
first quartile = the 25th percentile;
third quartile = the 75th percentile;
first decile = the 10th percentile;
ninth decile = the 90th percentile.

A *percentile* in this context is a rank below which a given percent of cases fall. To calculate the first decile in each study, we must count down 10% of the cases from the top of each frequency list. In Study A, the first two ranks contain exactly 10% of the cases. The first decile is assigned the rank of 1.5, which is midway between the second and third rank. In Study B the ranks 0, 1, 2, 3, and 4 are necessary to include 10% of the cases, but since this percent is exceeded by a small margin, the following formula is used:

$$D_1 = U_r - \frac{cf_i - E}{f_i}$$

where D_1 = the first decile;

U_r = the upper limit of the interval that included the case necessary to reach 10%;

f_i = the frequency in the interval;

cf_i = the cumulative frequency up through the interval;

E = the number of cases that equals 10% of the total.

In the example we find that

$$D_1 = 4.5 - \frac{12 - 10}{3} = 4.5 - .67 = 3.83$$

Using a more generalized version of the above formula,

$$C_i = U_r - \frac{cf_i - E}{f_i} \tag{9.3}$$

where C_i is any percentile and U_r and E correspond to the appropriate percent of cases rather than specifically 10%.

Calculating the interdecile and interquartile ranges, therefore, requires the following steps:

Study A:

$$D_1 = D_{10} = 1.5 \ (\text{direct interpolation})$$

$$D_9 = C_{90} = 11.5 \ (\text{direct interpolation})$$

$$\text{Interdecile Range} = D_9 - D_1 = 10$$

$$Q_1 = C_{25} = 3.5 - \frac{35 - 25}{13} = 3.5 - .77 = 2.73$$

$$Q_3 = C_{75} = 7.5 - \frac{79 - 75}{6} = 7.5 - .67 = 6.83$$

$$\text{Interquartile Range} = Q_3 - Q_1 = 4.10$$

Study B:

$$D_1 = C_{10} = 4.5 - \frac{12 - 10}{3} = 4.5 - .67 = 3.83$$

$$D_9 = C_{90} = 12.5 - \frac{92 - 90}{4} = 12.5 - .5 = 12$$

$$\text{Interdecile Range} = D_9 - D_1 = 8.17$$

$$Q_1 = C_{25} = 6.5 - \frac{29 - 25}{11} = 6.5 - .36 = 6.14$$

$$Q_3 = C_{75} = 10.5 - \frac{82 - 75}{8} = 10.5 - .88 = 9.62$$

$$\text{Interquartile Range} = Q_3 - Q_1 = 3.48$$

Comparing the two studies, we see that for Study A the ranges are larger (10 and 4.1) than for Study B (8.17 and 3.48). The results *might* be interpreted to mean that there is less consensus in the first administrative agency than in the second over the accomplishment of organizational goals— a result, by the way, that is not obvious from a quick look at the information.

It is important to remember when dealing with ranks in the above manner that each numeric rank is given an interval that extends a distance of .5 on each side of the rank. In the example, the range of ranks is −.5 to 16.5, or a total of 17. As explained earlier, however, we do not know that these intervals are of the same distance. Thus, it is risky to conclude that there is more consensus in one agency than the other. If the "true" degree of consensus were known through some independent test, we might find that those in the first six ranks are actually much closer together than those in the second six ranks. Since in Study A most of the cases are in the first six ranks, the above procedure could exaggerate the range of the distribution. Though such a finding would be highly unusual, it is possible, and it is necessary to keep in mind that ordinal measures of dispersion assess the range of ranks and not the range of true values. The main justification for the use of such measures is that they would tend to be less of a distortion of the data than would interval measures of dispersion. The grounds for this point of view will be examined more carefully after a discussion of the interval measures.

There are a number of other statistics derived from the percentile rationale for ordinal data. One of the most common is called either the *semi-interquartile range* or the *quartile deviation,* and it is defined as

$$Q = \frac{Q_3 - Q_1}{2} \qquad (9.4)$$

In the two studies, $Q = 4.1/2 = 2.05$, and $Q = 3.48/2 = 1.74$. The formula can be stated more simply as

$$Q = .5\ (Q_3 - Q_1)$$

The larger the value of Q for a given number of ranks, the flatter or less peaked the frequency distribution. Perhaps the best measure of the *peakedness* or *kurtosis* of an ordinal variable expresses the ratio of the semi-interquartile range to the interdecile range. Symbolically,

$$K = .5\ (Q_3 - Q_1)/(D_9 - D_1) \tag{9.5}$$

In the two hypothetical studies,

$$K = .5\ (4.1)/(10) = .20$$
$$K = .5\ (3.48)/(8.17) = .21$$

The measure has the advantage of standardizing the result and it incorporates two pieces of knowledge about the distribution. It is used, for example, in the oblimax rotation technique in factor analysis. By this measure there is very little difference between the two distributions. The measure is actually intended for symmetrical distributions, and not the distribution given for Study A.

To test for the *asymmetry* or *skewness* of the distribution within this context, we suggest using an expression that compares the range between the first decile and first quartile with the range between the third quartile and ninth quartile, modified (or standardized) by one-half the interdecile range. Symbolically,

$$SK = \frac{(D_9 - Q_3) - (Q_1 - D_1)}{.5\ (D_9 - D_1)} \tag{9.6}$$

In our example,

Study A: $SK = \dfrac{(11.5 - 6.83) - (2.73 - 1.5)}{.5\ (10)} = \dfrac{2.44}{5} = .49$

Study B: $SK = \dfrac{(12 - 9.62) - (6.14 - 3.83)}{.5\ (8.17)} = \dfrac{.07}{4.08} = .017$

SK can vary from -1.0 to $+1.0$. If SK is negative, the tail of the distribution will be on the left; and if SK is positive, the tail of the distribution is on the right. The distribution for Study A is positively skewed (.49), whereas the distribution for Study B is almost symmetrical, where perfect symmetry would yield a value of 0. The SK formula is most appropriate for unimodal distributions. For bimodal and multimodal distributions, it is usually better to compare the ranges on each side of the median.

In contrast to ordinal measures of dispersion, *interval* measures of dispersion utilize every value in the distribution. Thus, even though the ordinal measures can be applied to interval data in an informative manner, it is generally even more informative to employ an interval statistic. The most common of these are the mean deviation, the mean variance, and the standard deviation. The *mean deviation* is the sum of the differences between each value and the mean, ignoring the minus signs, divided by the number of cases. We may write:

$$\text{Mean deviation} = \frac{\Sigma\,|X_i - \overline{X}|}{N} \tag{9.7}$$

If the values in a distribution were 20, 15, 10, 3, and 2, the mean, $\overline{X}$, would equal 50/5 or 10. Subtracting 10 from each of the values, we get 10, 5, 0, 7, and 8 as absolute differences. Their sum equals 30 and the mean deviation, 30/5, equals 6. On the average, the scores depart from the mean by a value of 6.

The mean deviation, while easy to understand, is not very important for statistical analysis. The mean variance and standard deviation, in contrast, are at the center of interval or parametric statistics. Although in this chapter only the calculations and basic features of the latter two measures will be discussed, it should be pointed out that the notion of variance will be important in all succeeding chapters. Statistical analysis of interval variables is essentially built on the concept of variance, and the mean variance is the primitive estimate from which statistical theory proceeds.

The *mean variance* is the sum of the squared differences divided by the number of cases, or:

$$s^2 = \frac{\Sigma\,(X_i - \overline{X})^2}{N} \tag{9.8}$$

Each difference is squared first, and then they are summed. The squaring process has the effect of emphasizing the larger differences. Thus, if we were to take two sets of observations:

A. 0, 4, 5, 6, 10
B. 2, 2, 5, 8, 8

the mean of each is 5, and the absolute differences are:

A. 5, 1, 0, 1, 5
B. 3, 3, 0, 3, 3

In each case the sum of the differences is 12 and the mean deviation is 2.4. However, we may observe that the *sum of squares* is not the same:

A. $25 + 1 + 0 + 1 + 25 = 52$
B. $9 + 9 + 0 + 9 + 9 = 36$

Dividing by N, the variance in the first case is 10.4, and in the second case, 7.2. The mean variance suggests that there is greater dispersion about the mean in distribution A than in distribution B.

The *standard deviation* is the square root of the mean variance, described by the equation:

$$s = \sqrt{\frac{\Sigma\,(X_1 - \overline{X})^2}{N}} \tag{9.9}$$

In terms of the relative emphasis given to extreme values, the standard deviation falls between the mean deviation and the mean variance. For distribution A above, $s = 3.2$, and for distribution B, $s = 2.7$, in rounded values. To see very clearly how the three measures of dispersion compare, their application to three distributions may be examined as follows:

Distribution	A.	0,	4,	5,	6,	10	
of	B.	1,	3,	4,	7,	9	X_i
Values	C.	2,	2,	5,	8,	8	

Distribution	A.	5,	1,	0,	1,	5	
of	B.	4,	2,	0,	2,	4	$X_i - \overline{X}$
Differences	C.	3,	3,	0,	3,	3	

Distribution	A.	25,	1,	0,	1,	25	
of	B.	16,	4,	0,	4,	16	$(X_1 - \overline{X})^2$
Squares	C.	9,	9,	0,	9,	9	

Mean	A.	2.4
Deviation	B.	2.4
	C.	2.4

Standard	A.	3.22	
Deviation	B.	2.83	(.39)
	C.	2.68	(.15)

Mean	A.	10.4	
Variance	B.	8.0	(2.4)
	C.	7.2	(.8)

In the three distributions, the values are systematically changed when moving from A to C, the first and fourth value being increased by one unit and the second and fifth value being decreased by one unit. This keeps the mean deviation constant for all three sets. Because of the squaring process, however, both the variances and the standard deviation will decrease. Distribution B has less extreme values than A, and distribution C has less extreme values than B, as reflected in the distribution of differences between the mean and each observation. The degree of absolute change in the mean variance is substantially greater than for the standard deviation.

Selection from the three measures of dispersion is especially important when assessing the extent to which distributions depart from a particular norm, such as equal income or equal apportionment. The mean variance will make extreme departures from the mean stand out, whereas the mean deviation will not be very sensitive. The standard deviation has the advantage of retaining the potential for calculating the mean variance while bringing the magnitude of the dispersion estimate within the range of the original values. This latter feature of the standard deviation can be appreciated when analyzing raw data that appear in large numbers or in decimal fractions. For example, the distribution of state expenditures per capita in Table 9.1 gives a mean value of $181.38, and maximum and minimum values of $283.69 and $110.47, respectively. The variance about the mean for this distribution is 1699.31, whereas the standard deviation about the mean is 41.22. The second certainly has more intuitive appeal in relation to the mean. Both the variance and the standard deviation have important theoretical properties in advanced statistical analysis. Later it will be necessary to utilize the term *mean variance* for the above statistics to distinguish it from other variance calculations. The standard deviation is important to the interpretation of the *normal* curve.

For practical research problems, there is one important mathematical identity that will make the calculation of the mean variance and the standard deviation much more convenient. It has been shown that the *sum of squares,*

$$\Sigma\,(X_i - \overline{X})^2 = \Sigma X_i^2 - \frac{(\Sigma X_i)^2}{N} \tag{9.10}$$

Normally for large data sets, the right-hand term will be easier to calculate by hand or with a desk calculator, and easier to program for computer analysis. In hand calculations the mean is usually not a whole number, but the observations very often are whole numbers. The right-hand term avoids this tedium, and with the use of a table of squares, can be used with considerable accuracy. It is also an advantage to avoid decimal places on a desk calculator. In computer programming the left-hand term requires instructing the computer to scan through the data twice—once to calculate the mean and once to calculate the squared differences—whereas, the right-hand term requires scanning through the data only once. Of course, computer programs for these standard formulae have been prewritten and are available in software packages in almost all computing centers.

Interval measures of kurtosis and skewness are less commonly employed, but can be of considerable aid in the early stages of analysis. The formula for skewness is:

$$Sk = \frac{(1/N)\,\Sigma\,(X_i - \overline{X})^3}{s^3} \tag{9.11}$$

where the numerator is the sum of the cubed deviations from the mean divided by N, and the denominator is the cube of the standard deviation. When the deviations are squared, as in the calculation of the mean variance, the signs all become positive. Cubing the deviations, however, preserves the signs of the original differences. Summing the cubed values yields a net plus or minus value, unless the distribution is symmetrical, in which case the net value is 0. When Sk is negative, the distribution is negatively skewed, and the distribution is positively skewed when Sk is positive. Unfortunately, the range of Sk is not definite and thus it is not so easily interpreted. The application of this formula by Schubert and Press to measure malapportionment in the states gave values as high as 6.55 when applied to 101 apportionment plans.[1]

The kurtosis or peakedness of a distribution is measured by raising the deviations from the mean to the fourth power, such that

$$Ku = \frac{(1/N) \; \Sigma \; (X_i - \overline{X})^4}{s^4} \tag{9.12}$$

Raising the deviations to the fourth power produces positive values, regardless of the original signs. As with *Sk*, the range of *Ku* is not definite. In the same study, Schubert and Press report a value of 58.73 for kurtosis, as well as several minus values. It is known, however, that when *Ku* = 3.00, the distribution conforms to the probability distribution of the *normal* curve, the exact nature of which will be discussed shortly. When *Ku* exceeds 3.00, the distribution is more peaked than the normal curve, and when it is less than 3.00, the distribution is flatter—or leptokurtic and platykurtic, respectively.

When it is the purpose of research to compare a variety of distributions, it is important to recognize that these measures of dispersion (mean deviation, *s*, s^2, *Sk*, and *Ku*) are not necessarily comparable from study to study. They have not been standardized for such a purpose. The quickest way to overcome this problem is to convert all raw scores to *standard scores,* so that they will all have the same mean, after which the measures of dispersion may be calculated. The procedure for doing this is explained in Chapter 6. Standard scores should not be confused with T-scores or standard *normal* scores.

The *normal* curve is a mathematically defined distribution, the formula for which is not important except for purely statistical or mathematical research. The curve may be viewed as a chance model for the distribution of values of a *continuous* variable, that is, a variable that may take on any value. Naturally, it is felt that many variables do distribute normally; otherwise the curve would be of very limited utility. A better case can probably be made for psychological characteristics and opinion surveys than for other kinds of social science information, and we would guess that many political scientists would claim that they seldom encounter a normally distributed variable. Nevertheless, normal curve assumptions have taken an important place in the interpretation of data and can be useful in a variety of circumstances.

Since the normal curve is symmetrical and unimodal, the mean of the distribution is at the center and highest point. The distinguishing feature of the normal curve is that its formula produces the exact relationship between any linear distance from the mean, and the area between that distance and the mean. As illustrated in Figure 9.3, the horizontal distance from the mean is associated with the area under the curve. The horizontal distance is measured in *standard deviation units,* and the area is expressed as a proportion of the total area. Literally, .62 standard deviation is one-half the

FIGURE 9.3

Areas under the normal curve and standard deviation units from mean

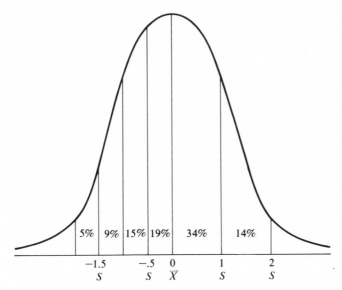

distance of 1.24 standard deviations from the mean. The area traversed by these distances can be obtained by consulting a table of areas of the normal curve (Table A). Find that .62 units traverses .2324, or about 23% of the area. The area traversed by one (1.0) standard deviation from the mean is .3413 of the total area. Thus, the area traversed by one standard deviation unit extending on both sides of the mean is .6826 of the total.

It is very convenient to determine whether a particular empirical distribution approaches the normal curve. Calculate the standard deviation, which, as indicated earlier, will give an intuitively reasonable distance from the mean within the range of the raw values. Using state expenditures per capita to illustrate, the mean is 181.38 and the standard deviation is 41.22. Thus, if the distribution is normal,

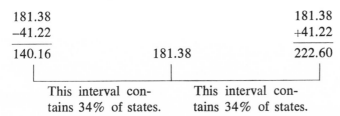

$$\begin{array}{ccc} 181.38 & & 181.38 \\ -41.22 & & +41.22 \\ \hline 140.16 & 181.38 & 222.60 \end{array}$$

This interval con-   This interval contains 34% of states.   tains 34% of states.

In reality, we find that the interval to the left of the mean contains the values for 21 states, or about 44%, and the interval to the right of the mean contains 29% of the values. The distribution does not approach the normal curve. Even if the distribution did satisfy this single test, other

273

multiples of the standard deviation should be checked. For most problems, one should at least examine the proportion of cases on each side of the mean that fall within

.5 (s) ———— about 19% of cases
s ———— about 34% of cases
1.5 (s) ———— about 43% of cases
2 (s) ———— about 48% of cases

For advanced multivariate problems proceeding under the normal curve assumption, one should calculate the Pearson correlation coefficient between the empirical distribution and the normal curve to see how well the normal curve "explains" the empirical distribution. The procedures for doing this are developed in Chapter 10. Here we simply caution the reader, having noted that in past studies it is not always clear that the validity of the normal curve assumption has been carefully examined. It is also possible to transform many distributions to a normal curve distribution. This procedure is discussed on pages 185–87 and 313–16.

A Measure of Cumulative Dispersion

In this section, $1 - $ *Gini Index of Inequality* is presented as a cumulative measure of dispersion. It is very much like the nominal coefficient of dispersion developed earlier in this chapter. It is quite different from the mean variance and standard deviation. Since we would like to avoid for the moment confusing this measure with the practical applications of the *Gini Index of Inequality,* we will call it simply a measure of *cumulative dispersion,* or D_c. The measure may be calculated from a cumulative frequency distribution converted to percentages. To apply the measure, one must first determine the kind of unit that is under study and call it the X variable. Typically, the X variable is made up of people or units of government. The Y variable is whatever is distributed among the X units. *A cumulative percentage distribution expresses the percentages of Y units that are distributed among a percentage of X units.*

Thus, if five agency bureaucrats and their salaries are each converted to cumulative distributions, as follows:

BUREAUCRATS	X_i	X_c	SALARIES	Y_i	Y_c
A	.2	.2	8,000	.10	.10
B	.2	.4	12,000	.15	.25
C	.2	(.6)	16,000	.20	(.45)
D	.2	.8	20,000	.25	.70
E	.2	1.0	24,000	.30	1.00

FIGURE 9.4

Cumulative dispersion

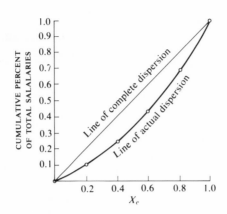

where X_i is the percent of employees represented by the bureaucrat, X_c is the cumulative percent, Y_i is the percent of total salaries received by the bureaucrat, and Y_c is the cumulative percent, it can be seen that 45% of the salaries are distributed among 60% of the employees. Important to the comparison is the *ordering* of bureaucrat salaries from lowest to highest. The X_c and Y_c coordinates can be plotted readily on a graph, illustrated by the curve in Figure 9.4. If all of the employees received the same salary, the plot would be the diagonal of the graph; the diagonal would represent complete dispersion.

For those who have worked with conventional measures of deviation, this formulation may seem the reverse of intuition, for it appears that the standard deviation of equal salaries is 0, indicating no dispersion. Essen-

FIGURE 9.5

Simple dispersion for five equal salaries

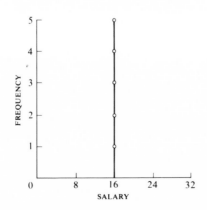

275

FIGURE 9.6

Cumulative dispersion for five equal salaries

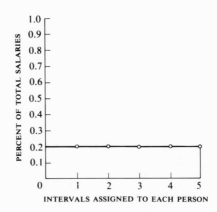

tially, here we are dealing with a *different* kind of dispersion—not the dispersion among numbers representing salaries, but the dispersion of salaries among people. Figures 9.5 and 9.6 pinpoint this distinction. Since there is no variation in salaries, the conventional "curve" is a straight vertical line, whereas the cumulative dispersion is represented by a rectangular distribution, each horizontal interval corresponding to percents of the population.

To determine dispersion in the cumulative distribution in Figure 9.4, it is necessary to calculate the area between the curve and the two sides of the lower triangle in Figure 9.4 as a proportion of the total area in the triangle, or, 1 – the area between the curve and the diagonal. Symbolically,

$$D_c = 1 - 2 \, \Sigma \, |Y_c - \overline{Y}_c| \, \Delta X_i \qquad (9.13)$$

where Y_c = the cumulative percentages of Y;

   $\overline{Y}_c$ = the cumulative percentages of the diagonal (as if every X unit had the mean share);

   ΔX_i = the horizontal percentage distances covered by each X unit, where $\Delta X_i = X_c - X_{c-1}$.

In Table 9.4, $D_c = 1 - 2(.10) = .80$, where D_c can range from 0 to 1.0. The formula actually works from the area in the total square of the graph so that the top triangle is the mirror image of the bottom triangle.

For convenience in calculation, it is actually not necessary to convert the values to percentages first; however, a slightly more detailed formula must be used, so that

$$D_c = 1 - \frac{2 \, \Sigma \, |Y_c - \overline{Y}_c| \, \Delta X_i}{\Sigma Y_i \, \Sigma X_i} \qquad (9.14)$$

where Y_c = the cumulative values of Y;
$\overline{Y}_c$ = the cumulative mean values;
X_i = the horizontal distances covered by each X unit.

When X_i is a constant, assume that it equals 1.0 and use the equation:

$$D_c = 1 - \frac{2 \, \Sigma \, |Y_c - \overline{Y}_c|}{\Sigma Y_i \, \Sigma X_i} \tag{9.15}$$

where any value of $X_i = 1.0$. Thus, in our example where ΔX_i is constant, we can write:

$$D_c = 1 - \frac{2 \, (40,000)}{80,000 \, (5)} = 1 - \frac{80,000}{400,000} = 1 - .20 = .80$$

The sum of the *absolute* differences in the numerator is calculated from the raw cumulative values, where $(8,000 - 16,000) + (20,000 - 32,000) + (36,000 - 48,000) + (56,000 - 64,000) + (80,000 - 80,000) = 40,000$.

TABLE 9.4
Calculation Table for Coefficient of Cumulative Dispersion

	Y_i	Y_c	$\overline{Y}_c$	$Y_c - \overline{Y}_c$	X_c	X_{c-1}	X_i	$Y_c - \overline{Y}_c \; X_i$
A.	.10	.10	.20	.10	.2	.0	.2	.02
B.	.15	.25	.40	.15	.4	.2	.2	.03
C.	.20	.45	.60	.15	.6	.4	.2	.03
D.	.25	.70	.80	.10	.8	.6	.2	.02
E.	.30	1.0	1.00	.0	1.0	.8	.2	.0
								$2 \times .10 = .20$

$$D_c = 1 - .20 = .80$$

As mentioned previously, the measure of cumulative dispersion, D_c, is the complement of the *Gini Index of Inequality,* and the *Gini Index* is actually calculated first in the previous equations. Thus, the simplified right-hand quantities in the calculation formulae may also be used to calculate the *Gini Index* when the appropriate conditions apply. The *Gini Index* is normally employed to demonstrate the extent to which a distribution departs from an equality norm, represented by the diagonal. Equality of distributions means the complete dispersion of something, such as money, legislative seats, or public services, among a given population. Usually it is said that the *Gini* coefficient can range from 0 to 1, and for large samples this is a fair assumption. Actually the coefficient can be no more than

$$1 - \frac{1}{N} \text{ or } 1 - \frac{1}{\Sigma X_i}$$

assuming that the values of X_i are 1.0. For problems with varying intervals, the smallest interval or last interval may be viewed as a limit. Correspondingly, D_c has a lower limit of $1 / \Sigma X_i$.

To accommodate the above problem for cases where X_i is constant and the sum of X_i is small, the following formula is suggested:

$$D_c = 1 - \frac{2 \, \Sigma \, |Y_c - \bar{Y}_c|}{\Sigma Y_i \, (\Sigma \bar{X}_i - 1)} \qquad (9.16)$$

Applying this formulation to the previous example, we obtain:

$$D_c = 1 - \frac{2 \, (40,000)}{(80,000) \, (4)} = 1 - \frac{80,000}{320,000} = 1 - .25 = .75$$

or a slightly more conservative estimate of the degree of dispersion.

Summary and Evaluation

The starting point in statistical analysis is in the description of frequency distributions. In conversational language, frequency distributions are referred to as symmetrical or asymmetrical, unimodal, bimodal, or multimodal, skewed to the left or skewed to the right, highly peaked or flat, or even normal. The distributions are given more precise definitions through the use of measures of central tendency and measures of dispersion. The primary measures of central tendency are the mean, median, and mode. Measures of dispersion may be divided into three broad categories: those intended for nominal, ordinal, and interval data. They may also be classified as measures of simple dispersion and measures of cumulative dispersion. For nominal data, we suggest using either:

> A. The Nominal Coefficient of Dispersion—CD (9.2)
>
> B. The Measure of Cumulative Dispersion—D_c (9.16)

Both require the preordering of the data distribution, from the category with the lowest frequency to the category with the highest frequency, to achieve the appropriate graphic display, although the nominal coefficient of dispersion, for calculation purposes, does not require preordering. One must be careful, of course, to keep in mind that the width of nominal categories is not known, and the results need to be viewed with caution. The assumption of equal widths of nominal categories may be open to question. For example, one might measure the distribution of calorie intake or food consumption among a set of people, where each person occupies one unit. The result might be misleading unless the size of each person (requiring different levels of food consumption) is taken into account. In any case, the coefficient value is the degree of dispersion that a classification system produces when each category is given the same weight.

Ordinal measures of dispersion are derived from percentiles. A percentile is a rank below which a given percent of cases fall. There are 99 percentiles, 9 deciles, and 3 quartiles, which divide up a population into 100, 10, and 4 parts, respectively. These divisions yield the following measures:

C. Interdecile Range
D. Interquartile Range
E. Semi-Interquartile Range, Q (9.4)
F. Kurtosis, K (9.5)
G. Skewness, SK (9.6)

The main reason that these ordinal measures are used is that they are less likely to magnify the error that results when the distances between numbers have not been ascertained. Raising deviations to the second, third, and fourth power, as with interval measures of dispersion, can accentuate original measurement errors.

There are certain circumstances, however, that lower the risk in the application of interval measures to ordinally measured data. Most important are (1) a large sample size, and (2) a symmetrical distribution. With a symmetrical distribution, errors reflected in the deviations on each side of the mean are more likely to cancel out, and with a large sample size they are even more likely to cancel out. Of course, it would be helpful to know that the *true* distribution is symmetrical, but such knowledge is rare when this kind of choice arises. Analysts generally prefer interval measures—sometimes to an extent that ignores the measurement procedures—because of the wide variety of advanced statistical packages for interval data and the consequent theoretical sophistication that can be achieved. The interval measures of dispersion include:

H. Mean Deviation   (9.7)
I. Mean Variance, s^2 or s_m^2 (9.8)
J. Standard Deviation, s (9.9)
K. Kurtosis, Ku (9.11)
L. Skewness, Sk (9.12)

The standard deviation is employed as a base for defining the characteristic normal curve. The mean variance is employed as a base for comparison in correlational analysis. The kurtosis and skewness measures are usually employed to determine the extent to which a distribution fits the normal curve. When the distribution is perfectly normal, $K = 3$ and $Sk = 0$.

Several alternative formulations of the measure of cumulative dispersion are possible, depending on the data circumstances. The measure and its parent *Gini Index* are usually treated separately from measures of simple dispersion. By our calculations, a strict normal curve will produce a value of .50 for either D_c or the *Gini* coefficient. For application to small samples (where N is less than 200), the correction factor in Equation (9.16) is recommended.

These many measures of dispersion should be viewed as summary devices. They allow the analyst to operationalize what might otherwise be a simple visual inspection of frequency distributions. But since they are only summary devices, they are not a complete substitute for a graphic plot or portrayal. Experience with these measures, in combination with a frequent "eyeballing" of graphic aids, will increase the sensitivity of the user to both and should increase the reliability of reported work and research. More advanced stages of statistical application are more exciting, and once they are learned, reverting to the examination of frequency distributions becomes a test of patience. Failure to begin at the beginning, however, can lead to an enormous waste of energy.

NOTES

1. Glendon Schubert and Charles Press, "Measuring Malapportionment," *American Political Science Review,* 63 (1964). See pages 966–970.

Chapter 10

MEASURES OF ASSOCIATION

This chapter will be concerned with bivariate relationships, taking two variables at a time. Multivariate relationships are considered in later chapters. Generally, we take the approach that measures of association should correspond to the level of measurement—nominal, ordinal, or interval; however, this does not rule out the possibility that a somewhat flexible approach might be more illuminating for certain problems. The need for flexibility arises especially in multivariate analysis, but even within a bivariate framework it is not always easy to decide whether a variable has an interval or ordinal measurement base, and it is conceivable that the nominal-ordinal distinction will be fuzzy for certain attributes. In any case, it makes sense to assume that the analyst is better able to cope with chameleon variables if he knows the basic organization of statistical measures. Following Freeman, we will use levels of measurement to organize statistical measures of association, so that there are six basic types of relationships: [1]

$$V_1 \qquad V_2$$

Nominal	—	Nominal
Nominal	—	Ordinal
Nominal	—	Interval
Ordinal	—	Ordinal
Ordinal	—	Interval
Interval	—	Interval

The first variable may be nominal, ordinal, or interval, and the second variable may be one of the three as well.

In discussing the relationship between two variables, it will also be important to distinguish between an independent and dependent relationship. If two variables are independent of each other, they are often said to be unrelated. There are two general categories of dependence, linear and nonlinear. A measure of association estimates the degree of dependence, and by convention, a value of zero or near zero signifies independence, whereas a high (+ or −) value, often approaching 1.0, signifies a high degree of dependence or association. An estimate of linear dependence may be 0, but an estimate of nonlinear dependence for the same two variables may be 1.0. To help us develop these distinctions and to aid in the selection of statistical measures, we commence with a series of tables and plots, keeping in mind the original frequency distributions that make up the variables from which the tables and plots are generated.

Independence

The notion of independence between two variables is derived directly from observation of their frequency distributions. Essentially, given the way two variables distribute, and given that they describe the same set of people or things, is there nothing more that can be said about the relationship between them? If not, they are independent. Put another way, the intersections between the two variables are completely predictable from the frequency distributions.

For example, suppose that we make a study of 100 officeholders and compare the type of office held with parent's occupational background. If the relationship shown in Table 10.1 were found, the frequency within each

TABLE 10.1
Strict Independence: Nominal Variables

	PROFESSION	BUSINESS	OTHER	
Legislator	16	16	8	40
Administrator	12	12	6	30
Judge	12	12	6	30
	40	40	20	$N = 100$

cell would be completely predictable from the totals in the margins. To predict how many legislators come from backgrounds other than professional or business, multiply the appropriate row total by the appropriate column total and divide by N, or $(40 \times 20)/100 = 8$. The cells of the table can be filled in by reference to the margin totals. Another way to interpret the information is to divide each margin total by N first. Then the multiplication of any row total by any column total will give the percent of cases in the appropriate cell.

The above example included two *nominal* variables. The same principle applies to two *interval* variables. Suppose that we wish to determine whether the percent of campaign funds spent for television is independent of the percent of votes won by 200 candidates for office. If the number of

TABLE 10.2

Independence: Interval Variables

| | | PERCENT VOTE | | | |
		0–24.99	25–49.99	50–74.99	75–100	
	0–33.33	8	12	12	8	40
Percent Funds for	33.34–66.67	18	27	27	18	90
Television	66.68–100	14	21	21	14	70
		40	60	60	40	N = 200

cases falling within equidistant points is established, as in the margin totals of Table 10.2, and the cell frequencies are again calculable from the margin totals, one variable is independent of the other. It is possible to collapse the first two columns, making the interval 0-49.99 and the column total 100, and the new frequencies may be calculated from the margin (e.g., $100 \times 40/200 + 20$). It is evident that, regardless of the level of measurement of either variable, the same rationale applies. Strict independence means that only the frequency distributions are responsible for the cell frequencies.

The condition of independence is very often referred to as the "chance model." It is a condition against which analysts compete when they hypothesize that one variable is a good predictor of another. In Table 10.2, percent funds for television do not help predict percent vote won by the candidates. Technically, to say that the relationship between two variables is attributed to chance is to say that when comparing the two variables, the matrix intersections are accounted for by the frequency distributions.

Of course, in the examination of interval variables it can be misleading to categorize the information. The plotted points on a graph would represent the data more accurately.

To generalize the notion of independence for interval scales, we would posit that when controlling for the frequency distributions in a bivariate comparison:

1. The outer limits of the plotted points will approach a circular shape (connecting the outer points to enclose all intersections within the shape).
2. The points on the boundary and within the circular or equilateral shape are spaced at equal intervals from each other.

A typical set of plotted points would not be directly interpretable, since the frequency distributions influence the location of point intersections. Because of this problem, analysts frequently collapse the data into a table with class intervals when they wish to determine how independent two variables are in relation to each other.

Linearity

The chance or independence model is relevant for all bivariate relationships, regardless of the level of measurement applied to each variable. A *linear* model makes sense only when ordinal or interval scales are employed for *both* variables; that is, when both are ordinal, both are interval, or when one is ordinal and one is interval. A strict linear relationship means, graphically, that the plotted point intersections all fall precisely on a straight line. The linear model is in direct competition with the independence model. If two variables are linearly dependent, they cannot be independent of each other. However, if the two variables are not linearly dependent, they may still fit some other dependence model.

Only when the two frequency distributions of a pair of variables are identical can the plotted points fall precisely on a straight line. To illustrate, let us take a set of five observations for variable X and a number of alternative arrays for variable Y:

	X	Y_1	Y_2	Y_3	Y_4
1.	1	2	1	2	1
2.	3	4	2	3	5
3.	8	9	3	3	6
4.	9	10	4	3	7
5.	10	11	5	4	10

Of course, with only five observations, there isn't much of a distribution, but we might say that the first two distributions (X and Y_1) are skewed, the third rectangular, and the last two unimodal and fairly symmetrical. All of the distributions give equal or increasing values when moving from the first to the fifth case, but only Y_1 will yield a straight line plot when compared with X, as illustrated in Figure 10.1. Even though the values of Y_1 are different, they yield the identical distribution.

To find two variables with *identical* distributions is very rare. With a large number of cases the probability is remote. One can expect to find, however, many pairs of variables with similar distributions. Identical distributions are achieved primarily through a mathematical transformation. Perhaps the most common is the rank-order transformation. For example, the values of X and the values of Y_4 can be ranked in each case according to their magnitudes, so that

	X	Y_4
1.	5	5.
2.	4	4
3.	3	3
4.	2	2
5.	1	1

FIGURE 10.1

Comparing different distributions of Y with a skewed distribution of X

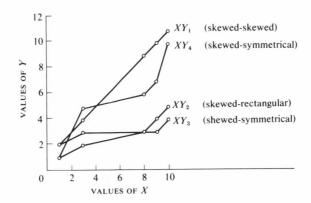

Now the plotted points fit a straight line. One can see, of course, that a loss of information is precipitated by the transformation. If the original magnitudes did not consistently increase in one of the variables, then even a rank-order transformation will not produce a straight line fit. Aside from the rank-order transformation, the most common are the normal curve and logarithmic transformations. These are all called nonlinear transformations because they destroy the original distances between values. The transformations are frequently utilized to accommodate linear reasoning. See pages 313–16 for further detail.

There are those analysts who prefer to transform data, and there are those who take a slightly different approach. Those in the second group ask: Regardless of the frequency distributions, how well does a straight line describe the plotted points? For ordinal and/or interval data, it is possible to find the "best fit" straight line. Conventionally, this is the line that minimizes the sum of the squared distances between it and the points around it. For any of the plots in Figure 10.1, one can see that a carefully drawn straight line would not grossly distort the relationship. Following the point of view of the second group, there is an important corollary question: What proportion of the minimized sum of squared distance is attributable to the frequency distributions? One way to acquire insight into the matter is to transform the distributions in order that they are identical.

Nonlinearity

The distinction between linearity and nonlinearity, of course, does not arise when one of the two variables is a nominal classification, since the categories can be rearranged at will to produce different matrix pictures. For ordinal and interval variable comparisons, it is important to observe not only whether the data exhibit a linear relationship, but also whether an identifiable non-linear pattern exists. The possibilities are numerous, but generally the status and quality of data collection and theory construction in most social science areas do not warrant exact mathematical representation of highly complex patterns. More than likely, the analyst will not be interested in going beyond the representation of accelerating or decelerating curves and parabola-like curves. A good fit for any distinct curve will be made possible by the frequency distributions. An accelerating or decelerating curve is more likely when one distribution is symmetrical and the other highly skewed, and virtually impossible if the distributions are identical. Parabola-like curves are possible in most situations. For example, the following two rectangular distributions:

	X	Y
1.	1	1
2.	2	3
3.	3	5
4.	4	4
5.	5	2

will produce a change in direction in the slope, from positive to negative. A parabolic relationship has two characteristics, roughly stated:

1. Middle-range values of X are paired with high (or low, but not both) values of Y.
2. Extreme values of X are paired with low (or high, but not both) values of Y.

A straight line is a very poor representation of a parabolic relationship, depending, of course, on just how exaggerated the parabolic-like plot is, whereas most accelerating or decelerating curves will be reflected to a considerable extent in a straight line fit. Realistically, analysts do not always examine plots, especially when a large number of variables are analyzed. It is a tedious and often unrewarding procedure, although computer plotting options are now available at most centers. It is advisable to employ one or more of the short-cut procedures suggested on pages 313–16.

Linear measures of association are usually satisfactory for rough summary purposes, with one important exception: the description of a parabolic-type relationship. Later we suggest utilizing a semilinear *mean difference transformation* to avoid concluding that there is no relationship between two variables when a parabolic-like plot exists. The procedure involves simply converting the values of one variable to their absolute differences from the mean value.

Criteria for Selection of a Measure of Association

At this writing no one has reported a thorough comparison of the behavior of *all* statistical measures in relation to *all* types of data arrays. The selection of a statistic will need to be based more on the skeletal features of both the data and the statistic. The statistic should correspond to the level of measurement characteristic of each of the two variables. For combinations including at least one nominal variable, it is desirable to use a statistic whose possible values range between 0 and 1.0. For linear measures of association on ordinal and interval data, it is desirable to have a statistic that ranges between -1.0 and $+1.0$ to indicate whether the relationship is inverse or direct. The measures are much easier to interpret when the range is standardized. All of the statistics presented *in detail* in this chapter do have a standardized range of either 0 to 1 or -1 to $+1$. This does not mean, of course, that they behave in the same way over the entire range and in response to different kinds of frequency distributions. These criteria—level of measurement and range—lead us to elaborate on the following measures: [2]

Nominal-Nominal	Cramer's V
	Guttman's (or Goodman and Kruskal's) lambda
Nominal-Ordinal	Freeman's theta
Nominal-Interval	Eta coefficient
Ordinal-Ordinal	Goodman and Kruskal's gamma
	Kendall's tau$_c$
	Spearman's rho
Ordinal-Interval	Jaspen's M
Interval-Interval	Pearson's r

Nonlinear Nominal Measures

Measures of bivariate association, including at least one nominal variable, are nonlinear in character. They are intended to convey the extent to which two variables are dependent, and their values range from 0 to 1.0. The problem for the researcher, of course, will be to select the measure that neither underestimates nor overestimates the level of measurement of each variable. An underestimate results in the loss of information and potential distortion. Within this group of nominal-nominal, nominal-ordinal, and nominal-interval measures, the most common errors, in our opinion, occur in the use of a nominal-nominal measure for a nominal-ordinal relationship, and somewhat

TABLE 10.3

Relationship Between Method of Selection and Declaration of Party Affiliation for 924 Judges in Twelve States: Calculation of Chi-Square and Cramer's V

METHOD OF SELECTION	DECLARED PARTY AFFILIATION	NO DECLARED PARTY AFFILIATION	
Legislative	52 (35.3)	4 (20.7)	56
Appointive	113 (102.2)	49 (59.8)	162
Partisan Election	234 (211.4)	101 (123.6)	335
Nonpartisan Election	178 (219.6)	170 (128.4)	348
Missouri Plan	6 (14.5)	17 (8.5)	23
Totals:	583	341	924

(Numbers in parentheses give expected frequencies.)

less frequently, in the use of a nominal-interval measure for a nominal-ordinal relationship.

TWO NOMINAL VARIABLES

To illustrate Cramer's V, and lambda (the two recommended statistics for nominal-nominal associations), the results of a 12-state study of 924 judges are reported in Table 10.3. This table represents the relationship between the method by which the judges were selected and whether, when asked, they do or do not declare a party affiliation.[3] Does the method of selection make a difference in the kind of response provided?

Cramer's V, as well as several other statistics, requires first the calculation of a Chi-square value, symbolized χ^2. Chi-square is calculated by comparing the actual frequencies in the table with the expected frequencies under the condition of total independence. As explained earlier, total independence would mean that the cell frequencies can be calculated from the margin totals, so that for any given cell,

$$E = \frac{\text{Column Total} \times \text{Row Total}}{N}$$

where E is the expected frequency of the appropriate cell. The numbers in parentheses in each cell in Table 10.3 are the *expected* frequencies. The numbers above each diagonal are the *observed* frequencies. From these paired values, Chi-square is developed:

$$\chi^2 = \sum \frac{(0 - E)^2}{E} \qquad (10.1)$$

Taking the difference between the expected and observed for each cell, squaring each result and dividing by the respective expected value, and finally summing the quotients, produces the Chi-square value. For the ten cells in this problem, commencing in the top left corner of this table:

$$\frac{(16.7)^2}{35.3} = 7.90 \qquad\qquad \frac{(22.6)^2}{123.6} = 4.13$$

$$\frac{(16.7)^2}{20.7} = 13.47 \qquad\qquad \frac{(41.6)^2}{219.6} = 7.88$$

$$\frac{(10.8)^2}{102.2} = 1.14 \qquad\qquad \frac{(41.6)^2}{128.4} = 13.48$$

$$\frac{(10.8)^2}{59.8} = 1.95 \qquad\qquad \frac{(8.5)^2}{14.5} = 4.98$$

$$\frac{(22.6)^2}{211.4} = \underline{2.41} \qquad\qquad \frac{(8.5)^2}{8.5} = \underline{8.50}$$

Summing the above, $\chi^2 = 65.84$

Cramer's V is calculated from the formula:

$$V = \sqrt{\frac{\chi^2}{mN}} \qquad\qquad (10.2)$$

where m is the number of rows *or* the number of columns minus 1.0, whichever is less ($r - 1$ or $c - 1$). Thus,

$$V = \sqrt{\frac{65.84}{(1)\,(924)}}$$

$$= \sqrt{.071}$$

$$= .27$$

V is a measure of the extent to which the cell frequencies depart from an independence model. A slight disadvantage to this statistic is that it cannot quite reach the value of 1.0, unless the row totals give a frequency distribution identical to the column totals.[4] In the above example the maximum value of V is about .97. For smaller tables the maximum value tends to be lower. Some analysts prefer to divide V by V_{max}, to control, in a sense, for the frequency distributions; or, alternatively, one could divide the Chi-square value by the maximum Chi-square value.

A number of very similar measures based on Chi-square, but with less appealing properties include:

Pearson's C, where mN is replaced by $X^2 + N$. The values cannot achieve 1.0

Tschuprow's T, where mN is replaced by $N \sqrt{(r-1)\,(c-1)}$. The values can achieve 1.0 only for square tables.

The Phi coefficient, where mN is replaced by N, confined to 2×2 tables.

For any of these measures, it is advisable that the *expected* cell frequencies exceed the value of 5.0; otherwise the table should be reduced in size.

The coefficient lambda, suggested by Guttman and developed by Goodman and Kruskal, does not utilize the Chi-square criterion. It is based on how well the frequencies of the nominal categories of one variable offer predictive evidence about the frequencies of the second nominal variable. In the study of judges, the question may be put in three ways, and for each, lambda offers a calculation formula:

1. How well does method of selection predict party affiliation or non-affiliation responses?
2. How well do party affiliation-nonaffiliation responses predict method of selection?
3. How mutually predictive are the two variables?

The first two questions are answered through the use of what we may call a *one-way lambda,* where the analyst must decide which variable is the independent variable (the one doing the explaining or predicting) and which is the dependent variable (the one being explained or predicted).

The first question above implies that "method of selection" is the independent variable. Suppose that we did not know the method of selection of each judge, and that only the totals of affiliation and nonaffiliation responses were known, so that

A. Affiliation Responses = 583
B. Nonaffiliation Responses = 341

Category A gives a mode of 583. If the mode is used to predict or guess the response distribution, 341 errors are committed, or $924 - 583$. In the lambda statistic, this quantity is symbolized $N - F_d$, where N = the number of cases, and F_d is the modal frequency of the dependent variable. The modal frequency is always found in the margin totals. The question is whether the use of the second nominal variable will reduce the number of errors, and by what proportion.

The next step requires finding the modal frequency within each subclass or category of the independent variable, symbolized f_i. In Table 10.3 the subclass modes may be totaled:

$$52$$
$$113$$
$$234$$
$$178$$
$$17$$
$$\Sigma f_i = \overline{594}$$

Using the subclass modes to predict affiliation-nonaffiliation leads to 330 errors, or $924 - 594$. The lambda formula, then, takes the reduction in error, $594 - 583$, and divides it by the original error of 341. The reduction in error may be symbolized in two ways, where

$$\Sigma f_i - F_d = (N - F_d) - (N - \Sigma f_i)$$
$$594 - 583 = (924 - 583) - (924 - 594)$$
$$11 = \quad 341 \quad - \quad 330$$

Modal	Submodal
Error	Error

Thus, one-way lambda is:

$$\lambda d = \frac{f_i - F_d}{N - F_d} \tag{10.3}$$

$$= \frac{\text{Submodal Reduction in Error}}{\text{Modal Error}}$$

$$= \frac{594 - 583}{924 - 583} = \frac{11}{341} = .03$$

Since lambda ranges from 0 to 1.0, method of selection is a poor predictor of affiliation-nonaffiliation responses.

The problem may also be reversed to predict method of selection from the responses, giving

$$\lambda d = \frac{(234 + 170) - 348}{924 - 348}$$

$$= \frac{56}{576}$$

$$= .10$$

Either way, lambda is quite low.

Two-way lambda always falls between the one-way lambda coefficients and can be calculated directly from the equation:

$$\lambda = \frac{\Sigma f_r + \Sigma f_c - (F_r + F_c)}{2N - (F_r + F_c)} \tag{10.4}$$

where f_r is the modal frequency within a row;
f_c is the modal frequency within a column;
F_r is the modal frequency in a row total;
F_c is the modal frequency in a column total.

In our problem,

$$\lambda = \frac{594 + 404 - (538 + 348)}{1848 - (583 + 348)} = \frac{67}{917} = .073$$

In a very direct manner, lambda, in these three applications, suggests that predicting judges' responses from the way they were selected will probably reduce the number of errors by 3%—a very weak improvement;

predicting method of selection from responses (a strange prediction) has a probable reduction of error of 10%. Slightly more abstract, the mutual predictive error will be reduced by about 7.3%. Lambda can be applied to all nominal-nominal tables, and it can always range from 0 to 1.0. As can be seen, the lambda values are much lower than the Cramer's V value of .27, a pattern to be expected, since it can be shown that where lambda is zero, V can be greater than zero; however, the reverse cannot be true. When $V = 0$, $\lambda = 0$.

In general, the Chi-square based measure is more interesting theoretically, but lambda is more practical. Lambda does have the same weakness as the mode. The mode becomes less and less attractive as the number of categories for a variable increases. Similarly, lambda becomes less attractive as the size of the table or matrix increases. The modes and submodes, even together, ignore much of the information in a large table. Thus, the best policy is to calculate both V and lambda.

One Nominal and One Ordinal Variable. Freeman's coefficient of differentiation, called theta, is preferable over V or lambda when one of the variables is ordinal rather than nominal.[5] For example, V and lambda will not distinguish between the following two arrays:

	RANKS						RANKS				
	4	3	2	1			4	3	2	1	
A.	10	0	0	0	10	A.	10	0	0	0	10
B.	0	10	0	0	10	B.	0	0	10	0	10
C.	0	0	10	10	20	C.	0	10	0	10	20
	10	10	10	10			10	10	10	10	

(NOMINAL CATEGORIES — left of rows A, B, C)

Assuming that the top variable is ordinal, it is clear that the classification system in the left matrix (A, B, and C) helps predict order in the second variable, whereas in the right matrix the classification system is less informative.

Calculation of theta is a bit tedious. It requires examining the ordinal structure for each pair of nominal classifications. In the above illustration, there are three pairs to compare: A with B, A with C, and B with C. To compare A with B, take the frequency of A under the highest rank and multiply it by the number of frequencies in B with lower ranks:

$$\text{Left Matrix: } (10)\ (10) = 100$$
$$\text{Right Matrix: } (10)\ (10) = 100$$

Then take the next highest rank, in this case 3, and multiply the A frequency by the number of B cases with lower ranks, and so on. Since the frequency of A is zero under the remaining ranks, the sum of these remaining calculations will be zero in both matrices. Thus, symbolically for both matrices: $f_b = 100$, where f_b signifies a quantity calculated from moving to the right and *below* the ranks of the A frequencies.

Still comparing A and B, it is now necessary to modify f_b by f_a, starting with the lowest rank (1) and multiplying the A frequency by the number of B cases with higher ranks, or (0) (10). Move them to the next lowest rank, and so on, applying the same reasoning. As it turns out in this example, f_a for A and B is zero in both matrices, and thus for

$$\text{A,B: } f_b - f_a = 100 - 0 = 100$$

Comparing A and C categories, one proceeds in the same manner, obtaining the following results:

LEFT MATRIX	RIGHT MATRIX
Rank 4: (10) (0 + 10 + 10) = 200	Rank 4: (10) (10 + 0 + 10) = 200
Rank 3: (0) (10 + 10) = 0	Rank 3: (0) (0 + 10) = 0
Rank 2: (0) (10) = 0	Rank 2: (0) (10) = 0
Rank 1: (0) (0) = 0	Rank 1: (0) (0) = 0
$f_b = 200$	$f_b = 200$
Rank 1: (0) (10 + 0 + 0) = 0	Rank 1: (0) (0 + 10 + 0) = 0
Rank 2: (0) (0 + 0) = 0	Rank 2: (0) (10 + 0) = 0
Rank 3: (0) (0) = 0	Rank 3: (0) (0) = 0
Rank 4: (10) (0) = 0	Rank 4: (10) (0) = 0
$f_a =$ 0	$f_a =$ 0

For both matrices: A,C: $f_b - f_a = 200 - 0 = 200$.
   The final comparison, between B and C, differentiates the two matrices, as can be seen:

LEFT MATRIX	RIGHT MATRIX
Rank 4: (0) (0 + 10 + 10) = 0	Rank 4: (0) (10 + 0 + 10) = 0
Rank 3: (10) (10 + 10) = 200	Rank 3: (0) (0 + 10) = 0
Rank 2: (0) (10) = 0	Rank 2: (10) (10) = 100
Rank 1: (0) (0) = 0	Rank 1: (0) (0) = 0
$f_b = 200$	$f_b = 100$
Rank 1: (0) (10 + 0 + 0) = 0	Rank 1: (0) (0 + 10 + 0) = 0
Rank 2: (0) (0 + 0) = 0	Rank 2: (10) (10 + 0) = 100
Rank 3: (10) (–) = 0	Rank 3: (0) (0) = 0
Rank 4: (0) (0) = 0	Rank 4: (0) (0) = 0
$f_a =$ 0	$f_a = 100$

For the two matrices: Left B,C: $f_b - f_a = 200 - 0 = 200$
   Right B,C: $f_b - f_a = 100 - 100 = 0$

The above calculations complete the tedium necessary when theta is not calculated by computer. The remainder of the theta equation is much easier to satisfy. The equation may read:

$$\theta = \frac{|\Sigma f_b - \Sigma f_a|}{T_2} \tag{10.5}$$

$$= \frac{\Sigma D_1}{T_2} \text{ by substitution,}$$

where T_2 is a combinatorial multiplication of the nominal category frequencies in the margin totals. In this example,

$$T_2 = (N_A) \ (N_B) + (N_A) \ (N_C) + (N_B) \ (N_C)$$
$$= (10) \ (10) + (10) \ (20) + (10) \ (20)$$
$$= 500$$

Using the full equation for each matrix example, we find that

Left: $\theta \dfrac{(100 + 200 + 200) - (0 + 0 + 0)}{500} = 1.0$

Right: $\theta \dfrac{(100 + 200 + 100) - (0 + 0 + 100)}{500} = .60$

The theta coefficient clearly conveys that the left matrix is a perfect nominal-ordinal relationship, while the right matrix is much less so. Cramer's V and Guttman's lambda give values of 1.0 for both matrices. Theta, then, signifies the extent to which order can be predicted on the basis of a classification system. The statistic should be very useful, for example, when comparing the attitudes or opinions of different categories of political elites. It should be clear that the nominal categories can appear in any order in the frequency matrix. The coefficient will not be affected, since all possible pairs of nominal categories are taken up in turn. A similar procedure is used in the calculation of the ordinal-ordinal statistic, gamma, but the steps are less tedious due to the order in both variables. It may be easier for some readers to work out the gamma procedures before taking up theta.

One Nominal and One Interval Variable. There is only one statistic for measuring the degree of association between one nominal and one interval variable, the eta coefficient, η, sometimes called the "correlation ratio." By convention, the interval variable is given the symbol Y, and the nominal variable, X. In certain ways, the eta coefficient is similar to the Pearson r statistic for interval-interval relationships, but it is much easier to comprehend, and an excellent intermediate step when learning.

The basic question that usually calls for the use of eta is: To what extent will a classification system explain or predict a set of numeric scores? For instance, suppose that we collected a group of congressional proposals introduced in the House of Representatives. These proposals included a variety of motions: to pass a bill, to recommit a bill, to amend, to resolve, and so on. All of these proposals were followed by a House vote. The proposals were classified into the following groups:

1. Those that both majority and minority leaders supported.
2. Those that majority leaders supported (no funding or appropriation).
3. Those allocating funds or appropriations and supported by majority leaders.
4. Those supported by minority leaders.

TABLE 10.4

Selected Characteristics of Foreign Affairs Roll Call Votes
(Eighty-Eighth Congress)

ROLL CALL MEASURE		MAJORITY PARTY LEADERS' SUPPORT	FUNDING INCREASE	MINORITY PARTY LEADERS' SUPPORT	ACTUAL VOTE	MEAN * SCORES (ROUNDED)
HR	4374	X		X	378–21	
HR	3872	X		X	379–11	380–7
HJ	Res 1145	X		X	416–0	
H	Res 836	X		X	375–3	
H	Con Res 343	X		X	352–0	
HR	5207	X			234–166	
HR	8864	X			181–145	
HR	9499	X			182–95	
HR	9499	X			202–105	225–112
HR	9499	X			189–158	
S	1627	X			268–89	
S	2701	X			320–23	
HR	7885	X	X		224–186	
H	Report 863	X	X		251–134	
HR	7885	X	X		195–164	230–161
HR	9499	X	X		250–135	
HR	11380	X	X		230–175	
HR	11812	X	X		231–174	
HR	5517			X	207–190	
HR	7885			X	222–188	
HR	9499			X	218–169	
HR	9499 (Recommittal motions)			X	141–136	
HR	9022			X	208–189	179–205
S	2455			X	90–309	
S	2214			X	132–247	
HR	11380			X	193–211	
HR	11812			X	198–208	
					6466,3631	

* $\Sigma Y_i^2 - \dfrac{(\Sigma Y_i)^2}{N}$ was used to calculate sum of squared differences.

These are mutually exclusive groups in this example, and all of the proposals are in the area of foreign affairs. Will these groups of proposals help
explain or predict the number of supporting and opposing votes cast by
members of the House of Representatives?

For this problem, the set of data, consolidated by Cherryholmes and
Shapiro in their study of House roll call voting, is presented in Table 10.4
in a revised form.[6] The X's indicate which conditions apply to each pro-
posal. It can be seen that the mean scores for the subgroups do differ, and
that perhaps the classification system will help. But we must estimate how
much the classification system improves our knowledge of the scores. To do
so, we commence with a summary measure of dispersion for the total set of
data, the mean variance, defined as

$$s_m^2 = \frac{\Sigma\,(Y_i - \overline{Y})^2}{N}$$

where the numerator is the sum of the squared distances from the mean.

In Congress, the number absent on votes varies considerably; thus, it is probably better to calculate the variance first for all 27 supporting votes, and then for all 27 opposing votes, giving us essentially two nominal-interval relationships to examine. Let us take up the supporting votes first. The mean, $\overline{Y}$, for supporting votes is 239.48. The mean variance gives an estimate of how poorly the mean describes the distribution. The higher the mean variance, the less descriptive is the mean. For supporting votes,

$$s_m^2 = \frac{171751}{27} = 6361$$

The question is whether the sum of the squared differences, divided by N, of the nominal *subgroups* is less than the *overall* mean variance, and by what proportion. Thus, the same formula is used to calculate the variance within each subgroup, yielding

Subgroup 1. $\Sigma\,(Y_i - \overline{Y})^2 = \Sigma\,(Y_i - 380)^2 = 2110$

2. $ = \Sigma\,(Y_i - 225)^2 = 16565$

3. $ = \Sigma\,(Y_i - 230)^2 = 2103$

4. $ = \Sigma\,(Y_i - 179)^2 = \underline{17126}$

$$ 37904$$

$$s_w^2 = \frac{37904}{27} = 1404$$

The variance within the subgroups is much less than the mean variance for the entire array. The within-group variance is less by the following proportion:

$$\eta^2 = \frac{s_m^2 - s_w^2}{s_m^2} = \frac{6361 - 1404}{6361} = .78 \qquad (10.6)$$

where the result is the square of the eta coefficient. The classification system improved on the mean variance by 78%. One would not expect to find such an improvement if the support votes were placed randomly into the subgroups.

The mean variance for opposing votes was found to be 6344, and the within-group variance, 1333. In the same manner,

$$\eta^2 = \frac{6344 - 1333}{6344} = .79$$

The nominal subgroups improved on the mean variance by about 79%. The eta coefficients simply require taking the square roots of the eta proportions.

Here:

$$\eta = \sqrt{.78} = .88$$

$$\eta = \sqrt{.79} = .89$$

Both η^2 and η range between 0 and 1.0, but the former is easier to interpret, and it is almost always calculated first.

There is a less intuitive but much quicker way to calculate the eta values, given by the equation:

$$\eta^2 = \frac{\displaystyle\sum_{i=1}^{k} n_j \, (\overline{Y}_j - \overline{\overline{Y}})^2}{\displaystyle\sum_{i=1}^{N} (Y_i - \overline{\overline{Y}})^2} \tag{10.7}$$

where $\overline{Y}_j$ is a subgroup mean;
$\quad n_j$ is the number of cases in a subgroup;
$\quad \overline{\overline{Y}}$ is the mean for the entire array;
$\quad k$ is the number of subgroups.

The denominator for this equation is the sum of squared differences for the total distribution. The numerator sums the products resulting from multiplying each subgroup n by the squared difference between its mean and the grand mean. For supporting votes,

$$\eta = \frac{(5) \, (380 - 239.5)^2 + (7) \, (225 - 239.5)^2 + (6) \, (230 - 239.5)^2 + (9) \, (179 - 239.5)^2}{171751}$$

$$= .78$$

The above figures in the numerator are rounded for the purpose of illustration. The grand mean is subtracted from each subgroup mean and the resulting quantity squared before multiplying by each subgroup n and summing. The numerator is commonly called the *sum of squares between groups*.

The calculation formula is derived from the knowledge that the total sum of squares (calculated from the grand mean) is equal to the sum of squares between groups *plus* the sum of squares within groups. Thus, eta can be calculated through the use of either the within-group sum of squares or the between-group sum of squares. Given the equations:

$$\sum_{i=1}^{N}(Y_i - \overline{\overline{Y}})^2 = \sum_{j=1}^{k} n_j \, (\overline{Y}_j - \overline{\overline{Y}})^2 + \sum_{j=1}^{k}\sum_{i=1}^{n}(Y_i - \overline{Y}_j)^2 \tag{10.8}$$

substituting: $T = B + W$

$$\text{and } \eta^2 = \frac{S_m{}^2 - S_w{}^2}{S_m{}^2} = \frac{\dfrac{T}{N} - \dfrac{W}{N}}{\dfrac{T}{N}} = \frac{T - W}{T}$$

$$\text{then } \eta^2 = \frac{B + W - W}{T}$$

$$= \frac{B}{T} \text{ or Equation (10.7)}$$

One final note: It is usually more accurate and convenient in the calculation of between-group sum of squares to utilize the right-hand expression in the following identity:

$$\sum_{j=1}^{k} n_j \, (\overline{Y}_j - \overline{Y})^2 = \sum n_j \, (\overline{Y}_j)^2 - \frac{(\Sigma n_j \overline{Y}_j)^2}{N}$$

Linear Measures of Association

Linear measures of association make sense when each of two variables in a comparison is measured by either an ordinal or an interval scale. The coefficients produced from the linear formulas range from -1.0 to $+1.0$ to indicate the direction of linear relationship. If the values of one variable increase while the values of the second variable decrease, a linear measure of association will give a negative correlation. If there is no linear relationship between the two sets of values, the correlation will be 0. Correspondingly, if both sets of values increase, or both sets decrease, the correlation will be positive.

Two Ordinal Variables. Three statistics are widely used in the measurement of linear relationship between two ordinal variables: Goodman and

TABLE 10.5

Hypothetical Relationship Between Two Ordinal Attitude Items (100 Responses)

			STRONG	MODERATE	LITTLE	NONE	
			1	2	3	4	
Do you favor increase in federal spending in next fiscal year?	Yes	1	a 15	b 15	c 5	d 5	40
	Und.	2	e 10	f 5	g 5	h 12	32
	No	3	i 0	j 5	k 15	l 8	28
			25	25	25	25	100

INTENDED SUPPORT FOR ENVIRONMENTAL BILL

Kruskal's gamma, Kendall's tau_c, and Spearman's rho. The first two are very similar in rationale and can be developed simultaneously; rho is based on somewhat different assumptions. The basic assumption underlying these statistics is that the exact distances between the numbers on each variable are not known.

To illustrate gamma and tau_c, hypothetical responses to two attitude items are presented in Table 10.5. The immediate purpose is to measure the extent to which a legislator's attitude toward increased spending is related to the degree he or she intends to support a pending environmental bill. A cursory examination of the table should reveal that a majority of the cases fall near the diagonal running from the top left to the bottom right corner. In gamma-tau language:

1. If a case falls *below* and to the *right* of another case, the two cases make up a *concordant* pair.
2. If a case falls *below* and to the *left* of another case, the two cases make up a *discordant* pair.

By convention here, the total number of concordant pairs in a table is symbolized P, and the total number of discordant pairs is symbolized Q. Gamma is symbolized as

$$G = \frac{P - Q}{P + Q} \qquad (10.9)$$

whereas tau_c is symbolized:

$$T_c = \frac{(P - Q)\ (2z)}{N^2\ (z - 1)} \qquad (10.10)$$

where z is the number of columns or number of rows, whichever is less. The primary feature of both statistics is the difference between the number of concordant and discordant pairs.

Working from the interval cells of Table 10.5, we find 15 cases in the top left corner cell. Below and to the right of it are $5 + 5 + 12 + 5 + 15 + 8$, or 50 cases. Multiplying 15 by 50 will give the number of concordant pairs, 750, for the top left cell alone. Following the same procedure for every cell with cases below and to the right yields

$$
\begin{array}{llll}
\text{Cell a:} & (15)\ (5 + 5 + 12 + 5 + 15 + 8) & = 750 \\
\text{b:} & (15)\ (5 + 12 + 15 + 8) & = 600 \\
\text{c:} & (5)\ (12 + 8) & = 100 \\
\text{e:} & (10)\ (5 + 15 + 8) & = 280 \\
\text{f:} & (5)\ (15 + 8) & = 115 \\
\text{g:} & (5)\ (8) & = 40 \\
& & \overline{1885} = P
\end{array}
$$

Cells d, h, i, j, k, and l have no cases below and to the right of them. The number of discordant pairs is calculated by starting in the top right corner and counting the number of cases below and to the left, so that

Cell d: (5) (5 + 5 + 10 + 15 + 5 + 0) = 200
  c: (5) (5 + 10 + 0)   = 100
  b: (15) (10 + 0)   = 150
  h: (12) (15 + 5 + 0)   = 240
  g: (5) (5 + 0)   = 25
  f: (5) (0)   = 0

$$\overline{715} = Q$$

Given the above calculations of P and Q, both gamma and tau_c can be satisfied:

$$G = \frac{P - Q}{P + Q} = \frac{1885 - 715}{1885 + 715} = \frac{1170}{2600} = .45$$

$$T_c = \frac{(P - Q)\,(2z)}{N^2\,(z - 1)} = \frac{+\,(1885 - 715)\,2\,(3)}{10,000\,(3 - 1)} = \frac{7020}{20,000} = .35$$

Note that the procedures for calculating P and Q emphasize order and not distance. For example, the cases below and to the right of the top left cell are simply counted without regard to how far below and to the right such cases are. Gamma may be more preferable because its interpretation is more direct (although in statistical theory the question is still open). A positive value of gamma gives the net number of concordant pairs as a percentage of the total number of pairs. A negative value (favoring the off-diagonal rather than the main diagonal) gives the net number of discordant pairs as a percentage of the total number of pairs. When there are no tied ranks on either variable, gamma and tau_c produce identical values. The authors recommend the use of tau_c, however, whenever the margin totals are highly skewed. Under such conditions, gamma can yield values that are deceptively high.

  Spearman's rho is usually employed only when tied ranks are either few in number or nonexistent, and seldom when there are many tied ranks as in the above example. Its use is almost always preceded by a data transformation whereby the researcher, not confident of the exact values assigned to a set of subjects or other units of observation, or wishing to ignore idiosyncratic frequency distributions, decides to rank-order the values. The values: .90, .82, .50, .50, .40, .35, and .33 would be ranked 1, 2, 3.5, 3.5, 5, 6 and 7 respectively. The two tied ranks are given the average value of what their ranks would be if they were not tied. Thus, the third and fourth values above are given the rank of $(3 + 4)/2$. With no tied ranks, the rank-order procedure produces perfect rectangular distributions. If the original data values can be trusted to give only order and not distance, then why not rank-order the values and use the ranks for analysis purposes?

  In reality, the Spearman formula does not ignore distance; distances between numbers are simply made less important by the prior rank-ordering procedure. Spearman's rho is represented symbolically as

$$r' = 1 - \frac{6 \Sigma (X_i - Y_i)^2}{N (N^2 - 1)} \tag{10.11}$$

$$= 1 - \frac{6 \sum D_i^2}{N (N^2 - 1)} \tag{10.12}$$

where X_i is the rank assigned to a unit of observation on variable X;
Y_i is the rank assigned to a unit of observation on variable Y;
$D_i = X_i - Y_i$;
N = the number of cases.

The value of r' may range from -1.0 to $+1.0$. The squaring procedure in the numerator will give greater than proportional weight to large values of D.

The Spearman formula is actually a special version of the interval-interval statistic, Pearson's r, to be presented later in this chapter. Both statistics will give the same value when applied to rank values. Because of this fact, the full rationale for rho will be postponed until the Pearson statistic is introduced. The purpose of this section can be best served by comparing calculated rho values to calculated gamma and tau$_c$ values.

Spearman's rho is so easy to calculate when there are no tied ranks that only brief examples are necessary. Taking a first example of ranks for five observations, we have:

	X	Y	D	D²	
1.	1	2	1	1	$r' = 1 = \dfrac{6\,(4)}{5\,(5^2 - 1)}$
2.	2	1	1	1	
3.	3	4	1	1	$= 1 - \dfrac{24}{120}$
4.	4	3	1	1	
5.	5	5	0	0	$= .80$
				4	$G = .60 \qquad T_c = .60$

A second example produces the following results:

	X	Y	D	D²	
1.	1	3	2	4	$r' = 1 - \dfrac{6\,(10)}{5\,(5^2 - 1)}$
2.	2	2	0	0	
3.	3	1	2	4	$= 1 - \dfrac{60}{120}$
4.	4	5	1	1	
5.	5	4	1	1	$= .50$
				10	$G = .20 \qquad T_c = .20$

As others have noted, we may note that the gamma and tau$_c$ values are closer to r'^2 than r'. The squared values of r' are .64 and .25, respectively. The next example, however, shows that such an interpretation is risky:

	X	Y	D	D²
1.	1	2	1	1
2.	2	4	2	4
3.	3	1	2	4
4.	4	3	1	1
5.	5	5	0	0
				10

$$r' = 1 - \frac{6\,(10)}{5\,(5^2 - 1)}$$

$$= 1 - \frac{60}{120}$$

$$= .50$$

$$G = .40 \qquad T_c = .40$$

In this example the values of gamma and tau_c are closer to r' than its square. Rho does not vary consistently with the gamma-tau values because it clearly takes into account the distances between the paired ordinal numbers.

Given the above lack of correspondence, it is difficult to know what stance to take toward the rank-order correlation coefficient rho. One way to view the problem is to ask for the conditions that would make rho the best candidate. The following conditions favor the use of r':

1. Tied ranks are rare or nonexistent.
2. It is suspected that the original data contain a small number of serious measurement errors (which would be reflected too strongly in an interval statistic).
3. It is suspected that errors in the original data are more likely to be located at the tails rather than the center of the original frequency distributions (otherwise, a normal curve transformation might be more appropriate).
4. It is felt that the true distribution is rectangular.
5. The original data distributions are fairly rectangular or, if not, they are clearly affected by the measuring instrument.
6. It is felt that if the distances between numbers are ignored entirely, the estimate of association will be too conservative.

The last point can be illustrated by the following array:

X	Y	D	D²
1	2	1	1
2	1	1	1
3	4	1	1
4	3	1	1
5	6	1	1
6	5	1	1
7	8	1	1
8	7	1	1
9	10	1	1
10	9	1	1
			10

$$r' = 1 - \frac{6\,(10)}{10\,(10^2 - 1)}$$

$$= 1 - \frac{60}{990}$$

$$= .94$$

$$G = .78 \qquad T_c = .78$$

$$r'^2 = .88$$

The D quantities are a product of "local" differences and the squared value of r' is much higher than the values for gamma and tau_c.

Calculation of P and Q, when there are no tied ranks, can proceed in the same manner as illustrated earlier. In the above case, simply create a 10 by 10 matrix, enter the frequencies (all of which will be 1) and proceed as shown earlier. For a large number of cases, do not create the matrix, but work from the parallel listing of ranks as above. Ignore the X ranks, since they are in perfect order. Start with the last Y rank (9 above) and count the Y ranks above it that should be below it to produce a ranking identical to the X ranking. Do the same to the next value up the Y list, and so on. Summing the results, this procedure in the above example will give a Q value of 5. To calculate P, start with the last Y value again and count the number of ranks above it that should be above it. Do the same to the next value up the list, and so on. Summing in the above example will give a P value of 40, and $G = 35/45 = .78$. As a check, it is helpful to know that when there are no tied ranks, $P + Q = .5(N^2 - N)$. To avoid mistakes, it is important first to list by rank-order one variable and then to assign the appropriate ranks to the second variable. One must be able to ignore the X ranks, so that

Y	Q	P
3		
2	1	0
1	2	0
5	0	3
4	1	3
	4	6

$$G = \frac{6 - 4}{6 + 4} = .20$$

Other ordinal-ordinal statistics include Kendall's tau_b and Somer's d, both of which have undesirable ranges when a matrix does not have the same number of columns and rows. Yules' Q was developed for 2 by 2 tables and produces the same values as gamma.

One Ordinal and One Interval Variable. There is only one general statistic for an ordinal-interval relationship, Jaspen's Coefficient of Multiserial Correlation, and it is not used very often. To use it, the analyst must be willing to assume that the ordinal variable is normally distributed given a sufficient number of properly selected observations and a sufficiently refined measurement technique. The formula is used primarily when the analyst has been able to use only broad ordinal categories on one variable, a situation that arises frequently in the use of open-end questions in interview studies. Like Spearman's rho, the multiserial correlation, M, is a special version of Pearson's r.

Suppose that in a study of 20 governors an open-end question regarding their attitude toward deficit spending was administered, and that the responses

TABLE 10.6
Calculation of M *for Ordinal-Interval Relationship*

ATTITUDE

X_i	P_j	Y_i	Y_i^2	$\overline{Y}_j$	$(0_b - 0_a)_j$	$(0_b - 0_a)_j^2$	$\overline{Y}_j (0_b - 0_a)_j$	$\dfrac{(0_b - 0_a)_j^2}{p_j}$
1		2.4	5.76					
1	.20	4.0	16.	2.5	.28	.0784	.70	.392
1		1.6	2.56					
1		2.0	4.					
2		3.0	9.					
2		2.6	6.76					
2		1.2	1.44					
2	.40	1.0	1.00	1.5	.1063	.0113	.1595	.0282
2		1.9	3.61					
2		0	0					
2		1.6	2.56					
2		.7	.49					
3		1.4	1.96					
3		1.2	1.44					
3	.25	1.0	1.00	.7	.1531	.0234	.1072	.0936
3		.1	.01					
3		-.2	.04					
4		.7	.49					
4	.15	-1.0	1.00	-.3	.2332	.0544	.07	.3627
4		-.3	.09					
		24.9	59.31				1.0367	.8765

$$s_Y \sqrt{\dfrac{59.31 - 29.9^2}{20}}$$

$$= 1.19$$

$$M = \dfrac{1.0367}{(1.19)\,(.8765)}$$

$$= \dfrac{1.0367}{1.043} = .994$$

allowed the analyst to separate the governors into four groups: favor, slightly favor, slightly opposed, opposed, corresponding to the ordinal ranks of 1, 2, 3, and 4. Later, the percent debt increase or decrease actually recommended by the governors for the next fiscal period was recorded. Is there any relationship between their attitudes and their recommendations? The hypothetical data are presented in Table 10.6, the first column containing the attitude score (X_i), and the third column the percent increase or decrease in debt (Y_i). The distribution among ranks on the attitudinal variable is as follows:

RANK	FREQUENCY	PROPORTION
1	4	.20
2	8	.40
3	5	.25
4	3	.15
	20	1.00

The ranks are assumed to be very crude categories and the distances between them may vary considerably. A better measuring instrument might produce a normal distribution. Since we do know the proportion of cases, *p*, falling within each rank, we might assume that these proportions represent areas under the normal curve, as illustrated in Figure 9.3. This would allow us to locate the normal curve deviates dividing the governors into four groups. Using Table A in the Appendix, we find:

(P_j) PROPORTION	CUMULATIVE PROPORTION	z
.20	.20	−.8416
.40	.60	.2533
.25	.85	1.0364

These calculations indicate that 20% of the cases fall at least .8416 standard deviation units to the left or below the mean, 40% of the cases fall between −.8416 and .2533 units from the mean, 25% of the cases fall between .2533 and 1.0364 units to the right of the mean, and 15% of the cases fall at least 1.0364 standard deviation units to the right of the mean. The problem now is to find the mean *z* value for each of the four segments, since the mean is the best single estimate of where the scores fall within the segment.

The mean value, *z*, is found by consulting the height of the curve, referred to as the height of the *ordinate,* at each point segmenting the curve. The ordinates are found in Table B of the Appendix. The mean value of *z* for any segment is determined by subtracting the height of the ordinate above the segment from the height of the ordinate below the segment and dividing by the proportion of cases. Symbolically,

$$\bar{z}_i = \frac{0_b - 0_a}{P_i}$$

$$\bar{z}_1 = \frac{0 - .28}{.20} = -1.4$$

$$\bar{z}_2 = \frac{.28 - .3863}{.40} = -.2657$$

$$\bar{z}_3 = \frac{.3863 - .2332}{.25} = .6124$$

$$\bar{z}_4 = \frac{.2332 - 0}{.15} = 1.555$$

These $\bar{z}$ values can replace the ranks, after which the Pearson correlation coefficient can be applied. However, the resulting correlation must be divided by the standard deviation of *z* to correct for the use of broad categories. The use of broad categories tends to lower the variance of its distribution. In any case, we may note that

$$M = \frac{r}{s_z}$$

where r is the Pearson correlation coefficient.
M may be calculated directly from the equation:

$$M = \frac{\Sigma \overline{Y}_j (O_b - O_a)_j}{s_y \sum \frac{(O_b - O_a)_j^2}{p_j}} \tag{10.13}$$

where $\overline{Y}_j$ is the mean of a subgroup corresponding to an ordinal rank;

$(O_b - O_a)_j$ is the lower ordinate minus the higher ordinate for a sub-group;

s_y is the standard deviation for all values of Y, the interval variable:

p is the proportion of cases in a subgroup.

Consulting the calculation table, we find that this formula yields a correlation coefficient of .994 for the hypothetical relationship between attitudes toward deficit spending and percent increase/decrease in debt recommended.

Two Interval Variables. The most important concept in the assessment of interval-interval relationships is that of *variance*. The concept underlies not only the Pearson statistic, r, of course, but also the eta coefficient, the rank-order correlation coefficient rho, and Jaspen's M. There are two types of variance of interest here: the first is the mean variance, calculated from the equation:

$$s_m^2 = \frac{\Sigma (Y_i - \overline{Y})^2}{N}$$

The mean variance may be viewed as a function of the amount of error that results from predicting (or postdicting) the values of Y_i from the mean, $\overline{Y}$. The mean is the best *least-squares* guess; that is, take any other value and substitute it for the mean and it will produce a larger value for s^2. In statistical application what we wish to do is to choose a second variable that will produce less variance than does the mean of the first variable when the values of Y_i are predicted from the values of the second variable X. This second type of variance is symbolized:

$$s_y^2 = \frac{\Sigma (Y_i - Y_i')^2}{N}$$

where Y_i' is the predicted value of Y_i from a value of X. Pearson's r allows us to state by what proportion we have improved upon the mean variance.

Schematically, when the values of X give exact predictions of the values of Y, the plotted points will fall on a straight line. When this happens, $s_y^2 = 0$, indicating no error, and

$$\frac{s_m^2 - s_y^2}{s_m^2} = 1.0$$

indicating that the X predictions have improved by 100% over the Y predictions.

The basic puzzle is one of determining how to make predictions of Y from the X values. Schematically, this puzzle amounts to finding *the* straight line that minimizes the sum of the squared distances between the plotted points and the line. The line is found algebraically, commencing with the equation:

$$Y_i = a + bX_i$$

where b is the slope coefficient, and a is the value of Y_i when $X_i = 0$. The slope coefficient reveals how many units of change in X accompany a single unit of change in Y. The slope of X on Y is defined as

$$b = \frac{\Sigma (X_i - \overline{X}) (Y_i - \overline{Y})}{\Sigma (X_i - \overline{X})^2} \qquad (10.14)$$

Calculation of the slope requires first the calculation of the two means. Since it is known that the best-fit line must pass through the intersection of the two means,

$$\overline{Y} = a + b\overline{X}, \text{ and}$$
$$a = \overline{Y} - b\overline{X}$$

Just as the best single-value least-squares prediction is the mean of Y, the best-fit regression line prediction will be a line that passes through the intersection of the two means.

To illustrate, we can take a set of data presented by Peterson in a study of voting participation in poverty districts for Community Action Council candidates.[7] The question is whether the number of candidates living in particular sections of a district is related to the percent of people actually voting in such sections. The data for 12 sections appear in Table 10.7. The mean number of candidates, $\overline{X}$, is 5.9. The mean percent voting, $\overline{Y}$, is 1.88. The numerator for the slope formula may be applied to the data as follows:

1. $(12 - 5.9) (5.6 - 1.88) = 22.692$
2. $(12 - 5.9) (5.7 - 1.88) = 23.302$
3. $(10 - 5.9) (2.2 - 1.88) = 1.312$
4. $(8 - 5.9) (1.4 - 1.88) = -1.008$
5. $(8 - 5.9) (1.2 - 1.88) = -1.428$
6. $(6 - 5.9) (2.3 - 1.88) = .042$
7. $(6 - 5.9) (.9 - 1.88) = -.098$
8. $(5 - 5.9) (2.0 - 1.88) = -.108$
9. $(4 - 5.9) (.7 - 1.88) = 2.242$
10. $(0 - 5.9) (.4 - 1.88) = 8.732$
11. $(0 - 5.9) (.1 - 1.88) = 10.502$
12. $(0 - 5.9) (.1 - 1.88) = 10.502$

$$\Sigma = \overline{76.684}$$

The sum of squares for X in the denominator of the slope formula yields a value of 208.92. Thus,

$$b = \frac{76.684}{208.92} = .367$$

TABLE 10.7

*Calculation Table for Pearson's r: Community Action Council
Candidates and Voting*

NUMBER LIVING IN POVERTY SECTION X	X^2	PERCENT VOTING Y	Y^2	XY
12	144	5.6	31.36	67.2
12	144	5.7	32.49	68.4
10	100	2.2	4.84	22.0
8	64	1.4	1.96	11.2
8	64	1.2	1.44	9.6
6	36	2.3	5.29	13.8
6	36	.9	.81	5.4
5	25	2.0	4.00	10.0
4	16	.7	.49	2.8
0	0	.4	.16	0
0	0	.1	.01	0
0	0	.1	.01	0
71	629	22.6	82.86	210.4

Adapted from Paul E. Peterson, "Forms of Representation: Participation of the Poor in the Community Action Program," *American Political Science Review*, 64 (June 1970), Table 3.

For every unit change in Y, there is a .367 change in X units. The constant, a, as indicated, may now be directly calculated:

$$a = \overline{Y} - b\overline{X}$$

$$= 1.88 - .367 (5.9)$$

$$= 1.88 - 2.165$$

$$= -.285$$

Thus, the linear regression equation for this problem is:

$$Y_i = -.285 + .367X_i$$

The linear regression equation is utilized to predict the values of Y by substituting the actual values of X to see what values of Y result. We can symbolize the predicted values of Y as Y_i' to distinguish them from the actual values of Y. For ease of comparison of Y_i' and Y_i, the above equation can be reversed, so that

	a	+	b	$(X_i) =$	Y_i'	Y_i	$Y_i - Y_i'$	$(Y_i - Y_i')^2$
1.	−.285	+	(.367)	(12) =	4.119	5.6	1.481	2.1933
2.	−.285	+	(.367)	(12) =	4.119	5.7	1.581	2.4996
3.	−.285	+	(.367)	(10) =	3.385	2.2	−1.185	1.4043
4.	−.285	+	(.367)	(8) =	2.651	1.4	−1.251	1.5650
5.	−.285	+	(.367)	(8) =	2.651	1.2	−1.451	2.1054
6.	−.285	+	(.367)	(6) =	1.917	2.3	.383	.1467
7.	−.285	+	(.367)	(6) =	1.917	.9	−1.017	1.0343

8. $-.285 + (.367)$ (5) $= 1.55$	2.0	.45	.2025
9. $-.285 + (.367)$ (4) $= 1.183$	.7	$-.483$	.2333
10. $-.285 + (.367)$ (0) $= -.285$	.4	.685	.4692
11. $-.285 + (.367)$ (0) $= -.285$	.1	.385	.1482
12. $-.285 + (.367)$ (0) $= -.285$	.1	.385	.1482
			12.151

The errors in prediction are given under $Y_i - Y_i'$, ranging from slightly over 1.5% to less than four-tenths of 1%. Summing the absolute values and dividing by N produces an average error of about .9%. Squaring each error value and summing yields the sum of squared differences, 12.151. Dividing this value by N, or 12, gives the variance, where

$$s_y^2 = \frac{\Sigma (Y_i - Y_i')^2}{N}$$

$$= \frac{12.151}{12} \qquad (10.15)$$

$$= 1.0126$$

The mean variance for Y is calculated most easily through the use of an identity, where

$$s_m^2 = \frac{\Sigma (Y_i - \bar{Y})^2}{N} = \frac{\Sigma Y^2 - \frac{(\Sigma Y)^2}{N}}{N}$$

$$= \frac{82.86 - 42.56}{12}$$

$$= \frac{40.3}{12}$$

$$= 3.3583$$

One can see that the amount of variance produced by using the values of X to predict Y is substantially less than the mean variance. It should be noted that s_y^2 can never exceed s_m^2, although it is possible that the two values will be equal. For this reason, it is legitimate to ask by what proportion the second variable has improved upon the mean in estimating the values of Y. This proportion is given at least three labels by various authors: the coefficient of determination, the explained variance, and symbolically, r^2. In this example,

$$r^2 = \frac{s_m^2 - s_y^2}{s_m^2}$$

$$= \frac{3.3583 - 1.0126}{3.3583}$$

$$= \frac{2.3457}{3.3583}$$

$$= .70$$

This value is the square of the Pearson correlation coefficient, r. The square root of .70 is .84.

The above procedures illustrate the rationale of linear regression analysis, but they should never be used, except for understanding what underlies the Pearson statistic. The procedures involve too many fractions and arithmetic operations, and unless a computer is utilized, calculation errors are very likely. The steps for the recommended calculation formula appear in Table 10.7 in order to satisfy

$$r = \frac{\Sigma X_i Y_i - \frac{\Sigma X_i \, \Sigma Y_i}{N}}{\sqrt{\left(\Sigma X_i^2 - \frac{(\Sigma X_i)^2}{N}\right)\left(\Sigma Y_i^2 - \frac{(\Sigma Y_i)^2}{N}\right)}} \tag{10.16}$$

$$= \frac{210.4 - \frac{71(22.6)}{12}}{\sqrt{\left(629 - \frac{71^2}{12}\right)\left(82.86 - \frac{22.6^2}{12}\right)}}$$

$$= \frac{76.7}{91.6}$$

$$= .84 \qquad\qquad r^2 = .706$$

The value of r may range from -1.0 to $+1.0$, whereas r^2 is always positive. The more laborious procedure does not give the sign of r directly, although a simple check of the sign of the slope coefficient will.

Because the procedures relating to the Pearson statistic have had a relatively long history in many fields of inquiry, the terminology that has developed to describe its many features can be confusing to the infrequent user or beginning student. Below is a list of values from the above problem, the associated notation, and the narrative terms applied at least occasionally in various sources.

1. $r = .84$ — Pearson product-moment correlation coefficient
Product-moment correlation coefficient
Zero-order correlation coefficient
Simple correlation coefficient
Pearson's r (Pearson developed other statistics)

2. $r^2 = .706$ — Explained variance (proportion of total implied)
Reduction in variance
Coefficient of determination

3. $b = .367$ Slope
Slope coefficient
Regression coefficient
Least-squares regression coefficient

4. $s_m^2 = 3.3583$ Mean variance
Original variance
Total variance

5. $s_y^2 = 1.0126$ Error variance
Regression variance
Unexplained variance

6. $s_m^2 - s_y^2 = 2.3457$ Explained variance

7. $\Sigma (Y_i - \overline{Y})^2 = 40.3$ Total sum of squares
Mean sum of squares

8. $\Sigma (Y_i - Y_i')^2 = 12.151$ Unexplained sum of squares
Residual sum of squares

It may be noted that in real life circumstances, decision-makers may be more interested in the average error resulting from $Y_i - Y_i'$ than in the abstract notion of variance.

When the variables are normally distributed, it is much better to use the *standard error of the estimate* and not the average error. The estimate is calculated from either of the following formulae:

$$s_{yx} = \sqrt{\frac{\Sigma (Y_i - Y_i')^2}{N-2}}$$

$$= \sqrt{\frac{\Sigma Y_i^2 - \frac{(\Sigma X_i Y_i)^2}{\Sigma X_i^2}}{N-2}} \tag{10.17}$$

$$= \sqrt{\frac{82.86 - \frac{210.4^2}{629}}{10}} = 1.115$$

The last formula is used because the necessary values were previously determined for the r formula. The result may be interpreted to mean that 68% of the cases can be expected to fall within 1.115% of the predicted voting percent when X is the number of candidates within a poverty section and the calculated linear equation is used. The normal curve makes this kind of sensible prediction possible. Correspondingly, 95% of the time the prediction will be within 2.23 of the actual voting percentage.

NONLINEARITY

Most statisticians would probably admit that without accurate data and extensive observation or well-developed theoretical principles, linear estimates of association should suffice, at least at the earlier stages of analysis. Graphically, unless a pattern of relationship, other than linear, is fairly pronounced, it is probably not worth the effort to change the statistical model. With modern computing facilities, however, less and less effort is being required to alter the statistical model. In one convenient alteration, for example, the values of one variable are converted to logarithms, after which the Pearson statistic is applied to estimate the degree of relationship. Essentially, the linear mathematical operations are retained while testing for a particular curvilinear relationship. It appears that this kind of adjustment to test for alternative patterns of relationship is becoming more vital as analysts begin to produce large matrices of intercorrelations.

Parabolic-Type Relationships. A type of relationship that is especially easy to overlook, since a direct application of r will not index it, is one that resembles, precisely or roughly (even crudely), a parabola. The idea is that the plotted relationship changes direction, producing what is called a *second-order polynomial*. What we will suggest here is a two-directional linear fit that requires a mean-based semilinear transformation. The notion is less complex than it sounds. Suppose the following values for X and Y were observed:

	X	Y
1.	1	1
2.	2	3
3.	3	5
4.	4	4
5.	5	2

Calculating r for this relationship yields a value of .40. But now suppose that we transform the values of X so that

$$X'_i = |X_i - \overline{X}|$$

X'_i is the absolute difference between X_i and the mean $\overline{X}$. The correlation between Y and the transformed values of X may be calculated:

X'	Y	X'Y	X²	Y²
2	1	2	4	1
1	3	3	1	9
0	5	0	0	25
1	4	4	1	16
2	2	4	4	4
6	15	13	10	55

$$r = \frac{13 - \dfrac{6\,(15)}{5}}{\sqrt{\left(10 - \dfrac{36}{5}\right)\left(55 - \dfrac{225}{5}\right)}}$$

$$= \frac{-5}{5.3}$$

$$= -.94$$

The two-directional model provides a much better fit. The correlation is based on variation around two straight lines, one with a positive slope and one with a negative slope. The two lines meet at the mean of X. In essence, the two regression lines form two sides of a triangle. If the correlation coefficient has a negative sign, as above, the peak of the triangle is at the top of the graph. If the sign is positive, the peak is at the bottom of the graph, assuming that X is the horizontal axis. In other words, the sign gives the *second* direction of the two-directional fit.

The semilinear transformation can be used for ordinal variables as well, by utilizing the median rank as the new point of origin rather than the mean. Before applying gamma or tau_c, however, it is necessary to reorder the transformed variable such that the matrix will follow the magnitudes of the transformed ranks. If the X variable is transformed, the columns of the table or matrix will need to be reshuffled accordingly. When there are many ties, some analysts prefer to use the Chi-square based statistic, Cramer's V, which will indicate whether there is *some* pattern of nonlinear dependence. The disadvantage to V, however, is that it cannot be compared directly to gamma or tau_c.

The mean-based semilinear transformation works best when the original distribution of the transformed variable is *symmetrical*. Even when the condition of symmetry is satisfied, the correlation derived as a result of the transformation must be substantially higher than the original correlation before it is treated seriously. That is, one would not want to accept a more complex model when a slightly better fit may have resulted from measurement error. For *asymmetrical* frequency distributions the analyst may wish to revert to the eta coefficient. To use eta, the independent variable X_i is divided into a number of subgroups based on the magnitudes of the observed values. The remaining procedures are identical to those presented on pages 294–98. Again, this is a shortcut protective device, having the disadvantages of ignoring the unique values of X_i once the subgroups are formed, but having the advantage of indexing *any* type of curvilinear relationship.

Using Transformations to Achieve Normality. The mean-based two-directional test, it has been pointed out, is much more effective when the original distributions are symmetrical, whereupon the mean will divide the cases in approximately two equal groups. It appears to us that, in general, much more effort to achieve symmetrical distributions will be required of future social science statistics. The present procedures for rank-ordering, and normalizing after rank-ordering, are mathematically inferior methods for achieving symmetry, primarily because rank-ordering is a one-way transformation. The analyst cannot return to the original values through a formal mathematical statement. Much more promising are the mathematically determined reciprocal transformations of frequency distributions. We are in debt to Rummel for his catalog of some of these devices.[8]

The purpose of a reciprocal transformation is to approximate a normal distribution with a set of X_i^* values, so that, if necessary, the analyst may return to the original X_i values. Using the X_i^* values in a subsequent correlation analysis will tend to reduce the number of curvilinear relationships; that is, assuming that all of the distributions are approximately normal, curvilinear relationships are less likely to appear. Furthermore, the symmetry of the normal distribution makes the variance, s^2, a much better estimate of dispersion. In essence, the analyst tries to *delegate the complexity* of the problem to the transformations. By doing so, the regression analysis is more manageable. The gains are not so apparent for bivariate measures of association, but in statistical significance testing, multiple regression analysis, and factor analysis, all discussed in later chapters, normalized distributions help clean up the analysis.

Reciprocal transformations may be divided into four groups:

1. Positively skewed (tail to the right) to approximate normal.
2. Negatively skewed (tail to the left) to approximate normal.
3. Platykurtic (low peak) to approximate normal.
4. Leptokurtic (high peak) to approximate normal.

Positively skewed distributions are highly typical of monetary measures, both in the study of individual-based data and aggregate data relating to countries, states, or cities. Ordinarily, variables that reflect purchasing power or resource distribution (radios per capita, doctors per capita) are also positively skewed. The root and log functions are the most commonly used in this situation, where

$$X_i^* = \sqrt[n]{X_i}$$
$$X_i^* = \log X_i$$

To see the effects of the above equations, we can take four contrived values to represent a skewed distribution and then examine the square roots, cube roots, and logs of those values:

Values:	4	9	16	36
Square Roots:	2	3	4	6
Cube Roots:	1.58	2.08	2.51	3.3
Logs:	.60	.95	1.20	1.56

In this example it can be seen that the logs are the best approximation of a normal distribution. The two middle values (.95 and 1.20) yield a smaller interval than the intervals between the first and second values and between the third and fourth values, and the latter two intervals are almost identical (.35 and .36), giving a symmetrical shape to the distribution. In other examples, of course, the log transformation might be too powerful. Root transformations require that no values are negative, whereas log transformations of this kind require that all values exceed zero.

In preparing for these transformations, the analyst may wish to add the maximum absolute value, X_{max}, of each distribution, plus 1.0, to each of the original values in the respective distributions. In selecting the best of these possible transformations, the skewness and kurtosis measures [Equations (9.11) and (9.12)] applied to the X_i^* values may be utilized. The skewness of the distribution is the most important characteristic. Kurtosis values are not comparable unless the distributions are symmetrical. Ideally, $Sk = 0$ and $Ku = 3$.

Negatively skewed distributions (tail to the left) may be transformed by raising the values in the distributions to successive powers, assuming the values are all positive, until Sk and Ku are satisfied. Another group of transformations presumes that the original values have been reduced to a range of positive decimal fractions. Setting X_i equal to $X_i + |X_{max}| + 1$ and dividing by the largest resulting value, plus 1.0, will prepare the data for all of these applications. The transformations include $X_i^* = \log(X_i/(1 - X_i))$, $X_i^* = \frac{1}{2} \log((1 + X_i)/(1 - X_i))$ and $X_i^* = \arcsin(X_i)^{1/2}$.

Distributions that satisfy the test of symmetry, where Sk approaches zero, may still be too flat or too peaked. While trigonometric functions may be used here as well, it may be easier to work with roots and powers of deviations from the mean. If the distribution is too flat, the transformation

$$X_i^* = (X_i - \bar{X})^3 / \sqrt{(X_i - \bar{X})^2}$$

will produce a higher peak and spread out the tails of the distribution while at the same time saving the sign of the quantity $X_i - \bar{X}$. Obviously, if the distribution previously had a mean of zero, the formula is reduced to $X_i^* = X_i^3/\sqrt{X_i^2}$. If the peak of the distribution is too high, the transformation

$$X_i^* = (X_i - \bar{X}) / \sqrt[3]{(X_i - \bar{X})^2}$$

may be used. The transformation should reduce the value of Ku.

The above transformations are but a few of the many possible ways to approach normal distributions. In no way do these transformations "eliminate" curvilinear relationships between variables. They are for mathematical and statistical convenience in the generation of theoretical constructs. Prediction equations developed from transformed variables need to be viewed with care, remembering that the transformations are part of the equations. For example, the equation $Y_i' = a + bX_i$ may produce a poor least-squares fit, whereas the equation $Y_i' = a + bX_i^*$ may produce a good fit. Depending on the transformation used, the latter equation may be expressed in more elaborate form, such as

$$Y'_i = a + b \log X_i$$

$$Y'_i = a + bX_i^3$$

$$Y'_i = a + b\left((X_i - \overline{X})^3 / \sqrt{(X_i - \overline{X})^2} \right)$$

It is too early to know, of course, whether the transformation "approach" will have a high return in application. Further experimentation is clearly needed. At the present time, the approach may be viewed as a way of preserving a simple statistical model, one that conforms to the normal distribution condition and allows the use of statistical methods wherein the condition must be met.

NOTES

1. Linton C. Freeman, *Elementary Applied Statistics* (New York: John Wiley & Sons, Inc., 1965). Freeman organizes the chapters of his introductory text according to these level-of-measurement guidelines, for the purpose of describing both statistical association and statistical testing. Although we introduce additional materials and use a different sequence, we do adopt, as others have, the basic idea present in his extraordinarily clear work. For this and the succeeding chapters, a number of sources have been helpful, especially G. David Garson, *Handbook of Political Science Methods* (Boston: Holbrook Press, Inc., 1971) for its compilation of tests and measures.

2. For a further evaluation of desirable and undesirable characteristics of statistical measures, see Johan Galtung, *Theory and Methods of Social Research* (New York: Columbia University Press, 1967), pp. 207–14.

3. Kenneth N. Vines, "Courts as Political and Governmental Agencies," in *Politics in the American States,* Chapter 7, pp. 239–87, eds. Herbert Jacob and Kenneth N. Vines (Boston: Little, Brown and Company, 1965). The data for Table 10.3 were derived from Tables 6 and 13 in the chapter by Vines.

4. Actually, this is not quite true. Sometimes a table can be collapsed to give identical frequencies. In such cases, the full table can yield a V of 1.0.

5. Freeman, *Elementary Applied Statistics,* Chapter 10.

6. Cleo Cherryholmes and Michael T. Shapiro, *Representatives and Roll Calls* (Indianapolis: The Bobbs-Merrill Co., Inc., 1969), pp. 130–32.

7. Paul E. Peterson, "Forms of Representation: Participation of the Poor in the Community Action Program," *American Political Science Review,* 64 (June 1970), 491–507.

8. R.J. Rummel, *Applied Factor Analysis* (Evanston: Northwestern University Press, 1970), Chapter 11, especially pp. 280–86.

Chapter 11

TESTS OF SIGNIFICANCE

Historically statistical tests of significance have been developed to estimate the likelihood that an observed relationship between two or more variables may be due to *random* sources of error. The most vivid case arises when the total population under study cannot be observed, whereupon a random sampling procedure is implemented (see Chapter 4). Simply by chance, false representations of the total population may result; therefore, it is crucial to estimate the probability that a sample finding will be upheld by a full study.

There are many tests of significance, but they all have the following features:

1. A mathematical formula to calculate the *significance value.*
2. A sensitivity to the *size of the sample.*
3. A *probability value* associated with the significance value.

Since the number of significance values and probability values is infinite, convenient tables have been developed to allow one to find the approximate probability value for a given sample size or table size and the computed significance value.

By convention, statisticians distinguish between two types of hypotheses, a *research* hypothesis and a *null* hypothesis. Normally the researcher hypothesizes that two variables are associated or correlated in some way; the null hypothesis is the contrived contradiction that the two variables are not associated. In a very probabilistic manner, a significance test allows us to come to one of two conclusions:

1. Reject the null hypothesis and tentatively accept the research hypothesis.
2. Reject the research hypothesis and tentatively accept (or not reject) the null hypothesis.

To either conclusion it is possible to attach a probability value that will indicate the likelihood that it is incorrect. If conclusion 1 is incorrect, the analyst has made a *Type I* error, and if conclusion 2 is incorrect, he has made a *Type II* error.

The probability of a Type II error is *not* the complement of a Type I error, but the two are inversely related. The more stringent the researcher is about avoiding a Type I error, the more likely he is to make a Type II error; however, it is known that the larger the sample, the less likely a Type II error will be made, and in balance, the analyst can be more cautious about making a Type I error in large samples. In practice this means:

1. In large samples, adopt a probability level of .001 or .01 to protect against a Type I error.
2. In small samples, adopt a probability level of .05 or even .10 to protect against a Type I error and a Type II error.

Of course the analyst may have a particular reason for wanting to avoid one type of error or the other; in such a case the above suggestion should be modified. The probability level that a significance value actually satisfies is determined by consulting the appropriate significance table in the Appendix. The procedures will be described in more detail when the individual tests are considered.

Unfortunately, the problem of testing significance is not as straightforward as it may seem.[1] Rarely can one be certain that the only sources of error are random in nature. When a simple random sample is drawn from a population, accompanied by a very low refusal rate in surveys or very complete reports in aggregated data, tests of significance have the greatest meaning since *a* random source of error can be pinpointed. It is, essentially, random sampling error. In large populations, simple random samples are seldom taken (as suggested in Chapter 4), but through *stratified* random sampling, guided by prior knowledge of certain characteristics of the total population (geographic area, occupation, ethnic makeup, and the like), simulated random samples are drawn. As long as the sampling procedure adheres to the notion that each person in the population has an equal chance of becoming part of the sample, supported by convincing evidence and a low refusal rate, a test that takes into account sampling error makes sense. The test of significance helps one make better guesses about the larger population.

There are many situations, however, in which a significance test does not really help one make better guesses about the larger population. If the sample is unrepresentative of the total population by virtue of a nonrandom selection procedure, or if the sample includes all or nearly all the members of the population, drawing inferences from significance tests can be misleading, and at best, superfluous. Probably the greatest bulk of studies in political science are *not* based on random samples.

Frequently in full sample studies of the American states involving aggregate data about the characteristics of those states it is tempting to utilize tests of significance knowing that there is probably a bit of random error in the derivation of the data. But in fact the test of significance is superfluous. First of all, in comparing any two variables from such a study, the N does not vary enough to make sample size a concern. In other words, one has the same confidence in correlations that are identical for different variables. The actual *correlations* are sufficient to select both the most prominent relationships *and* the relationships least likely to be overturned by more accurate data. Second, unless the study has an ample longitudinal dimension, it cannot be regarded as a representative sample of different time intervals. One can test for significance for measurements that are taken at different points in time, but it would not make sense to apply the test to a 30-year average score calculated for each of 50 states for two variables. One should not be persuaded by the argument that the significance tests for a single year's study necessarily indicate the likelihood that the relationships will be confirmed in a subsequent study of a later year. Such an argument presupposes knowledge of the variability in the observed behavior over time.

While in full samples significance tests are superfluous, in biased samples they are misleading, at least to the novice. The novice may conclude that the probability levels derived from a cross-national study of noncommunist countries are realistic estimates of the firmness of a relationship for all countries, or that an individual-based study of the full membership of a single legislative chamber offers realistic probability levels for its sister chamber.

A natural question arises: Are significance tests *ever* useful for purposes other than estimating the possible effects of random sampling error? The answer is a cautious "yes." There are certain problems where the probability levels may serve as a decision aid. In some situations the analyst may find it necessary to *order* a set of findings, strongest to weakest, for some probabilistic purpose. At the present time it is extremely difficult to compare the correlation magnitudes of different statistical measures of association. The bridge between the different combinations of nominal-ordinal-interval measures may be closed somewhat by considering the probability levels. In another case the analyst may be comparing findings with a highly variable N. Correlation or prediction levels, by themselves, without considering the N's, would be unsatisfactory as a decision criterion. Significance tests have the virtue of taking N into account. These applications usually come up in advanced statistical problems, and there is no need to go into detail here. Suffice it to say that tests of significance are useful in limited ways for purposes other than accounting for random sampling error, but generally they are designed for random sample studies.

CRITERIA FOR SELECTION OF STATISTICAL TESTS OF SIGNIFICANCE

As in the selection of measures of association in Chapter 10, the tests of significance described in this chapter are classified by the level of measurement of each of the two variables in question. The tests for nominal-nominal, nominal-ordinal, and nominal-interval combinations are tests against the null hypothesis that the two variables are independent; for ordinal-ordinal, ordinal-interval, and interval-interval combinations the tests compete against the null hypothesis that the two variables are linearly unrelated. The same general organization will be followed in this chapter.

It would be convenient if for every measure of association a statistical test had been developed, but unfortunately the sampling distributions for certain statistics are not known. To develop a significance test for a particular measure of association, it is necessary to know the probability that the correlation will be zero in a random sample if the two variables are truly unrelated, and further the probability that the correlation will be .05, .10, .25, .35, and so on. For any statistic the sampling distribution will vary with the size of the sample, or the number of categories (e.g., the number of rows and columns in a nominal-nominal table), or both, but the point is that these probabilities have not been calculated for all measures of association. Where possible, the tests of significance described below correspond to the measures of association presented in Chapter 10.

To avoid a considerable amount of redundant discussion, significance tests that duplicate much of the procedure for their previously described measures of association will be covered only briefly, leaving room for some of the differences that arise because of small samples, tied ranks, and extensions. The tests may be listed as follows:

Nominal-Nominal	Chi-square, χ^2 and χ_c^2
	Fisher's Exact Probability Test, p
Nominal-Ordinal	Mann-Whitney U-test
	Kruskal-Wallis extension, H
Nominal-Interval	F-test

Ordinal-Ordinal	Significance of gamma and tau$_c$, z
	Significance of rho, t or F
Ordinal-Interval	Significance of M, F
Interval-Interval	Significance of r, F
	Significance of multiple R, F_R
	Significance of partial r, F_P

To fully understand some of the above tests, the reader may wish to consult the chapters on multiple regression and time-series.

There are five tables in the Appendix to service the application of the above tests. The matching of tables to significance tests yields:

TABLE C.   Table of Chi-square values
      1. Chi-square test, χ^2 or χ_c^2
      2. Kruskal-Wallis, H

TABLE D. Table of U values
         1. Mann-Whitney U-test

TABLE E. Table of G values and normalized z
         1. z-test for both gamma and tau$_c$ correlations
         2. Direct test for gamma when N is less than 41

TABLE F. Table of F values
         1. F-test for nominal-interval relationships
         2. Simple, partial, and multiple product-moment correlation coefficient tests, F, F_P, and F_R
         3. F-test for rho and M

TABLE G. Table of t values
         1. Simple and partial product-moment correlation coefficients
         2. Tests for rho and M
         Note: $F = t^2$

Null Hypothesis Stated as Independence

When at least one of the two compared variables is a nominal variable, the analyst is usually interested in rejecting the null hypothesis that they are independent; however, before this particular approach is taken, it should be emphasized that in multivariate analysis it is frequently as important to reject the research hypothesis that two variables are dependent. Consequently, it is not unusual to encounter uses of the Chi-square and F criteria at all levels of measurement. They have the virtue of indexing any kind of relationship, linear or curvilinear. Interval and ordinal variables can be arranged into classes or groups, at the loss of information, but with the advantage of submitting to the independence-dependence criteria.

One possible confusion may arise for those readers who have consulted other sources for the test statistics that are presented in this section. Several authors distinguish between tests that are designed for dependent and independent samples. For example, a random sample of voters in each of three cities consists of three *independent* samples. The three cities make up the nominal variable, and presumably additional variables are derived from the interviews. In this section it is assumed that the categories of the nominal variable represent mutually exclusive populations. This does not mean that the researcher has necessarily designed separate subsamples for each category. Normally a single random sample is implemented, and at least some of the information will allow the creation of an exhaustive set of nominal categories. Each person in the sample will fall into one of the mutually exclusive categories (such as primary occupation categories). The people in a given category represent a sample of the entire population having that same characteristic. By definition, a nominal variable is a set of mutually exclusive categories representing mutually exclusive subsets of the population, and when the members of each nominal category are randomly selected, statistical tests are appropriate.

TWO NOMINAL VARIABLES

In describing nominal-nominal associations, two statistics were illustrated, Cramer's V and lambda. The probability distribution for lambda is unknown, but V was actually built upon what was known as Pearson's Chi-square test of significance. Chi-square is calculated from the formula:

$$\chi^2 = \sum \frac{(O - E)^2}{E} \qquad (11.1)$$

where O is the observed frequency in a cell of the table;

E is the expected frequency in a cell of the table, or ,

(column total × row total)/N.

Summing the results for each cell in the table yields χ^2. The sampling distribution of this statistic will vary with the number of rows and columns in the table to which it is applied; thus it is necessary to calculate the *degrees of freedom* in the table, where $df = (c - 1)(r - 1)$. In a 3 by 4 table, $df = (3 - 1)(4 - 1) = 6$.

Let us say that $\chi^2 = 16.9$ and that $df = 6$. Consulting Table C in the Appendix, we find for 6 degrees of freedom that the significance value exceeds the tabled value of 16.81 where $p = .01$. For such a relationship it may be concluded that the probability is less than 1 in 100 that there is actually no relationship between the two variables; therefore, the null hypothesis is rejected. Whenever the χ^2 value exceeds the tabled value at a given probability level, the null hypothesis at that level is rejected. If the 3 by 4 table were presented in a professional journal, the author would list these values with the table ($\chi^2 = 16.9$, $df = 6$, $p < .01$).

The Chi-square statistic requires that the *expected* frequency in each cell is at least 5; thus it may be necessary to collapse some tables so that they have fewer columns or rows. When the sample is very small, a 2 by 2 table may be the only reasonable way to exhibit the data, and even then an expected frequency may be less than 5. When this occurs, Fisher's Exact Probability Test can be used. Fisher's test requires constructing all of the tables that are stronger than the observed one, and for *each* of these tables, including the observed one, applying the following formula:

$$p = \frac{\Sigma\,(M_i!)}{N!\,\Sigma\,(f_i!)} \qquad (11.2)$$

where $M_i!$ is the factorial of a row total or column total (4 in all);

$f_i!$ is the factorial of a cell frequency (4 in all);

$N!$ is the factorial of the number of cases.

The probabilities are summed, and normally if the sum is less than .10 the null hypothesis would be rejected, remembering here that if the probability level for rejecting the null hypothesis is too low, the likelihood of Type II error is great. In constructing the "stronger" tables for this test, the column and row totals must remain fixed. It is only the cell frequencies that are altered. For example, p would be calculated for the following three tables and summed, assuming that the first is the observed relationship:

OBSERVED

6	2	
	4	6
8	6	14

STRONGER

7	1	8
1	5	6
8	6	14

STRONGEST

8	0	8
0	6	6
8	6	14

For large samples, 2 by 2 tables are undesirable unless the attributes are truly dichotomous, but since attributes frequently do appear in dichotomous form. Yates' correction for continuity should be employed when applying the Chi-square test. A value of .5 must be subtracted from each absolute difference between the observed and expected frequencies, such that,

$$\chi_c^2 = \frac{(0 - E - .5)^2}{E} \tag{11.3}$$

There are several other nominal-nominal tests of significance, including Yule's Q and Yule's Y, and the McNemar test for before-after samples of the same people. These tests are limited to 2 by 2 tables. The McNemar test might be useful for experimental designs or for matched pairs problems. In the first case, a group of subjects might be divided into two groups according to some attribute, then exposed to a set of stimuli, and then classified again according to the attribute. To determine whether the stimuli had any effect, the formula $\chi^2 = (|a - d| - 1)^2 / (a + d)$ may be applied to the following representation of the characteristic table:

		AFTER	
		Y	N
	Y	a	b
BEFORE			
	N	c	d

where Y and N refer to a "yes" or "no" answer to a particular question. The Chi-square value is treated in the same manner when consulting the distribution table, where $df = (r - 1)(c - 1)$ as before. The expected frequencies for cells a and d must be at least 5. The same formula would be used if from two separate samples, pairs of subjects (one from each sample in a pair) had been matched on several characteristics in order to rule out the ex-

TABLE 11.1
Preliminary Calculation Table for Mann-Whitney U-Test

		SD	WD	ID	I	IR	WR	SR	
				PARTY IDENTIFICATION					
(f_{ij})	Black	173	139	48	34	24	43	19	480
	White	203	223	52	46	33	46	52	655
	F_j	376	362	100	80	57	89	71	1135
	cF_j	376	738	838	918	975	1064	1135	
Mean Rank (M_j)		188.5	557.5	788.5	878.5	947	1020	1100	

Multiply M_j by f_{ij} where $w_{ij} = M_j(f_{ij})$

	Black	White
SD	32610.5	38265.5
WD	77492.5	124322.5
ID	37848.	41002.
I	29869.	40411.
IR	22728.	31251.
WR	43860.	46920.
SR	20900.	57200.
	265308.0	379372.0

$\Sigma w_{Bj} = 265308$ $\quad$ $\Sigma w_{Wj} = 379372$

planatory significance of those characteristics. For tables larger than 2 by 2, the reader should consult the Cochran Q-test.[2]

ONE NOMINAL AND ONE ORDINAL VARIABLE

For nominal-ordinal comparisons, Freeman's theta was offered as a measure of association. Here again, the sampling distribution of theta is not known; therefore we take the Mann-Whitney U-test to derive a significance value. For samples that are larger than 20, the distribution of the U statistic is approximately *normal*. Since most random samples in political science do exceed an N of 20, we can illustrate the statistic under this assumption.

As an example we can take data from the Matthews-Prothro study of the Southern electorate.[3] The question raised by Table 11.1 is whether there is a significant difference between the party identifications of black and white persons in the South in 1961. The table includes only those persons who identified with one of the two major parties. The study was made well before the Goldwater campaign and well before Governor Wallace of Alabama sought support for the office of the President. It is worth noting that the table is difficult to interpret without the aid of a statistic.

There are several ways to actually calculate the values necessary for the U-test; the easiest method begins by determining the cumulative frequencies for the ordinal variable, where F_j is the total number of cases having a particular rank, and cF_j is the total number of cases up through a particular rank, as illustrated in the third and fourth rows in Table 11.1. From the cumulative frequencies it is possible to compute the mean rank of each group, assuming that the ranks range from 1 to N. Symbolically,

$$M_j = \frac{cF_j + cF_{j-1} + 1}{2} \qquad (11.4)$$

where M_j is the mean rank of an ordinal class;
    cF_j is the cumulative frequency of the class;
  cF_{j-1} is the cumulative frequency of the previous class.

The same result would be achieved by summing all of the ranks assigned to an ordinal class and then dividing by two, but the procedure is much more time-consuming. Applying the formula to persons identified as *Strong Democrats* and *Weak Democrats,* for example:

$$M_1 = \frac{376 + 0 + 1}{2} = 188.5$$

$$M_2 = \frac{738 + 376 + 1}{2} = \frac{1115}{2} = 557.5$$

The second basic step requires weighting the original cell frequencies by the respective mean rank values such that

$$w_{ij} = f_{ij} (M_j) \qquad (11.5)$$

Here it is important to note that the subscript i refers to the nominal class and j refers to the ordinal class. The weighted frequencies in each nominal class are then summed, yielding what might be considered as weighted row totals in this problem. Consulting Table 11.1, we can let

$$W_1 = \Sigma w_{1j} = 265308$$

$$W_2 = \Sigma w_{2j} = 379372$$

From these values we may compute corresponding U values from the formula:

$$U_i = W_i - \frac{n_i (n_i + 1)}{2} \qquad (11.6)$$

$$U_1 = 265308 - \frac{480 (481)}{2} = 265308 - 115440 = 149868$$

$$U_2 = 379372 - \frac{655 (656)}{2} = 379372 - 214840 = 164532$$

Now we may ask what the expected value of U would be if there were no relationship between the two variables. In that case U_1 would equal U_2, and the expected value of 0 would be $(U_1 + U_2)/2$, or

$$\frac{149868 + 164532}{2} = 157200$$

More directly, the expected value of U, symbolized $\hat{U}$, may be calculated as follows:

325

$$\hat{U} = \frac{n_1 n_2}{2} \tag{11.7}$$

$$= \frac{480 \ (655)}{2} = \frac{314400}{2} = 157200$$

Thus it is the difference between U and U_i that provides the basis for the statistical test. To enter the table for the U-test, however, it is still necessary to convert that difference to a standard deviation unit, where

$$z = \frac{U_i - \hat{U}}{s_u} \tag{11.8}$$

where

$$s_u = \sqrt{\left(\frac{n_1 n_2}{N \ (N-1)}\right)\left(\frac{N^3 - N}{12} - \Sigma T_j\right)} \tag{11.9}$$

and where T_j is calculated for each ordinal class according to the formula:

$$T_j = \frac{F_j^3 - F_j}{12} \tag{11.10}$$

where F_j is the total number of cases in the ordinal class.

Applying T_j to each of the seven ordinal classes in our example, we find that

$$T_1 = \frac{376^3 - 376}{12} = 4429750$$

$$T_2 = \frac{362^3 - 362}{12} = 3953130.5$$

$$\begin{matrix} \cdot & & \cdot \\ \cdot & & \cdot \\ \cdot & & \cdot \\ \cdot & & \cdot \end{matrix}$$

$$\Sigma T_j = 8612853.5$$

Substituting in Equation (11.9),

$$s_u = \sqrt{\frac{480 \ (655)}{1135 \ (1134)}\left(\frac{1135^3 - 1135}{12} - 8612853.5\right)}$$

$$= \sqrt{\frac{314400}{1287090}\left(\frac{1462134240}{12} - 8612853.5\right)}$$

$$= \sqrt{(.0345) \ (113231666.5)}$$

$$= \sqrt{3906492.5}$$

$$= 1976.5$$

Finally, the z value for entering the significance table may be computed:

$$z = \frac{U_i - \hat{U}}{s_u}$$

$$= \frac{149868 - 157200}{1976.5} = \frac{-7332}{1976.5} = -3.71$$

Either U_1 or U_2 could be used in calculating the z value, since the absolute result is the same, and in Table D of the Appendix it is the absolute magnitude of the value that must exceed the tabled value. Since this sample exceeds 20, one need only consult at the bottom of the page the z value corresponding to the selected level of significance. Thus we find that 3.71 exceeds the tabled z value of 2.576 at the .01 level of significance. There is a significant difference between the party identifications of black and white respondents.

SMALL SAMPLES

When each of the two nominal classes has 20 or fewer cases the test of significance is much less tedious. It is not necessary to compute the z value. Simply calculate U_1 and then derive U_2 from the equation:

$$U_2 = n_1 n_2 - U_1 \tag{11.11}$$

Take whichever U value is smallest and consult the appropriate intersection in Table D of the Appendix. If the calculated value is larger than the tabled value, the null hypothesis is rejected.

THE KRUSKAL-WALLIS EXTENSION

When there are more than two nominal categories it is advisable to employ the Kruskal-Wallis test, which is similar in rationale, but whose values approximate the Chi-square distribution. For this test the degrees of freedom are defined as the number of nominal classes minus 1.0, or $k - 1$. The formula for the test statistic is:

$$H = \frac{\left(\dfrac{12}{N(N-1)}\right) \sum \dfrac{W_i^2}{n_i} - 3(N+1)}{1 - \Sigma T_j / (N^3 - N)} \tag{11.12}$$

We may note that all of the symbols on the right-hand side of the equation are used in the Mann-Whitney test, and they are calculated in the same way. While this test is a bit less intuitive, it has the virtue that it may be used for any size table. Substituting the values from the Matthews-Prothro study of the Southern electorate,

$$H = \frac{\left(\dfrac{12}{1135(1134)} \left(\dfrac{265308^2}{480} + \dfrac{379372^2}{655}\right)\right) - 3(1136)}{1 - 8612853.5 / (1135^3 - 1135)} = 7.89$$

327

Consulting the X^2 table for 1 degree of freedom, we find that the relationship is significant at the .01 level, since H exceeds the tabled value of 6.64.

ONE NOMINAL AND ONE INTERVAL VARIABLE

In Chapter 10 the eta coefficient was presented as the statistic for measuring the degree of association between a nominal classification (so-called "nominal variable") and an interval variable. The statistic is based upon the analysis of variance. Three types of variance illustrate the rationale behind the statistic.

1. Total variance = mean variance = $s_m^2 = \dfrac{\sum\limits_1^N (Y_i - \overline{Y})^2}{N}$

2. Between-group variance = $s_B^2 = \dfrac{\sum\limits_1^k n_j (\overline{Y}_j - \overline{Y})^2}{N}$

3. Within-group variance = $s_W^2 = \dfrac{\sum\limits_1^k \sum\limits_1^n (Y_i - \overline{Y}_j)^2}{N}$

where N = the number of cases;
$\overline{Y}$ = the mean for all cases;
$\overline{Y}_j$ = the mean for a subgroup;
k = the number of subgroups;
n_j or n = the number of cases in a subgroup.

The between-group variance is the average sum of squared differences between the subgroup means and the grand mean, weighted by the number of cases in each subgroup. The within-group variance is essentially the sum of the subgroup mean variances.

The mean variance, s_m^2, is equal to $s_B^2 + s_W^2$. If the nominal classification is useful in explaining the interval values, the between-group variance will make up a substantial portion of the mean (or total) variance. Thus

$$\text{eta}^2 = \eta^2 = \frac{s_B^2}{s_m^2}$$

By convention, the test of significance for this statistic is called the F-test, where

$$F = \frac{\left(\sum\limits_1^k n_j (\overline{Y}_j - \overline{Y})^2\right) \Big/ k-1}{\left(\sum\limits_1^k \sum\limits_1^n (Y_i - \overline{Y}_j)^2\right) \Big/ N-k} \tag{11.13}$$

F is the ratio of the between-group variance to the within-group variance, as modified by the degrees of freedom.

The degrees of freedom may be understood by first referring to the mean variance for the entire distribution. Since it is assumed that F is applied to a sample, not to the entire population, the unbiased estimate of the mean variance is actually

$$s_m^2 = \frac{\sum_{1}^{N} (Y_i - \overline{Y})^2}{N - 1} \qquad (11.14)$$

where one degree of freedom is lost due to the calculation of the mean. Likewise, in calculating the within-group variance in the denominator above, k degrees of freedom are lost, one for each of the subgroup means. In the numerator, one degree of freedom is lost for the grand mean. The subgroup means in the between-group computation are treated in effect as if they were observations, numbering k. It may be noted that $N - 1 = (k - 1) + (N - k)$. Allowance for the loss of degrees of freedom in samples does give a better estimate of the true variance in the entire population. As explained earlier, a random sample tends to give lower variance estimates unless the degrees of freedom are taken into account.

Let us assume that we have a random sample of 27 cases and a nominal variable with four subgroups $(k = 4)$. Suppose that it is found that

Sum of squared differences between groups = 143847

Sum of squared differences within groups = 37904

Applying the F test,

$$F = \frac{143847 / (4 - 1)}{37904 / (27 - 1)} = \frac{47949}{1648} = 29.1$$

With this value one may now consult the sampling distribution in Table F of the Appendix. To find the appropriate place in the table, use the degrees of freedom calculated for the between- and within-group variances. In this example,

Between-group degrees of freedom $(df) = k - 1 = 3$

Within-group degrees of freedom (df) $= N - k = 23$

The value for $k - 1$ is located at the top of the table, and the value for $N - k$ at the left side of the table. At the intersection of the column and row are two values, one for .05 level of significance, and one for .01 level of significance, or 3.03 and 4.76, respectively. If the observed F value is higher than the tabled F value, the null hypothesis that there is no relationship may be rejected. Since the observed F in this case is 29.1, the relationship would be significant at either probability level.

In discussing the eta coefficient in Chapter 10, it was assumed that a *random* sample had not been administered, and thus it was not necessary to take the degrees of freedom into account. For random samples, however, it is advisable to modify the estimate of association as follows:

$$\hat{\eta}^2 = \frac{\eta^2 (N-1) - (k-1)}{N-k} \qquad (11.15)$$

For the data supplied for the above example, $\eta^2 = .78$, but

$$\hat{\eta}^2 = \frac{.78 (27-1) - (4-1)}{27-4}$$

$$= \frac{20.28 - 3}{23}$$

$$= .75$$

Taking into account the degrees of freedom will always give a more conservative estimate of the degree of association.

The F statistic can be applied regardless of the number of nominal classes, but it should be recognized that a significant F value speaks only for the total differentiating power of the classification system, and not for any given pair of classes. As a matter of practice it is helpful to list the subgroup means according to magnitude. The relative distances between the subgroup means will give a rough idea of which subgroups are the most distinct. The F-test can then be applied to adjacent subgroups, where in each case, $k = 2$. If any of the resulting F values are insignificant, the analyst may wish to consider whether it makes theoretic sense to collapse the corresponding nominal classes, perhaps providing a new label. From a purely statistical point of view, the analyst should calculate $\hat{\eta}^2$ for each of the insignificant F values, collapse the two subgroups yielding the lowest $\hat{\eta}^2$, and then calculate $\hat{\eta}^2$ for the entire relationship to determine how much explanatory power is lost. Thus if one began with four nominal classes, yielding a correlation of .75, and found that after reducing the number of nominal classes to three (by collapsing), the correlation was .74, it would be evident that the fourfold classification system is statistically unnecessary. The same process could be applied to the new threefold classification system. The calculations, of course, are tedious unless a computer is utilized.

The above learning procedure is most helpful when the original F value is significant and when the magnitude of $\hat{\eta}^2$ is fairly high. A similar procedure can be used, working strictly with the eta values, when the study is not based upon random sampling. In a random sampling context the purpose of the above procedure is to avoid accepting an ambiguous research hypothesis. By the same token, one would also like to avoid a tentative acceptance of an ambiguous null hypothesis. If the original F value for the nominal-interval relationship is insignificant, it may be found upon further investigation that there is a significant difference between certain nominal classes. Such significant findings will necessarily apply to smaller portions of the sample, meaning that the universality and exhaustiveness of the classification system will be lost unless a new way of differentiating the remaining cases is developed.

The subject of this section is frequently described in the statistical literature as the *analysis of variance*. In this literature one will find alternative statistics, such as: (1) the *t*-test of significant difference between means for dichotomous nominal variables, where $t^2 = F$; (2) the Scheffe test for all possible comparisons, which has the virtue of being a little easier to calculate than *F*, but is less sensitive to the differences between subgroups; and (3) the Dunnett test for comparing experimental results to a control group.[4] The *t*-test is obviously subsumed by the *F*-test. Both the Scheffe and Dunnett tests are conservative in the sense that they protect against a Type I error (making a Type II error more likely). The *t* and *F* statistics have been used frequently with simple bivariate versions of the experimental designs discussed in Chapter 3.[5]

TWO NOMINAL VARIABLES AND ONE INTERVAL VARIABLE

The analysis of variance extends in theory to multivariate problems, generally known as the *multiple classification analysis of variance*. However, there is no single accepted procedure for testing all mixtures of nominal and interval variables. The major problem arises in the assessment of *interaction effects,* or, simply, interaction between variables. The procedures are most clear and better developed for problems designed to give equal or proportional subgroups, and for this reason it is in experimental work that multiple classification analysis is most often used, since the size of subgroups can be prearranged.[6] For more advanced and detailed treatment of this subject, the reader is referred to other sources.[7]

The most typical need for analysis of variance arises when the analyst has a single *dependent* variable that is intervally measured, and two or more independent nominal variables. Suppose, for example, that the test scores for knowledge of American politics served as the dependent variable in a sample of college graduates between the ages of 30 and 35, implemented, perhaps, in a study of political participation. One might hypothesize that the major field in college would make a difference in future test scores, but that also the political consciousness of the family during childhood would make a difference. If the sample were designed to produce an equal number of cases in each of the following cells,

	SCIENCE AND ENGINEERING	HUMANITIES	SOCIAL SCIENCES
FAMILY POLITICAL			

the scores would be entered, and the problem would be approached in a very direct manner.

Recall that the F-test for a single nominal variable was based upon partitioning the total sum of squared differences into that found *within* subgroups and that found *between* subgroups. We could have symbolized the basic equation as

$$SS_T = SS_W + SS_B$$

The F-test value was the ratio of the between-group sum of squares over the within-group sum of squares, each modified by the degrees of freedom. In this problem, however, we must partition the total sum of squares in a more detailed manner. In separate F-tests we could have determined whether major field in college and family political consciousness was each significantly related to later political knowledge, but this would not take into account the possible *interaction* between the two nominal variables. Social science training, compared to training in the humanities, may make a difference only when the family is nonpolitical. Or perhaps the combination of a political family and social science training leads to large test score differences.

To reveal the significance of interaction, the total sum of squares may be partitioned into four parts:

$$SS_T = SS_C + SS_R + SS_W + SS_I \qquad (11.16)$$

where SS_T is the total sum of squares;
$\quad SS_C$ is the sum of squares between columns;
$\quad SS_R$ is the sum of squares between rows;
$\quad SS_W$ is the sum of squares within cells;
$\quad SS_I$ is the sum of squares for interaction.

Except for SS_I, the above values are calculated directly, SS_T just as in a simple F-test, SS_C from the column totals and SS_R from the row totals in the same manner that SS_B is calculated in a simple F-test, and SS_W from the values within each cell just as SS_W is calculated in a simple F-test. These values, of course, will need to be modified by the degrees of freedom to derive F values.

The interaction sum of squares is calculated from

$$SS_I = SS_{\text{cells}} - SS_C - SS_R \qquad (11.17)$$

where SS_{cells} is the sum of squares *between* cells. The degree of freedom for each term in Equation (11.16) may be represented by a partitioning formula such that

$$N - 1 = (C - 1) + (R - 1) + (C - 1)\ (R - 1) + (N - RC)$$

Thus if we began with a sample of 30 college graduates, the terms would reduce to

$$29 = 2 + 1 + 2 + 24$$

$$29 = 29$$

In this two-way classification problem there will be three applications of the F-test, one for *between columns,* one for *between rows,* and one for *interaction,* where

$$F = \frac{SS_C / (C-1)}{SS_W / (N-RC)} \qquad (11.18)$$

$$F = \frac{SS_R / (R-1)}{SS_W / (N-RC)} \qquad (11.19)$$

$$F = \frac{SS_I / (C-1)(R-1)}{SS_W / (N-RC)} \qquad (11.20)$$

The degree of freedom in the numerator and denominator are used to find the appropriate intersection in the F-value table. If the F value for interaction is significant (exceeding the tabled value), it means that the row effects upon the scores are not constant from column to column, and that the column effects are not constant from row to row.

If the interaction effects are not significant, the effects of the two nominal variables may be treated independently, that is, as having independent effects upon the dependent interval variable. If interaction *is* significant, the row and column effects are not additive, even if significant by the F-test criterion. In this situation it is usually advisable to go back to simple analysis of variance, taking each row separately (ignoring half of the sample in each application for the above example), and then taking each column separately (ignoring two-thirds of the sample in each application).

In nonexperimental research the analyst usually begins with a random sample wherein the nominal variables have unequal subgroups. If the analyst finds that the nominal variables are uncorrelated for the total sample, he should consider this evidence for their additivity. Drawing secondary samples from the larger sample to equalize subgroups for each cell will probably produce very little interaction effect in a subsequent two-way analysis of variance. Likewise, if the two variables were highly correlated, interaction effects are clearly present, and any subsequent secondary finding to the contrary is a distortion. Thus in nonexperimental research, if the analyst is seeking additivity, he should not use two-way analysis of variance, but should use Cramer's V and the Chi-square test to determine the strength and significance of the correlation between the nominal variables. If they are uncorrelated, calculation of the nominal-interval statistic, eta², for each nominal-interval relationship, plus the simple F-test, will provide all of the information necessary. The only possible reason for implementing two-way analysis of variance would be to find out how much interaction is present. The F values are more comparable than are the values of Cramer's V and eta².

ONE NOMINAL VARIABLE AND TWO INTERVAL VARIABLES

Another set of statistical procedures, consisting of what is usually called the *analysis of covariance,* is designed to test for significance when the problem includes one nominal variable and two or more interval variables. Here we illustrate with only two interval variables and a dichotomous nominal variable. It is assumed that the same number of observations are made for each variable. For example, the analyst may have industrialization and urbanization values for a sample of 50 counties in the United States. The counties are also divided into Southern and non-Southern, depending upon their location. Geographic location can be considered a proxy for cultural differences that may have an effect upon the relationship between the two interval variables. The analysis may begin by identifying the *total covariance* between the two interval variables, such that

$$\text{cov} = \frac{\Sigma \, (X_i - \overline{X}) \, (Y_i - \overline{Y})}{N} \tag{11.21}$$

The numerator is frequently called the *sum of the cross-products,* since it may be reduced to $\Sigma X_i Y_i - \Sigma X_i \, \Sigma Y_i / N$, and if the means were standardized to equal zero, the last term would drop out.

To simplify our equations, we can let the numerator of Equation (11.21) equal SP_T, the *total* sum of cross-products. The cross-products fall into one of two groups, depending upon whether they apply to a Southern or non-Southern county, giving two *sub*-cross-product sums, SP_s and SP_{ns}, for Southern and non-Southern counties respectively. The two subgroup sums add up to the within-groups sum of cross-products, or SP_W, when each subgroup has the same number of cases. Generally, it is easier to calculate SP_B, the between-group sum of cross-products first, where

$$SP_B = \sum_{j=1}^{k} \frac{\Sigma X_{ij} \, \Sigma Y_{ij}}{n_j} - \frac{\Sigma X_i \, \Sigma Y_i}{N} \tag{11.22}$$

where k is the number of subgroups and j refers to the specific subgroup. We may then derive the within-group sum of cross-products:

$$SP_W = SP_T - SP_B$$

As a preliminary estimate, if the between-group sum of cross-products is large in relation to the within-group sum, the nominal variable would appear to be an important factor. However, certain adjustments are necessary to complete the problem.

The next step requires estimating the slope of one of the interval variables (X) from the equation.

$$b = SP_W \, / \, SS_{WX}$$

where SS_{WX} is the within-sum of *squares* for the X variable, calculated as described in the last section. The values of Y may now be predicted from the conventional regression equation, $Y_i = bX_i + e$ (assuming zero means), or $Y'_i = bX_i$. It is essentially the difference between the actual values of Y and the predicted values of Y that yields the adjusted score for each case.

The adjusted value of Y, symbolized Y^*, is equal to $Y - Y'$, or $Y_i^* = Y_i - Y_i'$. These adjusted scores provide the basis for the final analysis. The following steps lead to the significance value, F:

$$SS_{TY}^* = SS_{TY} - (SP_T)^2 / SS_{WX}$$

$$SS_{WX}^* = SS_{WY} - (SP_W)^2 / SS_{WX}$$

$$SS_{BY}^* = SS_{TY}^* - SS_{WY}^*$$

$$F = \frac{SS_{BY}^* / (k-1)}{SS_{WY}^* / N - k - 1)} \qquad (11.23)$$

As usual, the F value is compared to the tabled value for the appropriate degrees of freedom, $k-1$, and $N-k-1$, or $2-1$ and $50-2-1$ for 50 counties divided into Southern and non-Southern counties. If the empirical value is larger than the tabled value, one would conclude that region did make a difference in accounting for the values of Y, even when controlling for X, and the null hypothesis would be rejected. However, the conclusion may be premature. The above procedure assumes *homogeneity of regression,* that is, assumes that the slope of X on Y is about the same in each subgroup. The test for homogeneity is:

$$F = \frac{(SS_{WY}^* - SS_{WR}) / (k-1)}{SS_{WR} / (N - 2k)} \qquad (11.24)$$

where

$$SS_{WR} = SS_{WY} - \sum_{j=1}^{k} SP_j^2 / SS_{Xj}$$

If the test value is below the tabled value for the appropriate degrees of freedom $(k-1$ and $N-2k)$, the slopes are not significantly different, suggesting that there is very little interaction effect in the problem.

Null Hypothesis Stated as No Linear Relationship

This section is concerned with tests of significance for linear relationships. The research hypothesis is limited to the notion that the variables in question yield a relationship sufficiently characterized by a straight line so that a full sample is *unlikely* to produce a relationship for which a straight line provides no information. As explained much earlier, the best-fit line may be curvilinear, or the variables may be fully independent. But tests of linear relationships ignore the other possibilities. A linear test of significance is based upon a linear measure of association. Thus the null hypothesis for a linear test is that there is no measurable degree of linear fit in the full population. These tests are applicable, depending upon the choice, to variables based upon ordinal or interval scales.

There are certain problems for which the research hypothesis can be split. The analyst might hypothesize that there is a *positive* linear relationship between two variables. Either a negative linear relationship or no linear relationship will be evidence against the hypothesis. In statistical terms, a *one-tailed* test rather than a *two-tailed* test could be applied to the corresponding data. Obviously the null hypothesis is altered to state that there is no positive linear relationship. In a very pedestrian sense, the difference between one-tailed and two-tailed hypotheses means that the probabilities are different and that we must consult different points in the significance tables developed from the sampling distributions. The calculation formulae are identical.

Knowing this, one need consider only when it is appropriate to use a one-tailed or two-tailed test. Two-tailed tests should be used in all exploratory work and in any situation where there is some evidence or reasoned argument that the relationships could go in either direction, positive or negative. One-tailed tests could be used when there is ample prior evidence that the relationships will be in a given direction, and the researcher simply wishes to add a confirmation. One-tailed tests could be used also when an "opposite" finding would be either clearly due to sampling error, or just simply uninteresting. If your opponent in a coin-tossing contest appeared to be winning frequently by betting "heads," you might wish to run a precise test on the coin to determine whether it was rigged to land heads. If, on the contrary, it lands tails 8 out of 10 tosses, not only would you reject your one-tailed hypothesis, but also you would not even test the contrary hypothesis that the coin was rigged to land tails. If we hypothesize that party leaders in power are inflating economic growth reports during the year prior to regularly scheduled elections, and we have sampled reports at many times in many countries to satisfy the criterion of randomness, we might use a one-tailed test because a contrary (rather than null) finding of lower economic estimates would be theoretically uninteresting if not suspect.

Due to the lack of scientific theory in most social science areas, one-tailed tests are usually inappropriate. An "explanation" can almost always be provided in a tentative way for any finding, positive or negative. It has been argued that a one-tailed test should be applied if the researcher has stated the hypothesis before examining the data. But a significance test is not a test of the researcher's insight; it is a test of whether the relationship may have resulted from sampling error. The prestating of an hypothesis, by itself, has nothing to do with the probability that a relationship will hold up for the entire population under study. Otherwise, two different researchers looking at identical data might apply different standards. Thus it would appear that it is only the preponderance of prior evidence that might lead one to employ a one-tailed test. Even here, however, it would seem more appropriate to test for whether there is a significant difference between the correlation of earlier studies and the correlation of the new study.

TWO ORDINAL VARIABLES

There are several tests of significance for ordinal variables, but here we will be concerned with only those tests related to the measures of association presented in Chapter 10—Goodman and Kruskal's gamma, Kendall's tau_c, and Spearman's rho. The test statistics for these measures are easier to calculate when there are no tied ranks (or nearly none). When there are many tied ranks, rho is *not* recommended. Both gamma and tau_c are based upon the relative number of concordant and discordant pairs, symbolized P and Q, respectively. The reader may wish to review the rationale presented earlier (pages 298–300) before continuing with this section.

The Significance of Gamma (G) & Tau_c

When there are no ties or nearly no ties present, one may simply take the value of G, where $G = (P - Q) / (P + Q)$, and consult Table E of the Appendix, which specifies the necessary magnitude of G for problems including samples of 40 or less. In most problems, however, either the N will be large and/or there will be many tied ranks. Assuming that the sample includes at least 10 cases, it is possible to compute a z value. In other words, the sampling distribution of the test statistic is approximately normal, and it is necessary to determine whether z, where

$$z = \frac{\hat{S}}{s_s} \tag{11.25}$$

exceeds the value at the bottom of the page of Table E in the Appendix under the selected significance level of .05 or .01.

To compute z, the following uncomplicated steps must be completed:

1. $S = P - Q$

2. $\hat{S} = |S| - \dfrac{N}{(2)\,(r-1)\,(c-1)}$ (11.26)

where r = the number of rows in the table;

c = the number of columns in the table;

$|S|$ = the absolute value of S;

N = the number of observations.

3. $S_{s_s} = \sqrt{\dfrac{R_2 C_2}{N-1} - \dfrac{R_2 C_3 C_2 R_3}{N\,(N-1)} + \dfrac{R_3 C_3}{N\,(N-1)\,(N-2)}}$ (11.27)

where R_2 is the sum of the products of the row totals taken two at a time;

R_3 is the sum of the products of the row totals taken three at a time;

C_2 is the sum of the products of the column totals taken two at a time;

337

C_3 is the sum of the products of the column totals taken three at a time. The standard z value derived from these steps is the test value for both gamma and tau$_c$.

The Significance of Rho

For ranked data with very few ties one may calculate Spearman's rho, where

$$r^1 = \frac{6 \, \Sigma D^2}{N \, (N^2 - 1)}$$

The significance of the rho value is computed from the formula:

$$t = \frac{r \sqrt{N - 2}}{\sqrt{1 - r^2}} \tag{11.28}$$

The t value is used to enter Table G in the Appendix. If the value is larger than the tabled value at the selected level of significance, the null hypothesis is rejected. One may also square this t value and enter the F table as explained in the section on interval-interval significance tests. In either case, there are $N - 2$ degrees of freedom.

ONE ORDINAL AND ONE INTERVAL VARIABLE

The rationale for Jaspen's M was presented in an earlier chapter. Recall that M is a version of the Pearson correlation coefficient, r, corrected for broad categories in the normally distributed ordinal variable. Furthermore, the ordinal variable was transformed from its original values to new normalized z values. To test for significance, one may simply calculate Pearson's r for the relationship between the z values and the interval variable and then use the procedures outlined in the next section. Alternatively, one may "unconvert" M by use of the following formula:

$$r^1 = M \sqrt{\sum \frac{(O_b - O_a)^2}{P}} \tag{11.29}$$

where $\Sigma \, (O_b - O_a)^2 / p$ appears in the denominator of the equation for Jaspen's M. After r is reestablished, the procedures in the next section may be used.

TWO OR MORE INTERVAL VARIABLES

The tests of significance for the Pearson product-moment correlation, r, the multiple coefficient, R, and the partial coefficients (e.g., $r_{12.3}$) are all based upon the same sampling distribution and are very similar in rationale. For all three we may use the F distribution in Table F of the Appendix, the same table used for nominal-interval relationships. It must be assumed here that the variables are normally distributed, possibly through transformations; otherwise the tests do not have a precise meaning and can be used only as a rough guide.

In the case of Pearson's r, the F value represents the ratio of the explained variance, r^2, to the unexplained variance, $1 - r^2$, modified by the degrees of freedom, $N - 2$, such that

$$F = \frac{r^2 (N - 2)}{1 - r^2} \qquad (11.30)$$

In fitting a regression line, two degrees of freedom are lost, since in two-dimensional space a line cannot be calculated without prespecifying two characteristics: the slope of the line, and the value of one variable when the other equals zero. In an equation this line is defined by two coefficients, b and a. In three-dimensional space the line would be defined by three coefficients, b_1, b_2, and a.

As an example we can return to Peterson's sample of 12 poverty districts, where the percent voting for Community Action Council candidates was found to be related to the number of candidates living in the poverty district ($r^2 = .7$). We find that

$$F = \frac{.7 (12 - 2)}{1 - .7} = \frac{7}{.3} = 23.3$$

Checking in the first column of the F distribution table for 10 degrees of freedom, we find that the computed value exceeds the tabled values of 4.96 and 10.04 for .05 and .01 levels of significance. Thus we may reject the null hypothesis that there is no linear relationship in the larger population of poverty districts.

Turning to the multiple coefficients of correlation, we again take the ratio of explained variance to unexplained variance, modified by the degrees of freedom:

$$F_R = \frac{R^2 (N - (k + 1))}{(1 - R^2) (k)} \qquad (11.31)$$

where k is the number of independent variables. Suppose that Peterson had used three independent variables instead of one, arriving at an R^2 of .7. Substituting the values,

$$F_R = \frac{.7 (12 - (3 + 1))}{(1 - .7) (3)}$$

$$= \frac{.7 (8)}{.3 (3)}$$

$$= 6.22$$

Note that there are 8 degrees of freedom in the numerator and 3 in the denominator, the latter corresponding to the number of independent variables. Checking in the F table the third column and its intersection with 8 degrees of freedom, we observe that at the .05 level a value of 4.07 is required, and at the .01 level a value of 7.59. The computed value falls in between these two tabled values. Less than 5 times in 100, but more than 1 time in 100, an F of 6.22 will result from sampling error.

Testing the significance of a partial correlation coefficient is quite similar. Let us assume that $r^2_{ij.kl} = .3$ for the above example (see pages 348 for explanation of partial equation); that is, controlling for variables k and 1, the correlation (squared) between i and j is only .3. Then,

$$F_P = \frac{r^2_{ij.kl} \ (N - (k + 1))}{1 - r^2_{ij.kl}} \qquad (11.32)$$

$$= \frac{.3 \ (8)}{.7}$$

$$= 3.43$$

Consulting the first column of the F table for 8 degrees of freedom, we find that the computed F value is not significant at either level. It does not exceed 5.32 at the .05 level.

Several observations can be made regarding the use of these tests. First, as with any significance test, if the sample is large enough, "significant" relationships may have little explanatory value. The degree of correlation is theoretically more interesting. Second, it is helpful to observe in the F distribution that the significance values begin to stabilize as the degrees of freedom in the left margin becomes larger; therefore the table becomes less informative for large F values when N is also large. If the degrees of freedom in the numerator of the F equation exceed 21, any F_r or F_p value that exceeds 8.00 will be significant at the .01 level, and for any size population F_r or F_p must be at least 6.64 to be significant at the .01 level. Thus for samples ranging from about 25 to infinity the range of significance is only about 1.36 $(8.00 - 6.64)$.

Many analysts report t values rather than F values for simple and partial correlations. Since $t^2 = F$, a translation is made without difficulty. Simply square the t value and look in the first column of the F table for the appropriate degrees of freedom, or, consult the t table (Table G in the Appendix). As a matter of practice in many multiple regression problems, the t values are reported for each partial slope coefficient and used to assess and alter the regression model. See Chapter 12 for a clarification of the relationship between a partial slope coefficient and a partial correlation coefficient. Here we need point out only that the test of the partial coefficient is probably the most important type of significance testing in multivariate theory-building.

Comments

Significance tests are designed to protect against the consequences of random sampling error. Unlike statistical measures of association, they are relatively insensitive to the strength of relationship between variables. In large samples, variables that are correlated only slightly will produce "significant" test values. For example, in a random sample of 1,000 cases, a product-moment correlation between two variables of .081 is significant at the .01 level, yet obviously the relationship by itself is theoretically uninteresting. One variable "explains" only .0066 (r^2) of the variance in the other variable. The reader should be careful about tabled relationships for which *only* significance test values are reported, especially when the respective samples are large. Social science theory builds upon the location of high correlations. Significant test values are used primarily to avoid probabilistic pitfalls.

There are certain types of problems in which both test values and correlation values are easily misinterpreted. Frequently data that are collected from individuals are later reported in grouped form, by city, by county, by state, or by country, giving the percentage of people within the geographic units that possess various characteristics. It is then convenient for the analyst to run correlations across units, or perhaps a sample of units, requiring significance tests. Unfortunately, the derived statistical values do not apply to individuals: they apply to unit groupings. The actual individual correlations may contradict the unit correlations. A significant test value at the unit level may prove to be insignificant at the individual level. What this means in essence is that the between-group and within-group variances have not entered the problem in a manner that was illustrated in the section on covariance. If it were possible to control for the unit grouping, the correlation between two individual-based variables, X and Y, may be near zero. The reader is referred to other sources for a more technical discussion of this problem.[8] The point we wish to make here is that when data are grouped into aggregate units such as states, a nominal classification (or variable) has been imposed upon the analysis. Failure to treat the nominal variable explicitly can lead to erroneous conclusions.

NOTES

1. For a debate on this subject see Hanan C. Selvin, "A Critique of Tests of Significance in Survey Research," *American Sociological Review,* 22 (October 1957); and Robert McGinnis, "Randomization and Inference in Sociological Research," *American Sociological Review,* 23 (August 1958), 408–14.

2. Sidney Siegal, *Nonparametric Statistics for the Behavioral Sciences,* (New York: McGraw-Hill Book Company, 1965), pp. 161–66.

3. Donald R. Matthews and James W. Prothro, "The Concept of Party Image and Its Importance for the Southern Electorate," Chapter 8 in M. Kent Jennings and Harmon Zeigler (eds.), *The Electoral Process* (Englewood Cliffs, N.J.: Prentice-Hall, Inc., 1966).

4. See John T. Roscoe, *Fundamental Research Statistics for the Behavioral Sciences* (New York: Holt, Rinehart and Winston, Inc., 1969), pp. 238–42 for descriptions of the Scheffe and Dunnett tests.

5. Roscoe, *Fundamental Research Statistics,* Chapter 24. See modifications of the *t*-test for related samples.

6. Equal subgroups can be achieved by sampling within a sample, a feasible approach when the differences are minor. Actually, it is the requirement of *proportionality* of subgroups that must be met, of which *equal* subgroups is a special case. Thus in a matrix with six cells, representing a dichotomous and a trichotomous nominal variable, the number of cases in each cell of the first row, n_{11}, n_{12}, and n_{13}, must yield the same ratio when divided by the cell just below it. What this means is that the nominal scales, in regard to frequencies, must be totally independent of each other. Cramer's V and Guttman's lambda should equal 0.

7. Allen L. Edwards, *Statistical Methods for the Behavioral Sciences* (New York: Rinehart & Co., 1960), Chapters 16 and 17; Hubert M. Blalock, *Social Statistics* (New York: McGraw-Hill Book Company, 1960), Chapters 16 and 20; E.A. Haggard, *Intraclass Correlation and the Analysis of Variance* (New York: Dryden Press, 1958), Chapters 1–5. For this section and the one to follow we are in debt to the clear presentation and notation system of Roscoe, *Fundamental Research Statistics,* Chapters 37 and 38.

8. W.S. Robinson, "Ecological Correlations and the Behavior of Individuals," *American Sociological Review,* 15 (June 1950), 351–57; L.A. Goodman, "Ecological Regression and Behavior of Individuals," *American Sociological Review,* 18 (December 1953), 663–64; L.A. Goodman "Some Alternatives to Ecological Correlation," *American Journal of Sociology,* 64 (May 1965), 610–25; and Hubert M. Blalock, Jr., *Causal Inferences in Nonexperimental Research* (Chapel Hill: University of North Carolina Press, 1961), Chapter 4.

Chapter 12

MULTIPLE REGRESSION ANALYSIS

The analyst cannot progress very far into multivariate analysis without understanding the features of regression equations. In this chapter we commence with a discussion of simple and partial slope coefficients, beta weights, error terms, and partial and multiple correlation coefficients, setting the stage for a later discussion of causal inference models and time-series analysis. We confine our discussion to linear models, the simplicity of which most researchers find appealing and not nearly as restrictive as it may seem. It is often possible to transform data in a precise mathematical way to preserve the simplicity of linear equations, yet not in any real way lose the values associated with the original observations. In addition, it is advisable in any case to determine how well the linear model works. In preparation for this chapter, the reader may find it helpful to review the section on the Pearson statistic, r, in Chapter 10.

Multiple Regression Equations

The linear regression equation for two variables, $Y_i = a + bX_i$, produces predictions of Y based on the values of X, modified by a slope and constant. The slope, b, conveys how many units of change in X are associated with each unit of change in Y. The constant, a, gives the value of Y when X is zero. When the equation is stated in the above way, Y is called the *dependent* variable and X the *independent* variable. Intuitively, Y is the variable the analyst is trying to explain and X is the variable offered to do the explaining. When the equation reads $X_i = a + bY_i$, X is called the dependent variable and Y the independent variable.

343

For any bivariate relationship, there are two slope coefficients: b_{yx} and b_{xy}. They may be calculated from the equations:

$$b_{yx} = \frac{\Sigma \ (X_i - \bar{X}) \ (Y_i - \bar{Y})}{\Sigma \ (X_i - \bar{X})^2} \qquad (12.1)$$

$$b_{xy} = \frac{\Sigma \ (X_i - \bar{X}) \ (Y_i - \bar{Y})}{\Sigma \ (Y_i - \bar{Y})^2}$$

Only the denominators in the formulae differ. Using the same subscript designations, the constants are calculated from

$$a_{yx} = \bar{Y} - b_{yx} \ \bar{X}$$

$$a_{xy} = \bar{X} - b_{xy} \ \bar{Y} \qquad (12.2)$$

The subscript notations are seldom used in bivariate analysis because it is understood by the form of the equation which constant and slope are on the right-hand side of the expression.

Now we take the regression equation for three variables:

$$Y_i = a + bX_i + bZ_i$$

where Z is the third variable. In this case Y is the dependent variable and X and Z are the so-called independent variables. Actually, the above expression is a bit clumsy. The subscript i is unnecessary, since we may assume that the values associated with the use of the equation apply to the respective units of observation (individuals, governments, and so on). Furthermore, in longer equations it is somewhat unappealing to select a new letter for each variable. More frequently, the above equation is written as

$$Y_i = a + bX_i + bZ_i$$

where the subscript now refers to a variable. The variables X_1, X_2, and X_3 correspond to Y, X, and Z, respectively.

The three-variable equation, however, contains one other important element, which can be easily overlooked, leading to confusion when one is reading advanced materials. The slope coefficients are not simple slope coefficients: they are *partial* slope coefficients. Whenever the term "partial" is employed in statistics, it is referring to the relationship between two variables, *controlling* for the effects of one or more additional variables. Referring to slope coefficients:

$b_{12.3}X_2$ is the slope of X_2 on X_1, controlling for the slope of X_3;

$b_{yx.z}X_i$ is the slope of X on Y, controlling for the slope of Z;

$b_{13.2}X_3$ is the slope of X_3 on X_1, controlling for the slope of X_2.

Thus, the full regression equation for the above example is:

$$X_1 = a + b_{12.3}X_2 + b_{13.2}X_3$$

The constant, a, is again determined by substituting the mean values of X_1, X_2, and X_3 and solving.

By convention, the subscripts in the partial slope term give, before the period, the two variables for which the slope is calculated, and, after the period, the variable(s) controlled. For four variables;

$$X_1 = a + b_{12.34}X_2 + b_{13.24}X_3 + b_{14.23}X_4$$

For any expression of a multiple linear regression equation, at least some of the slopes on the right-hand side of the equation *must* be partials. Otherwise the equation does not make sense. This is so well understood that frequently, when *all* additional independent variables are controlled, the detailed subscripts for the partial slopes are left out of the equation. The right-hand variables are called the *independent* variables. They are seldom actually independent of each other. It is only that the dependence between them is "partialed out."

Calculation of a partial slope depends on the number of variables controlled. If one variable is controlled, it is called a *first-order* partial slope; if two variables are controlled, it is called a *second-order* partial slope, and so on. First-order partial slopes are calculated from the simple, or zero-order, slope coefficients. Second-order partial slopes are calculated from the first-order slope coefficients, and so on. If we take the three-variable equation above, the two formulae needed are the first-order slope coefficients:

$$b_{12.3} = \frac{b_{12} - b_{13}\,b_{32}}{1 - b_{23}\,b_{32}} \qquad (12.3)$$

$$b_{13.2} = \frac{b_{13} - b_{12}\,b_{23}}{1 - b_{32}\,b_{23}}$$

Recalling the formula for *simple* slopes discussed earlier, we may multiply b_{23} by b_{32}, so that

$$b_{23}b_{32} = \frac{\Sigma\,(X_3 - \bar{X}_3)\,(X_2 - \bar{X}_2)}{\Sigma\,(X_3 - \bar{X}_3)^2} \times \frac{\Sigma\,(X_3 - \bar{X}_3)\,(X_2 - \bar{X}_2)}{\Sigma\,(X_2 - \bar{X}_2)^2}$$

$$= \frac{(\Sigma\,(X_3 - \bar{X}_3)\,(X_2 - \bar{X}_2))^2}{\Sigma\,(X_3 - \bar{X}_3)^2\,\Sigma\,(X_2 - \bar{X}_2)^2}$$

Turning to one formula for the Pearson correlation coefficient, r:

$$r_{23} = \frac{\Sigma\,(X_3 - \bar{X}_3)\,(X_2 - \bar{X}_2)}{\sqrt{\Sigma\,(X_3 - \bar{X}_3)^2\,\Sigma\,(X_2 - \bar{X}_2)^2}}$$

$$r_{23}^2 = \frac{(\Sigma(X_3 - \bar{X}_3)\,(X_2 - \bar{X}_2))^2}{\Sigma\,(X_3 - \bar{X}_3)^2\,\Sigma\,(X_2 - \bar{X}_2)^2}$$

Thus we see that

$$b_{23}b_{32} = r_{23}^2 \text{ and } 1 - b_{23}b_{32} = 1 - r_{23}^2$$

The rationale may be expanded to any number of control variables. The second-order partials may be calculated directly from the first-order partials. For example:

$$b_{12.34} = \frac{b_{12.3} - b_{14.3}b_{42.3}}{1 - b_{24.3}b_{42.3}} \qquad (12.4)$$

For second- and higher-order partial slopes, the calculations are overwhelming and very susceptible to human error, and one should normally allow a computer to do the work.

In summary, since it is assumed that slope coefficients appearing on the right-hand side of linear regression equations are partial slopes, such equations are more efficiently written as

$$X_1 = a + b_2X_2 + b_3X_3 + b_4X_4 \ldots \ldots$$

The constant, a, is always calculated after the slopes are derived and by substituting the slope values and the mean values in the equation. Thus, there will be a unique constant for each unique equation. In an equation with four variables:

$$a = \overline{X}_1 - (b_2\overline{X}_2 + b_3\overline{X}_3 + b_4\overline{X}_4) \qquad (12.5)$$

Frequently, the above regression equations are expressed without the a term, so that, for example;

$$X_1 = b_2X_2 + b_3X_3 + b_4X_4$$

When this is done, it means that a transformation has been applied to each variable, setting the mean of each variable to 0. For instance, the values 1, 2, 2, 4, 4, and 5 can be transformed to −2, −1, −1, 1, 1 and 2, changing the mean from 3 to 0. When all variables are transformed to have a mean of 0, it can be seen that

$$a = 0 - [b_2 (0) + b_3 (0) + b_4 (0)]$$

$$= 0$$

In an earlier chapter it was noted that the least-squares regression line must always pass through the intersection of the means of the compared variables. Transforming to zero means takes advantage of this knowledge and simplifies the equations. As long as the transformation involves nothing more than subtracting the mean from each value for one or more variables, preserving the relative distances between numbers, the magnitudes and signs of the slope coefficients and correlation coefficients will not be affected. If, however, each value is further divided by the standard deviation $((X_i - \overline{X})/s)$, the slope coefficients (not the correlation coefficients) will be affected.

BETA WEIGHTS

Slope coefficients do not necessarily spell out the degree of importance of each independent variable in relation to the dependent variable. Frequently the independent variables are measured in different units (money, years, attitude scale scores, and so forth). Some analysts prefer to adjust the slope coefficients by using the ratio of standard deviations of the two variables in question. Thus:

$$\beta_{12.3} = b_{12.3}\ (s_2\ /\ s_1)$$

$$\beta_{13.2} = b_{13.2}\ (s_3\ /\ s_1) \qquad (12.6)$$

$$\beta_{12.34} = b_{12.34}\ (s_2\ /\ s_1)$$

The values of β are substituted in the regression equation, and they are called beta weights. The beta weights are *standardized* values. It is important to recognize that if all of the original values of X_1, X_2, and X_3, for instance, were converted to z scores through the formula $(X_1 - \overline{X})/s$, the partial slopes would be beta weights. It is much more convenient to standardize *after* the partial slopes have been calculated.

Since standardized z scores yield a mean of zero, the constant in the consequent beta weight linear equation disappears. Thus the following two equations have identical predictive value:

$$X_1 = a + b_2X_2 + b_3X_3 + b_4X_4$$

$$X_1 = \beta_2X_2 + \beta_3X_3 + \beta_4X_4$$

Standardized z scores, of course, are not the same as normalized z scores. Standardized z scores represent a linear transformation, whereas normalized z scores constitute an alteration of the original distances between values.

There is a slight difference, however, between standardizing the original values of *all* variables and standardizing the slope coefficients directly. When the original values are standardized, the constant, *a,* will equal zero, since in solving for it, the mean of each variable will be zero. Calculation of the beta weights directly will not automatically set the constant to zero. The constant may be calculated from the equation:

$$a = X_1 - \frac{(b_2s_2\overline{X}_2 + b_3s_3\overline{X}_3 + \ldots + b_ks_k\overline{X}_k)}{s_1} \qquad (12.7)$$

The advantage of this procedure is that the linear equation gives predictions in the range of the original values of X_1 and not within a transformed range of z values for X_1.

NOTATIONAL SUMMARY

In all expressions of the linear regression equation, the term on the left-hand side of the equation is called the dependent variable and the terms on the right-hand side of the equation are called the independent variables. When three or more variables are in the equation, the b designations indicate partial slopes. Reading statistical materials will be easier if it is recognized that for the same set of data and the same multivariate relationship, the notational style can vary considerably. Any of the following alternatives could be encountered:

$Y_i = a + bX_i + bZ_i$

$Y_i = a + bX_1 + bX_2$

$Y_i = a + b_1X_1 + b_2X_2$

$Y_i = b_1X_1 + b_2X_2$ (original values adjusted to give means of 0)

$Y_i = \beta_1X_1 + \beta_2X_2$ (original values adjusted to standardized z scores)

$X_1 = a + b_2X_2 + b_3X_3$

$X_1 = a + b_{12.3}X_2 + b_{13.2}X_3$

$X_1 = \beta_{12.3}X_2 + \beta_{13.2}X_3$

$X_1 = b_2X_2 + b_3X_3$

$X_1 = a + \beta_2X_2 + \beta_3X_3$ (partial slopes converted to beta weights)

PARTIAL CORRELATION

The partial correlation coefficient is an expression of the degree of relationship between two variables, controlling for one or more additional variables. With accurate data, partial correlation coefficients serve as a very powerful base for theory-building. Along with linear regression equations, partial correlations are the crux of most of advanced statistical analysis. The basic equations for the partial for three and four variables are:

$$r_{ij.k} = \frac{r_{ij} - (r_{ik})\,(r_{jk})}{\sqrt{(1 - r_{ik}^2)\,(1 - r_{jk}^2)}} \qquad (12.8)$$

$$r_{ij.kl} = \frac{r_{ij.k} - (r_{il.k})\,(r_{jl.k})}{\sqrt{(1 - r_{il.k}^2)\,(1 - r_{jl.k}^2)}} \qquad (12.9)$$

Note that $r_{ij.k}$ is called a first-order partial and that it is calculated from the simple or zero-order correlation coefficients. The second-order partial, $r_{ij.kl}$, in turn, is calculated from the first-order partial correlations.

For three variables, X_1, X_2, and X_3, there are three possible first-order partial correlations: $r_{12.3}, r_{13.2}, r_{23.1}$.

For four variables we can solve for the above three first-order partials plus

$r_{12.4}$	$r_{24.1}$	$r_{13.24}$
$r_{13.4}$	$r_{24.3}$	$r_{14.23}$
$r_{23.4}$	$r_{34.1}$	$r_{23.14}$
$r_{14.2}$	$r_{34.2}$	$r_{24.13}$
$r_{14.3}$	$r_{12.34}$	$r_{34.12}$

Once four or more variables are introduced, the computations required to give all partial correlations become quite laborious, and a canned computer program should be used. Frequently, of course, it will not make theoretic sense to calculate all partial correlations. For example, if the analyst can decide upon the *dependent* variable, it will not make sense to control for that variable and the corresponding partials are not necessary. In the above listing, if X_1 is the dependent variable, then $r_{23.1}$, $r_{24.1}$, $r_{34.1}$, and the last three second-order partials are not meaningful.

ERROR TERMS IN REGRESSION EQUATIONS

More and more, typical linear regression equations include the use of an error term. The error term is expressed by the notation e_i or u_i, and a common equation would read:

$$X_1 = b_2 X_2 + b_3 X_3 + e_1.$$

To understand why the error term is used, we can take the elementary prediction equation $Y_i' = a + b X_i$ as an example. In practice the equation yields predictions of the values of Y from the values of X. The predicted values of Y are to be distinguished from the actual values of Y. Thus, notationally, it is customary to signify the predicted values by Y_i'. The difference between Y_i and Y_i' conveys the magnitude of error in the prediction. In the strictest sense, unless the two values are equal, the equation $Y_i = a + b X_i$ is incorrect. One must write:

$$Y_i' = a + b X_i$$

or

$$Y_i = a + b X_i + e_i$$

where e_i = the difference between the predicted and actual value of Y.

Specification of the error term becomes more important in multiple regression problems. In causal modeling, for example, evaluation of the error terms is required before any particular causal structure is accepted. Here we need to note only that frequently one must find that the values for different error terms are *uncorrelated*. For each linear equation there is an error term. For example, the following two equations may be part of a model:

$$X_2 = b_{21} X_1 + e_2$$
$$X_3 = b_{31.2} X_1 + b_{32.1} X_2 + e_3$$

Typically, if there were 100 observations of X_1, X_2, and X_3, producing 100 values of e_2 and e_3, the analyst will calculate the correlation between e_2 and e_3 as one test of the adequacy of the model. The reason for doing this will become clear later.

MULTIPLE CORRELATION

When confronted with three or more variables, one of which is identified as the dependent variable, it may be helpful to calculate the multiple corre-

349

lation coefficient, *R,* or the multiple coefficient of determination, R^2. Either estimate expresses how well two or more independent variables account for the values of the dependent variable. For three variables,

$$R_{1.23} = \sqrt{r_{12}^2 + r_{13.2}^2 \, (1 - r_{12}^2)} \qquad (12.10)$$

$$R_{1.23}^2 = r_{12}^2 + r_{13.2}^2 \, (1 - r_{12}^2) \qquad (12.11)$$

where the subscripts identify the variables. In this example variable 1 is the dependent variable. Obviously the subscripts *x, y,* and *z* could be substituted for 1, 2, and 3. To calculate $R^2_{1.23}$, it is first necessary to calculate the variance in variable 1 explained by variable 2 (r^2_{12}), then the partial correlation coefficient squared, which signifies the variance explained by variable 3 when controlling for variable 2. The latter quantity is multiplied by the variance not explained by variable 2 ($1 - r^2_{12}$). The above formulae may be expanded to any number of variables. Thus for four variables,

$$R_{1.234}^2 = R_{1.23}^2 + r_{14.23}^2 \, (1 - R_{1.23}^2) \qquad (12.12)$$

In most computer routines for the above calculations, a *stepwise* procedure is used; that is, the variables are taken up according to how well they explain the remaining variance in the dependent variable. If there were four variables in the problem, variable 1 serving as the dependent variable, r^2_{12} would represent the highest simple coefficient of determination, exceeding in value the other two possibilities, r^2_{13} and r^2_{14}. By the same token, $r^2_{13.2}$ exceeds $r^2_{14.2}$. The stepwise procedure can give the analyst some notion of how important the variables are, but the final result, $R^2_{1.234}$, will be identical regardless of the order by which the variables are selected.

Care must be given to the interpretation of the stepwise procedure. If two of the independent variables are highly correlated with each other, then the one that correlates least with the dependent variable will not improve much upon the "explanatory" or predictive power of the other. The stepwise procedure is likely to promote a third independent variable that correlates less well with the first two, even though the third variable by itself is not as highly correlated with the dependent variable. Thus if voter turnout is the dependent variable, two socio-economic status variables may be excellent individual predictors, but since they are highly correlated, one of them may be relegated in the multiple equation to a later position in preference for a campaign intensity variable, even though the latter variable is a relatively poor individual predictor.

It should be noted that the value of *R* cannot decrease by virtue of the introduction of additional variables. An impressively high multiple correlation can be manufactured from any large list of variables. The resulting *R* may be largely due to the effects of measurement and sampling error. For social science data it is generally inadvisable to treat the magnitude of *R* very seriously when more than four or five variables are included—at the very least, the problem must be evaluated in more detail. At a minimum, the successive values of R^2 need to be assessed. For example, the following data may be helpful:

PERCENT OF REMAINING
VARIANCE EXPLAINED

$r_{12}^2 = .60$		
$R_{1.23}^2 = .80$	50
$R_{1.234}^2 = .88$	40
$R_{1.2345}^2 = .92$	33
$R_{1.23456}^2 = .925$	6

Since the sixth variable explains only 6% of the remaining variance, its inclusion is highly questionable, even for predictive purposes.

MULTIPLE REGRESSION MODELS AND CAUSAL INFERENCE

Recent developments in statistical reasoning make it clear that multiple correlation as described in the previous section may impose a theoretically incorrect structure upon a set of variables. Generally it is assumed in the above correlation problems that the reality measured by the independent variables occurs earlier in time than the reality measured by the dependent variable; otherwise, the formal expressions would not make much theoretic or practical sense. But multiple correlation and the characteristic regression equation should be regarded as primarily *estimating* or prediction devices. The so-called independent variables are left in an ambiguous theoretical juxtaposition.

More recently analysts have turned their attention to the causal structure implied by the statistical relationships between a set of variables. Mathematically, the deciphering of causal structure is a natural extension of the interpretation of regression equations and correlation coefficients. In another sense, however, causal inference via statistical assessment is a direct translation of verbal propositions. An increase in educational level leads to an increase in political participation. Legislator A persuades legislator B to support the bill. The AFL-CIO influenced the outcome of the minimum wage bill. Constituency opinions influenced Congressional roll call voting. These are isolated causal statements, some of which are testable through statistical analysis. It is evident that causal inferences do assume a time sequence.

Use of the term "cause" need not lead, as it sometimes does, to an endless philosophical debate. It is essentially a convenient term for describing particular patterns of events. The root of the notion is in the definition of these patterns, and the word "cause" is a verbal device for referring to the definitions of such patterns. In the most primitive language, *cause* applies to cases where a change in X leads to a change in Y, a pattern that is easiest to observe in controlled experiments. In such experiments, as discussed in

Chapter 3, it is frequently possible to reduce the effects of other variables to a negligible amount, whereby the changes in Y, if any, almost certainly result from planned changes in X. At the present time many political and social problems are *non*experimental, making it very difficult to control a set of conditions in order that the "isolated" relationship between two variables can be examined. It is within this realm of nonexperimental work that causal inferences are the most elusive.

One way to approach the nonexperimental problem is to develop a statistical rationale that will take into account the complexity of real world events. For any event there may be multiple causes and multiple effects. The symbolic representations of all such events can take an enormous number of unique forms. A statistical rationale, at the very minimum, would allow us to reject some forms in favor of others. At the same time, it would take into account human measurement error and the effects of incomplete knowledge. This rationale, as developed by Herbert Simon and Hubert Blalock, is represented by the merging of three "symbolic" aids, causal diagrams, correlations, and simultaneous regression equations.[1]

Causal Diagrams. Even in the three-variable case, the alternative causal inference structures are numerous. Under ideal research conditions the analyst has established the sequence of "events." If the events that make up variable A occur before the events that make up variable B, which in turn occur before the events that make up variable C, then only four diagrams would be appropriate:

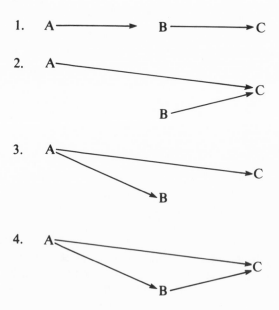

These models of one-way causation are candidates for the explanation of the relationship between three variables, given prior knowledge that A, B, and

C occur in the suggested time sequence. If the time sequence is not known, the number of possibilities obviously increases. Not only are the variables A, B, and C interchangeable in the construction of diagrams, but also the potential for two-way causation arises.

Theoretically, the notion of two-way causation (A causes B and B causes A) is unacceptable. Time is a continuous variable, measurable in units that are infinitely small. No two events can occur simultaneously. In practice, of course, observations are not infinitely discriminating. For example, the United States Bureau of the Census conducts its major study every ten years. From the 1970 census one could derive a measure of urbanization and a measure of industrialization for various areas of the country. Suppose that during the ten preceding years many firms built industrial sites in areas where they estimated there would be a concentrated labor supply due to rapid urbanization. In the same ten years thousands of people may have moved to areas where they thought the job market was expanding due to new industrial activity. From 1960 to 1970, or even from 1969 to 1970, both sequences of events occurred. Thus in a causal diagram,

$$U \qquad\qquad\qquad\qquad I$$

must imply that there is a sequence of the order,

$$U_1 \longrightarrow I_1 \longrightarrow U_2 \longrightarrow I_2 \longrightarrow U_3$$

underlying the relationship, or better yet, that there are several sequences of a similar nature. When research is not planned to acquire observations or measurements at the same place in each causal chain, modeling the process in a precise statistical way is a highly speculative endeavor.

While the problem of analyzing causal chains of the above nature is far from hopeless, it seems safe to say that recent statistical developments are geared more toward ferreting out the precise relationships between variables about which the time sequences have been ascertained. This does not mean that all variables in the model need to be measured by the analyst or others at definite intervals or in a definite time order, but only that the larger share of the model conforms. Some ambiguities can be tolerated, especially when there is some basis for estimating the degree of stability in the measured values of one or more variables. For example, if a national survey measured a particular psychological attribute in 1972, there may be evidence from studies limited to smaller geographic areas or populations that individual scores on such an attribute remained constant over at least a three-year period. Thus it would be fairly safe to assume that an earlier survey would have produced the same results, and in a model the variable could be in-

353

serted prior to a second variable made up of events that were observed in 1972.

Using Correlations in Causal Inference. For intervally measured variables, it is possible to acquire statistical *advice* about the presence of causal patterns. We can begin with a three-variable problem for which the time sequence has been empirically ascertained. X occurs before Y, which in turn occurs before Z. X can represent the proportionate wealth of a political candidate for office; Y, the proportion of nonpersonal campaign expenditures committed by the respective candidate prior to the election; and Z, the proportion of votes received. Correlating the results for a large number of political candidates for different offices might lead to one of the following three alternatives:

1. $r_{XY} = .5$, $r_{YZ} = .6$, $r_{XZ} = .3$ and $r_{XZ.Y} = 0$

Tentative Conclusions: Controlling for campaign expenditures, wealth does not correlate with voting support. It appears, however, that increased wealth does lead to increased nonpersonal campaign expenditures, which then leads to increased voting support.

2. $r_{XY} = 0$, $r_{YZ} = .6$, $r_{XZ} = .5$

Tentative Conclusions: It appears as if wealth and campaign expenditures have independent effects upon voting support. Note that $R^2 = r^2_{YZ} + r^2_{XZ}$.

3. $r_{XY} = .5$, $r_{YZ} = .3$, $r_{XZ} = .6$ and $r_{YZ.X} = 0$

Tentative Conclusions: Controlling for wealth, campaign expenditures do not correlate with voting support. It appears as if wealth leads to increased voting support and increased campaign expenditures, but that the latter does not affect voting support.

354

From a set of actual intercorrelations it is possible to determine whether any one of the above models fits the data. The first case is an example of a *developmental* sequence. The partial correlation, $r_{xz.y}$, vanishes, as can be seen by inserting the correlations into the appropriate formula:

$$r_{xz.y} = \frac{.3 - (.5)\,(.6)}{\sqrt{(1 - r_{xy}^2)\,(1 - r_{yz}^2)}} = 0$$

In practice, it is not necessary to consult the partial formula to acquire the desired advice, but instead simply note that $r_{xz} = r_{xy} \cdot r_{\hat{y}z}$. Likewise in the third case, $r_{yz} = r_{xy} \cdot r_{xz}$. The third case falls under the general category of *multiple effects*, whereby the effects are correlated by virtue of the prior variable. In both cases, one of the partials is predicted to be zero.

In contrast, *multiple cause* patterns, illustrated by the second case, are characterized by uncorrelated prior variables. In all of these examples it is assumed, of course, that the correlations are high enough in absolute magnitude to be interesting when represented by the diagrammatic arrows, and that in sampling problems the statistical significance is taken into account.

Seldom will real data provide a precise fit for the above models in social science work, but it is frequently possible to determine the most likely candidate and to rule out others. The problem is complicated when the time sequence is ambiguous. Assuming that one cannot ascertain which of two variables X and Y occurs first, but that Z does occur at a later point in time, two additional models become directly competitive with the developmental sequence and multiple effects models previously specified. Through the correlations alone, one cannot distinguish between the developmental sequence, $X \xrightarrow{.5} Y \xrightarrow{.6} Z$, and the double effect,

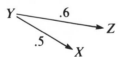

One of the two must be incorrect. Similarly, one cannot distinguish between the sequence, $Y \xrightarrow{.5} X \xrightarrow{.6} Z$, and the double effect,

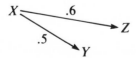

The ambiguity need not remain if a fourth variable can be brought into the model. If it is known, for example, that the events represented by the fourth variable, W, occur before the X and Y events, the resulting correlations may possibly clarify the original dilemma. Thus in the following problem the four-variable developmental sequence would be tentatively accepted:

$$r_{WX} = .6 \qquad\qquad r_{XZ} = .3$$
$$r_{WY} = .3$$
$$r_{WZ} = .18$$

$$W \xrightarrow{.6} X \xrightarrow{.5} Y \xrightarrow{.6} Z \qquad r_{WY.Z} = 0$$
$$r_{WZ.XY} = 0$$
$$W \xrightarrow{.3} Y \qquad\qquad \xrightarrow{.6} Z \qquad r_{WZ.Y} = 0$$
$$\qquad\qquad\qquad \searrow{.5}\; X \qquad\qquad r_{WX.Y} = 0$$

Taking a second example with less tidy results requires a more careful evaluation, assuming that

$$r_{WX} = .6 \qquad\qquad r_{XZ} = .3$$
$$r_{WY} = .35$$
$$r_{WZ} = .25$$

Here it is helpful to create a prediction table to elicit the lack of fit of each model. Table 12.1 compares the correlation predictions with the actual correlations for the nonarrowed paths in each of the two models, yielding the degree of error in the last column. It is clear that the second model is unacceptable due to the large amount of error for the second prediction. The first model, however, fits pretty well, and in an actual problem one must judge whether the model makes theoretic sense. The discrepancies between the predicted and actual correlations may be due to a number of incorrect entries in the original data, or to minor variables whose inclusion is not worth the loss in parsimony.

Using Regression Equations in Causal Inference. Even if a correlational fit yields negligible discrepancies, it is advisable to examine the regression structure of the model. The primary purpose for doing so is to evaluate the error terms (e_i), but secondarily, the regression structure helps *identify* the model for both theoretical and practical purposes. In the correlational diagrams it was apparent that the nonarrowed paths are accompanied by correlations that may be predicted from the causal paths. In essence, the theoretical model is simplified when a good fit is found. One should expect that the regression structure will also undergo certain simplifications.

The format for developing regression equations in a multivariate model requires that an equation be written for each variable such that the left side specifies the variable in question and the right side of the equation spells out the prior variables, including the slope coefficients and the error term. We

TABLE 12.1

Prediction Table for Comparing Alternate Models

	EQUATION	PREDICTION	ACTUAL	DISCREPANCY
	$r_{WX} \cdot r_{XY} = r_{WY}$	.30	.35	.05
(1)	$r_{XY} \cdot r_{YZ} = r_{XZ}$	.30	.30	.00
	$r_{WX} \cdot r_{XY} \cdot r_{YZ} = r_{WZ}$	.18	.25	.07
	$r_{WY} \cdot r_{YZ} = r_{WZ}$	.21	.25	.04
(2)	$r_{WY} \cdot r_{YX} = r_{WX}$	.175	.6	.425
	$r_{YZ} \cdot r_{YX} = r_{XZ}$	.30	.30	.00

can begin by writing the equations for three variables, X, Y, and Z, assuming standardized means of zero to eliminate the constant in each equation:

$$X = e$$

$$Y = b_{yx}X + e_1$$

$$Z = b_{zy.x}Y + e_2 \qquad \text{where } b_{zx.y} = 0$$

In this example, X is the prior (exogenous) variable, the causes of which are unknown and represented by e. Y is caused by X as modified by the slope coefficient and error term. Z is caused by Y. X does not appear in the third equation because it was found that $b_{zx.y} = 0$ and thus $b_{zx.y}X = 0$.

In setting down the simultaneous equations for a causal structure, the right-hand side of each equation must contain all of the variables causally prior to the variable on the left side of the equation, *unless* the partial slope coefficient of a prior variable vanishes. The vanishing partials are a necessary condition for asserting the lack of direct causal connections (e.g., a non-arrowed connection) in a developmental sequence or multiple effects model. As Simon has clarified, when a partial slope coefficient, $b_{ij.k}$, equals zero, then the partial correlation coefficient, $r_{ij.k}$, will also equal zero, and vice versa. Thus whether the analyst is working with slope coefficients or correlation coefficients, the two sets of results will be consistent and mutually informative.

Through the error terms, the regression equations bring greater clarity. In positing a causal inference model, one would prefer to have confidence that he or she is not vulnerable to the peculiar effects of variables not included in the model; otherwise the inferences might well be spurious. In the above simultaneous equations the values of e_1 equal the differences between the actual values of Y and the predicted values of Y, or $Y_i - Y_i'$, and the values of e_2 equal the respective values of $Z_i - Z_i'$. Symbolically, it is customary to treat these residuals as error variables $E_1, E_2, \ldots E_n$. As Simon argues, to have confidence that the model stands by itself, the residuals must be uncorrelated, that is, in the example;

$$r_{E_1 E_2} = 0$$

If the correlation between E_1 and E_2 does not approach zero, the causal inferences in the three-variable model are not justified. Other variables apparently affect the relationships in a nonrandom fashion.

To illustrate, suppose that our earlier campaign example was confined to young candidates running for office for the first time, and that we had tentatively accepted the model:

Wealth   Nonpersonal   Voting
of   .5   Campaign   .6   Support
Candidate ──► Expenditures ──► (Z)
(X)   (Y)

Upon investigation of the error terms, however, it was found that $r_{E_1 E_2} \neq 0$, and further study revealed that the appropriate model was:

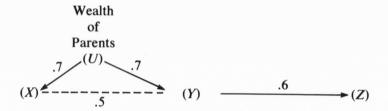

If this model meets all of the tests, it is evident that X does not cause Y, and that the errors in prediction of Y had to be correlated with the errors in prediction of Z in the first model. Essentially, evaluation of the error terms makes it possible to estimate whether there is a variable outside of the model that affects *more than one* variable in the model.

Since modeling is an ongoing process, calling for the revision, recasting, and elaboration of tentative explanations, the discovery of correlated error terms coterminous with an otherwise good fit should not lead one to discard the problem, but rather to search for a more elaborate explanation. In non-experimental research it would seem that statistically isolated models (external variables having random effects or no effect) are not a necessary outcome of insightful research and analysis. Correlated error terms provide a basis of instruction more than a basis for rejection. In practice, of course, the problem of evaluating the error term is made more complex and frequently insoluble by the presence of observational error made at the point of record-keeping. In this context, Blalock, and Siegel and Hodge discuss the problem of measurement error in ample detail.[2]

Students frequently have difficulty writing the appropriate regression equations for models that include more than three variables. The rules may be stated as follows:

1. There must be an equation for each variable in the model.
2. Variables that appear on the right-hand side of the equation must be

possible direct or indirect causes of the variable on the left-hand side of the equation.

3. Slope coefficients that appear in any single equation are of the same order (e.g., second-order slope coefficients).

4. The order of the slope coefficients in an equation depends upon the number of variables on the right-hand side. For example, if there is only one causal variable, it is modified by a zero-order coefficient, b_{ij}; if there are two causal variables, they are each modified by the first-order coefficients, $b_{ij.k}$ and $b_{ik.j}$.

5. The equations may be simplified by removing those variables whose slope coefficients approach zero.

These rules apply to recursive causal models expressed in simultaneous equations, and should *not* be generalized for regression equations written for other purposes.

To illustrate the application of these rules, we can take two four-variable models, the full equations for each, and the reduced equations assuming that the models are born out by the data:

$$X_1 \longrightarrow X_2 \longrightarrow X_3 \longrightarrow X_4 \qquad\qquad X_1 \longrightarrow X_3 \longrightarrow X_4$$
$$\searrow X_2$$

$$X_1 = e_1 \qquad\qquad\qquad\qquad X_1 = e_1$$
$$X_2 = b_{21}X_1 + e_2 \qquad\qquad\qquad X_2 = b_{21}X_1 + e_2$$
$$X_3 = b_{31.2}X_1 + b_{32.1}X_2 + e_3 \qquad\qquad X_3 = 0 + b_{32.1}X_2 + e_4$$
$$X_4 = b_{41.23}X_1 + b_{42.13}X_2 + b_{43.12}X_3 + e_4 \qquad X_4 = 0 + 0 + b_{43.12}X_3 + e_4$$

$$X_1 = e_1 \qquad\qquad\qquad\qquad X_1 = e_1$$
$$X_2 = b_{21.3}X_1 + b_{23.1}X_3 + e_2 \qquad\qquad X_2 = b_{21.3}X_1 + 0 + e_2$$
$$X_3 = b_{31.2}X_1 + b_{32.1}X_2 + e_3 \qquad\qquad X_3 = b_{31.2}X_1 + 0 + e_3$$
$$X_4 = b_{41.31}X_1 + b_{43.12}X_3 + b_{42.31}X_2 + e_4 \qquad X_4 = 0 + b_{43.12}X_3 + 0 + e_4$$

Here again it is important to note that many analysts will convert the original data in a multivariate problem to standard scores, such that each variable has a mean of 0 and a standard deviation of 1.0. As explained earlier, the transformation is *linear* and will not affect the relative distances between values for a single variable. The above equations will still hold. In fact, the simple and partial slope coefficients will be identical to their respective squared simple and partial correlation coefficients. Before transforming, one would normally find that $b_{12} \neq b_{21}$ and $b_{12.3} \neq b_{21.3}$. With standard scores, however,

$$b_{12} = b_{21} = r_{12}$$

$$b_{12.3} = b_{21.3} = r_{12.3}$$

$$b_{12.34} = b_{21.34} = r_{12.34}$$

From this perspective it is a bit easier to see the connection between the regression equations and direct correlational analysis. Whether one uses standardized or unstandardized slope coefficients is not, however, an unimportant matter.

Standardized slope coefficients give the researcher a better grip on the relative importance of two or more independent variables, and they eliminate unimportant differences in measurement procedures. For example, one researcher might employ total scores from a set of additive measurements, while another researcher decides to employ average scores. The difference is theoretically trivial and will be overcome by standardizing the data. For work involving the study of a single population it would appear that standardized coefficients are preferable and much easier to interpret. For comparative work over more than one population, however, it may be important to examine the unstandardized results, especially when the standard deviations for the same variables are not comparable for the different populations. The unstandardized slope coefficients will convey standard deviation differences. It is possible to have identical standardized regression coefficients in two populations but wildly different unstandardized slope coefficients. Without considering the latter possibility, it would be easy to overstate the pervasiveness of one's findings.

In the pursuit of statistical laws it is desirable to state how many units of change in X lead to how many units of change in Y. But take the following results for two populations:

POPULATION ONE			POPULATION TWO	
X	Y		X	Y
−1	−2		−3	−2
0	−1		0	−1
0	0		0	0
0	1		0	1
1	2		3	2

The correlations between X and Y for each population are identical (.9). The slope coefficients, however, yield:

$$\text{Population One } b_{yx} = 2$$

$$\text{Population Two } b_{yx} = .67$$

In population one, for every unit of change in X there are two units of change in Y, while in the second population, for every unit of change in X there are .67 units of change in Y—not the kind of result that would give confidence in the causal sequence. Of course the converse of this example may also occur—that is, the correlations will vary but one of the slopes remains constant. As Blalock has pointed out, overlooking a stable slope is ignoring the essence of scientific laws.[3]

CAUSAL INFERENCE AND MULTIPLE CORRELATION

As was seen earlier, the multiple coefficient of determination, R^2, is usually calculated in a stepwise fashion. The equation,

$$R^2_{1.234} = R^2_{1.23} + r^2_{14.23} (1 - R^2_{1.23})$$

connotes that variable 1 is the dependent variable, that the highest simple correlation with variable 1 is r_{12}, that the highest first-order partial correlation, controlling for variable 2, is $r_{13.2}$ (not $r_{14.2}$), and that variable 4 is the least helpful in explaining the variance of variable 1. The corresponding prediction equation,

$$X_1 = b_{12}X_2 + b_{13.2}X_3 + b_{14.23}X_4$$

provides the best least-squares guess of the X_1 values regardless of the way in which X_2, X_3, and X_4 are related to each other.

Assuming standardized z scores, let us see what would happen to these equations if certain good-fit causal models were found:

1. X_2, X_3, and X_4 are uncorrelated and each directly causes X_1.

$$R^2 = r^2_{12} + r^2_{13} + r^2_{14} \text{ (i.e., } r^2_{13} = r^2_{13.2} ; r^2_{14} = r^2_{14.23})$$
$$X_1 = b_{12}X_2 + b_{13}X_3 + b_{14}X_4$$

2. X_2 causes X_1; X_3 causes X_2; and X_4 causes X_3, following a strict developmental sequence.

$$R^2 = r^2_{12} \text{ (i.e., } r^2_{13.2} = 0; r^2_{14.23} = 0)$$
$$X_1 = b_{12}X_2$$

3. X_2 causes X_1, X_3, and X_4 in a multiple effects model.

$$R^2 = r^2_{12}$$
$$X_1 = b_{12}X_2$$

In these examples we may note that the multiple regression equations reduce to a predictable form, and that if, further, the error terms for the recursive simultaneous equations are uncorrelated, there is only one matter left unsettled—the explanation of $1 - R^2$. We might note that the last two examples are not differentiated by $R_{1.234}$ and its regression equation.

PATH ANALYSIS

A set of procedures closely related to the Simon-Blalock procedure goes under the name of *path analysis*. The reader is referred to other sources for a detailed explanation.[4] Here we can point out briefly that path analysis subsumes the Simon-Blalock technique, but also incorporates a procedure for determining whether the "history" of a causal system is relevant to the explanation of a dependent variable.[5] The typical problem is diagrammed as follows:

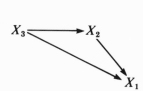

There are *two* paths from X_3 to X_1. Path analysis allows the weighting of these two paths in terms of variance explained. It takes into account the effects of the remote cause both directly and through X_2. If X_3 and X_2 were independent of each other $(r = 0)$, path analysis would not be used.

Path analysis requires that the original data be expressed in standard scores, but otherwise the assumptions are the same as they are for the Simon-Blalock technique. The variables are represented by *interval* scales; the relationships can be expressed as *linear* functions; the regression equation error terms are uncorrelated with each other; and the variables outside the system do not affect more than one of the named independent variables. Furthermore, it is generally understood that the intercorrelations are not so close to 1.0 so as to give rise to problems of multicollinearity, that all major subsets of population obey the same causal laws, and that in random samples the arrowed coefficients are statistically significant. Social science data, prone to errors in measurement and record-keeping, make it necessary to relax some of these assumptions in practice, and force a "tentativeness" upon all multivariate constructs, especially those built strictly on cross-sectional analysis.

NOTES

1. Herbert A. Simon, *Models of Man* (New York: John Wiley & Sons, Inc., 1957). Hubert M. Blalock, Jr., *Causal Inferences in Nonexperimental Research* (Chapel Hill: University of North Carolina Press, 1961).

2. Hubert M. Blalock, Jr., "A Causal Approach to Nonrandom Measurement Errors," *American Political Science Review*, 64 (December 1970), 1099–111; Paul M. Siegel and Robert W. Hodge, "A Causal Approach to the Study of Measurement Error," Chapter 2 in H.M. Blalock, Jr., and Ann B. Blalock (eds.), *Methodology in Social Research* (New York: McGraw-Hill Book Company, 1968).

3. Blalock, *Causal Inferences in Nonexperimental Research,* Chapter 4.

4. See Otis D. Duncan, "Path Analysis: Sociological Examples," *American Journal of Sociology*, 72 (July 1966), 1–16; and E.F. Borgatta, ed., *Sociological Methodology 1969* (San Francisco: Jossey-Bass, Inc., 1969), particularly chapters by Kenneth C. Land, David Heise, and Otis D. Duncan. A technical evaluation is given by Raymond Boudon in "A New Look at Correlation Analysis," in Blalock and Blalock (eds.), *Methodology in Social Research*, pp. 199–235.

5. Otis D. Duncan, "Contingencies in Constructing Causal Models," in Borgatta, (ed.), *Sociological Methodology*, p. 41.

Chapter 13

AN APPROACH TO FACTOR ANALYSIS

The term "factor analysis" applies to a wide variety of alternative mathematical procedures having the minimum purpose of reducing a complex variable matrix to a more simple and interpretable form. Above this minimum, factor analysis is used to create complex index constructs, and, more ambitiously, to develop or test causal theories. In this chapter it will not be possible to detail the large number of alternative procedures, many of which, in any case, are considered inferior. Unfortunately for most social science learners, the older and less satisfactory forms of factor analysis are the easiest to comprehend mathematically, while the now most commonly used and perhaps most widely accepted procedure, *principal-components* (or principal-axes) factor analysis, is relatively complex. The procedures are also sufficiently tedious that the use of a computer program is required.[1]

Principal-components factor analysis is offered in most computing center software packages; however, it is obvious that its accessibility has created a situation whereby many users of factor analysis may not understand the mathematical rationale underlying it. This in itself should not be overly disturbing, since most of us utilize technological devices as a matter of course without understanding how they operate. It is more important that the results be interpreted properly. For this reason we will postpone the actual calculation steps to the latter part of the chapter and will first focus on a typical setting for the application of factor analysis in social science.

The Problem

In the most common setting the analyst has developed a matrix of intercorrelations between a large number of variables. The correlations are *linear* estimates of the degree of relationship between each pair of variables. Normally, the values are simple Pearson product-moment correlation coefficients, but possibly they are covariance estimates or rank-order correlation coefficients. As long as the same kind of coefficient is in every cell, and the data are at least ordinal in nature, factor analysis may be helpful. But it must be ascertained whether the linear estimates are the appropriate estimates in each case. Hidden parabolic-type relationships or exponential relationships are not allowed. That is, the researcher must either remove variables that produce curvilinear relationships or transform them before calculating the correlations for the matrix that will provide the basis for the factor analysis.[2]

In a problem of this sort the analyst is usually lacking a firm theoretical structure for deciphering the intercorrelation matrix in an *a priori* manner. The images or patterns conveyed by the matrix are unclear and in any case dependent on how the variables are ordered in the presentation. At a minimum, the analyst wishes to have an optimal way to order or *group* the variables so that the matrix can be interpreted. The major contribution of factor analysis is that it provides a grouping principle.

The use of factor analysis embodies the hypothesis that one or more subsets of variables is "explained" by a unique underlying factor. When the hypothesis is correct, the $m \times m$ variable matrix will reduce to an $n \times k$ factor matrix, where m is the number of variables and k the number of factors. The factor may be thought of as an unknown, latent, or unobserved variable that finds meaning only through its correlations with observed variables. The variables that correlate most highly with the factor help convey its meaning. The common practice is to give the factor a label, normally a broad concept that captures the content of the empirical variables with the highest loadings on it.

Major Input and Output Matrices

In most applications the analyst begins with a *data* matrix, from which a *correlation* matrix is derived. The correlation matrix allows for the calculation of an *unrotated factor* matrix, then a *rotated factor* matrix, and finally, if desired, a matrix of *factor scores*. In addition, we would suggest that the analyst also examine a *reordered* correlation matrix, based on the groupings provided by the rotated factor matrix.

THE DATA MATRIX

For most political science studies, each observation applies to a property of either an individual or a particular governmental entity. For individual-based studies, the need for factor analysis seems to be more apparent when the investigator has developed a large number of psychological variables, made up largely from attitude and opinion items. Frequently the items are designed so that they fall into subsets, making up a number of attitude scales. The factor analysis may or may not verify the design. Assuming that the analyst might accept the factored groupings, he may also wish to calculate a factor *score* for each person on each factor. If so, it is important that the original assignment of numbers to response categories are standardized in order that all variables have a mean of 0 and a standard deviation of 1.0. Although it is a matter of judgment, the researcher may also wish to normalize the standard scores. Generally, the assumptions of factor analysis are better met when the frequency distributions are normal, or at least of the same symmetrical shape. If the frequency distributions differ, the assumption of linearity is less likely to hold.

Of course factor analysis can be applied to other individual-based data sets, such as the voting behavior of legislators, judges or United Nations delegates; and whenever factor scores are needed, one should consider standardizing the original data. In aggregate data studies of political or social units the measurement scales are usually quite mixed (dollar units, population, radios per 1,000 people, and so on), and the distributions are frequently far from normal. Here it is even more important to create standard scores and normalized z scores, or rank-ordered data may be desirable. In sum, we can offer the following rules, recognizing that the user's discretion must play a large part:

1. If factor scores for each unit of observation are desired, standardize the values for each variable.
2. Determine whether all bivariate relationships are represented adequately by a linear regression coefficient. If not, either eliminate the confounding variables, transform the confounding variables to produce linear relationships, and/or eliminate differences between frequency distributions.

THE CORRELATION MATRIX

The matrix of intercorrelations is a symmetrical $(m \times m)$ matrix, called $R_{m \times m}$. The diagonal cells may contain the value of 1.0 or the known communalities, as will be explained later. The individual correlations are represented as r_{12}, r_{13}, and so on.

THE UNROTATED FACTOR MATRIX

The unrotated matrix is an intermediate result, expressed in an $m \times k$ matrix where k is less than or equal to m. The matrix will have the following form:

	f_1	f_2	f_3	f_4 $\ldots\ldots\ldots f_k$
v_1	.78	.04	.10	.21 . . . .
v_2	.08	.83	.12	.01 . . . .
v_3	.85	.20	.01	.02 . . . .
v_4	.10	.65	.03	.28 . . . .
.	.	.	.	.
.	.	.	.	.
.	.	.	.	.
v_m	.	.	.	.

The entries in the cells of the matrix $(v_i f_j)$ are correlation coefficients between the respective variables and factors, frequently called "factor loadings." The first and third variables correlate highly with factor 1, and the second and fourth variables correlate highly with factor 2.

In the above matrix, the variance in each variable has been partitioned among the factors. The columns will be ordered by the magnitudes of their sums of squares. For example, one will find that

$$\Sigma \, (v_i f_1)^2 \geqslant \Sigma \, (v_i f_2)^2$$

or

$$(.78^2 + .08^2 + .85^2 + .10^2 + \ldots) \geqslant (.04^2 + .83^2 + .20^2 + .65^2 \ldots)$$

It may be observed that the addition of the row sums of squares will equal the addition of the column sums of squares. In factor analysis terminology, a column sum of squares is called a *latent root,* a term that is synonymous with the terms *eigenvalue* and *characteristic root.* Normally, most of the total variance in the matrix, $\Sigma \, (v_i f_j)^2$, will be in the first few columns, subsumed by the first few factors. Each latent root, or eigenvalue, may be divided by m to determine the percent variance in each factor. The resulting value is usually called the *percent trace.*

THE ROTATED MATRIX

The principal-axes solution will produce as many factors as there are variables in the *un*rotated matrix, unless at an earlier point the latent roots add up to the total variance, or unless a limit is imposed. Most computer programs impose or allow the use of the Kaiser criterion, which requires that a latent root must exceed 1.0 for the factor to be included. There is some debate over this criterion, but generally the debate is focused more on what should be entered in the diagonal cells of the original correlation matrix. Most would agree that if diagonal cells contain the value of 1.0, it makes sense to use the latent root criterion of 1.0, since the average row sum of squares is 1.0 in the unrotated version.

Thus, when the unrotated matrix is rotated, only those factors having a latent root exceeding 1.0 will be included. The efficiency of the factor analysis may be judged by the *cumulative* percent trace of the included factors. The cumulative percent will typically range between 50% and 90% for social science problems. The details of rotation will be explained later in conjunction with the *varimax* solution. The basic idea is that in multidimensional space each variable is at given distances from several axes that cut through that space. The axes are all at 90° angles to each other (orthogonal) and each represents a factor. All axes intersect at a common point. In unrotated form this multi-axis structure is in an arbitrary position, except for the common intersect. The rotation of the axes occurs without changing the common intersect.

In the new factor matrix the rotated loadings (correlations) will probably produce a more distinct picture. Most variables will be highly correlated with only one factor, and the magnitudes of the latent roots will be redistributed in a somewhat less skewed sequence. The actual magnitudes of the rotated correlations will depend in part on how *efficient* the original factor solution was, measured by the cumulative percent trace for the included factors, and in part on the magnitude of the communalities inserted in the diagonals.

To make sense out of the rotated factors, most analysts will at least underscore the variables having the highest loadings on each factor. Doing so may suggest the nature of the underlying factor. As will be seen shortly, however, the results should be examined with much greater care. The graphic result of the rotation is an $m \times k$ matrix, symbolized here as $F_{m \times k}$.

THE MATRIX OF FACTOR SCORES

When the analyst wishes to treat each factor as a "variable" by assigning scores on the factor to each unit of observation (people, countries, and so forth), an $N \times k$ matrix will be produced, and each cell will contain a *factor score*. The procedure involves taking each case of the N sample, multiplying the standard scores of each case for each variable by the respective rotated loadings on each factor, and summing the products within each factor. Taking a single case and a single factor, we could have the following result for a 10-variable study:

v_i	z_i	f_i	$z_i(f_i)$
1.	2.3	.9	2.07
2.	.3	.1	.03
3.	1.2	.8	.96
4.	1.1	.9	.99
5.	−.2	.1	−.02
6.	1.0	.0	.0
7.	−2.8	−.8	2.24
8.	.5	−.2	−.10
9.	−.5	−.1	.05
10.	.3	.1	.03
			6.25

where v_i refers to the factor-analyzed variables, z_i the standardized data values for the case in question, f_i the factor loadings of each variable on a particular factor, and $z_i f_i$ the product. The sum of the products, 6.25, is the factor score. The same case will receive a factor score for each of the remaining factors. Applying the procedure to each case in the study will produce a new, more abbreviated "data" matrix. The $N \times m$ matrix is reduced to an $N \times k$ matrix. On occasion, only the variables with the highest loadings are used to compute the factor score (e.g., variables 1, 3, 4, and 7 above). In attitude scaling, for example, an item that did not load highly with the other items of the predesigned scale on the same factor would be discarded for its failure to discriminate in the same way.

THE REORDERED CORRELATION MATRIX

Before utilizing factor scores, it is advisable that the analyst examine the rotated loadings in the F matrix in a number of ways. In the next section the importance of examining the causal inference structure will be pursued, but here we consider only a very simple device for gaining perspective. As stated earlier, the minimum purpose of factor analysis is to regroup the variables into a manageable form. The original correlation matrix typically presents a confusing if not bewildering pattern. The confusing pattern may be due to the order in which the variables are listed from left to right and from top to bottom. Since there are $m!$ (factorial) possible orders, a non-computerized reshuffling would be too tedious.

In orthogonal factor analysis the new matrix of intercorrelations may be constructed as follows:

1. Take the variable with the highest loading on the first factor and assign it to the first column and row. To the second column and row assign the variable with the second highest loading on the first factor, and so on, until a variable is reached that loads more highly with another factor.
2. Repeat the above steps for the remaining factors, and then fill in the original product-moment correlation coefficients.
3. Identify the factors in the matrix by drawing the appropriate squares along the diagonal as in Figures 13.1 and 13.2. Each square encloses the correlations between variables that load highest on a particular factor.

As a group, the correlation within the enclosures should be distinctly higher than the correlations outside the enclosures. If the distinction is weak, the factor analysis may be inappropriate to the problem. At the very least, the problem will need to be reexamined. In other words, if the distinctions are not apparent in the reordered correlation matrix, the factor model must be a poor one. Even here, however, it may be possible to extract some information from the matrix, or to revise the size or content of the variable list to produce a more informative result.

Factor Analysis Inference Structure

There are several different types of factor analysis, offering alternative models, but here we will focus on principal components factor analysis and varimax rotation. It is probably easiest to think of the factors as unknowns that account for the correlations between the known empirical variables. The

FIGURE 13.1

Reordered correlation matrix (sample data)

	1.	2.	3.	4.	5.	6.	7.	8.	9.	10.
1. Power		.66	.66	.55	-.07	-.10	.06	.25	-.02	.25
2. Trade	.66		.71	.93	.57	.70	.17	.30	.22	.55
3. Defense Budget	.66	.71		.79	-.18	-.07	.47	-.38	.14	.47
4. GNP Per Capita	.55	.93	.79		.58	.31	.17	.36	.34	.62
5. U.S. Agreement	-.07	.57	-.18	.58		.75	.11	.11	-.24	.36
6. Freedom of Opposition	-.10	.40	-.07	.31	.75		-.28	-.32	.57	.32
7. % GNP for Defense	.06	.17	.47	.17	.11	-.28		-.44	.24	.15
8. Foreign Conflict	.25	.30	-.38	.36	.11	-.32	-.44		-.04	.46
9. Int. Law Acceptance	-.02	.22	.14	.34	-.24	.59	-.24	-.04		.56
10. Stability	.25	.55	.49	.62	.36	.32	.15	.46	.56	

Adapted from a factor analysis problem presented by R.J. Rummel, *Applied Factor Analysis* (Evanston: Northwestern University Press, 1970), pp. 136, 146.

FIGURE 13.2

Reordered correlation matrix

	1.	2.	3.	4.	5.	6.	7.	8.	9.	10.
1. Military Participation		-.64	-.55	-.53	-.47	-.49	-.36	.10	-.06	.00
2. Representation Character	-.64		.76	.83	.81	.78	.74	-.39	.34	-.44
3. Political Leadership	-.55	.76		.80	.77	.73	.75	-.38	.47	-.29
4. Horizontal Power Distribution	-.53	.83	.80		.84	.85	.86	-.51	.49	-.37
5. Electoral System	-.47	.81	.77	.84		.87	.88	-.61	.60	-.22
6. Constitutional Status	-.49	.78	.73	.85	.87		.92	-.67	.71	-.13
7. Freedom of Group Opposition	-.36	.74	.75	.86	.88	.92		-.72	.75	-.36
8. System Style	.12	-.39	-.38	-.51	-.61	-.67	-.72		-.87	-.14
9. Non-Communist Regime	-.06	.34	.47	.49	.60	.71	.75	-.87		.15
10. Monarchical Type	.00	-.44	-.29	-.37	-.22	-.13	-.36	-.14	.15	

Adapted from a factor analysis problem presented by R.J. Rummel, *Applied Factor Analysis* (Evanston: Northwestern University Press, 1970), pp. 82, 379.

principal-axes solution will produce unknown variables that are *uncorrelated* with each other. In other words, if we were to calculate the factor scores for each observed case, we would find that the scores for any two factors are uncorrelated (save rounding error). It must be assumed, of course, that the rotation procedure is orthogonal, not oblique, such that all axes are at 90° angles to each other. Whether or not the unknown variables are uncorrelated is not a matter of debate; they are uncorrelated. They are, tentatively, "artificial" unknowns, mathematically determined. Only when an oblique rotation is employed can the unknown variables correlate. As will be explained, orthogonal axes can result from an oblique rotation, but since the former gives simpler models we can begin with it by considering a number of examples.

CASE ONE

The intercorrelations between all variables are identical, let us say .5. There will be only the one factor, illustrated as follows:

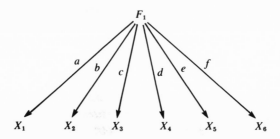

The empirical variables are symbolized by X_i, and the unknown by F_1. The factor loadings (correlations between F_1 and the variables) are represented by a, b, c, d, e, and f. This is so simple that we may solve directly for the loadings. The quantity $a(b)$ must equal $r_{X_1X_2}$, $a(c)$ must equal $r_{X_1X_3}$, $b(c)$ must equal $r_{X_2X_3}$, and so on, just as in the Simon-Blalock causal inference technique. Thus,

$$\begin{array}{llll}
(1)\ \ ab = .5 & (2)\ \ ab(ac) = .25 & (3)\ \ a^2bc = .25 \\
ac = .5 & ab(bc) = .25 & b^2ac = .25 \\
bc = .5 & ac(bc) = .25 & c^2ab = .25 \\[1em]
(4)\ \ a^2(.5) = .25 & (5)\ \ a^2 = .25/.5 & (6)\ \ a^2 = .5 & (7)\ \ a = .707 \\
b^2(.5) = .25 & b^2 = .25/.5 & b^2 = .5 & b = .707 \\
c^2(.5) = .25 & c^2 = .25/.5 & c^2 = .5 & c = .707 \\
\end{array}$$

The same result is derived for d, e, and f. There are other unique solutions for a single factor, but most arrays of intercorrelations for more than three variables will not fit a single-factor solution, at least not in a precise way.

CASE TWO

The intercorrelations between variables X_1, X_2, and X_3 are all .5; the intercorrelations between variables X_4, X_5, and X_6 are all .36; and the correlations $r_{X_1X_4}$, $r_{X_1X_5}$, $r_{X_1X_6}$, $r_{X_2X_4}$, $r_{X_2X_5}$, $r_{X_2X_6}$, $r_{X_3X_4}$, $r_{X_3X_5}$, and $r_{X_3X_6}$ all equal zero. In this example there will be two factors, and diagrammatically,

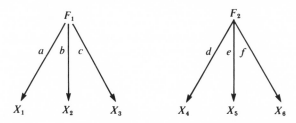

As in the previous case, a, b, and c each equals .707, but in contrast, solving in the same way for d, e, and f yields a value of .6 for each. The two-factor model accounts for all of the variance in the matrix. F_1 is uncorrelated with X_4, X_5, and X_6; and F_2 is uncorrelated with the first three variables.

CASE THREE

The intercorrelations between X_1, X_2, and X_3 are all .54; the intercorrelations between X_4, X_5, and X_6 are all .40; and all other intercorrelations are .2614. Again we have a two-factor solution, but this time all variables load on both factors, as follows:

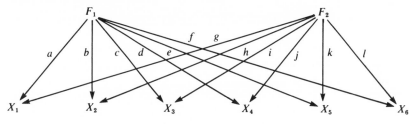

This problem is a bit more typical of a factor analysis result. Algebraically, one may demonstrate that

$$a = b = c$$

$$d = e = f = g = h = i$$

$$j = k = l$$

Then it is possible to derive, for example, that

$$g^2 = aj - .3842$$

where

$$\sqrt{.4(.54) - .2614^2} = .3842$$

Now we might substitute the loadings from the previous example such that $a = .707$ and $j = .6$, giving:

$$g^2 = .707(.6) - .3842$$

$$= .4242 - .3842$$

$$= .04$$

$$g = .2$$

Thus the loadings d through i are all .2.

We can check out this result by using the so-called rules of causal inference to "predict" three of the empirical correlations:

$$r_{X_1 X_2} = ab + gh = .707(.707) + .2(.2) = .54$$

$$r_{X_3 X_4} = cd + ij = .707(.2) \quad + .2(.6) = .2614$$

$$r_{X_4 X_5} = de + jk = .2(.2) \quad\quad + .6(.6) = .40$$

Of course this example was designed so that it would work out. A unique solution is assured only when there are as many factors as there are variables.

The above results represent an orthogonal solution; that is, the factors themselves are uncorrelated ($r_{F_1 F_2} = 0$), which means that the factor *scores* of each are uncorrelated. Although the reader is referred elsewhere for a discussion of oblique solutions, it may be pointed out here that an oblique solution may yield a more powerful solution. As Rummel emphasizes, an oblique rotation of the factor loadings may simply confirm the orthogonal solution by giving very low correlations between the factors.[3] In terms of our diagrams, an oblique solution may, however, require that an arrow be drawn between F_1 and F_2, thus alerting the analyst to possible causal inference patterns among the unknown variables.

Factor Matrix for Case Three

It has been stated that the results calculated for Case Three represent *a* solution for the correlation matrix. Placing the loadings in the conventional $m \times k$ matrix helps clarify the problem:

	f_1	f_2	h^2
X_1	.707	.2	.54
X_2	.707	.2	.54
X_3	.707	.2	.54
X_4	.2	.6	.40
X_5	.2	.6	.40
X_6	.2	.6	.40
latent root	1.62	1.20	
percent trace	.58	.42	

The column sums of squares are the latent roots, and the row sums of squares (h^2) are called the *communalities*. The neatness of the pattern, of course, is the product of the preselection of numbers that would work out neatly. An actual factor analysis program is constructed to manage any array of correlations. In this problem *all* of the variance is accounted for by two factors (or unknown variables). In most applications that we have seen, as many factors as variables are required to explain all of the variance. The principal-axes solution persists to the very end, running down sampling error, rounding error, and idiosyncratic variables. That is why the latent root value is used to determine which factors will be treated seriously.

Normally the communalities (h^2) are not known and they are frequently assumed to be 1.0. This assumption will obviously raise the magnitude of the correlations between variables and factors, since the total sum of squares is higher. But even if the above communalities are known and inserted in the diagonal of the $R_{m \times m}$ matrix, the *un*rotated solution will not give the same results. It will be found that the sum of the cross-products of loadings of any two adjacent factors will be zero. Thus, in unrotated form several loadings will necessarily have negative signs. In Tables 13.1 and 13.2 the rotated and unrotated loadings may be compared, in the first table using the communalities of .54 and .4 as above, and in the second using the value of 1.0.

TABLE 13.1

Unrotated and Rotated Loadings with Known Communalities *

	UNROTATED		ROTATED	
	FACTOR 1	FACTOR 2	FACTOR 1	FACTOR 2
Variable 1	.68	−.27	.70	.22
Variable 2	.68	−.27	.70	.22
Variable 3	.68	−.27	.70	.22
Variable 4	.52	.35	.19	.60
Variable 5	.52	.35	.19	.60
Variable 6	.52	.35	.19	.60

* These are rounded values, as were the correlations presented in Case Three. The slight discrepancies between the rotated loadings and the deduced loadings are due to rounding errors.

TABLE 13.2

Unrotated and Rotated Loadings with Communalities of 1.0,
Using the Kaiser Criterion for Rotation

	UNROTATED		ROTATED	
	FACTOR 1	FACTOR 2	FACTOR 1	FACTOR 2
Variable 1	.73	−.4	.81	.17
Variable 2	.73	−.4	.81	.17
Variable 3	.73	−.4	.81	.17
Variable 4	.61	.47	.16	.76
Variable 5	.61	.47	.16	.76
Variable 6	.61	.47	.16	.76

Calculation of Loadings

A hand calculation of factor loadings would be excessively tedious, especially for the principal-axes solution, and even for a small number of variables. To understand the computations, the user must be familiar with elementary matrix algebra. Most important is the row-by-column rule of matrix multiplication. In the principal-axes solution, the correlation matrix must be multiplied by itself, or squared, and the results successively squared until a solution is reached for the factor in question. In squaring the correlation matrix, one does not simply square the value in each cell. Take any cell in the correlation matrix. The value to go into the same cell of the squared matrix is the sum of the cross-products of the values in the row and column for that cell in the original matrix. Assuming that the following row and column are in the matrix,

$$
\begin{array}{c}
.6 \\
.5 \\
.3 \\
.3 \ .2 \ .4 \ .7 \ .5 \\
.4
\end{array}
$$

the squared matrix would contain $(.3) \ (.6) + (.2) \ (.5) + (.4) \ (.3) + .7^2 + (.5) \ (.4)$ in the cell where .7 is located; that is, it would contain the value of 1.09. The $R_{m \times m}$ matrix is replaced by a $R^2_{m \times m}$ matrix.

One basic procedure involves solving for the first factor loadings first, finding the residual correlations, solving for the second factor loadings from the residuals, and so on. The steps in solving for the first factor may be summarized as follows:

1. Sum the correlations in each column of the R matrix and divide each total by the *highest* column total. Treat the results as tentative loadings.
2. Square the R matrix, giving R^2, and repeat the above procedure for the squared matrix. If the new loadings are identical to the old (say to four places), go to step 5.
3. Square the R^2 matrix, giving R^4, and repeat the same procedure. If the new loadings are the same as those for step 2, go to step 5.
4. Power the matrix again. Repeat until agreement between tentative loadings for two successive matrices is reached.
5. Calculate the sum of the cross-products between the final tentative loadings and each row of the original correlation matrix, R, yielding a value for each column. The process may be symbolized as

$$v_j = R \ (c_j)$$

where c_j represents the tentative loadings, and v_j the weighted loadings.

6. Calculate each of the standardized loadings for the first factor from the formula:

$$a_1 = \frac{v_1}{\sqrt{\Sigma c_j v_j}}$$

Solve also for $a_2, a_3 \ldots a_m$.

7. Enter each of the standardized loadings in the first column of the factor matrix.

The above steps may be applied to succeeding factors as well, beginning each, of course, with a residual R matrix. We may label this the R' matrix with r'_{ij} representing the residual value in a cell, where

$$r'_{ij} = r_{ij} - a_i a_j$$

for the second factor. The residual correlation for a cell is the original correlation minus the product of the correlations of the respective two variables with the first factor. If two factors had been derived previously, then the sum of products of the two variables on each factor would be subtracted from the original correlation. The communalities in the diagonal are simply the difference between the first estimated communalities and the square of each respective loading (or sum of squares if more than one factor has been extracted).

Rotation

There are two general categories of rotation, orthogonal and oblique, and within each category there are several methods of rotation. It is easiest to understand the concept of rotation when there are only two factors, for it is difficult to visualize multidimensional space. A rotation, regardless of the particular method, is a *search* for an efficient description of an array of points. The points represent correlations between variables and factors. In a graphical solution the analyst can represent each factor by a straight line called an *axis*. For two factors the analysis begins with a horizontal axis for factor 1 and a vertical axis for factor 2. Each factor axis ranges from -1.0 to $+1.0$, and they intersect at 0.0, dividing the space into four quadrants. The intersection of each variable in this two-factor space is plotted very simply. If a variable is correlated .6 with the first factor and $-.2$ with the second, the intersection $(.6, -.2)$ is found in the lower right quadrant. After all points are entered in this manner, the axes are ready to be rotated.

The problem with graphic rotation, of course, is that it involves too much guesswork. It would be better if a rotation principle were established. In orthogonal rotation, where the axes must remain perpendicular to each other, the Kaiser *varimax* criterion is almost always used. The varimax criterion embodies the principle of *max*imizing the *vari*ance in each column of the factor matrix. This should not be misinterpreted to mean "maximizing the sum of *squares* of each column," but rather to the *fourth* power, as evidenced by the criterion equation:

$$V = m \sum_{j}^{p} \sum_{i}^{m} (b_{ij}/h_i)^4 - \sum_{j}^{p} \left(\sum_{i}^{m} b_{ij}^2 / h_i^2 \right)^2$$

where the b's are rotated loadings, the h's communalities, p the number of factors, and m the number of variables. The b's that give the maximum value of V are accepted as the rotated loadings.

In interpreting the meaning of the varimax equation graphically, the analyst must disregard the notion of a least-squares regression line to avoid confusion. The loading or correlation of a variable on a factor depends on the variable's distance from the factor axis. If a variable falls exactly on the horizontal axis, it is uncorrelated with factor 1. The further away the variable's point intersect is from the axis, the higher it is correlated with that factor. Thus the varimax rotation yields a position of the axes, if possible, whereby for each axis a small number of points are very far away from it and the remaining points are very close to it, corresponding to a few high loadings and many low loadings. Of course we are describing the typical solution, and there is no mathematically necessary reason why the few-to-many contrast must hold. In Case Three above, there are equal numbers of high and low loadings on each factor.

In Figures 13.3 and 13.4 the positions of the axis for Case Three are represented. In Figure 13.3 are the axes for when the true communalities were inserted in the diagonal of the correlation matrix. In Figure 13.4 the estimated communalities of 1.0 were inserted. In both cases, the horizontal and vertical axes represent the unrotated factors. The rotated axes in the two figures are identical to each other, even though the communalities were different in the original correlation matrix. This is an extremely simple example where two factors explain all of the variance in the correlation matrix and where there are only two unique point intersects; however, the procedures are not much different for more complex problems. In multifactor rotations, the factors may be taken two at a time, rotating the first and the second factor, then the second and third factor (using the new axis position of the second factor), and so on, until the cycle is completed. Additional follow-up cycles are usually necessary. When certain factors are not included in the rotation, as is typical, it should be remembered that the communalities of the rows in the factor matrix no longer add up to the original estimated communalities.

As mentioned earlier, oblique rotations do not have the restriction that the axes remain at 90° angles to each other. The procedures are much more complex, and there is no agreed-upon technique at this time. Rummel describes eight different techniques: oblimax, quartimin, covarimin, biquartimin,

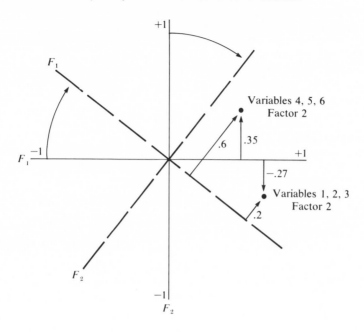

FIGURE 13.3

Rotation of two factors with known communalities

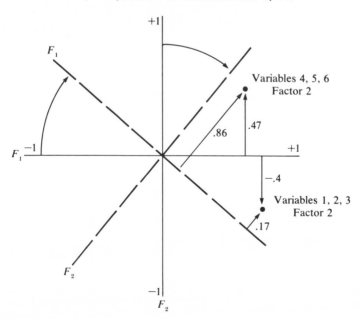

FIGURE 13.4

Rotation of two factors with communalities of 1.0

binormamin, maxplane, promax, and target rotation. He suggests that several techniques should be applied. If they yield similar interpretations, *"as usually appears to be the case in practice,"* the problem has been solved in a rough if not exact way.[4] Otherwise the analyst will need to exercise his or her substantive judgment. If some of the techniques yield nearly orthogonal results, giving low correlations between the factors, the original orthogonal solution is probably preferable.

Evaluating Orthogonal Results

As suggested earlier, factor analysis may be used for two related but distinct purposes: (1) to regroup a complex set of data into more manageable form, say for the purpose of index construction, scaling, or locating subsets of variables; and (2) to impose a causal structure on the data for the purpose of theory construction or testing. The success of the experiment cannot be divorced from its purpose. The extent to which the first purpose is satisfied may be judged by examining the patterns in the reordered correlation matrix, as illustrated earlier. Most of the higher correlation should fall along the diagonal within the square enclosures. Here we offer a simple device for summarizing the distinctiveness of the pattern, defined as

$$D = \frac{(\sum r_w^2) / n_w}{(\sum r_w^2) / n_w + (\sum r_o^2) / n_o}$$

where the numerator is the average sum of squares within the enclosures and the denominator is the numerator plus the average sum of squares outside the enclosures. We may note that if a variable is the only one having the highest loading on a factor, it falls outside the enclosures. Of course, in calculation of the above formula, only the cells above the diagonal need to be considered. In the two tables adapted from Rummel's work for illustrative purposes (Figures 13.1 and 13.2), the D values are .81 and .61, respectively. In the artificial example used in Case Three, $D = .77$.

Much of this discussion has assumed that the analyst is interested in grouping variables, but frequently the aim of the research is to group countries, states, cities, or people according to some variable having a dyadic quality analogous to that of a simple correlation coefficient. Roll call agreements, foreign trade, geographic distance, treaty partnerships, and migration are but a few of the many variables that can be arranged into a symmetric matrix analogous to a correlation matrix. The values in the matrix are usually percentages, either common to the index, such as percent agreement on roll calls, or modified by the maximum value in the raw data matrix, such as for trade. Frequently the analyst will be concerned with changes in the factor groupings over time. Using the formula for D, above, will connote

378

whether the overall patterns are becoming more or less distinct. Batteries of attitude items, for example, may with time lose their original distinctiveness.

When the purpose of the analysis is to develop a causal inference structure through the use of unknown variables, it must be realized that the factor matrix is usually nothing more than a preliminary mapping. The most severe limitation is that the model assumes that the known variables are not causally related. They are correlated only by virtue of the unknowns. Although it is certainly possible that unknowns will be detected in this manner, by and large the resulting structure cannot be taken literally. Problems resulting from the inclusion of confounding variables and measurement error alone require that caution be exercised, and that the causal structure be treated as a tentative arrangement of variance. Nevertheless, factor analysis may point to causal inference models that would be difficult to decipher otherwise.

Given the nature of factor analysis, it would appear that the analyst should first reexamine the variables that load highly on a given factor, primarily to determine whether they submit to a causal design based on path analysis techniques. In doing this, the analyst may find that the use of an unknown, deduced directly from the empirical correlations as in Case Two earlier, will be helpful. The unknown may be viewed as a variable, or simply a macroconcept as is usually the case for labels given to factors. This process may have the effect of eliminating certain confounding variables from the analysis. An approach for making this kind of evaluation may be taken directly from a rationale developed by Costner, as described and modified in the next section.

Algebraic Solutions

In a recent article Costner developed two desiderata for linking abstract concepts to specific measures through the use of simple correlation coefficients.[5] Our purpose here is to show how his procedures relate to factor analysis. If we were concerned, for example, with the relationship between socioeconomic status and political participation, it might be argued that these concepts are abstract and require more specific definition. Socioeconomic status can refer to annual income, level of education, and perceived occupational status, whereas political participation may refer to voting, membership in political and quasi-political organizations, and the amount of time spent discussing and reading about politics. Given specific measures for each of the subconcepts, Costner's rationale allows the derivation of "epistemic" coefficients between the abstract concepts and between each abstract concept and each measure. The epistemic coefficients are tentatively accepted only

FIGURE 13.5

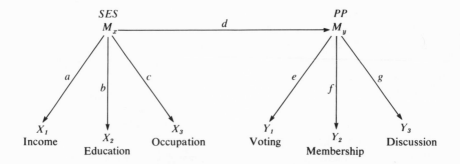

when certain criteria are met. These epistemic coefficients are *derived* correlation coefficients. Taking Figure 13.5 as the desired model, acceptance depends first on satisfaction of the equality:

$$\frac{(r_{X_iY_j})\ (r_{X_kY_l})}{(r_{X_iX_k})\ (r_{Y_jY_l})} = \frac{(r_{X_iY_l})\ (r_{X_kY_j})}{(r_{X_iX_k})\ (r_{Y_jY_l})}$$

for all unique subscript arrays where $i \neq k$ and $j \neq l$. Either side of the equation should yield d^2, the squared coefficients between the abstract variables, M_x and M_y. Omitting the common denominator, one should find, for example, that

$$(r_{X_1Y_1})\ (r_{X_2Y_2}) = (r_{X_1Y_2})\ (r_{X_2Y_1})$$

The second consistency criterion requires solving for the coefficients $a, b, c, e, f,$ and $g,$ in the manner previously described in relation to Cases One and Two, and as described by Costner. Once these coefficients have been solved, nine estimates of d—the link between the macroconcepts—are possible. For example, $r_{X_1Y_1} = ade$, according to causal linkage rules; thus, it may be shown that

$$d = \frac{r_{X_1Y_1}}{ae}$$

The consistency criterion stipulates that the nine estimates of d must be identical before the model is accepted. To use this test, there must be three or more operational variables under each macroconcept.

Suppose that we take the example developed under Case Three earlier, where the intercorrelations between X_1, X_2, and X_3 are all .54; the intercorrelations between Y_1, Y_2, and Y_3 are all .4; and the cross-correlations between the X's and Y's are all .2614. Instead of using the seven algebraic steps to solve for the coefficients between the empirical variables and the concepts, we may use a simplifying equation:

$$a = \sqrt{\frac{ac\,(ab)}{bc}} = \sqrt{\frac{.54\,(.54)}{.54}} = .73485$$

$b = .73485$ by same process

$c = .73485$ by same process

$$e = \sqrt{\frac{eg\,(ef)}{fg}} = \sqrt{\frac{.4\,(.4)}{.4}} = .63246$$

$f = .63246$ by same process

$g = .63246$ by same process

Now we may solve for d as follows:

$$d = \frac{r_{x_1 y_1}}{ae} = \frac{.2614}{.73485\,(.63246)} = .562$$

In this example all estimates of d will be identical and the first criterion will be satisfied as well.

We may note that this solution requires considerably fewer arrows to account for the empirical correlations than did the orthogonal factor analysis solution. In the factor analysis solution no arrow was drawn between the factors (macroconcepts, or unknowns), but an arrow had to be drawn between every variable and every factor.

An important *limit* to the Costner consistency criteria, developed in another work, may be observed by examining a general equation to solve for coefficients between macroconcepts and *three* empirical variables: [6]

$$r_{M_X X_1} = \sqrt{\frac{r_{x_1 x_2}\,(r_{x_1 x_3})}{r_{x_2 x_3}}}$$

It can be seen that if the denominator is less than the numerator within the radical sign, $r_{M_X X_1}$ will exceed 1.0. Take any three intercorrelations. If one of them is less in absolute value than the multiplication of the other two, one of the r_{MX} coefficients will exceed 1.0. Since these are standardized regression (or correlation) coefficients, a value that exceeds unity does not make sense. Also, it may be pointed out that the value within the radical sign must be positive, meaning the signs of the three intercorrelations must be either $+++$ or $+--$. When more than three operational variables are subsumed by a concept, the same limit applies, but then there will be more than one estimate of $r_{M_X X_1}$, and these estimates must be nearly identical.

In general we think that these algebraic solutions are appealing for future theory construction and causal inference models. The rejection criteria are explicit and demanding. The methods are direct and sensitive to human thinking and judgment. As Costner emphasizes, the methods provide a well-defined way of linking theoretical concepts to data. One of the problems in factor analysis—the inclusion of variables that create "noise" in the system—

is averted by virtue of the test criteria. Of course there are always the usual problems of measurement error, a fact that requires an air of tentativeness about any multivariate statistical solution.

NOTES

1. For a broad and detailed coverage of factor analysis, see R.J. Rummel, *Applied Factor Analysis* (Evanston: Northwestern University Press, 1970). The work by Benjamin Fruchter, *Introduction to Factor Analysis* (Princeton, N.J.: D. Van Nostrand Co., Inc., 1954) is helpful if the reader wishes to go through the precise numeric calculations of specific examples. For an excellent discussion and computer programming orientation to the subject, see William W. Cooley and Paul R. Lohnes, *Multivariate Procedures for the Behavioral Sciences* (New York: John Wiley & Sons, Inc., 1962), especially Chapter 8. For a discussion of the different purposes for which factor analysis is used, see Jack E. Vincent, *Factor Analysis in International Relations* (Gainsville: University of Florida Press, 1971).

2. If normal distributions cannot be achieved, it is advisable to use a *covariance* matrix. The covariance between two variables, X_i and Y_i, is defined as $(\Sigma(X_i - \bar{X})(Y_i - \bar{Y}))/N$, and with standardized means of zero, the formula is $\Sigma X_i Y_i/N$. See Donald Morrison, *Multivariate Statistical Methods* (New York: McGraw-Hill Book Company, 1967), pp. 221–24. Morrison suggests that when the variables are not too diverse in measurement base (e.g., dollars, votes, crime rates, etc.), but fairly similar, covariance values are preferable to correlation values in any case. The denominator in the simple correlation coefficient is a standardizing term that makes sense when the distributions are of the same symmetrical shape. In this chapter we work with correlation coefficients, primarily to integrate factor analysis with other forms of statistical analysis.

3. Rummel, *Applied Factor Analysis*, p. 171. The reader is also referred to Rummel's evaluation of oblique rotation models.

4. Rummel, *Applied Factor Analysis*, p. 141.

5. Herbert L. Costner, "Theory, Deduction and Rules of Correspondence," *American Journal of Sociology*, 75 (September 1969), 245–63.

6. Wayne L. Francis, "Toward Correspondence in Theoretic and Empirical Language: Covariance and Causal Inference" (paper delivered to Annual Meeting of Western Political Science Association, 1971).

Chapter 14

TIME-SERIES ANALYSIS

In recent years social science information banks, in their expansion, are affording increasing opportunities to analyze trends relating to political change. It seems evident that the statistical bases for evaluating and explaining trends will become increasingly important. Even so, it will no doubt be many years before political scientists find an interest in ongoing seasonal averages and fluctuations exemplified in the business and economic fields. Political scientists are more likely to be concerned with decennial or annual records, and more refined time distinctions only as they occur in special studies. We will need to show why more refined time-series collections are necessary. What will offset the cost of repetitive and systematic measurement?

The statistical tools for time-series analysis are essentially identical to those required for comparative studies of individuals or governments at a single point in time. It is only conceptually that the analysis differs. The conceptual differences are severe enough, however, that to take them lightly can lead to highly erroneous conclusions. In this chapter we will introduce the fundamentals necessary for doing more advanced time-series analysis and then briefly describe multivariate extensions.

Plotting Trends

Any set of values derived in the same manner at different points in time can be plotted as a trend line. These values can be raw data figures, percentages, *Gini Coefficient* values, standard deviations, ordinal ranks, correlation coefficients, and so on. In normal practice, time is represented on the horizontal axis, and the values producing the relationship are represented on the vertical axis. The trend line or curve may steadily increase, remain constant, decrease, or fluctuate up and down erratically.

There are three basic kinds of trends:

1. A trend of original values
2. A trend of distribution values
3. A trend of correlation values

In the first case, one might plot a trend of Democrat or Republican vote for a city, the number of treaties filed with the United Nations each year, the number of dollars spent by a campaign organization over the years, educational spending as a percent of total budget in a state, the percent unemployment in the country, and so on.

In the second kind of trend, a measure of *central tendency* or *dispersion* is utilized. For example, one could plot the mean income of federal employees and then separately plot the standard deviation around those calculated mean values. Or the same might be done for the age of judges in a court system.

A plotted measure of dispersion indicates the extent to which a set of values are distributed equally or unequally among a group of individuals or governmental units at different points in time. Trends in dispersion and trends in central tendency have the feature of exhibiting both comparative and longitudinal perspectives. Their relevance for the evaluation of programs, performance, and the achievement of goals is obvious. In randomized samples, the values making up the trend can be qualified by confidence intervals.

At a third, theoretically more sophisticated level, correlations derived in the same way can be plotted over time. Any of the correlation measures presented in Chapter 10 could be employed. The analyst would be interested in whether with time two variables are becoming more or less closely associated, or whether a rather constant degree of association is reflected. A correlation between the percent of votes and the percent of seats won by majority parties in the 50 states, for example, could be calculated for each of several years to determine whether a greater correspondence has resulted, perhaps due to Supreme Court apportionment decisions.

Causal Inference

In a time-series analysis it may be possible to risk a causal inference, such that an increase in X leads to an increase in Y, or an increase in X leads to a decrease in Y, or a decrease in X leads to an increase in Y, or a decrease in X leads to a decrease in Y. As an example, we can take two interval variables: (1) expenditures of all state governments of the United States in constant dollars and (2) population of the United States. The hypothesis could be: Increased state expenditures are caused by increases in population. By "constant dollars" it is meant that inflation is controlled so that the dollar estimates represent purchasing power units.

In this example, let Y_t = total state expenditures for a given year, and X_{t-1} = total population in the previous year. The data may be listed as follows:

	POPULATION (MILLIONS)	EXPENDITURE (BILLIONS)
1953	157	
1954		15.8
1955	163	
1956		17.5
1957	170	
1958	173	20.2
1959	176	21.8
1960		21.9

Both population and expenditures increase with time. A simple Pearson correlation coefficient will obviously be quite high. In fact the correlation between any two variables that consistently increase will be very high.

TABLE 14.1

Preliminary Calculations for r_{YT} *and* z_{YX}

Y_t	Y^2_t	T_{t-1}	T^2_{t-1}	X_{t-1}	X^2_{t-1}	$Y_t T_{t-1}$	$Y_t X_{t-1}$
0	0	0	0	0	0	0	0
1.7	2.89	2	4	6	36	3.4	10.2
4.4	19.36	4	16	13	169	17.6	57.2
6.	36.	5	25	16	256	30.	96.
6.1	37.21	6	36	19	361	36.6	115.9
18.2	95.46	17	81	54	822	87.6	279.3

To guard against a premature conclusion that increased population leads to increased state expenditures, time can be treated as a *dummy* variable. If population can do no better than time in explaining the values of state expenditure, population is perhaps an unnecessary variable in the analysis. To make the calculations, the magnitude of the above numbers can be reduced by subtracting the lowest value in each distribution from every value in the distribution. Using these transformations, we have:

T	X	Y
0	0	
1		0
2	6	
3		1.7
4	13	
5	16	4.4
6	19	6
7		6.1

The segmented lines indicate which values of time and population, alternatively, will be used to explain the variance in Y. Since the Pearson formula is based upon variation around the means, the transformed values will not affect the magnitudes of the resulting correlations. The correlation between time and expenditures is symbolized $r_{y_t T_{t-1}}$, or in this problem simply r_{YT}. Correspondingly, $r_{y_t x_{t-1}}$ can be written r_{YX}. Using the calculations in Table 14.1, we find:

$$r_{YT} = \frac{\Sigma YT - \dfrac{\Sigma Y \ \Sigma T}{N}}{\sqrt{\left(\Sigma Y^2 - \dfrac{(\Sigma Y)^2}{N}\right)\left(\Sigma T^2 - \dfrac{(\Sigma T)^2}{N}\right)}}$$

$$= \frac{87.6 - \dfrac{(18.2) \ (17)}{5}}{\sqrt{\left(95.46 - \dfrac{(18.2)^2}{5}\right)\left(81 - \dfrac{(17)^2}{5}\right)}}$$

$$= \frac{25.72}{26.03}$$

$$= .988$$

Substituting X for T in the same equation,

$$r_{YX} = \frac{279.3 - \dfrac{(18.2) \ (54)}{5}}{\sqrt{\left(95.46 - \dfrac{(18.2)^2}{5}\right)\left(822 - \dfrac{(54)^2}{5}\right)}}$$

$$= \frac{82.74}{83.52}$$

$$= .991$$

The correlations differ by only .003. For the above set of data, population barely improves upon the dummy variable, time. Of course the above set of data, adapted from data appearing in *The Book of the States, 1962–63,* are too limited to draw any conclusions whatsoever. A better study would encompass many more years. An even better study would also incorporate a state-by-state trend analysis. Furthermore, it may be that states respond to population increases two or three years rather than one year later. The $t-1$ model can be changed to a $t-2$ or $t-3$ model. The essential point here is that *in a linear regression analysis, the dummy variable, time, should be included to guard against making exaggerated inferences.*

If the linear equations for the above relationships were developed, say, solving for $Y_t = a + bT_{t-1}$, it would be found that X is a slightly better predictor of the values of Y than is T. These equations could be regarded as miniature models for the explanation and prediction of Y. The equation including time (T), however, is a dummy model, and generally it would be treated only as a prediction device. If another equation is to be described as the causal model, it ought to add to the predictive value of T. While these comments are addressed to two-variable equation models, the same rationale works its way into multivariate models, where T serves to eliminate unnecessary explanatory variables.

There is a third competitive equation, $Y_t = a + bY_{t-1}$, utilized in a variety of ways to clarify a time-series problem. The values in the Y distribution are predicted from its lagged values, where $t - k$ indicates how many time units are imposed upon the lag. Given N observations of Y, there will be only $N - 1$ values for Y_{t-1}, therefore, the above linear equation gives only $N - 1$ predictions, and the corresponding correlation coefficient will be over $N - 1$ cases. In the above problem there are missing values for Y (1957 and 1955), and an interpolation of those values is required. The original and transformed values in the computation of the correlation coefficient are:

	ORIGINAL				TRANSFORMED	
	Y_t	Y_{t-1}			Y_t	Y_{t-1}
1956	17.5	16.65	1955 (interpol.)		0	0
1958	20.2	18.85	1957 (interpol.)		2.7	2.2
1959	21.8	20.2	1958		4.3	3.55
1960	21.9	21.8	1959		4.4	5.15

Using the transformed values in the Pearson correlation coefficient yields a value $r_0 = .609$, where r_0 signifies that it is a correlation between a variable and its lagged values. For the data given, previous expenditure values are not, in relation to T and X, very good predictors of current expenditure values.

The general formula for r_0 is:

$$r_0 = \frac{\Sigma Y_t Y_{t-k} - \dfrac{\Sigma Y_t \left(\Sigma Y_{t-k}\right)}{N - k}}{\sqrt{\left(\Sigma Y_t^2 = \dfrac{(\Sigma Y_t)^2}{N - k}\right)\left(\Sigma Y_{t-k}^2 - \dfrac{(\Sigma Y_{t-k})^2}{N - k}\right)}} \qquad (14.1)$$

where N is the total number of observations of Y_t; and
$\quad$ k is the number of lagged time units.

In statistics, the above equation is called a *serial* correlation. It is used when one suspects that the observations of Y are not independent of each other. Generally, the shorter the time intervals between observations, the greater the likelihood that successive observation values will not be independent. Election results at 12-year intervals, for example, are more likely to be independent than election results at 2-year intervals. It is clearly possible that the serial correlation will be higher than r_{YX}, and when this occurs, it is tentative evidence against the original speculation that X explains Y.

The Variance Problem

Statistical analysis of interval variables is built upon the concept of *variance*. If every value in a distribution is identical to every other value, there is no variance, and statistically, there is nothing to explain or predict. If the turnout percent in state elections is the same for every election unit, then it would not be possible statistically to explain variations in turnout percent. The mean variance, $s_m^2 = 0$, a value that cannot be reduced by the introduction of another variable. In a time-series analysis, if the plot of a simple trend gives a perfect fit to a straight line, it is hopeless to introduce another variable for the purpose of making a statistical assertion of explanation or prediction. The variance in the variable is a strict function of time, and the model $Y_t = a + bT_{t-k}$ holds. Only in experimental work, say, where X can be altered to determine if the alteration affects the value of Y, would it make sense to consider an additional variable. Most statistical analysis in political science, sociology, and economics is nonexperimental.

In business and economics, trends have long been a subject of interest. In those fields a time-series is usually defined as

$$TS = T + C + S + I$$

which means that a time-series, TS, is equal to a *trend*, plus *cyclical* variation, plus *seasonal* variation, plus *irregular* variation. The symbol T is the same as our T in the linear regression equation. It refers to the extent to which the linear regression equation represents the data. Seasonal variation refers to monthly data and is usually not relevant to political science problems. Cyclical variation and irregular variation are what is left after *detrending* the data. In the context of this chapter, they compose the variation we hope to account for by introducing another variable; however, a shift in terminology will be helpful. We can distinguish between:

1. Variance accounted for by T_{t-k}
2. Variance accounted for by Y_{t-k}
3. Variance accounted for by X_{t-k}
4. Unaccounted-for variance

This type of problem is most readily managed in a multiple regression analysis, but there is one wrinkle in the analysis that distinguishes it from the usual comparative study. The analyst needs to decide whether the time variable and the lagged variable are of any theoretical interest. If not, it may be desirable to detrend and/or deserialize the data. It may not be the proportion of original variance in Y accounted for by X that is of interest, but rather the proportion of remaining variance in Y after T_{t-k} and Y_{t-1} have been evaluated. For example, it seems rather obvious that national budgets have increased over the past 25 years, and that previous years' budgets are employed as a guide to new budgets. Identifying a variable that accounts for the remaining variation in budget figures could be more significant in theoretical work.

Detrending

To detrend a set of data is a tedious but uncomplicated matter when the observations are over equal time intervals. It requires, first, solving for the linear regression equation for the relationship between time and the variable, as illustrated in Chapter 10. To solve for $Y_t = a + bT_{t-1}$, calculate the slope and then the constant. If the observations are over equal intervals, do not worry about the lag in time values, since the result will be the same. If the numbers are cumbersome, transform them. In Table 14.2 are the turnout percentages for Presidential elections spaced at four-year intervals. The years have been transformed, setting 1920 to 0, 1924 to 1, and so on. The linear equation for the relationship is:

$$Y_t = 46.9 + 1.57T_{t-1}$$

The second step involves calculating all of the predictions of Y from the equation, making sure to substitute the transformed values for T, and *not* the original years. The predicted values, symbolized Y_t', are given in the fourth column of Table 14.2. The table gives rounded values for ease of illustration. These predicted values represent the trend. When they are subtracted from the actual values of Y, the resulting values $(Y - Y')$ are the *detrended* values. Figure 14.1 illustrates that the fluctuations in the data have been retained. In a problem wherein it is obvious that the trend is generally

TABLE 14.2

Detrending Data: Presidential Election Turnout *

YEAR T_t	TRANSFORMED T_t	ACTUAL TURNOUT Y_t	PREDICTED TURNOUT Y'_t	DIFFERENCE $Y_t - Y'_t$ OR D_t
1920	0	44.2	46.9	-2.7
1924	1	44.3	48.5	-4.2
1928	2	52.3	50.1	2.2
1932	3	52.9	51.7	1.2
1936	4	57.5	53.3	4.2
1940	5	59.7	54.8	4.9
1944	6	56.3	56.4	-.1
1948	7	51.5	58.0	-6.5
1952	8	62.0	59.6	2.4
1956	9	60.1	61.1	-1.0
1960	10	63.8	62.6	1.2
1964	11	62.0	64.2	-2.2

* Based on regression equation, $Y_t = 46.9 + 1.57T_{t-1}$. All values are rounded. The constant Y may be added to each value of D.

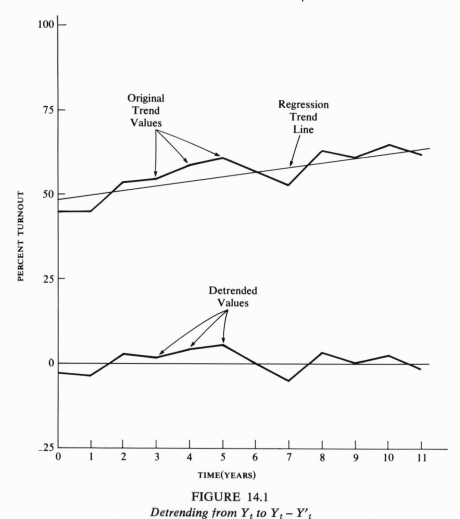

FIGURE 14.1
Detrending from Y_t to $Y_t - Y'_t$

upward, or generally downward, it is usually the fluctuations that are of theoretical interest, for if they can be explained, the analysis moves beyond mere extrapolation. The detrended values, symbolized D_t, may be treated directly for their relationship to values of other variables.

Deserializing

Deserializing is approached in the same way as detrending, through the calculation of the linear regression equation, in this case for

$$Y_t = a + bY_{t-k}$$

where k is a constant and may be set to 1 when the observations are spaced at equal time intervals. When a trend has a major change in direction, say, increasing for 20 years and then decreasing for 20 years, the detrending equation will not pick up the overall pattern, but the deserializing equation will. In a curvilinear trend of any type (assuming sufficient observations and rather prolonged shifts or patterns) the values of Y_{t-1} will pick up the "curves," since they follow the values of Y_t.

The equation and resulting correlation may be used simply to detect curvilinearity, or it may be felt that the trend values are dependent upon each other in a serial way. For example, voter turnout may be partly a product of whether people have participated in previous elections. The percent of those eligible who have voted in the previous election will make a difference in the turnout rate. The voting studies have shown that when new groups of people acquire suffrage or come of age they do not turn out at as high a rate as those who have previously voted. Variations in the number of people reaching voting age, variation in death rates, broadened voter franchise, and other factors make the problem of tracing seriality rather complex.

A set of trend values may be deserialized after it has been detrended. The values of D_t are predicted from D_{t-1} values, and the differences between D_t and D_t' represent the remaining fluctuation or variance in the trend. Normally, the problem is approached in a stepwise fashion; that is, the original trend values are detrended and deserialized separately to determine which explains away most of the variance in Y. Recall that $s_y^2 = (\Sigma\,(Y_t - Y_t')^2)/N$ and that the proportion of variance explained $r^2 = (s_m^2 - s_y^2)/s_m^2$. Thus the process that gives the best least-square estimates expressed by Y_t' and indexed by r^2 is implemented first.

It might be found that once the equation producing the highest value of r^2 is implemented, the equation representing the second process (detrending or deserializing) will have no effect upon the relative distribution of values. The quickest way to know whether the redundancy will occur is to calculate the correlation coefficients for the last $N-1$ cases, using the Pearson formula, r. The correlations between Y and T $(r_{YT_{t-1}})$, Y and Y_{t-1} $(r_{YY_{t-1}})$, and T and Y_{t-1} $(r_{T_{t-1}Y_{t-1}})$ will indicate a redundancy if it is found that

$$r_{YY_{t-1}} = (r_{YT_{t-1}})\,(r_{T_{t-1}Y_{t-1}})$$

Example: $.4 = (.8)\,(.5)$

$$r_{YT_{t-1}} = (r_{YY_{t-1}})\,(r_{T_{t-1}Y_{t-1}})$$

Example: $.36 = (.6)\,(.6)$

The first equation suggests that the correlation between Y and its lagged values is accounted for entirely by T. In the second equation, the correlation between Y and T is accounted for by the lagged values of Y. In the first case one would drop Y_{t-1} from the analysis, and in the second case T would be excluded.

Conclusion

When the analyst is interested in pure forecasting from a single variable, the above time and lag models are very useful. Furthermore they serve the purpose of evaluating whether additional variables do in fact add anything to the analysis. Many years ago, when computers and calculators were difficult to come by, and when few analysts were familiar with multivariate analysis, trend analysis bred a variety of microconcepts suited to highly specific purposes. It is probably correct to say that least-squares methods have pushed many of the older estimating devices aside, at least in theoretical work. One advantage of least-squares regression analysis may be found in its elaboration, wherein the relationship between several variables can be expressed at once in equation form. Evaluation of Y_t, T_{t-1}, Y_{t-1}, and X_{t-1} can proceed most efficiently through the use of the multivariate statistics.

Multivariate Extensions

The use of multiple regression techniques in time-series analysis is a complicated business, and this section can introduce only some of the elementary considerations.[1] It should be pointed out that the jump from cross-sectional or cross-unit analysis to time-series analysis is an artificial one. Any particular study may incorporate elements of both.

It has been stated previously that in time-series analysis it is necessary to consider the regression effects of detrending and deserializing the data. Taking Y as the dependent variable, it may be found that X has little explanatory value in competition with T (time) and Y_{t-1} (the lagged values of Y). The problem, then, is to have a multivariate framework, appropriate to longitudinal analysis, that will take time and lagged effects into account. In developing the framework, we can begin with a simple model, assuming interval data, continuous time, and standardized means of zero, and assuming that the observations are spaced equally over time. Taking X and Z as the independent variables, it is possible to solve for

$$Y_t = b_1 X_t + b_2 Z_t + b_3 Y_{t-1} + b_4 T_t + e_t$$

where the b's are partial slope coefficients, each controlling for all regressed independent terms. Suspecting lagged effects, the Y values have been lagged one interval. Lagging more than one interval will require a more complex equation.

In a time-series regression equation it is usually necessary to test for the significance of the partial slope terms, and in doing so it is possible to determine whether some terms are "irrelevant" to the explanation of variance in Y. The points in time at which the observations are made are treated as a random sample of all points of time within the range. If the analyst suspects that the observed points are atypical of the interim periods, the significance tests will not have much meaning. In such a case the problem would require additional evidence anyway and the above equation would be suspect.

To test for significance, the t-test is employed, where for the first slope, b_1, the equation:

$$t = \frac{b}{V(b)}$$

is read as   (14.2)

$$t = \frac{b_1}{V(b_1)}$$

where

$$V(b_1) = \frac{\sum e_t^2 / N - k - 1}{(\Sigma X^2)(1 - R^2_{X.ZY_{t-1}}T)}$$ (14.3)

The term $V(b)$ is the estimated variance of the regression coefficient which is calculated by dividing the *unique* variance of the variable in question (X_t here) into the standard error of the estimate for the entire equation, where $\Sigma e_t^2 = \Sigma(Y_t - Y_t')^2$ and k equals the number of regressed independent terms excluding the derived term, Y_{t-1}. The larger the value of t, the more significant the slope coefficient. Consulting Table G in the Appendix will reveal at what level (.10, .05, .01, etc.) the slope coefficient is significant, given the degrees of freedom, $N - k - 1$. That is, it will reveal the likelihood that the variance explained by the variable is due to sampling error. The same test is applied to each independent term and the results are compared.

In the next step the independent term with the lowest t value is eliminated if its significance level is weak, and the regression equation is restated without it. The procedure is repeated for the new equation. As a check against the loss of explanatory power, the multiple coefficient of determination, R^2, is calculated for each equation, adjusting for the degrees of freedom. R^2 corrected for the degrees of freedom is represented symbolically as

$$\hat{R}^2 = 1 - (\sum(Y_i - Y_i')^2 / \sum(Y_i - \bar{Y})^2)$$ (14.4)

The use of $\hat{R}^2$ together with the t values in this stepwise learning procedure will not necessarily lead to satisfying results, but it will reveal whether the model can be simplified without the loss of explanatory power, and it will protect against concluding too much about the importance of independent variables. Using this learning procedure, Richard Li, for example, in a re-examination of Winham's data on political development in the United States, is able to ferret out education as the most significant explanatory variable and eliminate communication as having a direct effect upon "democratic political development." The dummy variable, time, greatly reduces the independent predictive value of urbanization and lagged development.[2]

It cannot be overemphasized that the search for the best-fit equation is an experimental learning procedure, and that several alternatives need to be tried. There are actually four forms of evidence that may be drawn from the analysis to arrive at an appropriate model. First, the corrected multiple $\hat{R}^2$'s can remain relatively constant or change dramatically. A downward shift in magnitude from one model to another can mean a loss in predictive power, but only if the shift is large enough that it could not be attributed to measurement error. The same caution needs to be exercised in evaluating upward shifts in $\hat{R}^2$. It is important to keep in mind here the difference between postdiction and prediction. Variables that improve postdictions (predictions of known values through best-fit procedures) do not necessarily improve predictions.

The second form of evidence is the actual slope coefficient of each variable. If the slope coefficient of a variable remains relatively constant throughout the procedure, its degree of importance in the problem is well documented. The third form of evidence, the significance level of t for each slope (or beta weight), indicates how the model may be altered and the relative importance of each variable in a given model. A fourth form of evidence, not yet discussed, is based upon an evaluation of the error term, usually described under the heading of *autocorrelation* or *serial correlation* in time-series problems.

There are two approaches to autocorrelation in this context. One is to try to eliminate it mathematically from the regression equations; the other is to estimate it and deal with it explicitly as an important feature of the explanation. We will deal with it explicitly first. Autocorrelation refers to the correlation between successive error terms, where

$$r(1) = \frac{\sum e_t e_{t-1}}{\sqrt{\sum e_t^2 \sum e_{t-1}^2}} \tag{14.5}$$

is the formula for the lag of one time unit [using $r(2)$ and e^2_{t-2} for the lag of two time units]. Obviously the earliest observation in the data has no prior value, and the above equation will apply to $N-1$ error term comparisons. It needs to be understood that $\sum e_t e_{t-1}$ is merely a shortcut way of symbolizing the sum of $e_t e_{t-1} + e_{t-1} e_{t-2} + e_{t-2} e_{t-3} \ldots$.

When there are no lagged variables in the regression equation, the Durbin-Watson statistic is the standard instrument for testing the significance of the autocorrelation.[3] The test value, d, is calculated from

$$d = \frac{\sum_{t=2}^{N} (e_t - e_{t-1})^2}{\sum_{t=1}^{N} e_t^2} \tag{14.6}$$

The range of d is from 0 to 4. When d is near 2.0 there is very little autocorrelation, whereas values near 0 or 4 indicate positive or negative autocorrelation, respectively. This statistic should not be used when the lag is more than one time unit. Table H in the Appendix gives the precise range below and above 2.0, within which the null hypothesis may not be rejected.

When there is a significant degree of autocorrelation, the original regression model becomes suspect. Either there is a variable left out of the model that is producing the correlation, or the error term is time-dependent. In response to this dilemma, the analyst may wish to lag the dependent variable, producing a new term, Y_{t-1}, for the independent side of the equation. After calculating the new regression equation, it is then appropriate to use Durbin's h-test, where [4]

$$h = (1 - d/2) \sqrt{\frac{N}{1 - (N \cdot V(b_1))}} \qquad (14.7)$$

The d is calculated in the same way as in the Durbin-Watson statistic, N refers to the number of cases in the time-series, and $V(b_1)$ is the estimate of variance of b_1, where b_1 refers to the standardized slope coefficient or beta weight of the lagged variable, Y_{t-1}. The h-statistic has a theoretical *normal* distribution; thus Table G in the Appendix may be used to determine whether h exceeds the tabled value. If h exceeds the tabled value, autocorrelation is present. The h-statistic may not be used when $N \cdot V(b_1)$ exceeds unity, a possibility when there are too few degrees of freedom. Again, the presence of autocorrelation indicates that the model is inadequate.

A second way to deal with autocorrelation is through what is known as a *distributive lag model,* here described as a linear transformation of the regression model. The distributive lag model is designed to take into account the extent to which the dependent variable, Y_t, is influenced not just by X_t, but also by all past X's, expecting less influence from more remote X's, but nevertheless a cumulative impact upon Y_t. It seems reasonable to expect that in many cases the effects of past X's exponentially decline. The exponential weight is introduced by selecting a fraction, λ, to fit the equation:

$$Y_t = \lambda^0 b X_t + \lambda b X_{t-1} + \lambda^2 b X_{t-2} + \ldots \lambda^n b X_{t-n} + e_t$$

where the sum of $\lambda^i = 1.0$. The above equation reduces to

$$Y_t = b X_t + \lambda Y_{t-1} + v_t$$

where $v_t = e_t - \lambda e_{t-1}$. It may then be found that the correlation between the v_t error terms is zero.[5] We may note that if λ is set to one-half ($\frac{1}{2}$), that $\frac{1}{2} + \frac{1}{4} + \frac{1}{8} + \frac{1}{16} + \frac{1}{32} + \ldots$ approaches 1.0. Having made these adjustments, cleaning up the autocorrelation in the error term, the analyst may proceed with the learning steps previously elicited for the regression model.

In summary, the geometrically distributed lag model has the effect of reducing autocorrelation when originally the autocorrelation is fairly high. If originally the autocorrelation was negligible or very low, it wouldn't make much sense to complicate the model, and in fact distortions may result.[6] Thus the simpler model should be explored first, and if the resulting error terms are correlated, the distributed lag model can be applied.

NOTES

1. For background and more detailed analysis of time-series, see Edward J. Kane, *Economic Statistics and Econometrics* (New York: Harper & Row, 1968), especially Chapter 14, pp. 359–69; and Potluri Rao and Roger L. Miller, *Applied Econometrics* (Belmont, Calif.: Wadsworth Publishing Co., Inc., 1971), especially Chapter 5, pp. 121–26.

2. Richard Li, "A Retest of Lerner's Theory with the Distributed Lag Model: Negation of Winham's Findings," unpublished manuscript, 1972. Li also incorporates a geometrically distributed lag to reach his conclusions. The distributed lag model will be discussed shortly.

3. J. Durbin and G.S. Watson, "Testing for Serial Correlation in Least Squares Regression," *Biometrika*, 38 (1951), 159–77.

4. J. Durbin, "Testing for Serial Correlation in Least-Squares Regression When Some of the Regressions Are Lagged Dependent Variables," *Econometrica*, 38 (May 1970), pp. 410–421.

5. See Zvi Griliches, "A Note on Serial Correlation Bias in Estimates of Distributed Lag," *Econometrica*, 29 (January 1961), 65–73.

6. Potluri Rao and Zvi Griliches, "Small Sample Properties of Several Two Stage Methods in the Context of Auto-correlated Errors," *Journal of the American Statistical Association*, 64 (March 1969), 253–73.

TABLES

TABLE A

Areas of the Normal Curve

NORMAL DEVIATE z	.00	.01	.02	.03	.04	.05	.06	.07	.08	.09
0.0	.5000	.4960	.4920	.4880	.4840	.4801	.4761	.4721	.4681	.4641
0.1	.4602	.4562	.4522	.4483	.4443	.4404	.4364	.4325	.4286	.4247
0.2	.4207	.4168	.4129	.4090	.4052	.4013	.3974	.3936	.3897	.3859
0.3	.3821	.3783	.3745	.3707	.3669	.3632	.3594	.3557	.3520	.3483
0.4	.3446	.3409	.3372	.3336	.3300	.3264	.3228	.3192	.3156	.3121
0.5	.3085	.3050	.3015	.2981	.2946	.2912	.2877	.2843	.2810	.2776
0.6	.2743	.2709	.2676	.2643	.2611	.2578	.2546	.2514	.2483	.2451
0.7	.2420	.2389	.2358	.2327	.2296	.2266	.2236	.2206	.2177	.2148
0.8	.2119	.2090	.2061	.2033	.2005	.1977	.1949	.1922	.1894	.1867
0.9	.1841	.1814	.1788	.1762	.1736	.1711	.1685	.1660	.1635	.1611
1.0	.1587	.1562	.1539	.1515	.1492	.1469	.1446	.1423	.1401	.1379
1.1	.1357	.1335	.1314	.1292	.1271	.1251	.1230	.1210	.1190	.1170
1.2	.1151	.1131	.1112	.1093	.1075	.1056	.1038	.1020	.1003	.0985
1.3	.0968	.0951	.0934	.0918	.0901	.0885	.0869	.0853	.0838	.0823
1.4	.0808	.0793	.0778	.0764	.0749	.0735	.0721	.0708	.0694	.0681
1.5	.0668	.0655	.0643	.0630	.0618	.0606	.0594	.0582	.0571	.0559
1.6	.0548	.0537	.0526	.0516	.0505	.0495	.0485	.0475	.0465	.0455
1.7	.0446	.0436	.0427	.0418	.0409	.0401	.0392	.0384	.0375	.0367
1.8	.0359	.0351	.0344	.0336	.0329	.0322	.0314	.0307	.0301	.0294
1.9	.0287	.0281	.0274	.0268	.0262	.0256	.0250	.0244	.0239	.0223
2.0	.0228	.0222	.0217	.0212	.0207	.0202	.0197	.0192	.0188	.0183
2.1	.0179	.0174	.0170	.0166	.0162	.0158	.0154	.0150	.0146	.0143
2.2	.0139	.0136	.0132	.0129	.0125	.0122	.0119	.0116	.0113	.0110
2.3	.0107	.0104	.0102	.0099	.0096	.0094	.0091	.0089	.0087	.0084
2.4	.0082	.0080	.0078	.0075	.0073	.0071	.0069	.0068	.0066	.0064
2.5	.0062	.0060	.0059	.0057	.0055	.0054	.0052	.0051	.0049	.0048
2.6	.0047	.0045	.0044	.0043	.0041	.0040	.0039	.0038	.0037	.0036
2.7	.0035	.0034	.0033	.0032	.0031	.0030	.0029	.0028	.0027	.0026
2.8	.0026	.0025	.0024	.0023	.0023	.0022	.0021	.0021	.0020	.0019
2.9	.0019	.0018	.0018	.0017	.0016	.0016	.0015	.0015	.0014	.0014
3.0	.0013	.0013	.0013	.0012	.0012	.0011	.0011	.0011	.0010	.0010

Explanation: Standard deviation units are in left column, with second decimal places at tops of appropriate columns. To find proportion of area between the mean and a standard deviation value, subtract the tabled proportion from .50. For example, .62 standard deviations from the mean yields a tabled value of .2676, and .50 − .2676 = .2324, the proportion of area between the mean and .62 units from the mean.

TABLE B
Ordinates of the Normal Curve

z	.00	.01	.02	.03	.04	.05	.06	.07	.08	.09
.0	.3989	.3989	.3989	.3988	.3986	.3984	.3982	.3980	.3977	.3973
.1	.3970	.3965	.3961	.3956	.3951	.3945	.3939	.3932	.3925	.3918
.2	.3910	.3902	.3894	.3885	.3876	.3867	.3857	.3847	.3836	.3825
.3	.3814	.3802	.3790	.3778	.3765	.3752	.3739	.3725	.3712	.3697
.4	.3683	.3668	.3653	.3637	.3621	.3605	.3589	.3572	.3555	.3538
.5	.3521	.3503	.3485	.3467	.3448	.3429	.3410	.3391	.3372	.3352
.6	.3332	.3312	.3292	.3271	.3251	.3230	.3209	.3187	.3166	.3144
.7	.3123	.3101	.3079	.3056	.3034	.3011	.2989	.2966	.2943	.2920
.8	.2897	.2874	.2850	.2827	.2803	.2780	.2756	.2732	.2709	.2685
.9	.2661	.2637	.2613	.2589	.2565	.2541	.2516	.2492	.2468	.2444
1.0	.2420	.2396	.2371	.2347	.2323	.2299	.2275	.2251	.2227	.2203
1.1	.2179	.2155	.2131	.2107	.2083	.2059	.2036	.2012	.1989	.1965
1.2	.1942	.1919	.1895	.1872	.1849	.1826	.1804	.1781	.1758	.1736
1.3	.1714	.1691	.1669	.1647	.1626	.1604	.1582	.1561	.1539	.1518
1.4	.1497	.1476	.1456	.1435	.1415	.1394	.1374	.1354	.1334	.1315
1.5	.1295	.1276	.1257	.1238	.1219	.1200	.1182	.1163	.1145	.1127
1.6	.1109	.1092	.1074	.1057	.1040	.1023	.1006	.0989	.0973	.0957
1.7	.0940	.0925	.0909	.0893	.0878	.0863	.0848	.0833	.0818	.0804
1.8	.0790	.0775	.0761	.0748	.0734	.0721	.0707	.0694	.0681	.0669
1.9	.0656	.0644	.0632	.0620	.0608	.0596	.0584	.0573	.0562	.0551
2.0	.0540	.0529	.0519	.0508	.0498	.0488	.0478	.0468	.0459	.0449
2.1	.0440	.0431	.0422	.0413	.0404	.0396	.0387	.0379	.0371	.0363
2.2	.0355	.0347	.0339	.0332	.0325	.0317	.0310	.0303	.0297	.0290
2.3	.0283	.0277	.0270	.0264	.0258	.0252	.0246	.0241	.0235	.0229
2.4	.0224	.0219	.0213	.0208	.0203	.0198	.0194	.0189	.0184	.0180
2.5	.0175	.0171	.0167	.0163	.0158	.0154	.0151	.0147	.0143	.0139
2.6	.0136	.0132	.0129	.0126	.0122	.0119	.0116	.0113	.0110	.0107
2.7	.0104	.0101	.0099	.0096	.0093	.0091	.0088	.0086	.0084	.0081
2.8	.0079	.0077	.0075	.0073	.0071	.0069	.0067	.0065	.0063	.0061
2.9	.0060	.0058	.0056	.0055	.0053	.0051	.0050	.0048	.0047	.0046
3.0	.0044	.0043	.0042	.0040	.0039	.0038	.0037	.0036	.0035	.0034
3.1	.0033	.0032	.0031	.0030	.0029	.0028	.0027	.0026	.0025	.0025
3.2	.0024	.0023	.0022	.0022	.0021	.0020	.0020	.0019	.0018	.0018
3.3	.0017	.0017	.0016	.0016	.0015	.0015	.0014	.0014	.0013	.0013
3.4	.0012	.0012	.0012	.0011	.0011	.0010	.0010	.0010	.0009	.0009
3.5	.0009	.0008	.0008	.0008	.0008	.0007	.0007	.0007	.0007	.0006
3.6	.0006	.0006	.0006	.0005	.0005	.0005	.0005	.0005	.0005	.0004
3.7	.0004	.0004	.0004	.0004	.0004	.0004	.0003	.0003	.0003	.0003
3.8	.0003	.0003	.0003	.0003	.0003	.0002	.0002	.0002	.0002	.0002
3.9	.0002	.0002	.0002	.0002	.0002	.0002	.0002	.0002	.0001	.0001

TABLE C

Distribution of χ^2

df	.99	.98	.95	.90	.80	.70	.50	.30	.20	.10	.05	.02	.01	.001
1	$.0^3157$	$.0^3628$	$.0^3393$	.0158	.0642	.148	.455	1.074	1.642	2.706	3.841	5.412	6.635	10.827
2	.0201	.0404	.103	.211	.446	.713	1.386	2.408	3.219	4.605	5.991	7.824	9.210	13.815
3	.115	.185	.352	.584	1.005	1.424	2.366	3.665	4.642	6.251	7.815	9.837	11.341	16.268
4	.297	.429	.711	1.064	1.649	2.195	3.357	4.878	5.989	7.779	9.488	11.668	13.277	18.465
5	.554	.752	1.145	1.610	2.343	3.000	4.351	6.064	7.289	9.236	11.070	13.388	15.086	20.517
6	.872	1.134	1.635	2.204	3.070	3.828	5.348	7.231	8.558	10.645	12.592	15.033	16.812	22.457
7	1.239	1.564	2.167	2.833	3.822	4.671	6.346	8.383	9.803	12.017	14.067	16.622	18.475	24.322
8	1.646	2.032	2.733	3.490	4.594	5.527	7.344	9.524	11.030	13.362	15.507	18.168	20.090	26.125
9	2.088	2.532	3.325	4.168	5.380	6.393	8.343	10.656	12.242	14.684	16.919	19.679	21.666	27.877
10	2.558	3.059	3.940	4.865	6.179	7.267	9.342	11.781	13.442	15.987	18.307	21.161	23.209	29.588
11	3.053	3.609	4.575	5.578	6.989	8.148	10.341	12.899	14.631	17.275	19.675	22.618	24.725	31.264
12	3.571	4.178	5.226	6.304	7.807	9.034	11.340	14.011	15.812	18.549	21.026	24.054	26.217	32.909
13	4.107	4.765	5.892	7.042	8.634	9.926	12.340	15.119	16.985	19.812	22.362	25.472	27.688	34.528
14	4.660	5.368	6.571	7.790	9.467	10.821	13.339	16.222	18.151	21.064	23.685	26.873	29.141	36.123
15	5.229	5.985	7.261	8.547	10.307	11.721	14.339	17.322	19.311	22.307	24.996	28.259	30.578	37.697
16	5.812	6.614	7.962	9.312	11.152	12.624	15.338	18.418	20.465	23.542	26.296	29.633	32.000	39.252
17	6.408	7.255	8.672	10.085	12.002	13.531	16.338	19.511	21.615	24.769	27.587	30.995	33.409	40.790
18	7.015	7.906	9.390	10.865	12.857	14.440	17.338	20.601	22.760	25.989	28.869	32.346	34.805	42.312
19	7.633	8.567	10.117	11.651	13.716	15.352	18.338	21.689	23.900	27.204	30.144	33.687	36.191	43.820
20	8.260	9.237	10.851	12.443	14.578	16.266	19.337	22.775	25.038	28.412	31.410	35.020	37.566	45.315
21	8.897	9.915	11.591	13.240	15.445	17.182	20.337	23.858	26.171	29.615	32.671	36.343	38.932	46.797
22	9.542	10.600	12.338	14.041	16.314	18.101	21.337	24.939	27.301	30.813	33.924	37.659	40.289	48.268
23	10.196	11.293	13.091	14.848	17.187	19.021	22.337	26.018	28.429	32.007	35.172	38.968	41.638	49.728
24	10.856	11.992	13.848	15.659	18.062	19.943	23.337	27.096	29.553	33.196	36.415	40.270	42.980	51.179
25	11.524	12.697	14.611	16.473	18.940	20.867	24.337	28.172	30.675	34.382	37.652	41.566	44.314	52.620
26	12.198	13.409	15.379	17.292	19.820	21.792	25.336	29.246	31.795	35.563	38.885	42.856	45.642	54.052
27	12.879	14.125	16.151	18.114	20.703	22.719	26.336	30.319	32.912	36.741	40.113	44.140	46.963	55.476
28	13.565	14.847	16.928	18.939	21.588	23.647	27.336	31.391	34.027	37.916	41.337	45.419	48.278	56.893
29	14.256	15.574	17.708	19.768	22.475	24.577	28.336	32.461	35.139	39.087	42.557	46.693	49.588	58.302
30	14.953	16.306	18.493	20.599	23.364	25.508	29.336	33.530	36.250	40.256	43.773	47.962	50.892	59.703

For larger values of df, the expression $\sqrt{2\chi^2} - \sqrt{2df-1}$ may be used as a normal deviate with unit variance, remembering that the probability for χ^2 corresponds with that of a single tail of the normal curve.

SOURCE: Table I is reprinted from Table IV of R.A. Fisher and F. Yates, *Statistical Tables for Biological, Agricultural and Medical Research* (1948 ed.), published by Oliver & Boyd Ltd., Edinburgh and London, by permission of the authors and publishers.

TABLE D
Significant Values of U

Two-Tailed Test, $\alpha = .05$

N_1	3	4	5	6	7	8	9	10	11	12	13	14	15	16	17	18	19	20
1	–	–	–	–	–	–	–	–	–	–	–	–	–	–	–	–	–	–
2	–	–	–	–	–	0	0	0	0	1	1	1	1	1	2	2	2	2
3	–	–	0	1	1	2	2	3	3	4	4	5	5	6	6	7	7	8
4		0	1	2	3	4	4	5	6	7	8	9	10	11	11	12	13	13
5			2	3	5	6	7	8	9	11	12	13	14	15	17	18	19	20
6				5	6	8	10	11	13	14	16	17	19	21	22	24	25	27
7					8	10	12	14	16	18	20	22	24	26	28	30	32	34
8						13	15	17	19	22	24	26	29	31	34	36	38	41
9							17	20	23	26	28	31	34	37	39	42	45	48
10								23	26	29	33	36	39	42	45	48	52	55
11									30	33	37	40	44	47	51	55	58	62
12										37	41	45	49	53	57	61	65	69
13											45	50	54	59	63	67	72	76
14												55	59	64	67	74	78	83
15													64	70	75	80	85	90
16														75	81	86	92	98
17															87	93	99	105
18																99	106	112
19																	113	119
20																		127

$z = 1.960$

Two-Tailed Test, $\alpha = .01$

N_1	3	4	5	6	7	8	9	10	11	12	13	14	15	16	17	18	19	20
1	–	–	–	–	–	–	–	–	–	–	–	–	–	–	–	–	–	–
2	–	–	–	–	–	–	–	–	–	–	–	–	–	–	–	–	0	0
3	–	–	–	–	–	–	0	0	0	1	1	1	2	2	2	2	3	3
4		–	–	0	0	1	1	2	2	3	4	4	5	5	6	6	7	8
5			0	1	2	3	3	4	5	6	7	7	8	9	10	11	12	13
6				2	3	4	5	6	7	9	10	11	12	13	15	16	17	18
7					4	6	7	9	10	12	13	15	16	18	19	21	22	24
8						8	10	12	14	16	18	19	21	23	25	27	29	31
9							11	13	16	18	20	22	24	27	29	31	33	36
10								16	18	21	24	26	29	31	34	37	39	42
11									21	24	27	30	33	36	39	42	45	48
12										27	31	34	37	41	44	47	51	54
13											34	38	42	45	49	53	56	60
14												42	46	50	54	58	63	67
15													51	55	60	64	69	73
16														60	65	70	74	79
17															70	75	81	86
18																81	87	92
19																	93	99
20																		105

$z = 2.576$

TABLE E
Significant Values of Gamma and Tau$_c$

N	TWO-TAILED TEST		ONE-TAILED TEST	
	$\alpha = .05$	$\alpha = .01$	$\alpha = .05$	$\alpha = .01$
4			1.000	
5	1.000		0.800	1.000
6	0.867	1.000	0.733	0.867
7	0.714	0.905	0.619	0.810
8	0.643	0.786	0.571	0.714
9	0.556	0.722	0.500	0.667
10	0.511	0.644	0.467	0.600
11	0.491	0.600	0.418	0.564
12	0.455	0.576	0.394	0.545
13	0.436	0.564	0.359	0.513
14	0.407	0.516	0.363	0.473
15	0.390	0.505	0.333	0.467
16	0.383	0.483	0.317	0.433
17	0.368	0.471	0.309	0.426
18	0.346	0.451	0.294	0.412
19	0.333	0.439	0.287	0.392
20	0.326	0.421	0.274	0.379
21	0.314	0.410	0.267	0.371
22	0.307	0.394	0.264	0.359
23	0.296	0.391	0.257	0.352
24	0.290	0.377	0.246	0.341
25	0.287	0.367	0.240	0.333
26	0.280	0.360	0.237	0.329
27	0.271	0.356	0.231	0.322
28	0.265	0.344	0.228	0.312
29	0.261	0.340	0.222	0.310
30	0.255	0.333	0.218	0.301
31	0.252	0.325	0.213	0.295
32	0.246	0.323	0.210	0.290
33	0.242	0.314	0.205	0.288
34	0.237	0.312	0.201	0.280
35	0.234	0.304	0.197	0.277
36	0.232	0.302	0.194	0.273
37	0.228	0.297	0.192	0.267
38	0.223	0.292	0.189	0.263
39	0.220	0.287	0.188	0.260
40	0.218	0.285	0.185	0.256
z	1.960	2.576	1.645	2.326

Linton C. Freeman, *Elementary Applied Statistics* (New York: John Wiley & Sons, Inc., 1965), p. 249. Reprinted with permission.

TABLE F
Significant Values of F

5% (FIRST ROW ACROSS) AND 1% (SECOND ROW ACROSS) POINTS FOR THE DISTRIBUTION OF F

n_1 DEGREES OF FREEDOM (FIRST ROW ACROSS)

(FOR GREATER MEAN SQUARE)

n_2	1	2	3	4	5	6	7	8	9	10	11	12	14	16	20	24	30	40	50	75	100	200	500	∞
1	161	200	216	225	230	234	237	239	241	242	243	244	245	246	248	249	250	251	252	253	253	254	254	254
	4,052	4,999	5,403	5,625	5,764	5,859	5,928	5,981	6,022	6,056	6,082	6,106	6,142	6,169	6,208	6,234	6,258	6,286	6,302	6,323	6,334	6,352	6,361	6,366
2	18.51	19.00	19.16	19.25	19.30	19.33	19.36	19.37	19.38	19.39	19.40	19.41	19.42	19.43	19.44	19.45	19.46	19.47	19.47	19.48	19.49	19.49	19.50	19.50
	98.49	99.00	99.17	99.25	99.30	99.33	99.34	99.36	99.38	99.40	99.41	99.42	99.43	99.44	99.45	99.46	99.47	99.48	99.48	99.49	99.49	99.49	99.50	99.50
3	10.13	9.55	9.28	9.12	9.01	8.94	8.88	8.84	8.81	8.78	8.76	8.74	8.71	8.69	8.66	8.64	8.62	8.60	8.58	8.57	8.56	8.54	8.54	8.53
	34.12	30.82	29.46	28.71	28.24	27.91	27.67	27.49	27.34	27.23	27.13	27.05	26.92	26.83	26.69	26.60	26.50	26.41	26.35	26.27	26.23	26.18	26.14	26.12
4	7.71	6.94	6.59	6.39	6.26	6.16	6.09	6.04	6.00	5.96	5.93	5.91	5.87	5.84	5.80	5.77	5.74	5.71	5.70	5.68	5.66	5.65	5.64	5.63
	21.20	18.00	16.69	15.98	15.52	15.21	14.98	14.80	14.66	14.54	14.45	14.37	14.24	14.15	14.02	13.93	13.83	13.74	13.69	13.61	13.57	13.52	13.48	13.46
5	6.61	5.79	5.41	5.19	5.05	4.95	4.88	4.82	4.78	4.74	4.70	4.68	4.64	4.60	4.56	4.53	4.50	4.46	4.44	4.42	4.40	4.38	4.37	4.36
	16.26	13.27	12.06	11.39	10.97	10.67	10.45	10.27	10.15	10.05	9.96	9.89	9.77	9.68	9.55	9.47	9.38	9.29	9.24	9.17	9.13	9.07	9.04	9.02
6	5.99	5.14	4.76	4.53	4.39	4.28	4.21	4.15	4.10	4.06	4.03	4.00	3.96	3.92	3.87	3.84	3.81	3.77	3.75	3.72	3.71	3.69	3.68	3.67
	13.74	10.92	9.78	9.15	8.75	8.47	8.26	8.10	7.98	7.87	7.79	7.72	7.60	7.52	7.39	7.31	7.23	7.14	7.09	7.02	6.99	6.94	6.90	6.88
7	5.59	4.74	4.35	4.12	3.97	3.87	3.79	3.73	3.68	3.63	3.60	3.57	3.52	3.49	3.44	3.41	3.38	3.34	3.32	3.29	3.28	3.25	3.24	3.23
	12.25	9.55	8.45	7.85	7.46	7.19	7.00	6.84	6.71	6.62	6.54	6.47	6.35	6.27	6.15	6.07	5.98	5.90	5.85	5.78	5.75	5.70	5.67	5.65
8	5.32	4.46	4.07	3.84	3.69	3.58	3.50	3.44	3.39	3.34	3.31	3.28	3.23	3.20	3.15	3.12	3.08	3.05	3.03	3.00	2.98	2.96	2.94	2.93
	11.26	8.65	7.59	7.01	6.63	6.37	6.19	6.03	5.91	5.82	5.74	5.67	5.56	5.48	5.36	5.28	5.20	5.11	5.06	5.00	4.96	4.91	4.88	4.86
9	5.12	4.26	3.86	3.63	3.48	3.37	3.29	3.23	3.18	3.13	3.10	3.07	3.02	2.98	2.93	2.90	2.86	2.82	2.80	2.77	2.76	2.73	2.72	2.71
	10.56	8.02	6.99	6.42	6.06	5.80	5.62	5.47	5.35	5.26	5.18	5.11	5.00	4.92	4.80	4.73	4.64	4.56	4.51	4.45	4.41	4.36	4.33	4.31
10	4.96	4.10	3.71	3.48	3.33	3.22	3.14	3.07	3.02	2.97	2.94	2.91	2.86	2.82	2.77	2.74	2.70	2.67	2.64	2.61	2.59	2.56	2.55	2.54
	10.04	7.56	6.55	5.99	5.64	5.39	5.21	5.06	4.95	4.85	4.78	4.71	4.60	4.52	4.41	4.33	4.25	4.17	4.12	4.05	4.01	3.96	3.93	3.91
11	4.84	3.98	3.59	3.36	3.20	3.09	3.01	2.95	2.90	2.86	2.82	2.79	2.74	2.70	2.65	2.61	2.57	2.53	2.50	2.47	2.45	2.42	2.41	2.40
	9.65	7.20	6.22	5.67	5.32	5.07	4.88	4.74	4.63	4.54	4.46	4.40	4.29	4.21	4.10	4.02	3.94	3.86	3.80	3.74	3.70	3.66	3.62	3.60
12	4.75	3.88	3.49	3.26	3.11	3.00	2.92	2.85	2.80	2.76	2.72	2.69	2.64	2.60	2.54	2.50	2.46	2.42	2.40	2.36	2.35	2.32	2.31	2.30
	9.33	6.93	5.95	5.41	5.06	4.82	4.65	4.50	4.39	4.30	4.22	4.16	4.05	3.98	3.86	3.78	3.70	3.61	3.56	3.49	3.46	3.41	3.38	3.36
13	4.67	3.80	3.41	3.18	3.02	2.92	2.84	2.77	2.72	2.67	2.63	2.60	2.55	2.51	2.46	2.42	2.38	2.34	2.32	2.28	2.26	2.24	2.22	2.21
	9.07	6.70	5.74	5.20	4.86	4.62	4.44	4.30	4.19	4.10	4.02	3.96	3.85	3.78	3.67	3.59	3.51	3.42	3.37	3.30	3.27	3.21	3.18	3.16

TABLE F (continued)
Significant Values of F

5% (FIRST ROW ACROSS) AND 1% (SECOND ROW ACROSS) POINTS FOR THE DISTRIBUTION OF F

n_1 DEGREES OF FREEDOM (FOR GREATER MEAN SQUARE)

n_2	1	2	3	4	5	6	7	8	9	10	11	12	14	16	20	24	30	40	50	75	100	200	500	∞
14	4.60	3.74	3.34	3.11	2.96	2.85	2.77	2.70	2.65	2.60	2.56	2.53	2.48	2.44	2.39	2.35	2.31	2.27	2.24	2.21	2.19	2.16	2.14	2.13
	8.86	6.51	5.56	5.03	4.69	4.46	4.28	4.14	4.03	3.94	3.86	3.80	3.70	3.62	3.51	3.43	3.34	3.26	3.21	3.14	3.11	3.06	3.02	3.00
15	4.54	3.68	3.29	3.06	2.90	2.79	2.70	2.64	2.59	2.55	2.51	2.48	2.43	2.39	2.33	2.29	2.25	2.21	2.18	2.15	2.12	2.10	2.08	2.07
	8.68	6.36	5.42	4.89	4.56	4.32	4.14	4.00	3.89	3.80	3.73	3.67	3.56	3.48	3.36	3.29	3.20	3.12	3.07	3.00	2.97	2.92	2.89	2.87
16	4.49	3.63	3.24	3.01	2.85	2.74	2.66	2.59	2.54	2.49	2.45	2.42	2.37	2.33	2.28	2.24	2.20	2.16	2.13	2.09	2.07	2.04	2.02	2.01
	8.53	6.23	5.29	4.77	4.44	4.20	4.03	3.89	3.78	3.69	3.61	3.55	3.45	3.37	3.25	3.18	3.10	3.01	2.96	2.89	2.86	2.80	2.77	2.75
17	4.45	3.59	3.20	2.96	2.81	2.70	2.62	2.55	2.50	2.45	2.41	2.38	2.33	2.29	2.23	2.19	2.15	2.11	2.08	2.04	2.02	1.99	1.97	1.96
	8.40	6.11	5.18	4.67	4.34	4.10	3.93	3.79	3.68	3.59	3.52	3.45	3.35	3.27	3.16	3.08	3.00	2.92	2.86	2.79	2.76	2.70	2.67	2.65
18	4.41	3.55	3.16	2.93	2.77	2.66	2.58	2.51	2.46	2.41	2.37	2.34	2.29	2.25	2.19	2.15	2.11	2.07	2.04	2.00	1.98	1.95	1.93	1.92
	8.28	6.01	5.09	4.58	4.25	4.01	3.85	3.71	3.60	3.51	3.44	3.37	3.27	3.19	3.07	3.00	2.91	2.83	2.78	2.71	2.68	2.62	2.59	2.57
19	4.38	3.52	3.13	2.90	2.74	2.63	2.55	2.48	2.43	2.38	2.34	2.31	2.26	2.21	2.15	2.11	2.07	2.02	2.00	1.96	1.94	1.91	1.90	1.88
	8.18	5.93	5.01	4.50	4.17	3.94	3.77	3.63	3.52	3.43	3.36	3.30	3.19	3.12	3.00	2.92	2.84	2.76	2.70	2.63	2.60	2.54	2.51	2.49
20	4.35	3.49	3.10	2.87	2.71	2.60	2.52	2.45	2.40	2.35	2.31	2.28	2.23	2.18	2.12	2.08	2.04	1.99	1.96	1.92	1.90	1.87	1.85	1.84
	8.10	5.85	4.94	4.43	4.10	3.87	3.71	3.56	3.45	3.37	3.30	3.23	3.13	3.05	2.94	2.86	2.77	2.69	2.63	2.56	2.53	2.47	2.44	2.42
21	4.32	3.47	3.07	2.84	2.68	2.57	2.49	2.42	2.37	2.32	2.28	2.25	2.20	2.15	2.09	2.05	2.00	1.96	1.93	1.89	1.87	1.84	1.82	1.81
	8.02	5.78	4.87	4.37	4.04	3.81	3.65	3.51	3.40	3.31	3.24	3.17	3.07	2.99	2.88	2.80	2.72	2.63	2.58	2.51	2.47	2.42	2.38	2.36
22	4.30	3.44	3.05	2.82	2.66	2.55	2.47	2.40	2.35	2.30	2.26	2.23	2.18	2.13	2.07	2.03	1.98	1.93	1.91	1.87	1.84	1.81	1.80	1.78
	7.94	5.72	4.82	4.31	3.99	3.76	3.59	3.45	3.35	3.26	3.18	3.12	3.02	2.94	2.83	2.75	2.67	2.58	2.53	2.46	2.42	2.37	2.33	2.31
23	4.28	3.42	3.03	2.80	2.64	2.53	2.45	2.38	2.32	2.28	2.24	2.20	2.14	2.10	2.04	2.00	1.96	1.91	1.88	1.84	1.82	1.79	1.77	1.76
	7.88	5.66	4.76	4.26	3.94	3.71	3.54	3.41	3.30	3.21	3.14	3.07	2.97	2.89	2.78	2.70	2.62	2.53	2.48	2.41	2.37	2.32	2.28	2.26
24	4.26	3.40	3.01	2.78	2.62	2.51	2.43	2.36	2.30	2.26	2.22	2.18	2.13	2.09	2.02	1.98	1.94	1.89	1.86	1.82	1.80	1.76	1.74	1.73
	7.82	5.61	4.72	4.22	3.90	3.67	3.50	3.36	3.25	3.17	3.09	3.03	2.93	2.85	2.74	2.66	2.58	2.49	2.44	2.36	2.33	2.27	2.23	2.21
25	4.24	3.38	2.99	2.76	2.60	2.49	2.41	2.34	2.28	2.24	2.20	2.16	2.11	2.06	2.00	1.96	1.92	1.87	1.84	1.80	1.77	1.74	1.72	1.71
	7.77	5.57	4.65	4.18	3.86	3.63	3.46	3.32	3.21	3.13	3.05	2.99	2.89	2.81	2.70	2.62	2.54	2.45	2.40	2.32	2.29	2.23	2.19	2.17
26	4.22	3.37	2.98	2.74	2.59	2.47	2.39	2.32	2.27	2.22	2.18	2.15	2.10	2.05	1.99	1.95	1.90	1.85	1.82	1.78	1.76	1.72	1.70	1.69
	7.72	5.53	4.64	4.14	3.82	3.59	3.42	3.29	3.17	3.09	3.02	2.96	2.86	2.77	2.66	2.58	2.50	2.41	2.36	2.28	2.25	2.19	2.15	2.13

TABLE F (continued)
Significant Values of F

5% (FIRST ROW ACROSS) AND 1% (SECOND ROW ACROSS) POINTS FOR THE DISTRIBUTION OF F

n_1 DEGREES OF FREEDOM (FOR GREATER MEAN SQUARE)

n_2	1	2	3	4	5	6	7	8	9	10	11	12	14	16	20	24	30	40	50	75	100	200	500	∞	n_2
27	4.21	3.35	2.96	2.73	2.57	2.46	2.37	2.30	2.25	2.20	2.16	2.13	2.08	2.03	1.97	1.93	1.88	1.84	1.80	1.76	1.74	1.71	1.68	1.67	27
	7.68	5.49	4.60	4.11	3.79	3.56	3.39	3.26	3.14	3.06	2.98	2.93	2.83	2.74	2.63	2.55	2.47	2.38	2.33	2.25	2.21	2.16	2.12	2.10	
28	4.20	3.34	2.95	2.71	2.56	2.44	2.36	2.29	2.24	2.19	2.15	2.12	2.06	2.02	1.96	1.91	1.87	1.81	1.78	1.75	1.72	1.69	1.67	1.65	28
	7.64	5.45	4.57	4.07	3.76	3.53	3.36	3.23	3.11	3.03	2.95	2.90	2.80	2.71	2.60	2.52	2.44	2.35	2.30	2.22	2.18	2.13	2.09	2.06	
29	4.18	3.33	2.93	2.70	2.54	2.43	2.35	2.28	2.22	2.18	2.14	2.10	2.05	2.00	1.94	1.90	1.85	1.80	1.77	1.73	1.71	1.68	1.65	1.64	29
	7.60	5.42	4.54	4.04	3.73	3.50	3.33	3.20	3.08	3.00	2.92	2.87	2.77	2.68	2.57	2.49	2.41	2.32	2.27	2.19	2.15	2.10	2.06	2.03	
30	4.17	3.32	2.92	2.69	2.53	2.42	2.34	2.27	2.21	2.16	2.12	2.09	2.04	1.99	1.93	1.89	1.84	1.79	1.76	1.72	1.69	1.66	1.64	1.62	30
	7.56	5.39	4.51	4.02	3.70	3.47	3.30	3.17	3.06	2.98	2.90	2.84	2.74	2.66	2.55	2.47	2.38	2.29	2.24	2.16	2.13	2.07	2.03	2.01	
32	4.15	3.30	2.90	2.67	2.51	2.40	2.32	2.25	2.19	2.14	2.10	2.07	2.02	1.97	1.91	1.86	1.82	1.76	1.74	1.69	1.67	1.64	1.61	1.59	32
	7.50	5.34	4.46	3.97	3.66	3.42	3.25	3.12	3.01	2.94	2.86	2.80	2.70	2.62	2.51	2.42	2.34	2.25	2.20	2.12	2.08	2.02	1.98	1.96	
34	4.13	3.28	2.88	2.65	2.49	2.38	2.30	2.23	2.17	2.12	2.08	2.05	2.00	1.95	1.89	1.84	1.80	1.74	1.71	1.67	1.64	1.61	1.59	1.57	34
	7.44	5.29	4.42	3.93	3.61	3.38	3.21	3.08	2.97	2.89	2.82	2.76	2.66	2.58	2.47	2.38	2.30	2.21	2.15	2.08	2.04	1.98	1.94	1.91	
36	4.11	3.26	2.86	2.63	2.48	2.36	2.28	2.21	2.15	2.10	2.06	2.03	1.98	1.93	1.87	1.82	1.78	1.72	1.69	1.65	1.62	1.59	1.56	1.55	36
	7.39	5.25	4.38	3.89	3.58	3.35	3.18	3.04	2.94	2.86	2.78	2.72	2.62	2.54	2.43	2.35	2.26	2.17	2.12	2.04	2.00	1.94	1.90	1.87	
38	4.10	3.25	2.85	2.62	2.46	2.35	2.26	2.19	2.14	2.09	2.05	2.02	1.96	1.92	1.85	1.80	1.76	1.71	1.67	1.63	1.60	1.57	1.54	1.53	38
	7.35	5.21	4.34	3.86	3.54	3.32	3.15	3.02	2.91	2.82	2.75	2.69	2.59	2.51	2.40	2.32	2.22	2.14	2.08	2.00	1.97	1.90	1.86	1.84	
40	4.08	3.23	2.84	2.61	2.45	2.34	2.25	2.18	2.12	2.07	2.04	2.00	1.95	1.90	1.84	1.79	1.74	1.69	1.66	1.61	1.59	1.55	1.53	1.51	40
	7.31	5.18	4.31	3.83	3.51	3.29	3.12	2.99	2.88	2.80	2.73	2.66	2.56	2.49	2.37	2.29	2.20	2.11	2.05	1.97	1.94	1.88	1.84	1.81	
42	4.07	3.22	2.83	2.59	2.44	2.32	2.24	2.17	2.11	2.06	2.02	1.99	1.94	1.89	1.82	1.78	1.73	1.68	1.64	1.60	1.57	1.54	1.51	1.49	42
	7.27	5.15	4.29	3.80	3.49	3.26	3.10	2.96	2.86	2.77	2.70	2.64	2.54	2.46	2.35	2.26	2.17	2.08	2.02	1.94	1.91	1.85	1.80	1.78	
44	4.06	3.21	2.82	2.58	2.43	2.31	2.23	2.16	2.10	2.05	2.01	1.98	1.92	1.88	1.81	1.76	1.72	1.66	1.63	1.58	1.56	1.52	1.50	1.48	44
	7.24	5.12	4.26	3.78	3.46	3.24	3.07	2.94	2.84	2.75	2.68	2.62	2.52	2.44	2.32	2.24	2.15	2.06	2.00	1.92	1.88	1.82	1.78	1.75	
46	4.05	3.20	2.81	2.57	2.42	2.30	2.22	2.14	2.09	2.04	2.00	1.97	1.91	1.87	1.80	1.75	1.71	1.65	1.62	1.57	1.54	1.51	1.48	1.46	46
	7.21	5.10	4.24	3.76	3.44	3.22	3.05	2.92	2.82	2.73	2.66	2.60	2.50	2.42	2.30	2.22	2.13	2.04	1.98	1.90	1.86	1.80	1.76	1.72	
48	4.04	3.19	2.80	2.56	2.41	2.30	2.21	2.14	2.08	2.03	1.99	1.96	1.90	1.86	1.79	1.74	1.70	1.64	1.61	1.56	1.53	1.50	1.47	1.45	48
	7.19	5.08	4.22	3.74	3.42	3.20	3.04	2.90	2.80	2.71	2.64	2.58	2.48	2.40	2.28	2.20	2.11	2.02	1.96	1.88	1.84	1.78	1.73	1.70	

TABLE F (continued)
Significant Values of F

5% (FIRST ROW ACROSS) AND 1% (SECOND ROW ACROSS) POINTS FOR THE DISTRIBUTION OF F

n_1 DEGREES OF FREEDOM (FOR GREATER MEAN SQUARE)

n_2	1	2	3	4	5	6	7	8	9	10	11	12	14	16	20	24	30	40	50	75	100	200	500	∞	n_2
50	4.03	3.18	2.79	2.56	2.40	2.29	2.20	2.13	2.07	2.02	1.98	1.95	1.90	1.85	1.78	1.74	1.69	1.63	1.60	1.55	1.52	1.48	1.46	1.44	50
	7.17	5.06	4.20	3.72	3.41	3.18	3.02	2.88	2.78	2.70	2.62	2.56	2.46	2.39	2.26	2.18	2.10	2.00	1.94	1.86	1.82	1.76	1.71	1.68	
55	4.02	3.17	2.78	2.54	2.38	2.27	2.18	2.11	2.05	2.00	1.97	1.93	1.88	1.83	1.76	1.72	1.67	1.61	1.58	1.52	1.50	1.46	1.43	1.41	55
	7.12	5.01	4.16	3.68	3.37	3.15	2.98	2.85	2.75	2.66	2.59	2.53	2.43	2.35	2.23	2.15	2.06	1.96	1.90	1.82	1.78	1.71	1.66	1.64	
60	4.00	3.15	2.76	2.52	2.37	2.25	2.17	2.10	2.04	1.99	1.95	1.92	1.86	1.81	1.75	1.70	1.65	1.59	1.56	1.50	1.48	1.44	1.41	1.39	60
	7.08	4.98	4.13	3.65	3.34	3.12	2.95	2.82	2.72	2.63	2.56	2.50	2.40	2.32	2.20	2.12	2.03	1.93	1.87	1.79	1.74	1.68	1.63	1.60	
65	3.99	3.14	2.75	2.51	2.36	2.24	2.15	2.08	2.02	1.98	1.94	1.90	1.85	1.80	1.73	1.68	1.63	1.57	1.54	1.49	1.46	1.42	1.39	1.37	65
	7.04	4.95	4.10	3.62	3.31	3.09	2.93	2.79	2.70	2.61	2.54	2.47	2.37	2.30	2.18	2.09	2.00	1.90	1.84	1.76	1.71	1.64	1.60	1.56	
70	3.98	3.13	2.74	2.50	2.35	2.23	2.14	2.07	2.01	1.97	1.93	1.89	1.84	1.79	1.72	1.67	1.62	1.56	1.53	1.47	1.45	1.40	1.37	1.35	70
	7.01	4.92	4.08	3.60	3.29	3.07	2.91	2.77	2.67	2.59	2.51	2.45	2.35	2.28	2.15	2.07	1.98	1.88	1.82	1.74	1.69	1.62	1.56	1.53	
80	3.96	3.11	2.72	2.48	2.33	2.21	2.12	2.05	1.99	1.95	1.91	1.88	1.82	1.77	1.70	1.65	1.60	1.54	1.51	1.45	1.42	1.38	1.35	1.32	80
	6.96	4.88	4.04	3.56	3.25	3.04	2.87	2.74	2.64	2.55	2.48	2.41	2.32	2.24	2.11	2.03	1.94	1.84	1.78	1.70	1.65	1.57	1.52	1.49	
100	3.94	3.09	2.70	2.46	2.30	2.19	2.10	2.03	1.97	1.92	1.88	1.85	1.79	1.75	1.68	1.63	1.57	1.51	1.48	1.42	1.39	1.34	1.30	1.28	100
	6.90	4.82	3.98	3.51	3.20	2.99	2.82	2.69	2.59	2.51	2.43	2.36	2.26	2.19	2.06	1.98	1.89	1.79	1.73	1.64	1.59	1.51	1.46	1.43	
125	3.92	3.07	2.68	2.44	2.29	2.17	2.08	2.01	1.95	1.90	1.86	1.83	1.77	1.72	1.65	1.60	1.55	1.49	1.45	1.39	1.36	1.31	1.27	1.25	125
	6.84	4.78	3.94	3.47	3.17	2.95	2.79	2.65	2.56	2.47	2.40	2.33	2.23	2.15	2.03	1.94	1.85	1.75	1.68	1.59	1.54	1.46	1.40	1.37	
150	3.91	3.06	2.67	2.43	2.27	2.16	2.07	2.00	1.94	1.89	1.85	1.82	1.76	1.71	1.64	1.59	1.54	1.47	1.44	1.37	1.34	1.29	1.25	1.22	150
	6.81	4.75	3.91	3.44	3.14	2.92	2.76	2.62	2.53	2.44	2.37	2.30	2.20	2.12	2.00	1.91	1.83	1.72	1.66	1.56	1.51	1.43	1.37	1.33	
200	3.89	3.04	2.65	2.41	2.26	2.14	2.05	1.98	1.92	1.87	1.83	1.80	1.74	1.69	1.62	1.57	1.52	1.45	1.42	1.35	1.32	1.26	1.22	1.19	200
	6.76	4.71	3.88	3.41	3.11	2.90	2.73	2.60	2.50	2.41	2.34	2.28	2.17	2.09	1.97	1.88	1.79	1.69	1.62	1.53	1.48	1.39	1.33	1.28	
400	3.86	3.02	2.62	2.39	2.23	2.12	2.03	1.96	1.90	1.85	1.81	1.78	1.72	1.67	1.60	1.54	1.49	1.42	1.38	1.32	1.28	1.22	1.16	1.13	400
	6.70	4.66	3.83	3.36	3.06	2.85	2.69	2.55	2.46	2.37	2.29	2.23	2.12	2.04	1.92	1.84	1.74	1.64	1.57	1.47	1.42	1.32	1.24	1.19	
1000	3.85	3.00	2.61	2.38	2.22	2.10	2.02	1.95	1.89	1.84	1.80	1.76	1.70	1.65	1.58	1.53	1.47	1.41	1.36	1.30	1.26	1.19	1.13	1.08	1000
	6.66	4.62	3.80	3.34	3.04	2.82	2.66	2.53	2.43	2.34	2.26	2.20	2.09	2.01	1.89	1.81	1.71	1.61	1.54	1.44	1.38	1.28	1.19	1.11	
∞	3.84	2.99	2.60	2.37	2.21	2.09	2.01	1.94	1.88	1.83	1.79	1.75	1.69	1.64	1.57	1.52	1.46	1.40	1.35	1.28	1.24	1.17	1.11	1.00	∞
	6.64	4.60	3.78	3.32	3.02	2.80	2.64	2.51	2.41	2.32	2.24	2.18	2.07	1.99	1.87	1.79	1.69	1.59	1.52	1.41	1.36	1.25	1.15	1.00	

The function, $F = e$ with exponent $2z$, is computed in part from Fisher's table VI (7). Additional entries are by interpolation, mostly graphical. Reproduced from George W. Snedecor, *Statistical Methods*, 5th ed. (Ames, Iowa: The Iowa State University Press, 1956), pp. 246–49, by permission of the author and publishers.

TABLE G
Significant Values of t

df	LEVEL OF SIGNIFICANCE FOR ONE-TAILED TEST					
	.10	.05	.025	.01	.005	.0005
	LEVEL OF SIGNIFICANCE FOR TWO-TAILED TEST					
	.20	.10	.05	.02	.01	.001
1	3.078	6.314	12.706	31.821	63.657	636.619
2	1.886	2.920	4.303	6.965	9.925	31.598
3	1.638	2.353	3.182	4.541	5.841	12.941
4	1.533	2.132	2.776	3.747	4.604	8.610
5	1.476	2.015	2.571	3.365	4.032	6.859
6	1.440	1.943	2.447	3.143	3.707	5.959
7	1.415	1.895	2.365	2.998	3.499	5.405
8	1.397	1.860	2.306	2.896	3.355	5.041
9	1.383	1.833	2.262	2.821	3.250	4.781
10	1.372	1.812	2.228	2.764	3.169	4.587
11	1.363	1.796	2.201	2.718	3.106	4.437
12	1.356	1.782	2.179	2.681	3.055	4.318
13	1.350	1.771	2.160	2.650	3.012	4.221
14	1.345	1.761	2.145	2.624	2.977	4.140
15	1.341	1.753	2.131	2.602	2.947	4.073
16	1.337	1.746	2.120	2.583	2.921	4.015
17	1.333	1.740	2.110	2.567	2.898	3.965
18	1.330	1.734	2.101	2.552	2.878	3.922
19	1.328	1.729	2.093	2.539	2.861	3.883
20	1.325	1.725	2.086	2.528	2.845	3.850
21	1.323	1.721	2.080	2.518	2.831	3.819
22	1.321	1.717	2.074	2.508	2.819	3.792
23	1.319	1.714	2.069	2.500	2.807	3.767
24	1.318	1.711	2.064	2.492	2.797	3.745
25	1.316	1.708	2.060	2.485	2.787	3.725
26	1.315	1.706	2.056	2.479	2.779	3.707
27	1.314	1.703	2.052	2.473	2.771	3.690
28	1.313	1.701	2.048	2.467	2.763	3.674
29	1.311	1.699	2.045	2.462	2.756	3.659
30	1.310	1.697	2.042	2.457	2.750	3.646
40	1.303	1.684	2.021	2.423	2.704	3.551
60	1.296	1.671	2.000	2.390	2.660	3.460
120	1.289	1.658	1.980	2.358	2.617	3.373
∞	1.282	1.645	1.960	2.326	2.576	3.291

Abridged from Table III of R. A. Fisher and F. Yates, *Statistical Tables for Biological, Agricultural and Medical Research* (Edinburgh and London: Oliver & Boyd, Ltd., 1948), by permission of the authors and publishers.

TABLE H

Critical Values of d *for Dorbin-Watson Test (.05, two-tailed)*

n	k' = 1		k' = 2		k' = 3		k' = 4		k' = 5	
	d_l	d_u	d_l	d_u	d_l	d_u	d_l	d_u	d_l	d_u
15	0.95	1.23	0.83	1.40	0.71	1.61	0.59	1.84	0.48	2.09
16	0.98	1.24	0.86	1.40	0.75	1.59	0.64	1.80	0.53	2.03
17	1.01	1.25	0.90	1.40	0.79	1.58	0.68	1.77	0.57	1.98
18	1.03	1.26	0.93	1.40	0.82	1.56	0.72	1.74	0.62	1.93
19	1.06	1.28	0.96	1.41	0.86	1.55	0.76	1.72	0.66	1.90
20	1.08	1.28	0.99	1.41	0.89	1.55	0.79	1.70	0.70	1.87
21	1.10	1.30	1.01	1.41	0.92	1.54	0.83	1.69	0.73	1.84
22	1.12	1.31	1.04	1.42	0.95	1.54	0.86	1.68	0.77	1.82
23	1.14	1.32	1.06	1.42	0.97	1.54	0.89	1.67	0.80	1.80
24	1.16	1.33	1.08	1.43	1.00	1.54	0.91	1.66	0.83	1.79
25	1.18	1.34	1.10	1.43	1.02	1.54	0.94	1.65	0.86	1.77
26	1.19	1.35	1.12	1.44	1.04	1.54	0.96	1.65	0.88	1.76
27	1.21	1.36	1.13	1.44	1.06	1.54	0.99	1.64	0.91	1.75
28	1.22	1.37	1.15	1.45	1.08	1.54	1.01	1.64	0.93	1.74
29	1.24	1.38	1.17	1.45	1.10	1.54	1.03	1.63	0.96	1.73
30	1.25	1.38	1.18	1.46	1.12	1.54	1.05	1.63	0.98	1.73
31	1.26	1.39	1.20	1.47	1.13	1.55	1.07	1.63	1.00	1.72
32	1.27	1.40	1.21	1.47	1.15	1.55	1.08	1.63	1.02	1.71
33	1.28	1.41	1.22	1.48	1.16	1.55	1.10	1.63	1.04	1.71
34	1.29	1.41	1.24	1.48	1.17	1.55	1.12	1.63	1.06	1.70
35	1.30	1.42	1.25	1.48	1.19	1.55	1.13	1.63	1.07	1.70
36	1.31	1.43	1.26	1.49	1.20	1.56	1.15	1.63	1.09	1.70
37	1.32	1.43	1.27	1.49	1.21	1.56	1.16	1.62	1.10	1.70
38	1.33	1.44	1.28	1.50	1.23	1.56	1.17	1.62	1.12	1.70
39	1.34	1.44	1.29	1.50	1.24	1.56	1.19	1.63	1.13	1.69
40	1.35	1.45	1.30	1.51	1.25	1.57	1.20	1.63	1.15	1.69
45	1.39	1.48	1.34	1.53	1.30	1.58	1.25	1.63	1.21	1.69
50	1.42	1.50	1.38	1.54	1.34	1.59	1.30	1.64	1.26	1.69
55	1.45	1.52	1.41	1.56	1.37	1.60	1.33	1.64	1.30	1.69
60	1.47	1.54	1.44	1.57	1.40	1.61	1.37	1.65	1.33	1.69
65	1.49	1.55	1.46	1.59	1.43	1.62	1.40	1.66	1.36	1.69
70	1.51	1.57	1.48	1.60	1.45	1.63	1.42	1.66	1.39	1.70
75	1.53	1.58	1.50	1.61	1.47	1.64	1.45	1.67	1.42	1.70
80	1.54	1.59	1.52	1.62	1.49	1.65	1.47	1.67	1.44	1.70
85	1.56	1.60	1.53	1.63	1.51	1.65	1.49	1.68	1.46	1.71
90	1.57	1.61	1.55	1.64	1.53	1.66	1.50	1.69	1.48	1.71
95	1.58	1.62	1.56	1.65	1.54	1.67	1.52	1.69	1.50	1.71
100	1.59	1.63	1.57	1.65	1.55	1.67	1.53	1.70	1.51	1.72

J. Durbin and G. S. Watson, "Testing for Serial Correlation in Least Squares Regression," *Biometrika,* 38 (1951), 159–77. Reprinted with the permission of the authors and the Trustees of *Biometrika.*

INDEX